TRANS

S

A
Historical Dictionary of the
RAILWAYS
of the British Isles

Architect of mainline railway electrification, Sir Herbert Ashcombe Walker (1868-1949) has been regarded by many as one of the greatest railwaymen of all time, and was famous for ensuring that projects were always good value for money. (NRM BTC collection 3592/64)

A
Historical Dictionary of the
RAILWAYS
of the British Isles

DAVID WRAGG

Wharncliffe Books

First published in Great Britain in 2009
Wharncliffe Local History
an imprint of
Pen and Sword Books Limited,
47 Church Street, Barnsley,
South Yorkshire. S70 2AS

Copyright © David Wragg, 2009

ISBN: 978 1 844680 47 4

The right of David Wragg to be identified as
Author of this Work has been asserted by him
in accordance with the Copyright, Designs and Patents Act, 1988.

A CIP catalogue record of this book is available from the
British Library.

Typeset in Sabon by
Pen and Sword Books Ltd

Printed in the United Kingdom by the
MPG Books Group

Pen & Sword Books Ltd incorporates the imprints of
Pen & Sword Aviation, Pen & Sword Maritime,
Pen & Sword Military, Wharncliffe Local History, Pen & Sword Select,
Pen & Sword Military Classics and Leo Cooper.

For a complete list of Pen & Sword titles please contact:
PEN & SWORD BOOKS LIMITED
47 Church Street, Barnsley, South Yorkshire, S70 2AS, England.
E-mail: enquiries@pen-and-sword.co.uk
Website: www.pen-and-sword.co.uk

Contents

Acknowledgements

In writing any book such as this, an author is always indebted to those who help with such important matters as, for example, the quest for photographs. In this case, I am especially grateful to Mr A E W 'Bert' Colbourn of the Historic Model Railway Society for the use of their considerable archive of material, while thanks are also due to the staff of the National Railway Museum at York.

Introduction

The railways were one of the many great influences that shaped not just our country, but many others as well, making travel easier and cheaper than ever before, and not just travel: not only did the railways dramatically cut the cost of moving goods, they created whole new markets and broadened the range of products available to the consumer, bringing fish and dairy products daily to the big cities while they were still fresh. The cities themselves were able to grow, thanks to the railways. In 1920, Golders Green, on the Northern Line in London, was a muddy crossroads, but for well over half-a-century it has been a prosperous but built-up suburb and shopping centre. Seaside resorts sprung up, again because of the railway.

In preparing a reference book on the history of railways, it is easy enough to know where to start, but where should one finish? One could stick to the mainland, but the Isle of Wight is part of England and was part of the London, Brighton & South Coast and London & South Western Railways, who operated not only the ferry from Portsmouth to Ryde jointly, but also the line between Rye Pier Head and Ryde St John's, and then of course the entire system passed to the Southern Railway in 1923. Northern Ireland is part of the United Kingdom, but then too for most of the first hundred years of railways was the whole of Ireland, and in any case both the Midland Railway and the London & North Western Railway had lines on both sides of the Irish Sea, so obviously Ireland has to be included. Viewed in this light skipping the Isle of Man seems unfair, and it would be bizarre to include the Isle of Man and then exclude the Channel Islands, since the constitutional arrangements are similar.

There are several dictionaries that give railway technical terms, so this doesn't need to be another, except for such curiosities as wheel notation, for example, so it is easier to deal with the mass of railway companies, the prominent figures in the development of our railway system, and the impact of the railways on some of the major centres in the British Isles.

Then which period should be covered? Since this is a book on history, perhaps a good place to stop would be the privatised railway, not least because so many of the franchises change every seven years or so, and sometimes less if the franchisee runs into difficulties.

In fact, few books, if any, have covered railways in every corner of the British Isles, giving an overview of railway operation not just in England, Scotland and Wales, or even of Ireland as well, but also the Isle of Man, Jersey and Guernsey. In each case, public railways have been the defining characteristic, so private railways have been dropped, as have the German occupation lines in Jersey. On the other hand, matters such as the role of the railways in wartime, and major accidents, have also been included. A chronology at the end provides a list of the major events in railway history in the British Isles, and there is a select bibliography for further reading.

Readers' Note
Please note that within each A-Z entry any items featured in other listings (cross-references) are shown in **bold** type when mentioned for the first time.

A–Z Listing

THE HISTORICAL DICTIONARY

A

Aberdeen

Prior to the advent of the railway, Aberdeen was isolated and the most reliable means of transport was by sea. Such was the enthusiasm for the new mode of transport that the Harbour Board made a site available close to the centre of the city for a terminus. While a prospectus was issued for the Aberdeen Railway as early as 1844, proposing a link with the Northern Junction Railway at Forfar, difficulties in construction with a viaduct collapsing and a bridge being swept away in a flood, as well as the financial crisis of 1848, meant that the line did not open until 1850.

Meanwhile, the **Great North of Scotland Railway** approached the city from the north, using much of the route of the Aberdeen Canal which was abruptly drained for the purpose. The GNSR did not share the Guild Street terminus of the AR but instead stopped at Waterloo Quay, 1½ miles away. It was not until 1867 that a connecting line through the Denburn Valley was completed and a joint station opened. This was replaced in 1915 by the present station, completed in sandstone.

The opening of the railway benefited both the fishing industry and agriculture, with Aberdeenshire farmers specialising in cattle fattening. Instead of sending live cattle by sea, butchered meat could be sent south by rail. Initially the city was reached from the south by the **West Coast** route, but after the completion of the bridges over the **Forth** and **Tay**, overnight fish and meat trains could reach the London markets at Billingsgate and Smithfield. A small network of commuter services was also established around Aberdeen, with work-men's trains to the Stoneywood paperworks by 1870, and later a suburban service linking the city with Dyce, so that by the turn of a century, two million passengers a year were being carried. Nevertheless, these were short distance passengers and stations were close together, with eight in the six miles to Dyce, so the service was vulnerable when motorbus competition appeared after the First World War, and the suburban service ended in 1937.

Post **nationalisation**, many of the railway lines radiating from Aberdeen closed, with the exception of the line south to Dundee and **Edinburgh** and that to Inverness. Traffic through the port largely ended during the 1970s while road transport took over the fish traffic, and North Sea oil support vessels largely pushed most of the fishing fleet north to Peterhead. The oil business did bring some freight traffic, and in 1984 the station at Dyce re-opened both to serve the city's airport and also an expanding suburb.

Accidents/Accident Investigation

The Railway Regulation Act 1840 required the railway companies to report all accidents no matter how minor involving personal injury to passengers, but not necessarily staff, to the **Board of Trade**, which had the duty to appoint inspectors with the power to enter and inspect railway premises, track and rolling stock, but strangely did not have the power at this stage to actually investigate an accident! Even the subsequent Railway Regulation Act 1842 did not authorise the inspectors, who, with one exception, were all serving or recently retired officers from the Royal Engineers, to investigate all accidents, only serious accidents had to be investigated, meaning those inflicting serious injury to a member of the public. Nevertheless, at the time accidents generally resulted in serious injury, simply because of the circumstances. Frail wooden bodies on brittle iron underframes meant that even a minor collision could be serious, and this was compounded by the use of oil or gas-fired lighting within the carriages, a practice that persisted on some lines into the twentieth century. One essential provision of the 1842 Act was that no passenger-carrying railway line could be opened without the approval of an inspector. If an inspector was not satisfied, opening and operations could be delayed. The premature opening of a line before an inspector had given his approval made the railway company liable to a fine of £20 for each day of operation. This was a year's pay for many a working man at the time. The inspector's powers were used, with one of the most notable early cases being when the **London & South Western Railway** extended its line from Nine Elms to **Waterloo** in 1848. The inspector was concerned about the safety of one of the bridges and refused to allow the line to open as planned on 1 July, so opening was deferred for ten days.

Inevitably, when so much depended on the judgement of a single inspector, some veered on the side of caution. In 1850, the **Manchester, Sheffield & Lincolnshire Railway**, a predecessor of the **Great Central**, complained about an inspector's recommendation that it should not be allowed to open Torksey Bridge, and was allowed to proceed once other engineers declared that the inspector had been over-cautious.

In 1880, it took an accident on a very short stretch of line opened by the **Midland Railway** in 1872, before it was discovered that this line, an important link in the network, had never been submitted for inspection. The company paid accumulated fines totalling £60,000 (more than £3

million today). Under pressure from the Board of Trade, the Midland acknowledged its error, ensured that the line was of a suitable standard and then sought a formal inspection, after which the BoT waived the fines.

The army officers on whom the burden of investigation fell were certainly far better qualified to investigate a railway accident than any intelligent layman, but they too had much to learn about the new sciences, brought into widespread use by the railways. Metallurgy was little understood, and non-destructive testing simply not available. The inspectors were helped in the case of boiler explosions by the Board of Trade seconding experts from its Marine Department. Then there was so much to discover about signalling and the management of a busy stretch of railway line. The inspectors were not above criticism, but they have been universally regarded as having been diligent and honest, and they built up a massive body of experience and expertise through their work. The reports were never secret and always presented to Parliament, and after 1860 they could be bought by the public. Yet, their recommendations remained no more than advice. It was also the case that sometimes a new precautionary device would resolve one danger, and yet introduce a new one that would not be immediately apparent until exposed by a further accident. This was trial and error, simply because so much had to be learnt. The system endured the passage of time, including grouping and nationalisation, so that officers of the Royal Engineers continued in this role until 1982.

In chronological order, the major accidents over the years have included:

Clayton Tunnel, **London, Brighton & South Coast Railway,** *25 August 1861:*
Three trains left **Brighton** for **London** within a very short period of time. The

signalling failed and allowed the second train to approach the southern end of the tunnel before the first had cleared it, and entered before the signalman could stop the train with a red flag. The signalman was given the all clear indicating that the first train had cleared the tunnel and assumed that the second was also through, but the driver had glimpsed the red flag and stopped before setting back to see if all was well. The signalman then gave the white flag, which on the LB&SCR meant 'all clear' to the third train, which entered the tunnel at full speed and collided with the second train as it reversed to the entrance, killing 21 passengers and injuring 176.

*Staplehurst, **South Eastern Railway**, 9 June 1865:*
A bridge carrying the line over a stream near Staplehurst was being repaired, with little signalling and the workmen judging from the timetable how much time they had between trains when replacing the bridge timbers. The foreman checked the schedule for the boat train for the wrong day, as timings varied because at the time the harbour at Folkestone was tidal, and had less time than expected. The boat train hit the bridge at full speed while some of the bridge timbers had been removed. The locomotive and first carriage crashed down onto the bridge girders and almost got across, but the coupling between the first and second carriages broke and the frail wooden carriage crashed down into the stream, breaking up, killing 10 persons and injuring another 49, all of which was witnessed by a notable passenger, Charles Dickens.

*Abergele, **London & North Western Railway**, 20 August 1867:*
At the time, trains worked by time interval rather than by fixed signals. At Llandulas a goods train was being shunted, and six wagons and a guard's van sitting on the main line were accidentally bumped and sent down a gradient of 1 in 147: near Abergele they ran into the 'Irish Mail', paraffin barrels being carried in the last two wagons burst and the locomotive and four leading carriages of the express were drenched in paraffin, which was ignited by the firebox. No one on the locomotive or four leading carriages survived the resulting inferno, which killed 34.

*Wigan, **London & North Western Railway**, 1 August 1873:*
The night express from **Euston** to Scotland, double-headed with 24 four-wheeled carriages, was derailed as it passed through the station at 50mph, with the couplings breaking between the seventeenth and eighteenth carriages, while the locomotive pulled the rest of the carriages through the station trailing the derailed seventeenth carriage. The sparks from this alerted the driver of the second locomotive to the problem and he managed to stop the train. There was no continuous brake, and the last six carriages ran on unbraked, mounting the platform ramp and demolishing part of the station, while one landed upside down and collapsed, crushing its passengers. All in all, 13 were killed and 30 injured, possibly by the track widening out of gauge.

*Abbots Ripon, **Great Northern Railway**, 21 January 1876:*
A southbound coal train ran past signals frozen into the 'clear' position, but was stopped by hand lamp signals, but while being shunted off the main line, an express also raced through the frozen signal and into the back of the coal train. A northbound express then ran into the wreckage, scattered over both up and down lines. There were 13 killed and 24 injured.

*Tay Bridge, **North British Railway**, 28 December 1879: see **Tay Bridge**.*

*Penistone, **Manchester, Sheffield &
Lincolnshire Railway**, July 1884:*
The locomotive axle broke on an express
from **Manchester** to Grimsby and the sever-
ity of the jolt broke a defective coupling
between the tender and the leading carriage,
fitted with the non-automatic type of
vacuum brake, leaving the train without any
braking at all. While the locomotive and
tender remained on the line, the carriages
rolled over and down the embankment,
killing 24 passengers and injuring more
than 60.

*Armagh, **Great Northern Railway of
Ireland**, 12 June 1889:*
A heavy and overcrowded excursion train
was worked by a locomotive not powerful
enough, and stalled on a 1 in 75 gradient,
whereupon the driver decided to divide the
train. The train was fitted with a non-automatic vacuum brake, and once uncoupled,
the only brake available to these carriages
was a handbrake. As it set off with the rest
of the train, the locomotive slipped back
slightly, bumped into the uncoupled
carriages, knocked off the handbrake, and
ten carriages with 600 passengers aboard
began to run back down the gradient, where
they ran into a second train running at
around 25mph. In the collision, 78 passengers were killed and 250 injured, many of
them children.

*Preston, **London & North Western
Railway**, 15 August 1896:*
After the railway **races** to Scotland, schedules were very tight. The 8pm from Euston
to Scotland was double-headed but neither
driver had worked the train before or driven
an express not booked to stop at Preston,
where a sharp curve at the northern end had
a 15mph speed restriction. The two drivers
took the curve at around 50mph, derailing
the entire train, but fortunately, thanks to
the improved construction of rolling stock

and the lack of any obstacle, only one
person was killed.

*Wellingborough, **Midland Railway**,
2 September 1898:*
A barrow fell off a platform onto the line
just as a **St Pancras** to **Manchester** express
approached. The bogie of the locomotive
was derailed, and the locomotive then
struck a cross over, which completely
derailed the locomotive which swung round
blocking the path of the rest of the train,
which crashed into it killing 7 persons.

*Salisbury, **London & South Western
Railway**, 30 June 1906:*
With keen competition between the LSWR
and the **Great Western** for the ocean liner
traffic between Plymouth and **London**,
speeds were high. After an engine change at
Templecombe, the driver of an up-express
ran through Salisbury station, which had
sharp curves at both ends, at high speed and
the train was derailed. Out of just 43
passengers aboard, 24 were killed.

*Grantham, **Great Northern Railway**,
9 September 1906:*
A down passenger and mail express from
King's Cross raced through the station
instead of stopping, and then passed several
signals at danger, before taking the junction
with the line to Nottingham too fast. The
locomotive tender derailed first, dragging
the locomotive and the following carriages
off the line, with most either wrecked or
burnt out in the fire that followed, while 14
persons, including the enginemen, were
killed. No explanation has ever been uncov-
ered for this accident.

*Shrewsbury, **London & North Western
Railway**, 15 October 1907:*
The night mail from Crewe to the West of
England was due to stop and let a **Great
Western Railway** locomotive take over from

the LNWR one, which was driven around the tight curve on the station approach at around 60 mph, derailing itself and killing 18 people, including the footplatemen.

Hawes Junction, **Midland Railway**, 24 December 1910:

The signalman during the early hours was preoccupied with a large number oif light engine movements by banking locomotives that had assisted heavy trains to Aisgill summit. He forgot about two locomotives, coupled together to return to Carlisle, which he had moved on to the down main line. The midnight express from **St Pancras** to **Glasgow** approached under clear signals, and the crews of the two locomotives thought the signals were for them and moved off. They were overtaken by the express and in the resulting collision, cylinders containing compressed oil gas for carriage lighting burst open and caused a fire that killed 12 passengers. Track circuiting would have avoided this accident.

Aisgill, **Midland Railway**, 2 September 1913:

Two southbound sleeper expresses were given poor quality coal and steamed poorly as a result. The first raised so little steam that it could not operate the vacuum brake ejector, and the brakes engaged, stalling the train on a 1 in 100 gradient. The driver of the second train was so determined to force his train onwards that he misread the signals at Mallerstang, and in the darkness did not see anything ahead of him until it was too late, and he crashed into the rear carriage of the stalled train, causing fire to break out with the loss of 16 lives.

Quintinshill, **Caledonian Railway**, 22 May 1915:

The signalman due to start his shift at 6 am usually travelled on the 6.10 am down from Carlisle if he knew it was to be run into a siding at Quintinshill to allow the night express from **Euston** through. To cover up his late arrival, the night shift man would write the entries onto a piece of paper so that his colleague could copy them into the register after he arrived. On the day of the accident, the siding was occupied, so to clear the line for the express the local was run onto the up line. The signalman then forgot about the local, which he had just travelled on, and concentrated on transferring the paper entries into the register. He accepted an up troop special, and gave the all-clear. He then accepted the **London** to **Glasgow** and **Edinburgh** express. The troop train collided with the local train and the wreckage was immediately torn into by the express from London, which was double-headed. Fire broke out, and it is believed that 227 were killed and 246 injured, but the exact death toll will never be known as the military records were destroyed in the fire.

Abermule, **Cambrian Railway**, 26 January 1921:

On a single line section, one driver was given the single line tablet for the wrong section, which he failed to check. His train met an up-express from Aberystwyth, colliding head-on, with the loss of 17 lives and another 36 people injured.

Sevenoaks, **Southern Railway**, 24 August 1927:

The old **South Eastern & Chatham Railway** lines were often ballasted with shingle from the beach at Dungeness, which were round and smooth and did not offer stability, especially when wet. The K-class 2-6-4 tank engines were also known to roll dangerously. An express from **Cannon Street** to **Dover** hauled by one such engine started to roll and then derailed on the curve between Dunton Green and Sevenoaks, with a Pullman car striking the central pier of a bridge and jamming itself across the track, so that the rest of the carriages piled up against it. This accident killed 13 persons and injured another 61.

*Charfield, **London, Midland & Scottish Railway**, 10 December 1937:*
A **Leeds** to **Bristol** mail train was running at full speed as a goods train was being shunted into a siding. The enginemen on the mail were sure that the distant signal showed clear and hit the goods train under an overbridge, where the carriages piled up and the resultant fire burned for twelve hours, killing 15 people.

*Battersea Park, **Southern Railway**, 2 April 1937:*
The lock and block system used on the busy Southern lines was modified to allow a signalman to free the interlocking if the apparatus failed to reduce delays to traffic. When the signalman at Battersea found himself in difficulty, he cleared his instrument on the up local line, allowing a train to come forward into a section already occupied: in the resulting collision between two electric multiple unit trains, 10 people were killed and another 80 injured.

*Castlecary, **London & North Eastern Railway**, 10 December 1937:*
Points choked with snow meant that a goods train could not be diverted into a siding, and a Dundee to **Glasgow** train behind it ran past signals in a heavy snowstorm, but managed to stop, although its last carriage was out of sight of the signalbox. The signalman assumed that it had run straight through, forgetting about the obstruction on the line, and accepted an express from **Edinburgh** to Glasgow, which was running too fast for the conditions, which ran into the back of the train from Dundee and in the collision, 35 persons were killed and 179 injured.

*Norton Fitzwarren, **Great Western Railway**, 4 November 1940:*
The Great Western was one of the pioneers of automatic train control, although its system allowed the locomotive driver to cancel a warning, retaining full control of the train if he decided that an emergency brake application was unnecessary.

On the night of 4 November 1940, the driver of an overnight passenger train from **Paddington** to the West of England was routed onto the down relief line as he was running late. On the GWR, drivers sat on the right hand side of the cab, and the driver thought that the signals on the main line, set at 'clear' for a down newspaper train, were for his train, but the signals for the relief line were set at danger. When the alarm sounded, he cancelled it. The newspaper train began to overhaul his train and the two trains passed as they ran through the station. Only then did the driver of the passenger train realise his mistake and apply the brakes. A trap point took the relief line running into a dead end with soft ground on the other side. Although the driver braked hard there was not enough room for him to stop, and his locomotive ploughed into the soft ground and six of the carriages behind it were derailed, scattering over the tracks.

As with most wartime trains, there was severe overcrowding with an estimated 900 passengers on the train, of whom 27 were killed and another 75 injured.

*Bethnal Green, **London Passenger Transport Board**, 3 March 1943:*
The worst loss of life on the British railway system of the war years had little to do with enemy action. The still unopened **Central Line** station at Bethnal Green was being used as an air raid shelter, and as the warning sounded, the local population headed for what they thought would be safety. A woman carrying a baby tripped as she went down a short staircase of just nineteen steps,

with the press of those behind meaning that others fell. Within a few minutes 173 people, 62 of them children were killed by suffocation and crush injuries.

Harrow, **British Railways,**
8 October 1952:
The up-Perth sleeping car express was running late on a misty morning while the low-sun made it difficult for the driver and fireman to see the signals, which they over-ran at speed and collided with a local train sitting in the station. A down **Euston** to **Manchester** and **Liverpool** express ran into the wreckage, knocking down a footbridge and scattering carriages over a platform on which people were waiting for a **Bakerloo** tube train. At least 122 persons were killed.

Princess Victoria, **British Railways,**
31 January 1953:
One of the first drive-on/drive-off car ferries, *Princess Victoria* left Stranraer for Larne in a bad storm. As she made her crossing, water started to enter the vehicle deck and as she rolled in the storm, surged across the deck. Her engines failed and she signalled that she was 'not under command'. Despite a Royal Navy destroyer being sent to her aid, she sank, with the loss of 133 out of the 177 persons aboard, including her master and three prominent Ulster politicians, with just 34 passengers and ten crew surviving.

Lewisham, **British Railways,**
4 December 1957:
The driver of a Cannon Street to Ramsgate express was so concerned about the steaming of his locomotive that he overran two caution signals at full speed and did not brake until he had passed a red, crashing into the back of an electric multiple unit suburban train stopped at a signal under the flyover carrying the Nunhead line. The steam locomotive then struck the columns of the flyover, which collapsed on top of the wreckage, contributing to the 90 lives lost.

Hither Green, **British Railways,**
5 November 1967:
The line from **Charing Cross** to Hastings required special narrow-body rolling stock, and until electrified had diesel multiple units. One evening a down train was derailed by a broken rail, killing 49 people and injuring another 78. The casualty figures would have been far higher but for it being a Sunday evening on this busy commuter line.

Moorgate, **London Transport,**
28 February 1975:
An early morning **Northern Line** tube train on the City & Northern Branch ran into the station at full speed, overshot and went into the sand drag at the end and, still in tunnel, hit the cul-de-sac wall at the end, the first two carriages concertinaed. There were 43 persons killed and another 74 injured. The cause of the crash has never been fully explained.

King's Cross, *London Transport,*
18 November 1987:
A small fire under an up escalator from the **Piccadilly Line** platforms developed gradually over fifteen minutes until there was a sudden flash-over and a fireball swept up the escalator and into the booking hall which was below street level. The complex nature of the underground station meant that trains continued to arrive and disgorge passengers for some minutes after the fire started. In the inferno, 31 people died. It was later concluded that the fire had been started when a burning cigarette end was dropped through the escalator steps and it ignited grease, dust and rubbish under the escalator. A smoking ban was introduced on all London Underground trains and stations as a result.

*Clapham Junction, **British Railways,** 12 December 1988:*

A train had been brought to a stand on a stretch of line recently re-signalled while the signal behind the train continued to show clear. The stretch of track had a tight curve and the driver of the following up train from **Bournemouth** could not see the stopped train, and ran into it at high speed. This very busy section of line had quadruple tracks, arranged fast up, on which the accident occurred, fast down, slow up and slow down, and wreckage was scattered across adjoining tracks from the accident on the fast up, with a fast down train running into it, while a slow down to Portsmouth only just missed being hit. The cause was found to be a loose wire in the signal. The accident cost 35 lives and another 70 passengers were injured.

Adams, William, 1823-1904

Starting his career as a marine engineer, Adams helped build the **North London Railway** works at Bow, becoming their loco-motive superintendent in 1858. In 1863, he invented the Adams bogie, which moves side-ways while restrained by springs as well as pivot, and which allowed locomotives to enter curves more quickly and smoothly. He moved to the **Great Eastern Railway** in 1873 and in 1878 to the **London & South Western Railway,** staying there until ill health forced him to retire in 1895. His locomotives for the LSWR were elegant and economical in both fuel and maintenance, initially with outside cylinders, but he later adopted front-coupled locomotives. He introduced the 'Vortex' blast pipe, invented by his nephew Henry. His outstanding locomotives included 4-4-0s for expresses and mixed traffic, and 4-4-2 tanks for suburban services, although he was also famous for long-lasting 0-4-4 tanks, a number of them lasting in daily service on the **Isle of Wight** until the end of steam on the island in late 1966.

Advanced Passenger Train, APT – see **High Speed Trains**

Air Transport and Railways

The railways received Parliamentary authority to operate air services in 1929, a year after they obtained powers to operate road transport. The **Southern Railway** made a bid to acquire the European services of Imperial Airways, the state-sponsored national airline. Nevertheless, the '**Big Four**' railway companies were forced to enter the air transport market in 1932 to react to small airlines that were being established in several parts of the country. First to get airborne was the **Great Western Railway** in 1933, with a service between **Cardiff** and **Plymouth** – a long journey by road or rail. With the technical and operational support of Imperial Airways, the **Big Four** formed **Railway Air Services** in 1934, with its first service being sponsored by the **Southern Railway,** linking Croydon with the **Isle of Wight,** and closely followed by the GWR with a route between **Plymouth** and **Liverpool.** The **London, Midland & Scottish** then sponsored services linking **London,** Belfast, **Birmingham, Manchester** and **Glasgow.** Alone, the **London & North Eastern Railway** did not become involved beyond its shareholding in RAS.

The railway interest in air transport was primarily a defensive move against competi-tion from the independent airlines, and travel agents were even threatened with the loss of railway business should they sell tickets for airlines not handled by the **Railway Clearing House.** The creation of the prestige trains such as the 'Golden Arrow' and 'Night Ferry' were also defen-sive moves against the growing popularity of air transport. Many of the independent airlines collaborated with the railways in order to survive. The routes to the Channel Islands were sufficiently important for Great Western & Southern Air Services to

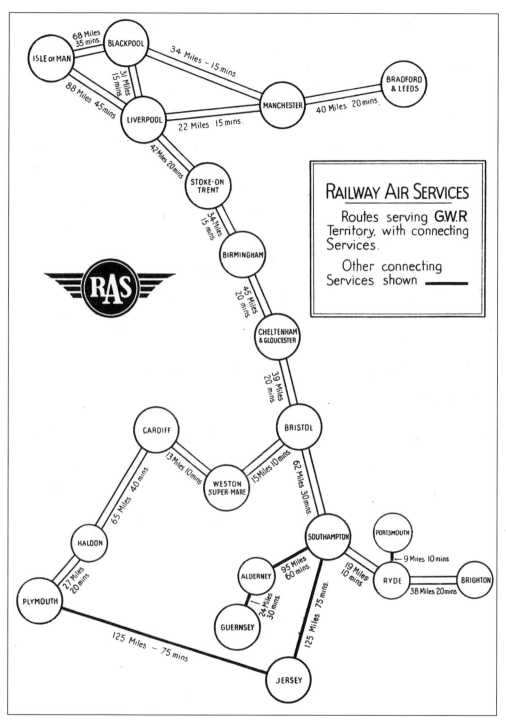

The railways were amongst the leaders in pioneering domestic air services in the British Isles, largely through Railway Air Services, with the Great Western and the Southern being the two most air-minded companies. This is the GWR network within RAS. The appeal of air transport on routes such as Cardiff to Weston Super Mare or Plymouth is obvious. (Great Western Railway Magazine)

be established as a separate entity. The SR also built the first airport stations at Gatwick and at Shoreham, which was actually a halt on the line between Brighton and Littlehampton.

While the Second World War saw most internal air services grounded, apart from those across the Irish Sea to Dublin, the railways nevertheless were active in buying out the smaller airlines and in 1944 published a plan for the development of post-war European air transport. The SR went further, and even acquired land in Kent for the construction of a post-war airport for **London**. All of these plans came to nothing when a Labour administration was elected in 1945. Nevertheless, **British Railways** retained air transport powers until 1993.

Alexandra (Newport & South Wales) Docks & Railway

As the name implies, this was originally a dock company, formed in 1865 to build a new dock at Newport. It took ten years to complete the work because of the company's financial weakness, but once it was finished local business interests argued that a railway connection with the Rhondda would enable it to attract a share of the booming South Wales coal traffic. In 1878, the Pontypridd Caerphilly & Newport Railway was established, with running powers over the lines of five other railways to bring coal to Newport docks, and this opened in 1884. In preparation for the opening of the new railways, the Alexandra changed from being a 'docks' company to a 'docks and railway' in 1882, and in 1887 it purchased the Pontypridd Caerphilly & Newport Railway. While freight, and especially coal, was the predominant traffic, a passenger service between Pontypridd and Newport was introduced, but this passed to the **Great Western** in 1899, leaving the Alexandra's passenger services confined to a service between Pontypridd and Caerphilly.

Meanwhile, the docks prospered and grew, with further expansion in the years leading up to the outbreak of the First World War, when the company managed to pay a dividend of 5 per cent. The actual railway route mileage owned by the company amounted to just 9.5 miles, making it the smallest of any of the constituent companies covered by the Railways Act 1921.

Allen, Cecil J, 1886-1973

One of the most prominent writers on railway matters of his day, Allen trained as an engineer before joining the **Great Eastern Railway** as a draughtsman in 1903, He was later transferred to the Permanent Way Department, and by 1908 was inspector of materials. He remained in the PWD until retiring from the **London & North Eastern Railway** in 1946. He had started writing in 1906 with a piece for the *Railway Magazine*, and in 1909, was one of four contributors to the long-running series 'British Locomotive Practice & Performance', becoming the only contributor in 1911 until the baton passed to O S **Nock** in 1958. He continued writing for *Trains Illustrated*. He started writing books in 1915, eventually writing 38, of which 8 were for children.

Allport, Sir James Joseph, 1811-1892

After joining the **Birmingham & Derby Junction Railway** in 1839, James Allport became manager in 1843, before moving to become manager of the Newcastle & Darlington Junction Railway in 1844, Manchester Sheffield & Lincolnshire Railway (predecessor of the **Great Central**) in 1850, before settling on the **Midland Railway** in 1853, but even here he was away from 1857 to 1860, managing a shipyard. Allport takes much of the credit for the MR's rapid growth. He found a railway whose boundaries were **Derby**, Leeds, Lincoln, **Bristol** and Rugby; he left a railway that reached Carlisle, Swansea and **London**, while jointly-owned lines took it to **Bournemouth, Liverpool** and Lowestoft. He introduced third-class accommodation on all MR trains from 1872, and in 1874 abolished second-class and withdrew third-class carriages, marking a major step forward in the welfare of the third-class passenger. He also introduced the first Pullman cars into the UK. On the debit side, he resisted interlocking for as long as possible. He was knighted in 1884, after retirement – another first as he was the first railway manager to be so recognised.

Arrol, Sir William, 1839-1913

Apprenticed to a blacksmith, in 1868 Arrol established a contracting business in **Glasgow**, and quickly gained a reputation for building iron railway bridges. In 1878, he was contracted to build a bridge over the Clyde and into the **Caledonian Railway's Glasgow Central Station**, but the contract awarded for a bridge across the **Forth** the following year was cancelled after the **Tay Bridge** disaster. Nevertheless, in 1882, his firm, by this time Tancred Arrol, was successful in gaining the contract for the new Forth Railway Bridge and he was knighted on completion in 1890. His firm had by this time a worldwide reputation and handled contracts around the world, including, closer to home, the Tower Bridge in **London**. Arrol was also a director of the Union Castle steamship line, a bank and a steelmaker.

Ashfield, Albert Henry Stanley, Lord, 1874-1948

The Knattries family migrated from Derby to the USA, and Albert Knattries started work as a messenger with the Detroit Street Railway in 1888. He moved to scheduling in 1893 on the first electrified line and by 1902, was general superintendent. The following year, he moved to the Public Service Corporation of New Jersey, and then in 1907 became general manager of the **Underground Electric Railways** of London, replacing the first general manager, **Gibb**, and given the task of making the **Metropolitan District** and the group's three tube lines profitable. He had adopted the surname Stanley in 1897.

During his first seven years in **London** he reorganised the **Underground** group and also acquired the London General Omnibus Company in 1912, creating an organisation referred to as the 'Combine'. He recognised the value of good publicity and appointed Frank **Pick**. He became a naturalised British subject in 1913, and in 1916-1919 he was President of the **Board of Trade** in Lloyd George's wartime government, for which he was knighted. Post-war, he returned to the **Underground** group as chairman and managing director, and began a process of coordination of bus and railway operations in London that effectively paved the way for the formation of the **London Passenger Transport Board** in 1933, a nationalised concern created by a Conservative government. He headed the new LPTB, but was disappointed that while the four mainline railway companies had to pool their suburban receipts with the LPTB's railway operations, there was no common management or coordination. Post-**nationalisation** of the railways, he became a full-time member of the **British Transport Commission**.

Aspinall, Sir John Audley Frederick, 1851-1937

Trained at **Crewe**, he moved to become locomotive superintendent of the **Great Southern & Western Railway of Ireland** in 1883, making a significant contribution to the efficiency of the vacuum brake. He moved to the **Lancashire & Yorkshire Railway** in 1886, completing the new works being built at Horwich, and where he completed the prototype of his famous 2-4-2 tank engines in 1889. Later he built his

'Highflyer' 4-4-2 locomotives with inside cylinders and 7 ft 3 in wheels. The L&CR promoted him to general manager in 1899, and he was active in promoting electrification starting with the Liverpool and Southport line in 1904, and then the Manchester-Bury line in 1915. He was appointed Associate Professor of Railway Engineering at Liverpool University, and after retirement in 1919 was in demand for his expertise, including conducting the enquiry into the Sevenoaks railway disaster in 1927.

B

Baker, Sir Benjamin, 1840-1907

After completing his apprenticeship at Neath Abbey ironworks in 1860, Baker worked for an associate of Sir John Fowler on Victoria Station and the associated Grosvenor Bridge, before joining Fowler in 1862 working on the Metropolitan Railway. Fowler persuaded Baker to remain in Britain rather than take his skills abroad, and in 1869, he became Fowler's chief assistant on the Metropolitan District Railway. Baker in due course became an authority on urban railways and tunnelling, and at home worked on the City & South London, Central London and Bakerloo, as well as going to the USA to work on the Hudson River Tunnel. He took the lead in designing the Forth Bridge, completed in 1890. He also built the first Aswan Dam in Egypt.

Baker, William, 1817-1878

Baker initially worked on the London & Birmingham and other railways, working under George Buck, until 1852, when he became the London & North Western's Southern Division engineer, and became the LNWR's chief engineer in 1859. His major projects included the Runcorn Bridge and the building of Birmingham's New Street

Station, reconstruction of Crewe, and building or reconstruction of other stations at Liverpool, Manchester and Preston. He also built new lines and widened existing ones, and built the Dundalk Newry & Greenore Railway in Ireland.

Baker Street & Waterloo Railway/ Bakerloo Line

Incorporated in 1893, little happened until 1897 when Whitaker Wright's London & Globe Finance Corporation took over the project. While work began in 1898 with a tunnel under the River Thames, the project stopped when LGFC collapsed in 1901, but the following year the American C T Yerkes' Underground Electric Railways Group took over, and the line eventually opened in 1906, going beyond Waterloo to Elephant & Castle, over 3.6 route miles. Initially, there was a flat fare of just 2d (less than 1p). The Baker Street & Waterloo Railway was nicknamed the 'Bakerloo' by the journalist G H F Nichols because it linked the two, but there was some dismay when the title was adopted officially. The editor of the Railway Magazine sniffly declared that '...for a railway itself to adopt its gutter title is not what we expect from a railway company.'

In 1910, the company passed to the recently formed London Electric Railway, along with the Charing Cross, Euston & Hampstead Railway, predecessor of the Northern Line. Steady extension then followed, with the line reaching Paddington in 1913, and in 1915 it reached Queen's Park where it connected to the London & North Western Railway, and in 1917 used the LNWR tracks to reach Watford. A plan to extend the line south to Camberwell was authorised in 1931, reconsidered in 1949, but then abandoned. The line passed to the newly formed London Passenger Transport Board in 1933. In 1939, it was used to reduce congestion on the inner section of the **Metropolitan Line** by providing a tube link between Baker Street to Finchley Road so that Bakerloo trains could run to Stanmore, by that time Bakerloo trains were operating over 32 route miles. In turn, the central London section of the Bakerloo itself became so congested that in 1979, the Stanmore branch achieved an independent existence as the **Jubilee Line**.

Ballycastle Railway
Supported by the **Belfast & Northern Counties Railway**, this 3ft gauge line ran for 16¼ miles from Ballymoney, on the BNCR mainline, to Ballycastle. It opened in 1880 and was absorbed by the **Northern Counties Committee**, successors to the BNCR, in 1928, making it a subsidiary of the **London, Midland & Scottish Railway**. It closed in 1950, after the NCC was **nationalised** in 1948.

Barlow, Peter William, 1809-1895
Brother of **William Henry Barlow**, he became a pupil of H R Palmer on the Birmingham & Liverpool Junction Canal and docks in London, before becoming **Sir William Cubitt**'s resident engineer on the **South Eastern Railway** (see **South Eastern & Chatham Railway**). He also worked on the Londonderry & Enniskillen and the Oswestry & Newtown, and on the over-ambitious Londonderry & Coleraine, which planned to run across Lough Foyle on reclaimed land. He took an interest in suspension bridges and was engineer for the suspension bridge at Lambeth, at the time the largest to use wire ropes. A proponent of underground railways, he became chairman of the Tower Subway Company, the first to use the Greathead shield.

Barlow, William Henry, 1812-1902
Younger brother of **Peter William Barlow**, he originally trained as a dock engineer, before working in Constantinople for the Turkish authorities between 1832 and 1838. He returned home to work for the **Manchester & Birmingham** and the **Midland Counties Railways**, before joining the **Midland** in 1844, where he retained a connection even after moving into private practice in 1857. In 1849, he patented the 'saddleback' form of rail, sometimes known as the 'Barlow Rail', which dispensed with sleepers and could sit in the ballast, but which was ultimately unsuccessful. His greatest work was the building of **St Pancras** in 1868. In 1879, he was asked to investigate the **Tay Bridge disaster**, and later was largely responsible for the second bridge.

Barry Railway
As demand for coal grew during the second half of the nineteenth century, the docks at **Cardiff** soon proved to be completely inadequate to meet the demand, and the pressure to use other ports for the export of the coal grew. A group of mine owners pressed to build a new dock at Barry, to the west of Cardiff, in 1883, but faced opposition from the **Taff Vale** and **Rhymney** railway companies, but in 1884 they were successful and obtained parliamentary approval. The company was allowed to build a 19 mile long line from Trehafod, to the north of Pontypridd, where it had a junction with the Taff Vale, and three short branches. Later, there were also connections with the **Great Western** at Bridgend, established in 1900, and with the **Brecon & Merthyr Railway** near Caerphilly in 1905. The line opened in February 1889, followed in July by the new port, with a dock area of 73 acres, which was increased to 120 acres in 1898.

The new port was an immediate success, so that by 1892, its traffic equalled a third of that of Cardiff, and by the outbreak of the First World War it handled as much coal as Cardiff and Penarth combined. It was the only truly railway-owned port, but depended on its connection with other railways for most of its traffic. The commercial success was reflected in the dividends paid, which during the period 1894-1920 averaged 9.5-10.0 per cent. On the debit side, much of this economic success was the result of over-zealous cost-cutting, with as many as a third of its locomotives out of service awaiting repairs.

Beattie, J H, 1804-1871.

Beattie became locomotive superintendent of the **London & South Western Railway** in 1850 until he died in office. Inventive, he patented many improvements in steam locomotive design and moved the railways away from locomotives with a single pair of driving wheels, introduced improvements in the burning of coal and achieved economy by condensing steam so to provide hot feed water. Nevertheless, some of his inventions required heavy maintenance which countered their other advantages.

Beeching, Lord, (1913-85)

Probably no one involved with Britain's railways in the twentieth century has been as controversial as Lord Beeching, associated by many with drastic and even damaging cuts to the country's railway network.

The then Richard Beeching graduated from Imperial College, **London**, and spent the Second World War on armaments research. As Dr Richard Beeching, he became technical director of Imperial Chemical Industries (ICI), in 1957. In 1961, he was appointed Chairman of the **British Transport Commission**, and then chairman-designate of the new **British Railways Board** when that was established in 1962. This was a period when the BRB was under strong political pressure to cut its mounting deficit. Beeching produced two reports, of which the better known was the first, *The Re-Shaping of British Railways*, which proposed closing some 2,000 stations and

withdrawing 250 train services. The resultant outcry, and the bitterness felt even today, has eclipsed his second report, *The Development of the Major Trunk Routes*, which proposed major investment in what would be a strong network.

Credited with the ability to grasp unfamiliar subjects and for his power of analysis, Beeching's methodology has been criticised. He analysed line by line, station by station and train service by train service, identifying where the losses were being incurred. This approach failed to identify those parts of the network that made a valuable contribution by feeding the trunk lines, or those, such as resort stations, which had relatively low ticket sales, but nevertheless were used by large numbers carrying return tickets bought elsewhere. He also failed to

Britain's railway network more or less at its peak in 1952, although a few minor lines had already been closed and many more were to come in the next few years, but all pre-Beeching.

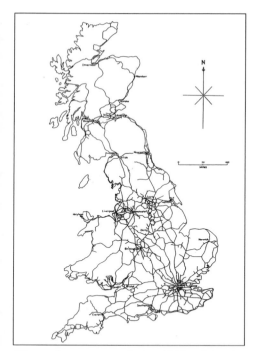

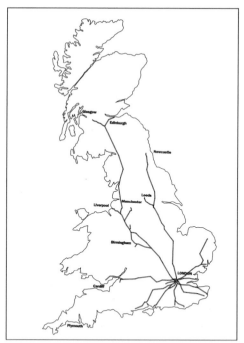

The railway network in 1985 after the Beeching cuts, and a number of post-Beeching cuts as well. Scotland, Wales, East Anglia and Yorkshire have taken the brunt of the cuts.

This is how Serpell would have re-shaped the railways, leaving very little left. Would the line from Newcastle south to London have been profitable without the Edinburgh and Aberdeen traffic? Would travellers from Plymouth have been prepared to catch the train at Bristol, or would they have kept on driving?

appreciate the scope for substantial cost savings in running rural branch lines. To be completely fair, however, he also sought to end much duplication and many of the services he wished to discontinue were almost impossible to justify.

Beeching called in his second report for more electrification and high speed freight trains, all demanding higher levels of investment.

Beeching disagreed with a new Labour government in 1964, and resigned in 1965, being made a life peer while also returning to ICI. He later chaired the Royal Commission that established the present English Crown Court system.

Belfast & County Down Railway

Incorporated in 1846, the first section of the Belfast & County Down Railway, built to

Irish standard gauge of 5 ft 3 ins was opened in 1848, running 44¼ miles from Belfast to Downpatrick, with branches to Holywood, on the outskirts of Belfast, the coastal resort of Bangor and Donaghadee, which with later extensions meant that the network reached 80 miles by 1912. Its longest line was to Newcastle, Co Down, close to what later became the border with the Irish Free State, now the Republic of Ireland. The peak rolling stock list comprised around 30 steam locomotives and 3 steam rail motors, 180 passenger carriages and 700 wagons. In 1948, it was taken over by the **Ulster Transport Authority**, and in 1950, most of the network was closed, with the exception of

Newcastle to Castlewellan, which connected with the **Great Northern Railway of Ireland**, but which closed in 1955, and Belfast to Bangor, which remains open.

Belfast & Northern Counties Railway

Formed in 1860 by the merger of four smaller railways: Belfast & Ballymena Railway, Ballymena Railway, Coleraine & Portrush Railway, and the Londonderry & Coleraine Railway, all of which were on Irish standard gauge of 5ft 3ins, and in 1884 acquired the 3ft gauge Ballymena, Cushendall & Red Bay Railway. In total, it had 201 miles of standard gauge and 48 miles on 3ft gauge, with a main line, single in places, 80 miles from Belfast to Londonderry, which with the line from Belfast to Larne, packet port for Stranraer in Scotland, and the branch to Portrush, remains in use.

The company faced direct competition with the **Great Northern Railway of Ireland** between Belfast and Londonderry, but had the faster line. In 1903, it was taken over by the expansive **Midland Railway**, whose livery it adopted, and which paid lip service to local control by establishing the **Northern Counties Committee**, NCC, which became its name. In 1923, it became part of the **London, Midland & Scottish Railway**, which provided it with re-gauged versions of its standard steam locomotives and carriages. It was acquired by the **British Transport Commission** on **nationalisation** of Britain's railways in 1948, but sold to the **Ulster Transport Authority** in 1949.

Most of the lines were closed in the 1960s, other than those to Londonderry, Portrush and Larne. One of the first actions of the UTA was to introduce the 'Belfast Express', which was introduced in 1949 and provided 2 hr 15 minute timing between Londonderry and the capital. An unusual feature of the main line to Londonderry is that at one point the line runs across the runway of an airfield built during the Second World War.

Belfast Holyrood & Bangor Railway

Opened in 1848 and extended to Bangor in 1865, this 12½ mile line of Irish standard gauge was absorbed by the **Belfast & County Down Railway** in 1884, and remains in use today.

Big Four

General term for the four grouped companies: the **London Midland & Scottish**, the **London & North Eastern**, the **Great Western** and the **Southern**.

Birmingham

Unlike many of the major centres nurtured by the advent of the railway age, Birmingham was already a growing industrial city, sometimes described as the 'workshop of the world', before the railways arrived. It was the hub of a canal network that served the Midlands and beyond, with the Grand Union Canal linking the city with London. Many of the canals were to pass into railway ownership. Birmingham was linked to London by rail in 1838 when the **London & Birmingham Railway** opened its line from Euston. The **Great Western Railway**'s advance on Birmingham was abruptly checked when the **Midland Railway** acquired the **Birmingham & Gloucester** and **Bristol & Gloucester** companies, to the relief of the **London & North Western Railway**, as the LBR had become by this time, that had been concerned about the disruption that would be caused by broad gauge lines running into the city if the Great Western was welcomed by the Midland into its terminus at New Street.

The GWR was determined to serve Birmingham, however, and indeed aimed to go further north to Merseyside. Its ambitions were to be satisfied by the acquisition of first the Birmingham & Oxford Railway, which opened in 1852, and followed this in 1854 by the acquisition of the Birmingham, Wolverhampton & Dudley Railway. Unable to enter New Street, a new terminus was built for these broad gauge companies at Snow Hill, which was also in the central district of Birmingham but approached through a tunnel to avoid demolition of valuable properties. All of the companies serving Birmingham, which included the **Grand Junction** as well as the GWR, LNWR and MR, were slow to develop a suburban network for the growing city, and it was not until the 1860s that suburban branches started to open. In the case of the GWR, its Birmingham branch network concentrated on the towns to the north and west of the city, including Wolverhampton, Dudley and Kidderminster, and south to Leamington Spa, while other areas were reached with the acquisition of the Birmingham & North Warwickshire Railway, which was to become part of a GWR line competing with the MR between Birmingham and Bristol, finally opened in 1907-08. Although Snow Hill was rebuilt in 1912 and in its new form was a spacious and elegant station, local trains also had their own terminus at Moor Street. By this time, a Paddington-Banbury direct route had been opened, in 1910, and the GWR's timings from **Paddington** were now competitive with those of the LNWR, whose route was in fact slightly longer. Great Western expresses were then able to cover the 110.5 miles between the two cities in two hours.

Birmingham & Derby Junction Railway

One of three railways authorised in 1836, with the others being a predecessor of the **North Midland Railway** and the **Midland Counties Railway**, there were proposals for the BDJR to connect with both these, extending what would be the NMR line from **Leeds** to **Derby**, while the alternative was to join the MCR line from **Derby** at Rugby or Northampton. The BDJR opened in 1839 and was followed by the others in 1840.

The BDJR and NMR both used George **Stephenson** as engineer until he was replaced by his son Robert in 1837. The line ran through flat country and presented no engineering difficulties,, although trains had to reverse at Hampton. In 1840, powers were obtained for a line from Whitacre into **Birmingham** instead of the original plan for a Stretchford line – never built – and this opened in 1842.

Competition between the BDJR and the MCR meant that both companies suffered, and the BDJR paid less than 2 per cent dividends. It was not until 1843 that the two companies amalgamated under the guidance of **George Hudson**, chairman of the NMR, resulting in the creation of the **Midland Railway** in 1844.

Birmingham & Gloucester Railway

Despite earlier plans for a railway between **Birmingham** and **Bristol**, it was not until 1836 that a line between Birmingham and Gloucester was authorised, supported by the **London & Birmingham** and **Grand Junction Railways** to prevent a broad gauge line being built between Bristol and Birmingham. The line had the major obstacle of the 300ft change in levels between the Lickey Hills and the plain, which most engineers sought to avoid using a detour. The BGR's engineer, W S Moorsom, disagreed, and had the support of his directors. The result was a two mile-long gradient at 1 in 38. Locomotives were imported from the USA to work the incline, but had no more success than the British product, and until the introduction of diesel locomotives, the line required banking locomotives for trains ascending the incline. The line opened in 1840.

The opening of the line did not deter the construction of the broad gauge **Bristol & Gloucester**, which reached Gloucester in 1843, leaving Gloucester as one of the transfer stations between the two gauges. Both companies were absorbed by the **Midland Railway** in 1846.

Bishop's Castle Railway

Authorised in 1861, it opened in 1865 running ten miles between Bishop's Castle on the **Shrewsbury & Hereford Railway** to Montgomery on the **Cambrian Railway**. It was bankrupt from the day it opened. It became known for such poor quality that passengers had to have umbrellas in wet weather, and water even entered through the floors. It survived for seventy years because the area it ran through could not even support the much more economical motorbus.

Blackfriars

From its opening in 1886 until 1937, the station now known as Blackfriars was known as St Paul's. The current name was adopted in 1937 to allow **London** Transport to rename the **Central Line** station until then known as 'Post Office' as St Paul's.

The construction of Blackfriars, or St Paul's, was brought about by the success of the London Chatham & Dover's (see **South Eastern & Chatham**) extension towards London. The LCDR had been allowed to extend to London by its Metropolitan Extension Act of 1860, which gave it powers to reach Victoria and, more ambitious still, to a junction with the **Metropolitan Railway** at Farringdon Street, offering considerable long-term potential that was not to be realised for many years. In fact, there was an earlier station with the name of **Blackfriars**, with the first one, opened on 1 June 1864, on the south bank of the River Thames at the junction of today's Southwark Street and the approach

to Blackfriars Bridge. It served as a terminus for just a little over six months until the railway bridge over the Thames was completed, allowing trains to stop at a temporary station at Little Earl Street on the north bank from 21 December 1864. It was not until 1 June 1865, that Ludgate Hill was opened, it too becoming a terminus until the Metropolitan Extension was completed to Farringdon Street on 1 January 1866. The LCDR had persuaded both the **Great Northern** and **London & South Western Railways** to subscribe more than £300,000 apiece towards the cost of the extension with the promise of through running powers, which they soon exercised, along with the **Midland Railway**, which started running trains through to **Victoria** in 1875. The LCDR itself sent trains from Herne Hill through to **Kings Cross** and then as far as Barnet.

The new station at Ludgate Hill and the extension through the City was a considerable success, although not used by anything so ambitious as the Brighton-Rugby services of recent years. Unfortunately, a shortage of space meant that Ludgate Hill offered just two island platforms, which soon proved insufficient for the traffic on offer and, as expansion was out of the question given the high cost of property and the LCDR's overstretched finances, an additional station was built on a spur off the Metropolitan Extension, and it was this that was named St Paul's when it opened on 10 May 1886, despite the fact that the name Blackfriars was already in use as the name of the adjacent District and Circle Line station.

Before the opening of St Paul's, the LCDR lines south of the Thames had been widened and a second bridge had been built across the Thames alongside the original bridge and to the east of it, carrying seven tracks. The new terminus was a necessity forced on the railway and was built as cheaply as possible without any great architectural pretensions, even having a wooden booking office. The cramped surroundings and the presence of the **Metropolitan District Railway** immediately under the station meant that there was no forecourt and no cab access to the tar-coated wooden platforms, which were reached by a dark and drab staircase. Only two of the platforms were given numbers, simply 1 and 2 between the eastern siding and the up and down loops. Despite this, in incised letters on the stones surrounding the doors, the names were given of fifty-four destinations that could be reached from the station, including St Petersburg and Vienna, with nothing to suggest that the intrepid traveller could expect to make several changes along the way. Rather more practical was the inclusion in this list of Westgate-on-Sea and Crystal Palace. Two through lines were lopped through the station, with another three terminating tracks. The roof was kept as short as possible, and constructed of iron and glass, although canopies were provided above the outer ends of the platforms.

Trains running to Holborn Viaduct generally stopped at Blackfriars, while it also took the City portions of trains from the new Gravesend branch, opened on the same day as the new terminus, and which were later joined by those from the Greenwich Park branch, opened in October 1888. The new station was the only one operated by the LCDR with direct access to the underground network. Ludgate Hill continued to prove inadequate for the traffic on offer and became the butt of much press criticism as it was the most convenient station for Fleet Street, then the home of almost all the national newspapers and of the London offices of many provincial dailies. Holborn Viaduct was generally regarded as being useless, being inconveniently sited. Despite these criticisms, it was not until well after the formation of the **South East & Chatham** that any attempt

was made to remedy the situation, with a minor reconstruction of Ludgate Hill between 1907 and 1912.

The First World War saw a dramatic reduction in services reflecting both the need to save resources and also to allow for the large number of military specials operated. These reductions hit Ludgate Hill especially hard, jammed between Blackfriars and Holborn Viaduct, and post-war, the station was open only during rush hours from 1919. **Electrification** failed to save the station, but rather hastened its end, with closure on 2 March 1929. Part of the problem was that the station was in too tight a spot for expansion, and its platform was too short for an eight car electric train by some 80 feet – roughly a carriage length and a third.

The **Southern Railway** introduced electric suburban trains to both **Holborn Viaduct** and St Paul's on 12 July 1925, initially from the latter station to Crystal Palace (High Level), Shortlands via the Catford loop, while a service from Holborn Viaduct to Shortlands and Orpington via Herne Hill also called at the station. The running roads at St Paul's were re-arranged so that trains on the local lines to Holborn Viaduct could operate in parallel with the main line trains terminating at St Paul's. There were also some modifications to the platforms, including extending all of them to take eight car trains, and at the river end these now provided some fine views of the Thames downstream. St Paul's, later Blackfriars, saw a steady extension of its electric services up until the outbreak of World War II, culminating in the extension to Gillingham and Maidstone on 2 July 1939.

The services using Blackfriars were reduced as a wartime emergency measure from 16 October 1939, including the complete withdrawal of rush hour services to Dartford via Lewisham. The First World War had spared the City termini from the worst of German bombing, with only the **Great Eastern's Liverpool Street** being hit, but the Second World War saw considerable damage inflicted, especially at the height of the 1940-41 blitz. The worst night of the blitz was that of 16/17 April 1941 when a bomb wrecked the old Blackfriars signal cabin on the south side of the river. Immediately, flagmen were put into position to signal trains through the section and work the points, but worse was to come when either a large bomb or landmine destroyed the bridge over Southwark Street and seven flagmen seeking refuge in a shelter were caught by the blast, with three being killed outright, another three dying in hospital from severe burns, and just one surviving to make a slow recovery in hospital. With military help, a temporary bridge with two running roads was ready in fifteen days, but a permanent replacement was not in place until 9 October 1942. The terminal roads at Blackfriars were locked out of use until the end of the war, while temporary signalling arrangements were provided.

It was not until 12 August 1946 that a full restoration of services could be made at **Blackfriars**, with wartime cuts in services reversed and a new signal cabin at Blackfriars opened on that day and the terminal roads re-opened. The station's platforms were numbered 1 to 5 from east to west at the same time.

Blackpool

The railways projected Blackpool from being a small seaside resort to one of the leading resorts in the British Isles. Expansion started when the **Preston & Wyre Railway** reached the town in 1846. A little more than half a century later, the number of visitors annually had soared from around 3,000 to more than 3 million. A second line running along the coast reached the town in 1861, although this was not connected to the line to **Preston** until 1874, by which time both lines into the resort were owned and operated jointly by the **Lancashire & Yorkshire Railway** and the **London & North Western Railway**, but both companies used separate termini, with the LYR using Talbot Road, which later became Blackpool North, and which was rebuilt in 1898 with 15 platforms, and the LNWR using Central, rebuilt in 1900 with 14 platforms. In 1903, the 1861 coast line had an avoiding line built that shortened the distance from Preston by five miles.

Between the world wars, motor coaches made inroads into the summer excursion traffic, and this increased post-war with the added competition from private cars. Nevertheless, the main factor in the decline of Blackpool as a resort and the reduction in railways services has been the growth of foreign package holidays. The direct line was closed in 1967 and services were concentrated on Blackpool North, rebuilt in 1974, while through services to and from London ended in 1992, although there are still direct services to **Manchester** and **Leeds**.

Blyth & Tyne Railway

Dating from 1852, the Blyth & Tyne Railway was a merger of a number of small railways in the area between Morpeth, Blyth and Tynemouth. At the time, the export trade of coal through Blyth was growing rapidly, as were landings of fish, and in 1862, the BTR agreed to exchange traffic at Morpeth with the **North British Railway**. In 1864, the BTR opened a branch line to **Newcastle**.

Meanwhile, the **North Eastern Railway** had been attempting to unite the many small railways in Northumberland and Durham, and the BTR remained the only significant independent company. The BTR was profitable, with average dividends during 1854-64 of 9 per cent, and continuing to improve afterwards, peaking at 12.5

per cent in 1872. It was predominantly a freight railway, with passenger traffic providing just a quarter of its revenue. Nevertheless, substantial investment was needed, with the harbour at Blyth needing dredging to allow larger ships to use the port, while the agreement with the NBR had failed to produce substantial traffic. The NER bought the BTR for a substantial sum in 1874.

The wealthy NER started work on the port at Blyth in 1880, by which time the port's coal traffic had fallen to 235,000 tons, but over the next three decades it rose to 4,164,000 tons, and it was to rise still further to peak at more than 6 million tons in the early 1960s.

Board of Trade

The Board of Trade was primarily concerned with British shipping, but as the railway network grew, it was felt that some form of government regulation would be necessary. The House of Commons appointed two committees to investigate the matters, and they recommended in 1838 that the railways should be regulated by a new board which would itself be answerable to the BoT. In 1840, the Railway Department of the Board of Trade was established. The BoT had already been collecting statistics on railways, and the head of its statistical department, G R Porter, became the first head of the Railway Department. The new department had five people when it was formed, but the entire staff of the BoT at the time totalled just thirty.

Not only was the BoT responsible to Parliament for examining new lines and certifying that they were safe to open, but it also acquired responsibility for investigation of accidents. The engineering expertise needed came from the Royal Engineers, whose officers soon acquired a sound reputation for their judgement and fairness, which was a considerable achievement as

their experience was in civil engineering rather than railway operation. Even so, given the novelty of the steam locomotive, in the early days weaknesses of design or construction were sometimes overlooked.

The BoT lost its responsibilities for the railways after the First World War with the creation of a separate **Ministry of Transport**.

Boat trains

From the outset, ports were important to the railways; what would be today described as 'traffic generators'. The early railways often linked inland towns or mining areas with the nearest port, a good example being the **Liverpool & Manchester**.

The **London & Blackwall Railway** was amongst the first to carry passenger traffic on its services to the pier at Blackwall, but these were not boat trains as such, and more akin to current services between **Waterloo** and **Portsmouth** carrying passengers for the **Isle of Wight** ferries. Nevertheless, there were also attempts to link ferries and trains at Greenock and Ardrossan, but at first disagreements between the railways and the shipping companies made this difficult, not least because ferry schedules were often dependent on tides and weather. These problems affected the quality of the connections provided at Dover and Folkestone between trains from London and ferries to Boulogne and Calais, which started during 1843-44.

The ferries to Ireland used ports that were less affected by the tides, and so the first british boat train was the **London & North Western Railway**'s 'Irish Mail', which conveyed passengers and mail between London and Holyhead at the same times daily. On some routes, notably the **Great Eastern Railway**'s boat trains from Liverpool Street to Harwich, only steamer passengers would be carried, but on other routes, non-ferry passengers were also allowed. Some railways, including the **South Eastern & Chatham**, built special sets for ferry passengers with a higher standard of comfort, and this practice was continued by the **Southern Railway** with its 'Golden Arrow' Pullman expresses. The **Great Western** also did this with its carriages for passengers joining and leaving transatlantic liners at **Plymouth**.

While the 'Irish Mail' was more of a description than a title, many of the boat trains were given special names and were amongst the more prominent **named** trains: the 'Golden Arrow' was one of the most famous, as was the 'Ocean Liner Express' between Waterloo and **Southampton** Docks, while there was also the 'Ulster Express' between **Euston** and Heysham.

Bombing – see **Railways at War**

Bonsor, Sir H Cosmo, Bt, 1848-1929
A man with widespread interests, Bonsor was MP for what is now Wimbledon, 1885-1900; a director of the Bank of England; a brewer; and succeeded Edward **Watkin** as chairman of the **South Eastern Railway** in 1898. He was made a baronet in 1925.

The SER was locked in ruinous competition with the **London Chatham & Dover Railway**, and Bonsor's contribution to railway history was the creation of a working arrangement between the two companies, the **South Eastern & Chatham Managing Committee**, of which he became chairman in 1899. The two railways were able to coordinate and rationalise services, and Dover Marine station was built to ease transfer between boat trains and **ferries**. The 'new' railway was in good shape to bear the demands made of it during the First World War.

Bonsor was sceptical over plans to nationalise the railways before and immediately after the First World War. He remained chairman of the SECR until the end of 1922, but faced hostility amongst LCDR shareholders over the terms for the company's merger into the **Southern Railway**.

Booth, Henry, 1788-1869
Secretary and treasurer of the committees formed in 1822 for the construction of the **Liverpool & Manchester Railway**, remaining with the company when it merged with the **Grand Junction** in 1845, and when this in turn merged into the **London & North Western** in 1848, he stayed until 1859. Although a corn merchant by trade, Booth became involved with railway technology, including the development of the multi-tube boiler and inventing a screw coupling. He also wrote on railway matters, and advocated 'railway time', that is a standard time for all railways throughout the British Isles and the predecessor of GMT.

Bouch, Sir Thomas, 1822-80
After training under Joseph **Locke**, Bouch became manager and engineer for the Edinburgh & Northern Railway, and is credited with designing the world's first train ferries to cross both the **Forth** and the **Tay**. He designed and built railways throughout Great Britain, although his work, valued for its economy, often required expensive rebuilding later. Nevertheless, his work on stone viaducts was good, and he also was responsible for the towering iron trestle viaducts at Belah and Deepdale on the Barnard Castle-Tebay line. He was knighted for his design of the Tay Bridge, but died early after its collapse in which seventy people died. The blame for the disaster can be shared between Bouch and the contractors, with poor design, poor supervision of work and bad workmanship, and the fact that the bridge was too high in order to meet the demands of the harbour commissioners at Perth.

Bournemouth

Effectively a backwater until the railways came, Bournemouth was by-passed by the main coaching routes, and by the railways when they first arrived in the area with a line from Ringwood to Poole in 1847. Local opposition meant that the Ringwood Christchurch & Bournemouth Railway did not reach the town until 1870, but this was leased to the **London & South Western Railway** from the outset. Five years later, the **Somerset & Dorset Railway** reached the town and the following year was leased and worked jointly by the **Midland Railway** and the LSWR, much to the dismay of the **Great Western Railway**, although this used the 'West' station while the LSWR had the 'East'. In 1888, the LSWR opened a shorter route from Brockenhurst to Christchurch and Bournemouth, reducing the distance from London to 108 miles, and finally linked its line to Bournemouth West as well as building the new Central station on a branch off the main line.

Prior to grouping, Bournemouth was just two hours from **London** and also had four trains a day from the Midlands. Post-grouping, the Southern improved services by accelerating trains and introducing the all-Pullman *Bournemouth Belle*, and had it not been for nationalisation, would have expected to electrify the line during the mid-1950s.

Bradshaw, George, 1801-1853

Apprenticed as an engraver in **Manchester**, his first notable work was a map of British canals, rivers and railways, published in 1830. In 1838, he started printing railway timetables, and in 1842, with his partner W J Adams, started to produce *Bradshaw's Monthly Railway Guide*, which continued until 1961. A companion *Continental Railway Guide* followed in 1847 and, with the exception of the First World War, remained a regular publication until September 1939. Other publications included the *Railway Manual, Official Directory* and *Shareholders' Guide*, all published annually between 1847 and 1942.

His most famous work, *Bradshaw's Monthly Railway Guide*, became the sole standard guide to all railway services in the British Isles, using proof sheets of timetables from the railway companies themselves. While the guide carried the usual disclaimer over inaccuracies, none could ever be attributed to the publication's own staff. On the other hand, this dependence on the railway companies meant that there was no uniformity to entries or instructions, and it was down to the reader to assess which of two or more competing routes was the best, although a comprehensive index helped. It was difficult to use, not helped by very small typefaces, and its bulk was increased by advertisements by hotels and for some railway services as well. On the other hand, it remains an invaluable insight to the development of railway passenger services, and one publisher, David & Charles, produced reprints of the *Guide* for significant dates in railway history.

During the 1930s, a companion volume was produced dealing with air services.

Bradshaw was an active member of the Society of Friends. He died early from cholera during a visit to Christiana (now Oslo).

Bradshaw's Railway Guide – see **Bradshaw, George**

Brampton Railway(s)

Originating as a group of railways serving collieries to south-east of Brampton in Cumberland and which started as horse-drawn wagonways, many of them dating from the eighteenth century. Initially, only freight was carried, but between 1836 and 1881 a horse-drawn carriage, or 'dandy' carried passengers between Brampton and Brampton Junction on the **North Eastern Railway**. Steam started to be introduced during the 1830s, but conversion was not complete until 1881, when the passenger service was also converted. Services were taken over by the NER, but reverted to the mine owners as many lines closed and after nationalisation the system was operated by the National Coal Board until final closure in 1953.

Brassey, Thomas, 1805-70
Having started his career as a land agent and surveyor, heavily involved in the development of Birkenhead, in 1834 he turned to contracting, with his first project being the New Chester Road at Bromborough. The following year, his first railway contract was for the Pendridge line on the **Grand Junction Railway**, working with Joseph Locke. The working relationship between the two men continued for the rest of Brassey's life, and included work throughout Great Britain and the Continent, including the **London & South Western Railway** and most of the Paris-Le Havre Railway.

By 1841, Brassey was one of the country's leading contractors. With William Mackenzie and John Stephenson, he built the **Lancaster & Carlisle Railway** and worked on the **Caledonian Railway**, but Stephenson died in 1848 and Mackenzie became seriously ill in 1849. One of his most important contracts was on the **Great Northern Railway** between London and Peterborough. He also became involved with other contractors, including Peto and Betts, involving work on the Grand Trunk Railway in Canada. This new partnership financed and built the Victoria Docks on the Thames, and the **London Tilbury & Southend Railway**, which was one of several also operated by Brassey, a true contractor's line. All in all, he built more than 6,500 miles of railway, including a

sixth of the British network. He was one of the few contractors to survive the failure of the bankers Overend Gurney, doubtless because of his own considerable wealth for he left a fortune of £3.2 million (around £150 million at today's values).

Brecon & Merthyr Tydfil Junction Railway
Given the size of some of the companies that became constituents of the new Great Western, and the financial problems besetting the **Cambrian**, it must have seemed strange that the Brecon & Merthyr Tydfil Junction Railway did not become a constituent company of the so-called western group of companies. Nevertheless, the BMTJR was a complex operation, basically being divided into two by a 2.5 mile section of the **Rhymney Railway** between Deri Junction and Bargoed South Junction, and although possessing running powers, this must have been viewed as a structural weakness.

The northern section of the BMTJR was authorised in 1858 and opened in 1867, running between Brecon and Merthyr Tydfil. South of the Rhymney Railway, the southern section ran to Basseleg and over three miles of the Great Western Railway to Newport. This was also achieved by buying the 'Old Rumney Railway' in 1861, and using its route down the left bank of the river to build a new railway that opened in 1865. The Old Rumney's upper portion was also pressed into use and in 1905 was linked to the Barry Railway so that coal and ore could be brought down for shipment at Barry. This complicated system led to many problems with its neighbouring lines and made profitability difficult to achieve, while much of the 60 route miles were difficult to operate.

Brighton
Brighton was a fashionable seaside resort well before the arrival of the railway, due to

the fashion for sea bathing and the patronage of the Prince Regent. By the time the first railways were proposed for the town, with six rival schemes mooted between 1834 and 1835, there were no less than sixteen coach services a day between **London** and Brighton, with the 50 mile journey taking 5¹/₂ hours.

In 1836, Parliament approved the LBSCR scheme, which was the most direct but also the costliest, and the railway opened in 1841. The resort was by this time no longer fashionable, but the railway created the day tripper market and the commuter market. The LBSCR made Brighton its railway town by moving its rolling stock and carriage works there in 1852, bringing to the resort its sole industrial activity. Both the SER and LCDR proposed routes to Brighton, but failed. Having reached Brighton, the LBSCR spread itself east and west along the coast, but also ensured that these towns also received direct trains from London.

The LBSCR had what would be regarded today as an up-market image, although sometimes this seems to have been at the price of neglecting its third class passengers. Pullman trains were operated and even on ordinary expresses, a Pullman car could often be found. This was not so extravagant as it might seem, since the short distances of even its trunk services were such that a conventional dining car would have been able to take just one sitting.

After the grouping, the Brighton line became Britain's first main line **electrification**, and in true LBSCR tradition, many of the comforts of the *Brighton Belle* all-Pullman train were to be found on other services as Pullman cars were inserted into otherwise standard electric multiple units.

Bristol

New docks had opened in Bristol in 1809, but it was not until 1841 that the city was linked to London by the new **Great Western**

Railway. To be fair, the railway could not have been ready to coincide with the opening of the docks, and as many of the early railways, such as the **Stockton and Darlington** and the **Liverpool and Manchester**, were short distance and met local needs, the delay in building what was from the start a trunk route seems understandable. At the start of the nineteenth century, an entrepreneur wanting to link two major cities would have been more likely to consider building a canal.

Nevertheless, the GWR arrived in Bristol to find that the next stage of the railway westwards, the Bristol to Bridgwater section of the **Bristol & Exeter Railway**, was already opened. Both lines were built to the broad gauge favoured by **Brunel**, engineer to both companies, but it was strange that the meeting of the two at Temple Meads, about a mile from the centre of Bristol, was at right angles, and a tight curving line with a separate 'express platform' cutting across the approach to the BER's station, proved necessary. That Bristol was to be not simply a terminus but a major junction and interchange was soon confirmed by the opening of the **Bristol & Gloucester Railway** in 1844, again engineered by Brunel, but his ambition to continue the line to **Birmingham** was foiled when the **Midland Railway** suddenly acquired both the Bristol & Gloucester and the **Birmingham & Gloucester** railways in 1845. The first standard gauge trains to reach Bristol were those of the Midland Railway from Birmingham in 1854. It was not until after the opening of the **Severn Tunnel** in 1886 that the GWR could open its own route to the Midlands via Shrewsbury, followed in 1908 by a route to Birmingham Snow Hill via Stratford-upon-Avon.

Brunel's dedication to the broad gauge made both him and the GWR unpopular in Bristol, where the influential local merchants and the council felt that it isolated the city from the national standard gauge network. Feeling on the matter ran so high that as early as 1861 the first plans for a standard gauge rival line to **London** were being promoted, with the Bristol & South Western Junction Railway running forty miles to join the **London & South Western Railway** line to **Waterloo** from Exeter. There was another scheme in 1882 and yet a third as late as 1902, by which time the broad gauge was history, but another factor in these schemes was the desire to build a central station in Bristol, although finding a suitable location for this would have been difficult.

Traffic between Bristol and South Wales had been strong for many years, with the distance between Bristol and Newport by sea being just twenty-five miles. A rail link between Bristol and South Wales was introduced in 1852 with trains running over the Bristol & Gloucester and **South Wales Railways**, although this meant that the distance between Bristol and Newport by train was eighty-two miles. In 1863, the broad gauge Bristol & South Wales Union Railway opened a line from Bristol to New Passage, connecting with a steam ferry to Portskewett, which was on a short branch off the South Wales Railway. The BSWUR line eventually was adapted to provide the route to the Severn Tunnel, which opened in 1886 and with a length of more than four miles was then the world's longest underwater tunnel. The opening of the tunnel meant that most of the traffic between London and South Wales worked through Bristol and Bath, a shorter and more direct route than that via Gloucester, with an avoiding line keeping through traffic away from Temple Meads.

Meanwhile, in 1878, an elegant new Temple Meads station was built by the GWR and MR, displacing the original station and that of the Bristol & Exeter. The original station became a goods station and then a car park before being used as an exhibition centre more recently. Despite the construction of a spacious new station, continued growth meant that Temple Meads continued to be congested, and several measures were taken, initially to ease pressure on the station and then, later, to reduce distances and journey times, ending the jibe that GWR stood for 'Great Way Round'. First, the Bristol Avoiding Line was built in 1892, close to Temple Meads, while far more ambitious the Castle Cary cut-off opened in 1906 reduced the route from **Paddington** to Taunton by twenty miles. Before this, the South Wales & Bristol Direct Railway opened in 1903, and often referred to as the 'Badminton Line', cut the Paddington to South Wales route by twenty-five miles compared to that via Gloucester and ten miles compared to the line through Bath and Bristol, and journey times were better than these figures might suggest as the new line enjoyed an excellent alignment. Using the Badminton Line, even the route to Bristol was reduced by a mile, and enabled the GWR to offer a two-hour Paddington to Bristol schedule.

Other routes continued to grow out of Bristol, including one to Southampton and Portsmouth which also shared part of its route with the line to Weymouth. A relatively small port development at Portishead was linked by broad gauge track to the Bristol & Exeter Railway in 1867. Later, both the GWR and the MR built lines to the docks at Avonmouth, where new docks opened in 1877 as ever larger deep sea ships could no longer reach Bristol up the spectacular, but narrow, Avon Gorge. Surprisingly, lines into the existing Bristol Docks did not enjoy the same urgency, although three short dock branches were built eventually. Avonmouth was also connected to the South Wales line.

The lines to Bristol benefited from quadrupling during the 1930s, and both the

GWR and the MR's successor, the **London, Midland & Scottish Railway**, were given powers to borrow money to finance improvements in the Bristol area and at Temple Meads.

Bristol & Exeter Railway

Authorised in 1836 and supported by the same Bristol merchants behind the **Great Western Railway**, the BER also used the GWR's engineer, Isambard Kingdom **Brunel** and was built to the same broad gauge. While both companies were independent, the fate of the BER depended on that of the GWR, and in 1840, before it opened, it was leased by the GWR until 1849. Bridgwater was reached in 1841 with a branch to Weston-super-Mare, while Exeter was reached in 1844. Further branches followed to Clevedon, Tiverton and Yeovilton between 1847 and 1853, while the company also worked the Exeter & Crediton Railway until 1862.

With the expiry of the GWR's lease, the BER took over operations itself, but remained as a partner in the traffic between **London** and **Plymouth**. Nevertheless, it suffered when the **London & South Western Railway** reached Plymouth in 1860 using standard gauge. Meanwhile, new branches were built, including Barnstaple, Chard, Minehead, Portishead and Wells. Between 1854 and 1861, it leased the Somerset Central Railway, but in 1862 the company merged with the Dorset Central to form the **Somerset & Dorset Railway**, leased to the **Midland** and the LSWR in 1875. This move is credited with forcing the merger of the BER and the GWR the following year.

The BER had a poor reputation for the quality of its trains and infrastructure, but it was reasonably profitable and was the first major railway to use the block system, operating throughout its life without a serious accident.

Bristol & Gloucester Railway

Incorporated in 1839, the Bristol & Gloucester incorporated a horse-drawn railway of the same name opened in 1832 to carry coal to Bristol from Coalpit Heath, a distance of just nine miles. Using the same engineer as the **Great Western**, Isambard Kingdom **Brunel**, and broad gauge, in 1843, three connections with other railways were authorised, linking with the GWR at Bristol; a junction with the broad gauge Cheltenham & Great Western Union Railway, which ran from Swindon to Gloucester, at Standish Junction, and with running powers over this to Gloucester, reached in 1844. At Gloucester, the BGR met the standard gauge **Birmingham & Gloucester**. The result was that passengers and goods between the two railways had to be transferred, leading to much chaos, delay and extra expense. Daniel **Gooch** designed special equipment for handling goods, but it was unsuccessful.

The situation at Gloucester led to a Royal Commission on Gauges being appointed as early as 1845, and they visited the city to see the situation for themselves. The Bristol and Birmingham companies agreed to unite as the Bristol & Birmingham, but before this could happen, they were both absorbed by the **Midland Railway** in 1846. Nevertheless, at this stage the MR was over-extending itself, and it took until 1854 before a third rail taking mixed gauge to Bristol could be completed.

British Railways/British Rail

On **nationalisation**, the operating identity of the new railway managed by the **British Transport Commission's Railway Executive** was British Railways. A corporate identity campaign during the mid-1960s saw the shorter title adopted.

British Railways inherited the assets and manpower of the 'Big Four' or grouped railway companies, which in order of size were the **London, Midland & Scottish, London & North Eastern, Great Western** and **Southern Railways,** four very different companies. The 'new' or combined railway inherited 19,639 route miles; 20,023 steam locomotives; 36,033 locomotive-hauled passenger carriages and 4,184 electric multiple unit carriages, with the latter mainly on the SR and to a lesser extent on the LMS. There were also 1,223,634 goods wagons of which half came from private owners, although the majority of these would have been the nationalised coal mines. There were also small numbers of diesel shunting locomotives and a number of diesel railcars, the latter mainly on the Great Western which also had a diesel multiple unit.

The relationship between the BTC and the Railway Executive was uneasy. After the general manager of the GWR, Sir James **Milne,** had turned the post down, Sir Eustace **Missenden** of the SR accepted it, possibly out of a sense of duty because it appears to have given him little satisfaction.

The new BR was divided into six regions, with the Southern Region approximating to the former operating area of the Southern Railway, while a similar situation existed with the Western Region and the GWR. The LNER was divided between the Eastern Region, the North Eastern Region and the Scottish Region; while the LMS was divided between the London Midland Region and the Scottish Region. The former joint lines were allocated to the region in which they existed, while the **London, Tilbury & Southend** was transferred to the Eastern Region. The boundary lines of the regions required some movement of responsibilities. Each region had a chief regional officer as the representative of the Railway Executive.

Naturally enough, one priority was to rationalise working practices and standardise new equipment. Another was to restore the railways to their pre-war standard after the ravages of enemy action and the neglect

that resulted from having insufficient skilled maintenance personnel and over-working locomotives and rolling stock to meet the demands of the war effort. There was considerable resistance to rationalisation and standardisation, with chief mechanical engineers in particular feeling that their way was best. One early casualty was Oliver **Bulleid** of the SR.

Relationships between the RE and the regions improved considerably after Sir John Elliott replaced Missenden in 1951, but his tenure was short as he was replaced by Sir Brian (later Lord) **Robertson** in 1953, the RE disbanded and area boards were created under the BTC. Nevertheless, the situation was deteriorating as a £19m operating surplus in 1948 became a deficit of £17m by 1955. That year, in an attempt to gain complete control of the development of the railways, the BTC published a modernisation plan valued at £1,240m, but soon increased to £1,500m, over fifteen years. This was meant to mark the replacement of steam by electric and diesel traction; widespread use of larger fitted (ie air or vacuum braked) goods wagons in place of smaller hand-braked goods wagons; modernisation of passenger and goods stations, with large mechanised goods yards replacing many small yards.

The truth was, of course, that after the war the RE had allowed steam locomotive construction to continue, and while wartime losses may have made some production necessary, no attempt had been made to switch to diesel or electric traction. The BTC had been unhappy about this.

Commitments under the Modernisation Scheme included the long-delayed electrification of suburban services from **Liverpool Street,** as well as those from **King's Cross** and the **Glasgow** suburban network, and the main lines from **London** to **Birmingham, Liverpool, Manchester** and **Leeds,** and possibly also York, and a grudging commitment to electrify the Southern Region lines into Kent. Where electrification was not regarded as viable, diesel locomotives would be introduced, with diesel multiple units for the less busy passenger services.

Priority was given to the **London, Midland Region** electrification, which was delayed because of the decision to switch from the proposed 1,500 V dc overhead system to the new 25kV ac system – the correct choice as it turned out. It was also beyond the available technical resources of both BR and industry to handle more than one significant scheme at any one time. By contrast, the introduction of diesels went ahead at a reckless pace, with too many locomotives of different types ordered in quantity, many of them underpowered and, ultimately, under-utilised before early withdrawal. The lack of experience in ordering diesel traction and multiple units also showed in the arrangements made for maintenance, often using steam depots with a consequent impact on reliability. Vacuum brakes had been specified for the new goods wagons, but this had to be reversed in favour of air brakes. The new marshalling yards were, in some cases, a waste of resources as freight traffic continued to decline. Nevertheless, within fifteen years, the railway was transformed, although electrification to **York** had to await electrification of the **East Coast** main line to **Edinburgh**, while also missing was electrification of the busy, and profitable, line to **Southampton and Bournemouth**, even though the Southern's 1937 electrification had taken the third rail as far as Brookwood, more than 25 miles from Waterloo. Not everything was as it should have been, with the new diesel locomotives, for example, continuing to have a two-man crew, despite not needing a fireman and indeed having the benefit of a dead man's handle!

The delay in electrifying to **Glasgow** and **Edinburgh** meant that as an interim solution these lines had to have diesel locomotives, and after the **West Coast** main line was electrified first, to provide a suitable standard of service to Edinburgh, the famous and successful Inter-City 125 or **High Speed Train** had to be introduced. What this meant was that the West Coast had within a few short years two generations of modern equipment, and the East Coast three, while a more comprehensive electrification scheme would have meant a straight steam to electric switch and better value for money.

The so-called 'sparks effect' meant that traffic on the newly electrified lines soared, but despite this the financial situation continued to worsen. The lines to Kent were in fact electrified in 1959 and 1961, using the Southern's less costly third-rail dc system. One conclusion that followed was that the BTC was too costly and unwieldy, and its demise lay in the Transport Act 1962, which broke it up. Its chairman, Dr Richard (later Lord) **Beeching** became the new chairman of the **British Railways Board**. The new organisation was much smaller, but many of the senior managers recruited by Beeching from outside the railway industry did not remain long.

Beeching immediately started to analyse the income and expenditure of the railway, line by line, train service by train service, he proposed substantial closures and withdrawal of many services in his report, *The Re-Shaping of British Railways*. This was announced to the public as cutting the railways by a third. Beeching became synonymous with rationalisation and closures of lines and stations in the public mind. In fact, much work had already been done. Many lightly-used rural lines had already been closed, including all but two lines on the **Isle of Wight**, while **Paddington** had lost its services to the Midlands and Waterloo lost its services beyond Exeter. It was also the case that Beeching called for more invest-ment and the introduction of new services more in tune with the needs of industry, such as the 'Liner Trains' of regular timetabled fast container trains that preceded the 'Freightliner' concept, and the 'Merry-go-Round' coal trains running non-stop from coal mines to power station, load-ing and unloading as they moved. Completion of modernisation was another Beeching initiative in a second report.

On the debit side, Beeching's method of analysis has since been proved to be faulty. As an example, the analysis of receipts at stations did not allow for inbound traffic with return tickets, so many stations at holi-day resorts showed a far worse passenger figure than was in fact the case. The role of branch lines in feeding the main lines was not given due weight, while the scope for lower cost branch operations was ignored. In short, the railway needed to be trimmed and productivity improved, but not as dras-tically as was in fact proposed. At the same time, before stations or lines could be closed, there had to be a public enquiry and the findings had to be confirmed by the Minister of Transport, so Beeching was never the sole culprit in closures.

Beeching retired in 1965 having been elevated to the peerage, and he was succeeded by Sir Stanley Raymond, but the deficit continued to rise and a new Labour administration with Barbara Castle as Minister of Transport introduced new arrangements, including a Joint Steering Group that reported to the BR Chairman and the Minister. The scene was set for constant friction. Raymond left under a cloud in 1967 and he was succeeded by a career railwayman, Sir Henry Johnson, who had been in charge of the London Midland electrification. Much of the pressure that had faced Beeching and Raymond was eased by the Transport Act 1968, which wrote off most of the capital debt of BR,

and also provided a system for making grants to cover loss-making socially neces-sary services. A new National Freight Corporation took over the burden of small consignments, or 'sundries' traffic in rail-way terms, but also received the growing Freightliner network. In addition, passenger transport authorities were established for the major conurbations outside London with the power to provide subsidies for local railway services which they regarded as essential for the local transport network.

The previous year, the London Midland electrification had been completed, and in 1968, **Euston** station's own reconstruction was completed. The line to Southampton and Bournemouth was also electrified in 1967, although diesel locomotives had to continue the journey for those trains termi-nating at Weymouth. Steam trains finally left the BR network in 1968, with a number of the locomotives being retired after less than a decade in service.

Line closures continued, but the decade saw a new modern logo, meant to represent 'coming and going' and a new blue and light grey colour scheme, which for most multi-ple units was blue all-over. The title of **British Rail** was adopted, although the legal entity remained the British Railways Board. Today, only the logo remains as the stan-dard railway station logo on direction signs in Great Britain. Behind the scenes, attempts were made to improve productivity, with single manning of locomotives and the with-drawal of the guard from goods trains with a continuous brake, while some closures continued, so that within less than a quarter of a century after nationalisation, BR had cut route miles by 41 per cent; passenger and goods stations by 67 per cent; passenger carriages by 57.5 per cent; goods wagons by 22 per cent; while 20,000 steam locomo-tives had disappeared leaving operations to 3,633 diesel locomotives and 317 electric engines, as well as a much larger number of electric and diesel multiple units. The longest railway line to have escaped passenger station closures completely was that between London Waterloo and **Portsmouth Harbour** via Guildford, known as the 'Portsmouth Direct', but even on that line the goods stations had been closed and many of the sidings surfaced to provide much-needed car parking for commuters. The longest stretch of line in the country without a station closure was on the Waterloo to Weymouth line, where for more than eighty miles stations remained open until one reached the New Forest, to the west of Southampton.

When Johnson retired in 1971, he was succeeded by a former Labour Minister of Transport, Richard, later Lord, Marsh. Yet another Railways Act in 1974 abandoned the provision of subsidies for unremunerative, but socially necessary services, with a lump sum known as the Public Service Obligation. Grants were made available to industry to build private sidings in an attempt to get freight back onto the railways. Even so, Marsh was openly critical of the limitations on investment imposed by the government. On the debit side, after much work by BR and by SNCF, the French nationalised railways, plans for a **Channel Tunnel** were scrapped. After difficult trials, the **Advanced Passenger Train** (**APT**), with its new tilting technology was scrapped, but in 1974, the first diesel **High Speed Trains**, or HSTs, also known as the IC125, were introduced and proved a great success. The brand 'Inter-City' was also created for fast long distance express services offering seat reservations and catering. Electrification continued, with the so-called Great Northern scheme from King's Cross to Welwyn and Hertford North, completed in 1976.

That was the same year that Marsh left to be succeeded by Sir Peter Parker, who agreed with Marsh that the railways needed further investment, and famously coined the phrase, 'crumbling edge of quality'. New investment did continue to be authorised, and Parker's early contribution was approval for electrification of the lines from Moorgate and **St Pancras** to Bedford, while the London, Midland electrification finally crossed the border to reach Glasgow in 1974, and that city's suburban electrification also continued to grow. Yet another Transport Act in 1978 saw Freightliners returned to BR from the NFC, while 'Speedlink', a timetabled fast long-distance freight trains augmented the original Freightliner concept, but had to be abandoned in 1991. Bulk traffic remained steady, although ironically, private owners' wagons, for so long the bane of the railway manager's life, were returning in greater numbers.

Productivity remain elusive, for despite earlier agreements on single-manning, opening of the electrified services between London and Bedford were delayed on this issue until 1983.

In the meantime, a Conservative government had been elected in 1979. BR was told to sell off its non-core activities, disposing of its ferry services, marketed as Sealink, and hotels, while British Rail Engineering was created to take control of the railway workshops, and a division was created between maintenance and manufacture, with the latter sold off in 1989. To make the railway more business-orientated, BR itself was divided into sectors, of which the main ones were Inter-City; London & South-East; Other Provincial Services, and Freight. Area management became more important, regional management less so. Sectorisation had its supporters, but created problems as the sector judged to be the main user of any stretch of track took responsibility for its maintenance, leaving Freight to complain about the high costs of track maintained to Inter-City standards, while Other Provincial

Services would complain about track maintained to Freight standards.

One of the railway managers involved with sectorisation was Sir Robert 'Bob' Reid, who took over from Parker in 1983. Reid was probably the strongest leader BR ever had, and this was coupled with political awareness. In the five years to 1988, he maintained a tight control on railway finances, which were boosted by a property boom that enabled the British Rail Property Board to become a useful income generator until the property slump of 1988. In the meantime, Reid also managed to persuade his political masters to electrify the East Coast main line to Edinburgh, while work was under way in completing the Eastern Region (which had been merged with the North Eastern in 1966) main line electrification. A low cost electrification had seen the third-rail reach Hastings, albeit with single-line working through the Mountfield Tunnel with clearances too tight for standard rolling stock, and with no additional rolling stock ordered, having to stretch productivity of the existing Southern Region emus.

At the same time, the railways had been subjected to another thorough review, which resulted in the Serpell Report, officially a 'Review of Railway Finances', published in January 1983. Sir David Serpell, who chaired the committee that produced the report, was a former permanent secretary at the Department of Transport and in retirement a part-time member of the British Railways Board. Serpell almost became a 'Beeching Mk2' as it concentrated solely on the commercial network and would have closed the railways north of Edinburgh and Glasgow, west of **Cardiff** and **Bristol,** while the Portsmouth line would have suffered the ultimate nonsense of being cut outside the city at Havant. Edinburgh would have been reached via the West Coast main line as the

line between Edinburgh and Newcastle would have been closed.

If Beeching's methodology had been flawed, that of Serpell was completely devoid of reason and ignored the fact that most railway lines became less profitable towards the end, what might be described as the 'country' terminus. There is with bus and railway routes, a taper effect. Perhaps realising this, a compromise report based on a reduced support network was produced, bringing Dundee and Aberdeen back into the network, but leaving Plymouth out of it.

The big problem that hit BR during Reid's tenure was the miners' strike of 1984, which cost BR £200 million in revenue, and by virtually killing off the British coal mining industry, struck a harsh blow at the bulk loads traffic, including the 'Merry-Go-Round' trains. Looking for further cuts, **Broad Street** was closed, but **Marylebone** survived despite plans to convert it into a coach station.

Despite the merger of the Eastern and North Eastern regions earlier, and the growing importance of the sectors, a new Anglia Region was created in 1988. The sectors were also divided into sub-sectors, giving many the impression that privatisation was looming. The Freight Sector divided into Railfreight Distribution, which was merged with Freightliner, and Trainload Freight, while parcels survived for a period as a separate sub-sector. 'Other Provincial Services' became 'Regional Railways', which no longer sounded as if it consisted of the odds and ends that no one wanted. The London & South-East Sector became 'Network South-East' with an identity of its own. The regions eventually disappeared in 1992.

Meanwhile, the **Channel Tunnel** project was resurrected in 1986, and BR became heavily involved with Union Railways, a company intended to design a high speed link between London and the tunnel, while

European Passenger Services was created to organise the railway services.

Cost cutting continued, with the increasing use of unstaffed stations, with growing vandalism, and conductor guards, which especially on crowded trains led to an increase in fare evasion. BR had the best productivity and lowest government funding of any European railway. Nevertheless, the East Coast main line was finally electrified, with an extension to Glasgow Central via Motherwell, a lengthy route because the direct line to Glasgow Queen Street ended at a terminus with very short platforms and little scope for expansion.

By this time, the West Coast main line was in dire need of modernisation, while on Network South-East, old slam door trains still ran, even though questions were by this time being raised about their safety. The upgrading of the main line between London and Folkestone, with new connections to enable trains to reach a new station at Waterloo International, in preparation for the Channel Tunnel made excessive demands on the funding being given by the government, or the taxpayer, and led to neglect in other areas. Indeed, in the south, passengers on the line to Portsmouth, at the time highly profitable, had to make do with the original 1937 electrification stock until 1968-69, while those on the London Midland had had two new fleets of carriages and first a diesel service and then electrification during that time.

Confusingly, 'Bob' Reid was followed by 'Bob Reid Mk II' when he retired in April 1990. The new Sir Robert 'Bob' Reid came from a very different background, having been chairman of Shell (UK), and faced a scene dominated by the needs of privatisation.

British Transport Commission

The railways were not the only form of transport nationalised under the Transport Act 1947, which also included canals and the docks, ferry services and bus companies owned by the railways, as well as the railways' hotel, road haulage and carrier interests. The operations of the **London Passenger Transport Board** were included for good measure. The ultimate intention was to nationalise all inland transport, but given the fragmented nature of public road transport and road haulage, this was impractical at the outset. Most narrow gauge railways also escaped. A number of major road hauliers were also taken, and two of the major bus operating groups, Thomas Tilling and Scottish Motor Traction, were also added, but the British Electric Traction Group avoided nationalisation until the late 1960s, although some of its bus companies had minority railway shareholdings that passed to the BTC.

The Act imposed on the BTC a duty to integrate all inland public transport and to balance its books, 'taking one year with another'. Clearly, the LPTB was to be a model, but the BTC was on an unprecedented scale.

The BTC operated through a series of executives, of which the Railways Executive and the London Transport Executive were just two, with others covering inland waterways, docks and road haulage. Over the executives at the BTC board, of which the first full-time members were the chairman, Sir Cyril (later Lord) Hurcombe, a retired civil servant; Sir William Wood, formerly of the **London, Midland & Scottish Railway**; John Benstead of the **National Union of Railwaymen** and Lord Rusholme from the Co-operative Movement. It seems clear that only one of these had substantial transport operating experience, and only two experience of managing a substantial commercial organisation.

Despite having delegated power to the executives for each mode of transport, the BTC's own staff duplicated much of their work by producing area schemes each of which was intended to produce regional monopolies, while for goods traffic, charges schemes were intended to draw traffic towards the most efficient and economic form of transport. These ambitions made little progress as at the level of the executives and below at company level, or in the case of the railways, at regional and area level, management dragged their feet. Staff attitudes were also hostile. Relations between the BTC and the executives were poor and especially so with the Railway Executive, which even the BTC considered over-centralised and resistant to new ideas.

In 1953, a Conservative government passed its own Transport Act, which retained London Transport but abolished the other executives, and attempted to establish area boards to decentralise the railways. The duty to integrate transport was dropped, while around two-thirds of the road haulage companies were sold off. All of the operations apart from London Transport reported directly to the BTC, which had to expand its own bureaucracy rapidly to cope with the demand. A new chairman, Sir Brian **Robertson**, a retired army officer, inherited a cumbersome operation. On top of this, growing road competition and increased car ownership, plunged the railways into loss, and in an attempt to reverse the situation, a Modernisation Plan was launched in 1955. Nevertheless, this struggled under pressure to show early benefits and from resistance from the railway unions.

When Robertson retired in 1961, he was replaced by Dr Richard **Beeching** from Imperial Chemical Industries, and when the BTC itself was abolished by the Transport Act 1962, Beeching became the first chairman of the new **British Railways** Board.

The BTC cannot be regarded as a success. It failed to achieve the elusive goal of integration, and the other goal of financial self-

sufficiency also faded away. It was a classic example of a political ideal being out of touch with the reality of business life.

Broad Street

No longer in existence, Broad Street was built as the City terminus for the **North London Railway**, which opened in 1850 as the East & West India Docks and Birmingham Junction Railway, dominated by the **London & North Western Railway**. The name of the original company showed that goods traffic was the aim, but by the time the simpler title of the North London Railway was adopted in 1853, it was clear that passenger traffic was of growing importance. At first the LNR used **Fenchurch Street** on the **London & Blackwall Railway**, but this involved a four-mile detour around East London.

The small NLR could only afford a terminus – sited at the junction of Broad Street and Liverpool Street – because the LNWR agreed to meet most of the cost as it needed a goods station in the City. To obtain Parliamentary approval for its extension, which was doubtful because of the number of homes that needed to be demolished, the NLR promised to provide workmen's trains from Dalston for a return fare of just one penny. Design and construction of Broad Street was entrusted to the LNWR's first chief engineer, William **Baker**. Three tracks connected the station with the rest of the LNR network. The platforms were approached by an external staircase on the eastern side of the station frontage, itself showing a mixture of styles and no record can be found of an architect.

Broad Street operated as a joint station with two booking halls, one for the NLR and the other for the LNWR, on either side of the clock tower. At platform level, there were two train sheds, initially having just four tracks between them. Opened on 1 November 1865, the initial service was a train every fifteen minutes to Bow, and another to Chalk Farm, as well as a service every half-hour to Kew via Hampstead Heath. In 1866, a service to Watford was introduced and in 1879, some Chalk Farm workings were extended to Willesden, but were cut back again in 1917. The LNWR goods yard was below the passenger platforms and wagons were raised and lowered by hydraulic lifts, but the goods sidings were to the west of the passenger station.

Despite having been built as cheaply as possible, the NLR and Broad Street proved to be a great success. The NLR's traffic doubled and increased still further when from January 1875, trains ran through to Broad Street from Great Northern Railway suburban stations. At one time, Broad Street was one of the busiest of the **London** termini, handling 712 trains daily with 80,000 passengers in 1906. A fourth track into the station had been completed in 1874, while the station had eventually grown to have eight stone platforms, although tracks were laid over engine pits, while each pair of platforms shared a coaling stage, an indication of the intensity of suburban working. In 1912, a booking hall was built beneath the forecourt of the terminus for the **Central London Railway**'s extension from the Bank to Liverpool Street.

Before 1910, Broad Street handled local trains only, but to compete with the **Great Western Railway**'s improved service to Birmingham, the LNWR introduced a weekday restaurant car express between Wolverhampton and Birmingham and Broad Street, and which had as a special feature a typist who would type letters for passengers during the journey. This service only lasted until the outbreak of the First World War and was never reinstated.

Despite the promising first forty years or so, by its very nature Broad Street's traffic was amongst the first to be seriously affected by the electric tram, the growth of the London Underground network and then the arrival of the motor bus. This first started to become noticeable in 1901, and by 1911, traffic was falling steadily. The answer lay in electrification, and although considered as early as 1904, it was not until after the LNWR took over the operations of the NLR in 1909 that progress began to be made. The LNWR's 1911 scheme used the third and fourth rail system and electric trains started operations to and from Broad Street in October 1916, when services to Kew Bridge and Richmond were converted from steam. Rush hour services to Watford followed in 1917, but the off-peak service was not introduced until 1922, by which time there were also electric trains to Dalston. The LNWR passed to the **London, Midland & Scottish Railway** on grouping, by which time an intensive electric service was being operated, but steam trains continued to run to Poplar, Tring and a number of stations on the **London & North Eastern Railway**. The LMSR lengthened platforms 1 and 2, and operated services to Grays, Tilbury and Southend from 1923. Despite this, traffic continued to decline, and the LNER service became rush hour-only, while enlargement of **Fenchurch Street** saw the Southend and Tilbury services disappear in 1935. The situation wasn't helped by the LMSR still using old NLR four-wheeled carriages up to 1938 on the Poplar service.

Fenchurch Street suffered some air raid damage during the First World War, with a thousand panes of glass being shattered, a wall demolished and horses wounded by bomb explosions in September 1915. This was nothing compared to the Second World War, when the terminus was put out of action on the night of 3/4 October 1940, and remained closed for several days. It also had to close on 13 October and 11 November following further enemy action.

Services to the LNER were cancelled to make way for war traffic, but reinstated post-war. Heavy air raids on London's East End also meant the withdrawal of services east of Dalston Junction, which were not reinstated after the war.

Post-war, Broad Street once again saw longer-distance trains as services to Cambridge were diverted to ease the pressure on **King's Cross**. Nevertheless, during the 1950s, the terminus saw further reductions in its services so that eventually its main traffic consisted of electric rush hour services to Watford and Croxley Green, as well as peak diesel services to and from Stevenage, Hertford North and Welwyn Garden City, with only the Richmond service operating through the day. By 1969, just 9,000 passengers were using the station daily, the trainshed cut-back and the number of platforms reduced to five, mainly without a roof. It was closed in 1986 and redeveloped as office space.

Brunel, Isambard Kingdom, 1806-1859
One of the most famous of the great railway engineers, Brunel's name is eternally associated with that of the **Great Western Railway** and the broad gauge. Brunel was born in Portsmouth of French parents, and educated in Paris before training in a watchmaker's workshops. He worked with his father, Marc Isambard, on the Thames Tunnel before producing the winning design for the Clifton suspension bridge over the Avon Gorge in **Bristol**.

Possibly as a result of his work in Bristol, he was appointed engineer for the GWR's main line between **London** and Bristol, using the 7ft broad gauge which he regarded as superior and which provided greater stability at high speeds. With the system of major companies sponsoring others providing useful extensions to their lines, Brunel was engaged as engineer on many other projects and altogether a thousand miles of

track were laid as broad gauge.

One of the last leading engineers not to specialise, his work included major steamships such as the *Great Britain* and *Great Eastern*, while he also worked on dock projects and designed prefabricated hospitals for the Crimean War. Much of his work was outstanding, including the Royal Albert Bridge over the River Tamar at Saltash and Box Tunnel near Bath, but his enthusiasm for innovation also led to problems and cost overruns, as with the original plan to work the **South Devon Railway** using atmospheric propulsion. To the public, he was an inspiration, and did much to advance the status of engineers in Victorian society, but he could also be overbearing to his subordinates and intolerant of opposition, as when he attempted to use force to remove the contractors at Campden Tunnel in 1851, despite the presence of armed troops and the reading of the Riot Act.

His single-minded advocacy of the broad gauge also landed his clients in serious difficulties and they incurred unnecessary expense when they had to eventually adopt the standard gauge. He was right to argue that the broad gauge had benefits, but ignored the extra costs, and the fact that the broad gauge would not be suitable in many areas. His weakness as an engineer was his indifference to money, whether his own or that of his clients.

He died in 1851, almost certainly due to overwork.

Bulleid, Oliver Vaughan Snell, 1882-1970
Oliver Bulleid was, like his predecessor **Maunsell,** a man of considerable experience at home and abroad. He started his career as an apprentice under Henry **Ivatt** on the **Great Northern Railway,** but in 1908 moved to become the assistant manager of the Westinghouse works in Paris, before returning to the UK in 1911 to become

personal assistant to Nigel **Gresley**, again on the GNR, for which company he was assistant carriage and wagon engineer in the three years before the grouping. Bulleid again became assistant to Gresley in 1923 when the former became the chief mechanical engineer of the new **London & North Eastern Railway**.

Bulleid took over as chief mechanical engineer at the **Southern Railway** in 1937, and inherited a railway in which development of larger and more powerful locomotives of the kind favoured by the LNER had been neglected, partly due to the demands of electrification., but also because of weight restrictions on many lines. He pressed successfully for the introduction of powerful 4-6-2 locomotives, and despite severe wartime restrictions on the type and size of locomotives that could be built, by claiming that his new designs were for mixed-traffic duties, succeeded in building no less than 140 Pacific locomotives of the Merchant Navy, West Country and Battle of Britain-classes, introducing many new features such as completely enclosed chain-driven valve gear and welded fireboxes, and an improved working environment for the enginemen. At the other end of the scale, he produced an austerity 0-6-0 freight locomotive, the Q1-class, of outstanding ugliness. The Bulleid Pacifics incorporated many features that were to be introduced into post-nationalisation designs, and were also more economical in their use of coal than the Britannia-class which in rebuilt form they closely resembled in appearance, but also had their weaknesses, including poor forward visibility and were prone to often catastrophic mechanical failures. His attempt at producing a steam locomotive capable of working at express speeds in either direction and based on current thinking on electric and diesel designs resulted in the Leader-class of C-C or 0-6-6-0 layout, which failed to pass the prototype stage, not least because of the great discomfort suffered by the fireman.

Far more successful and enduring was his work on new passenger rolling stock, using a design with widened bodies to provide greater comfort on mainline stock, and additional seating on suburban stock in the 4 SUB classes, with these features later carried over post-nationalisation onto the early 2 and 4 EPB and 2 HAP classes.

Post-war, Bulleid worked on a successful design for a prototype 1Co-1Co diesel-electric locomotive, the precursor of 350 locomotives for **British Railways**, but his anger at the rebuilding of his own Pacific classes, despite some of their features being incorporated in the new British Railways standard-classes, led him to resign in 1949 and join *Coras Iompair Eireann*, the Irish transport undertaking, as CME for the railways. He introduced diesel locomotives to Ireland and worked on new carriages and railcars as well as goods vehicles using welded production, and, as a final gesture to the steam locomotive, built yet another C-C design, but on this occasion designed to run on peat. He retired in 1958 to live in Malta.

Burry Port & Gwendraeth Valley Railway
Burry Port, to the west of Llanelli and south of Carmarthen, was one of the ports developed by the owners of the coal mines in response to the growing congestion at the older ports, despite the opening of new port facilities. The Burry Port & Gwendraeth Valleys Railway linked the port, which never became sizeable, with the mines in the Gwendraeth Valley, and was very much a minor player. The line was twenty-one miles long and officially not supposed to carry passengers, who arrived on the line as 'trespassers', but were tolerated so long as they paid 6d (2¹/₂p) for the carriage of their shopping basket.

Bus services

From early times, the railways were allowed to operate bus services that fed into their railway stations, which in many places was an operational necessity given that a considerable number of railway stations were some distance from the towns or villages they purported to serve. It was not until 1929 that the railways received the powers to operate bus services independently of their own network, and the **Big Four** moved quickly to either buy bus companies outright or take a shareholding in them. In some cases, they collaborated with railway companies operating in the same area sharing ownership of a bus company. The existing railway bus services were integrated into the companies that were acquired, sometimes to acquire an interest but often as a means of rationalising services. Different rules applied outside Great Britain, and in fact bus operation was the salvation of the **Londonderry & Lough Swilly Railway** and of the **County Donegal** in Ulster, which became bus operators, while in **Guernsey** the railway company never operated trains but went straight from trams to buses.

In some cases, the railway companies imposed a form of branding on the bus companies, with the **Southern Railway** having Southern Vectis on the **Isle of Wight** and Southern National in Dorset, for example, but this was not always the case and Hants & Dorset kept its name unchanged. One beneficiary was the **National Union of Railwaymen**, which started recruiting amongst the railway-owned bus companies.

C

Caledonian Railway

The largest Scottish company to be merged into the **London, Midland, Scottish** on 1 January 1923, the Caledonian Railway adopted the Royal Arms of Scotland as its crest and its locomotives were smartly presented in a blue livery. It was founded in 1845 to extend the West Coast mainline from Carlisle to **Glasgow** and **Edinburgh**, dividing at Carstairs, and at the time it was expected to be the only Anglo-Scottish line. The engineer was Joseph **Locke**. Initially, grand termini were planned in both cities, as well as a cross-country line, but these plans were thwarted.

The company reached Glasgow over the metals of the Grankirk & Glasgow (later renamed the Glasgow & Coatbridge) and the Wishaw & Coltness railways to Buchanan Street station, whose wooden trainsheds remained until **London & North Eastern Railway** days. Eventually three Glasgow termini were used, including, from 1849, the South Side station accessed via the Clydesdale Junction and the Glasgow Barrhead & Neilston Direct, and also shared Bridge Street with the **Glasgow & South Western**. South Side was closed when Central and St Enoch were opened in the 1870s, but Bridge Street continued to be used until 1906, after Central had been extended, eventually having seventeen platforms on two levels.

The line was extended north to **Aberdeen** using the **Scottish Central**, Scottish Midland Junction and Aberdeen Railways, and in 1856 the last two merged to form the Scottish North Eastern Railway, before all three were absorbed by the Caledonian in 1865-66. From 1880, the Caledonian served the Western Highlands over the **Callander & Oban Railway**, and then up to 1900, built a network of lines along the Clyde to compete with the **Glasgow & South Western and North British Railways**, giving the company a suburban and tourist network as well as serving steamer services, and the growing shipyards and the mines of Lanarkshire, for which many new lines and private sidings were built. The Caledonian's main routes were the finest in Scotland. The company moved into steamer services, including tourist steamers on Loch Lomond, with the main steamer-railway terminus being at Wemyss Bay. The further expansion of the Glasgow suburban network was cut short by the appearance of horse and, later, electric trams, with the Paisley & District line completed, but never opened for passenger trains.

Meanwhile, in Edinburgh, the unsatisfactory Lothian Road station was replaced by Princes Street, which later had the Caledonian Hotel added providing an impressive frontage. A network of suburban services was also created in the capital. Further north, the company built its own station at Stirling and took the lead in remodelling the joint stations at Perth and Aberdeen, and opened new tourist lines from Crieff to Lochearnhead and from Connel to Ballachulish.

The company provided railway links for all of the docks within its wide operating area, as well as owning those at Grangemouth, which it acquired with the Forth & Clyde Canal in 1867.

Intense competition arose with the Glasgow & South Western and, especially after the opening of the East Coast mainline, the North British, initially for traffic between Edinburgh and London, but after the **Tay** and **Forth** bridges were completed, this rivalry extended to Aberdeen. The hotel business extended from Glasgow and Edinburgh to include the famous hotel at Gleneagles. The company became famous for good design and high standards, with a strong awareness of the importance of public image. When merged into the London Midland & Scottish Railway in 1923, it contributed 1,057 route miles.

Callander & Oban Railway

Originally intended to be provided by the ill-fated Glasgow & North Western Railway, the idea of a line south from Oban to serve the growing resort and feed passengers to the steamer services to the islands, was revived during the 1860s. The cheapest route was 71 miles to Callander, connecting with the **Caledonian Railway**. Engineered by Blyth & Westland of Edinburgh, the line was amongst the first to use bowstring girder bridges on the section up Strathyre. Funding ran out leaving the line to terminate at Tyndrum with a stage coach connection to Oban, and it was only after extra capital was raised that the line to Oban was completed in 1880, using John Strain as engineer. The line suffered from steep gradients and the Caledonian had to design locomotives with small wheels and low axle weights to work the line, while a system of trip wires had to be used to operate signals if rocks fell on to the line. Three branches were built, the shortest to Killin opened in 1886; the longest opened in 1903 to Ballachulish; and then there was one to Comrie and Crief opened in 1905. The line to Comrie closed in 1964, the other branches in 1965, and the section of the line between Dublane and Crianlarich closed the following year, leaving the remainder of the line to be reached from the West Highland line.

Cambrian Railway

The Cambrian Railway was by far the largest of the constituent companies absorbed into the **Great Western** in 1923. Despite its title, a significant part of its overall route mileage of 295 miles lay over the border in England, including Oswestry, its headquarters and main works. Home territory for the Cambrian was the unlikely and sparsely-populated area of mid-Wales, so underdeveloped that its first locomotives for one of its predecessors, the Llanidloes & Newtown Railway opened in 1859, were delivered by horse teams.

The Cambrian Railway was formed in 1864 from four small companies, the

Llanidloes & Newtown Railway, Oswestry & Newton Railway, Newtown & Machynlleth Railway and the Oswestry, Ellesmere and Whitchurch Railway, as a defensive measure to keep the English railway companies away from mid-Wales. The new company was joined the following year by the Aberystwyth & Welsh Coast Railway, almost doubling its track mileage. A further major expansion came in 1888, when it took over the working of the Mid Wales Railway, which operated between Moat Lane and Talyllyn Junction, but had running powers through to Brecon. The largest town on the Cambrian network was Wrexham, served by the Wrexham & Ellesmere Railway which became part of the Cambrian in 1895. The Cambrian also absorbed or worked several other railways, including the 6.5 mile **Van Railway**, completed in 1871, the Mawddwy Railway, also of around 6.5 miles running through the Upper Dovey Valley, and the 19.5 mile Tanat Valley Light Railway, dating from 1904. There were also two narrow gauge lines, the 1ft 11½-in **Vale of Rheidol Railway**, opened in 1902, and the 2ft 6in gauge **Welshpool & Llanfair Railway** opened the following year.

Serving such a difficult area, the Cambrian, despite the nationalist leanings of its founders, soon became heavily dependent upon several of the major English companies for through traffic, and inevitably these included the Great Western at Oswestry as well as the **Midland** at Three Cocks Junction and, its closest associate, the **London & North Western** at Whitchurch and Welshpool. The two main lines for the Cambrian, both of which handled considerable holiday traffic, were the 96 miles between Whitchurch and Aberystwyth and the 54 miles from Dovey Junction to Pwllheli.

Given the unpromising traffic of its territory, the Cambrian remained impoverished for its existence, with much single track. It went bankrupt twice, and was often accused of being badly run. Nevertheless, in 1913, it carried three million passengers and a million tons of goods traffic. It suffered a major **accident at Abermule** in January 1921, when an express hit a stopping train head-on killing seventeen people and injuring many more, giving rise to much debate over the safety of single line railways.

The GWR was disappointed that the Cambrian became a constituent company, no doubt to the delight of the latter railway's shareholders who received a guaranteed income for the first time.

Camp Coaches

During the 1930s, old railway carriages had relatively little metal in them and were seldom valuable as items for scrap. They could be sold off, and the **Great Western** amongst others did indeed offer old carriages for sale and delivered them free of charge to stations on its network. The best an old carriage could expect was to be used as a summer cottage, but many simply became storage sheds or hen houses.

It was in 1933 that the **London & North Eastern Railway** hit upon the idea of converting surplus railway carriages to camping coaches, basically self-catering holiday accommodation, and located in disused sidings at stations that were in either tranquil surroundings or close to resorts. The Great Western was much taken with this idea, having a long running rivalry with the LNER over which company served the better holiday destinations, and eventually all of the **Big Four** offered camping coaches. In 1934, the first GWR 'Camp Coaches' appeared.

The coaches were old compartment six-wheel carriages, usually with about five compartments. In typical Great Western fashion, a booklet was commissioned, written and published, to introduce the public to the idea. Each camp coach would have one compartment fitted out as a kitchen, another two knocked into one as a living room with table, and the remaining two as sleeping cabins.

In the publicity material and the booklet, much was made of the fact that the company provided everything for its campers. The coaches all came with cutlery and crockery, saucepans, a cooking stove, tablecloths, towels, broom, blankets and sheets. A hurricane lamp was provided, with oil lamps for the sleeping cabins and another type of lamp for the living room, while the 'cooking stove' was a primus with an oven, while there was a jug for carrying paraffin and a bucket, as well as deck chairs so that the campers could sit outside. This may seem primitive to us today, but this was reasonable comfort for the day. These were non-corridor carriages so the sleeping cabins could only be reached by stepping outside. Charges were reasonable at £3 per week for up to six people, and employees of the Great Western could hire the coaches at a discount outside the main holiday season.

For the first season, there were just nineteen coaches, with locations including Penryn, Fowey, Blue Anchor and Princetown (handy for Dartmoor Prison), but this was soon extended and by 1939 there were sixty-five scattered throughout Cornwall, Devon, Somerset and rural Wales. Each season, demand exceeded the number of places available.

These ventures ended with the outbreak of war. Many of the camp coaches were used as emergency wartime accommodation, some of them being moved to new locations, but almost all seem to have suffered neglect and even misuse during the war years.

Canals

The canal age marked a significant advance in inland transport, especially for bulk loads such as coal, and it is a measure of the tremendous advance brought to inland transport by the railways that wherever a railway and a canal ran in parallel, it was the faster and cheaper railway that won. It was not surprising that the canal companies were amongst the most determined opponents of the railways when proposals for a new line were laid before Parliament. This opposition lasted until around 1845, when the start of the **railway mania** released so much money into the railway industry that many canal owners allowed themselves to be bought out. Some canal companies were persuaded to become railway companies, such as the Thames & Medway, a predecessor of the **South Eastern Railway**, while others leased themselves to railway companies. Many found that their route was as ideal for railway operation as it had been for canals, although sometimes problems with the water table could arise. In some cases, conversion was so rapid, as in Aberdeen, that boat owners found themselves stranded as water was drained away ready for the start of railway construction.

The railways did not always close the canals. The **London & North Western**, for example, used the Birmingham Canal to feed traffic to exchange depots, and in return paid a guaranteed dividend to shareholders. Others found that canal ownership was a quick and non-parliamentary means of penetrating the territory of a rival line. Eventually almost a third of the canal network fell into railway ownership, and while it is true that many were closed, converted or neglected, this was not always the case, and some continued to trade profitably into the twentieth century. Canals which had extensive development along their banks often did well. Like the railways, most canals were nationalised by the post-Second World War Labour government, eventually after the **British Transport Commission** control was passed to the British Waterways Board.

The Lancaster Canal actually leased a railway, which was illegal without parliamentary sanction.

Canals were very much slower than the railways, and while at first could offer to carry much larger loads, before long even this advantage was lost. The most impressive of the British canals was the Manchester Ship Canal, an integrated dock and canal system designed to end the city's dependence on the port of Liverpool, and which even had its own deep sea shipping company, Manchester Liners, operating transatlantic services. This was an exception on a scale more familiar in Europe or North America. There was no such thing as a standard gauge for canals, and they varied between those limited to the traditional, and many would say typical, 35-ton narrow boat to those capable of accommodating large barges of 300-tons. This meant that through traffic over long distances became difficult. The need to supply water was another cost and a complication, while they were vulnerable in drought or in very cold weather.

Although nationalisation and massive modernisation was advocated by a Royal Commission in 1911, railway opposition and the First World War delayed this. After the war, canal fortunes became far worse, not so much because of continued competition from the railways but from the massive growth in road transport, which also affected the railways with lower costs and doorstep to destination operation.

Cannon Street

Cannon Street was opened in 1866 as the City terminus for the **South Eastern Railway**, which had previously decanted its passengers at **London Bridge**, on the wrong side of the Thames. Earlier plans had been to provide two other stations on the extension line running to **Charing Cross**, but when the **London, Chatham & Dover Railway** was authorised to provide an extension to Ludgate Hill, the SER realised that it also needed a terminus on the north bank of the River Thames. It was even felt that there could be local traffic between Cannon Street and Charing Cross from those anxious to avoid the heavy congestion on the streets of London – these were the days before the construction of the **Circle** and **Metropolitan District Lines** and the prediction was to prove correct before these underground lines were built.

The extension to Cannon Street was authorised by an Act of 1861, with a bridge across the Thames and a triangular junction on viaducts with the line between London Bridge and Charing Cross. At first, and for many years, all trains running to and from Charing Cross called at Cannon Street. The triangular junction led on to an engine shed and turntable, so cramped that locomotives had to run over the turntable to enter or leave the shed, and coaling stages.

There were five tracks, four running roads and an engine road, on the bridge, which had pedestrian walkways on either side, with the one on the east reserved for railway personnel, while that on the west was available to the public on payment of a $\frac{1}{2}$d toll (0.2p). The station itself abutted immediately onto the bridge, with nine roads, and was a handsome building offering stunning views over the Thames, and with a hotel fronting the street. The roof was a single span of 190ft over 100ft above the rails and glazed over two-thirds of its surface, surmounted by a 22ft wide lantern running almost the whole 680ft length. There were seven platform faces, varying in length between 480 and 721ft, with the two longest faces incorporating a cab roadway, with another set of platform faces separated by three tracks to include a spare for rolling stock. The two longest platforms extended beyond the roof and on to the bridge.

The hotel, the City Terminus, was operated by an independent company and opened in May 1867, but was later acquired by the SER, and later renamed The Cannon Street Hotel. It managed, for reasons that remain obscure and can be nothing more than a coincidence, to become the venue for the creation of the Communist Party of Great Britain in July 1920. Falling business led to its closure in 1931, and while the public rooms were retained for meetings and functions, the remainder was converted to offices and let as Southern House.

When first opened on 1 September 1866, Cannon Street fulfilled its promise of being served by all trains proceeding to and from Charing Cross, including boat trains, and with these and a shuttle service between the two stations, there was a five minute frequency service between the West End and the City, taking seven minutes, and costing 6d (2¹/₂p) first class, 4d second class and 2d third class, compared with 3d for the horse bus. The local traffic was considerable, with 3.5 million of the 8 million passengers using Cannon Street in 1867 travelling solely between the City and the West End. This all came to an end with the opening of the District Railway between Westminster and **Blackfriars** in May, 1870, and which reached Mansion House in July, 1871, while the completion of the Circle Line on 6 October 1884 saw a station opened under the forecourt of Cannon Street.

One kind of specialised traffic had already disappeared before this. The seven minute run had proved a great draw to certain ladies who found that it combined with the comfort of a first class compartment to provide the ideal environment for the entertainment of their clients. Once a stop was introduced at **Waterloo** from 1 January 1869, the number of drawn blinds on trains running into and out of Charing Cross dropped dramatically.

Cannon Street was the exclusive preserve of the SER except during late 1867 and until the end of July, 1868, when the **London, Brighton & South Coast Railway** operated two up morning and two down evening trains to and from **Brighton**.

Growing traffic, with a train being handled every minute at peak periods, meant that the approach bridge had to be widened to ten tracks, including a siding on each side. This was completed on 13 February 1892. Inside the station, the cab road was shortened to provide another platform, while three platforms were extended further on to the first pier of the bridge. On the south bank, the locomotive facilities were extended.

The First World War saw the continental boat trains removed to Victoria, an arrangement that continued until the late 1930s, while severe reductions in services to save fuel also saw the practice of running Charing Cross trains into and out of the station finally come to an end on 31 December 1916. This must have been a welcome cut in journey times for passengers travelling to and from the West End terminus, and certainly could not have continued during the post-war years as traffic levels continued to rise. The next year saw the station closed on Sundays, and after 1 May 1918, it also closed on Saturdays after 15.00, and between 11.00 and 16.00 on weekdays. While these changes reflected the nature of the passenger traffic at Cannon Street, it also enabled the station to be used as a crew interchange point for the goods trains operating between the Midlands and North of England and the Channel ports, via Farrington and Ludgate Hill, and provided a marked improvement in productivity on these services.

Plans to electrify the suburban services were overtaken by the grouping, even though the **South Eastern & Chatham Railway** had first obtained powers for this as early as 1903.

Post grouping, the **Southern Railway**

remodelled the track, with electrification ending the need for light engine movements and the old layout designed to facilitate the operation of trains to and from Charing Cross being redundant. An extension of the system of non-conflicting parallel movements pioneered by the SECR in 1922 also increased the number of trains that could be handled at peak periods. The changes required Cannon Street to be closed from 15.00 on Saturday, 5 June 1926, until 04.00 on Monday, 28 June. The bay platform was abolished and the eight remaining platforms rearranged, providing lengths of between 567 and 752 ft, with numbers 1 to 5 electrified. Under the new timetable introduced with electrification on 19 July 1926, there were eight electric trains an hour off-peak and seventeen during the peak, with a total of just thirty-six steam trains daily, mainly for Chatham and stations beyond. Two further platforms were fitted with third rail in July 1939 when the services to Gillingham and Maidstone were electrified. The station re-opened on Sundays in summer, 1930, and a few trains returned between Charing Cross and Cannon Street in 1933, some of which continued to be operated until 1956. Continental boat trains returned during summer, 1936, to relieve pressure on Victoria, and this continued up to the outbreak of the Second World War.

Once again, wartime saw restrictions on the station's operating hours, closing between 10.00 and 16.00 and after 19.30 daily, and from 15.00 on Saturday until Monday morning with effect from 16 October 1939. Even rush hour services were severely curtailed in wartime, so that by 1944, there were just twenty-four peak hour departures, only one of which was for the Kent coast. Before this, on the night of 10/11 May 1941, the station was bombed and caught fire, with railwaymen braving molten glass dripping from the roof to rescue locomotives and carriages, but one of the former, *St Lawrence*, was caught by a bomb on the bridge.

Post-war, *Southern House* was patched up, but the station had to operate as a shell of its former self, as it was judged too badly damaged to ever carry the weight of a single span roof. Weekend services resumed after nationalisation, but after a period of ten years were dropped again.

Canterbury & Whitstable Railway

Authorised in 1825 with the backing of Canterbury residents and businesses anxious to improve the delivery of coal from the port of Whitstable, just six miles away, the line had the distinction of being the first in the world to use steam propulsion for both passengers and freight. The first engineer was William James, but he underestimated the costs and was replaced by George **Stephenson**. It opened in 1830. Despite the short distance, it had gradients of up to 1 in 28, and had a half-mile tunnel. Initially, stationary engines worked the trains, although a one mile stretch on the level was worked by the steam locomotive *Invicta*, until it failed in 1839 and traction was left to the stationary engines and horses.

Leased to the **South Eastern Railway** in 1844, two years before it reached Canterbury, which purchased the line in 1853, having first re-introduced steam locomotives throughout. It required locomotives with special low-cut chimneys to cope with the restricted headroom in the tunnel. It survived **Southern Railway** ownership, but after a period as a freight-only line, closed completely in 1952.

Cardiff

Oddly, the lords of the manor for Cardiff were the Marquises of Bute, whose business interests included the Cardiff docks. Originally a small town, smaller than

Merthyr Tydfil, Newport or Swansea, Cardiff enjoyed considerable expansion at the outset of the industrial revolution when the Glamorganshire Canal, opened in 1794, brought first iron ore and then coal from Merthyr Tydfil and the Taff Vale for shipment. The old docks were soon overwhelmed by the new traffic, and a new dock was built by the 2nd Marquess and opened in 1839, by which time the traffic had overtaken the capacity of the canal and relief came with the opening of the **Taff Vale Railway** from Merthyr in 1841. From this time onwards, Cardiff enjoyed rapid growth so that by 1881, it was the largest city in Wales. Meanwhile, a second new dock, the East Bute Dock, had been opened in 1859, and authorisation given to build a third, which was completed in 1887.

The railways played a considerable part in the development of Cardiff both as a port and as a city. The **Rhymney Railway** reached Cardiff in 1858, and with the Taff Vale was responsible for most of the coal and ore traffic, and to ease congestion on its lines and at Cardiff docks, the TVR also served the new dock at Penarth two miles away when it opened between 1859 and 1865. Meanwhile, the broad gauge **South Wales Railway** had entered the town in 1850, but this played little part in the coal and ore traffic until after its conversion to standard gauge in 1872, allowing through running of wagons between the 'valley' lines and the main line.

Cardiff's success and the resultant congestion was almost the port's undoing as, mentioned earlier, in 1882 the mine owners were behind the establishment of the **Rhondda & Swansea Bay Railway** intended to remove their business from Cardiff, while in 1884 others started to build a new dock at Barry served by the **Barry Railway**, which opened in 1889. Fortunately, with coal output doubling between 1889 and 1913, sufficient traffic

existed to ensure that all of these railways and docks were busy.

Nevertheless, after the coal miners' strike and the related General Strike in 1926, coal production declined sharply, falling from 50 million tons to 35 million tons between 1922 and 1938. The post-war boom had been short-lived and the years of recession also affected demand, but many export markets for Welsh coal were lost during the strike and never regained. Being heavily dependent on the port and its coal and ore traffic, the recession affected Cardiff especially badly. By this time, the **Great Western Railway** was the monopoly provider of railway services in and around Cardiff, and was accused of neglecting the area, and although there was little evidence to substantiate these claims, faced with sharply declining traffic and some duplication of routes, the GWR itself had to close some twenty-five miles of line to passenger traffic in the valleys.

Cardiff Railway

Cardiff had originally depended on a canal to bring coal to the docks for transhipment, but this proved inadequate as the demand for coal rose and the situation was not resolved until the **Taff Vale Railway** opened from Merthyr Tydfil in 1841. The TVR was later joined by the **Rhymney Railway** in 1858, while the docks at Cardiff continued to expand. Additional port facilities were opened two miles away at Penarth during 1859-1865, with a railway connection leased to the TVR. While the **Great Western Railway** had reached Cardiff as early as 1850, its broad gauge was ill-suited to the conditions in the valleys, where standard gauge ruled completely and so it carried little coal traffic until after the coal and iron masters succeeded in securing a conversion to standard gauge in 1872.

Nevertheless, the docks and the TVR and Rhymney lines to Cardiff had themselves become so congested by 1882 that the mine owners secured powers to build the **Rhondda & Swansea Bay Railway**, determined to move their traffic away from Cardiff. In 1884, other coal mining interests obtained authority to build a new port at Barry, eight miles from Cardiff, with its own Barry Railway operating down the Rhondda. The new port and railway opened in 1889, and with the support of the mine owners started to take traffic away from Cardiff, although the port survived as coal output doubled between 1889 and 1913, so that there was sufficient business to keep all of the port facilities busy. It was not until 1897 that the Cardiff Docks obtained parliamentary approval to change its name to the Cardiff Railway and build new lines northwards to connect with the Taff Vale at Treforest and at Pontypridd, creating a further 11.5 route miles in addition to the existing 120 track miles within the Bute Docks (named after the local landowner, the Marquis of Bute). The Cardiff Railway had its own locomotives and two steam railcars for passenger traffic. Nevertheless, given the heavy concentration of competing and connecting lines and inter-port rivalry, the company soon found itself in protracted disputes with other railways and costly litigation. This must have been a factor in the poor financial performance of the Cardiff Railway, with its shareholders getting a dividend of just 1 per cent in 1921 compared with 9 per cent at the Rhymney.

A proposal to merge with the Taff Vale in the years before the First World War was vetoed by Parliament, which a little more than a decade later was to force these two companies and others to combine into the new GWR. Nevertheless, even before the grouping the three companies came under a single general manager.

Carmarthenshire Railway

A predecessor of the **Llanelly & Mynydd Mawr Railway**, the Carmarthenshire was notable for being the first combined railway and dock undertaking. It was formed in 1802 as an early iron railway with edge rails mounted on stone blocks, and using horse traction. A busy line, it was not profitable and went into liquidation in 1844. It was purchased by the LMMR in 1875, and a new line was laid over the old track bed and steam locomotives introduced.

Cavan & Leitrim Light Railway

Incorporated in 1883 as the Cavan Leitrim & Roscommon Light Railway, a 3ft gauge line linking Dromod with Ballinamore and Belturbet, opened in 1887, with a branch from Ballinamore to Arigna opened the following year. It was renamed the Cavan & Leitrim Light Railway in 1895. In 1925, under Irish grouping, it passed into the **Great Southern Railways**, and in 1945 it was nationalised. It closed in 1959.

Central London Railway/Central Line

Authorised in 1892 and opened in 1900, the Central London Railway linked Shepherd's Bush with the Bank, a distance of $5^3/4$ miles, running under London's West End to the City. Initially, trains were drawn by electric locomotives, but there were complaints from those buildings along the line about vibration and in 1903, the locomotives and trailer carriages were replaced by the more practical self-propelled trains, the first multiple unit trains in the United Kingdom. Unusually, the stations were slightly higher than the running tube, so that braking was assisted by trains climbing a short slope to the platforms, and acceleration helped by the corresponding downward slope.

Until 1907, a flat fare of 2d (less than 1p) was charged.

In 1908, the western end of the line was extended by a loop to Wood Lane, close to the exhibition centre at White City, and then extended eastwards to **Liverpool Street** in 1912. The line was badly affected by competition from motor buses after 1910, and in 1913, it was acquired by the **Underground Group**. A further westward extension followed in 1920, running over **Great Western** tracks to Ealing Broadway.

Along with the rest of the Underground companies, the CLR became part of the newly-formed **London Passenger Transport Board** in 1933, and in 1937, it was renamed the **Central Line**. In the meantime, the line was modernised between 1935 and 1940 under the New Works Programme, designed to stimulate employment, and the original central third rail power supply was replaced by the LT standard third and fourth rail. The line was further extended eastwards to Leyton and then ran over **London & North Eastern** tracks to Hainault and Epping, with four miles of new tube tunnel, and this eventually opened between 1947 and 1949. A further extension to Ongar was electrified in 1957, but closed in 1994. To the west, what was by this time the Western Region of **British Railways** took the line to West Ruislip in 1948. West Ruislip to Epping was a distance of more than 34 miles, while overall, the Central peak route mileage in 1957 was 51½ miles.

Channel Tunnel

Although the Channel Tunnel was officially opened in 1994, the concept dated from early in the nineteenth century when the French mining engineer, Albert Mathieu-Favier, proposed two tunnels meeting in an artificial island to be constructed on the Varne Bank in mid-Channel. This was meant to be a road tunnel and the island would allow horses to be changed. Later, during the 1830s, the idea was taken up by Thome de Gramond, who spent the next twenty years investigating the rock strata under the Channel. The British and French governments agreed in 1875 that private companies could have a concession to build and operate a tunnel. Later that decade, one

French and two British companies started trial boring on both sides of the Channel, and using compressed-air boring machines they successfully completed a mile-long tunnel that dropped around 160 feet into the chalk beneath the sea. The work stopped because the British Army saw a potential threat to national security.

The concept was not taken seriously again until 1929, when a Royal Commission considered proposals for a broad gauge line from London to Paris, which was strange since it would have been incompatible with the gauges in use on either side. Nevertheless, it was not until 1955 that it was finally accepted that a tunnel presented little threat to national security.

Charing Cross

No **London** railway station is as well situated for the traveller as Charing Cross, at the end of The Strand and with Trafalgar Square just around the corner. It is really the only railway station actually in the West End, since **Victoria** and **Marylebone** are located on the fringes. The substantial forecourt and the impressive façade of the Charing Cross Hotel all serve to disguise the fact that the station is smaller than many in medium-sized provincial cities.

Plans for a railway terminus in this part of London were mooted as long ago as 1846, when the **South Eastern Railway** promoted a bill for an extension from Bricklayers Arms to Hungerford Bridge, but it was unsuccessful. The SER finally managed to obtain the approval of the **London, Brighton & South Coast Railway** for a line from **London Bridge** to the West End, and in 1857 settled on the Hungerford Market as the ideal site, with the prospect of a link to the **London & South Western Railway** at **Waterloo**. As with **Cannon Street**, the idea was that the two stations would pair well with a lucrative traffic between the City and the West End, and this was indeed the case until the **Metropolitan District** and then the **Circle lines** came into existence.

The Charing Cross Railway Company Act 1859 authorised the construction of a line one mile and sixty-eight chains in length, mainly on viaduct except for Hungerford Bridge which took it across the Thames and into the terminus. The new company was separate from the SER in theory, but obviously linked to it, with the SER providing £300,000 of the initial £800,000 capital, and later raising this investment to £650,000 as land purchase costs proved to be far heavier than anticipated. Much of the money was spent south of the river, with the governors of St Thomas Hospital exacting the heavy price of £296,000, and then, despite the poverty of the area at the time, the many slum landlords also managed to follow this example. The CCRC wisely decided to build three running tracks instead of two on the viaduct, and to build Hungerford Bridge with four tracks instead of two. The SER had to pay for the reconstruction of Borough Market as well as a 404ft iron viaduct over it, and oversee the removal of more than 7,000 corpses from the College Burial Ground of St Mary, Lambeth, and their removal and re-interment at Brookwood. The viaduct had 190 brick arches including fourteen crossing streets, seventeen iron bridges and two iron viaducts, including that at Borough Market. Later, in June, 1878, a new junction was opened to provide a link, Metropolitan Junction, with the LCDR line to **Blackfriars**.

The line also resulted in the removal and scrapping of **Brunel's** original Hungerford Bridge, but nothing was wasted as the bridge and iron work was used for the construction of Clifton Suspension Bridge at **Bristol**. As at Cannon Street, the bridge included a pedestrian walkway, in this case on the eastern side, for which a toll of a ½d (0.2p) was charged until 1878, when the Metropolitan Board of Works paid the SER £98,000 for pedestrians to enjoy free access.

Charing Cross opened on 11 January 1864, initially with just a limited service of trains to Greenwich and mid-Kent, but on 1 April, trains from the north of the county started to use the new station, and on 1 May, main line services followed. The train shed had a single arch, a pattern repeated at **Cannon Street**, with a span of 164ft, length of 510ft and was 98ft above the track. The station was not immediately popular. For every one of those who appreciated the location overlooking the Thames, there was another who found Charing Cross and Cannon Street monstrous. There was an additional edge to the opposition to Charing Cross, as there were those, including some town planners, who favoured closing the station so that a new road bridge could be built over the Thames to take traffic directly into Trafalgar Square.

The six platforms were all built in wood, ranged in length up to 690ft and extended on to the bridge. Platforms 1 and 2, the most westerly and reserved for mainline departures, incorporated a cab road with an exit through the front of the station under the hotel, and a ramp to bring cabs up from Villiers Street. At first, there were no engine sidings, but two were eventually provided, known as 'gussets', at the end of platforms 1 and 6.

The Charing Cross Hotel was designed by the architect E M Barry, with 250 bedrooms and almost wrapped itself around the station by extending down Villiers Street, and later had an annex across the street reached by a covered footbridge.

Powers were obtained in 1864 in The North Western & Charing Cross Railway Act to provide an underground line running just below the surface for goods and passenger trains from Charing Cross to **Euston**.

The LNWR and SER both gave guarantees to raise 5 per cent of the capital, but this was not enough to encourage investors and the scheme was abandoned in the financial crisis of 1866 that pushed the LCDR into Chancery. The Euston link surfaced again in 1885, with the two railway companies prepared to provide a third of the capital each, but floundered again. Had either line been built, they could have undermined financial backing for the Hampstead tube, but on the other hand, could also have provided the basis for a modern day regional express across the centre of **London**.

Hungerford Bridge was widened in 1887 on the western or upstream side to provide another three tracks, and later, in 1901, a fourth track was laid between **Waterloo** and Metropolitan Junction, with scissors crossings east of Waterloo Junction. Meanwhile, the SER started buying the freehold of property on either side of the station in readiness for much needed expansion. In 1900, powers were obtained to widen Hungerford Bridge on the east side and also to enlarge the terminus. Having got this far, the SER was then discouraged from any further move by the plans to replace the station and bridge with a road bridge.

During the afternoon of 5 December 1905, workmen were busy on roof maintenance work. At 15.45, there was a sudden noise: shortly afterwards, at 15.57, there was a deafening roar as 70ft of the roof at the outer end of the station collapsed into the station, while pushing outwards the western wall onto the Avenue Theatre in Craven Street. Inside the station, three men were killed as rubble, iron work and glass crashed on to the 15.50 express to Hastings, while at the Avenue Theatre, three men out of a hundred who, by unhappy coincidence, were also working on renovations to that building, were crushed under the rubble.

The **South Eastern & Chatham** closed Charing Cross at once, and traffic on Hungerford Bridge was stopped.

Investigation soon showed that a weakness in a wrought-iron tie rod next to the windscreen at the southern end of the roof was the main cause. The weakness was due to a fault that doubtless had occurred at the time of manufacture, and had grown worse over the years as it expanded and contracted as weather conditions changed. The SECR decided to take no chances, rebuilding the roof and walls at a reduced height and dispensing with the single span. Meanwhile, trains were diverted to Cannon Street and Charing Cross could not re-open to traffic until 19 March 1906, when a partial service was restored. The closure did have one beneficiary, as it enabled the Charing Cross Euston & Hampstead Railway, precursor of today's **Northern Line**, to dig down through the forecourt.

The opportunity was also taken to enhance many of the facilities at Charing Cross, with new booking offices and waiting rooms, including the then customary ladies' waiting room. These works were not completed until 1913. By this time the suburban services were beginning to feel the competition from the trams, while the underground network had already long removed the once heavy volume of traffic between Charing Cross and Cannon Street.

The First World War saw the SECR become very much Britain's frontline railway, with the heaviest responsibility for the movement of men and materials to the coast. Charing Cross also had the role of being Westminster's local station, and a special train, code-named *Imperial A* was held ready at all times for VIP journeys to the coast, being used for 283 journeys during the war years. This was a short-formed but luxurious operation, usually consisting of just a Pullman car and a brake composite. In addition, there was a military staff officers' train that operated daily from

Charing Cross to Folkestone, leaving at 12.20. Less happily, but an incredible achievement nevertheless, after the start of the Battle of Messines at dawn on 7 June 1917, the first wounded arrived at Charing Cross at 14.15 on the same day.

As early as late October 1914, a lookout was posted on Hungerford Bridge watching for Zeppelin raids, and if an air raid seemed possible, no trains were to be allowed on to the bridge. All boat trains were diverted to **Victoria** for the duration of the war, but there were many fewer of these as **Dover** was closed to civilian traffic on the outbreak of war, and the following year closure was extended to include Folkestone.

When the **Southern** inherited Charing Cross, it also took on the old controversy over the question of a road or rail crossing of the Thames. One reason for the Southern considering the various plans for the Hungerford Bridge and Charing Cross was that the bridge itself was beginning to show signs of weakness, and restrictions had to be imposed on the weight of trains and loco-motives using it. **Electrification**, because of the lighter weights of electric multiple units and the more even spread of weight throughout the train, gradually made the restrictions superfluous. All that was neces-sary was to swap around the main line and suburban services, with the former using the newer and stronger 1887 bridge, while the latter took over the original bridge. The changeover was made during the weekend of 22-24 August 1925, ready for the start of electric services to Addiscombe, Beckenham Junction, Bromley North, Hayes and Orpington on 28 February 1926, with services to Dartford following on 6 June. The success of the scheme can be judged by the fact that daily traffic increased from 48,800 in 1925 to 71,200 in 1930. For elec-trification, the platform numbers were reversed with the lines into platforms 1 to 3 electrified, number 1 now being at the east-ern or Villiers Street side of the station. A carriage road between the lines serving plat-forms 4 and 5 was removed and this enabled platform 4 to be widened, while all of the platforms were lengthened, so that lengths varied between 610 and 750ft.

The Second World War found Charing Cross left on the sidelines as with the evacu-ation of the BEF from Dunkirk, there was no longer any need for senior officers to make hasty trips to France. During 8 October 1940, a daylight raid inflicted serious damage on a train standing in the station, but the worst raid of all was during the night of 16/17 April 1941, with the hotel and station both badly damaged by fire and other fires started on Hungerford Bridge. Three trains in the terminus were set alight along with a fourth on the bridge, while further disruption was caused when a land-mine was discovered near the signal cabin with its parachute caught on the bridge gird-ers. The mine was eventually defused and removed, but not before a fire under plat-form 4 had come within four yards of it. Charing Cross was closed throughout 17 April. Another closure followed a further raid on the night of 10/11 May. On 18 June 1944, a flying bomb blew out a span of the original bridge near the south bank, but trains managed to continue using the station by using the newer section of the bridge, although full service could not be resumed until 4 December.

Charing Cross, Euston & Hampstead Railway

Known more usually as the 'Hampstead Line' or the 'Hampstead & Highgate', the Charing Cross Euston & Hampstead Railway was authorised in 1893, and after many variations opened in 1907 as part of the **Underground Electric Railway** tube lines. At the time, it was known as 'The Last Link'. It was to run from **Charing Cross** to Hampstead via **Euston**, with a branch to the

Midland **Railway's** suburban station at Kentish Town but before opening it was extended to Golders Green, then nothing more than a muddy country cross roads, and Highgate. In 1914, it was extended southwards to the **Metropolitan Railway's** Charing Cross station on the bank of the Thames to provide a loop that avoided the need to reverse trains.

Legislation in 1912 and 1913 permitted further extensions, and between 1923 and 1924, it was extended from Golders Green to Edgware, including a London County Council housing estate being built at Burnt Oak, and after this through trains were operated over the **City & South London Railway** south of Camden Town. To the south, the line was extended to Kennington to connect with the southern extension of the CSLR to Morden in 1926. The line, by this time known as the Edgware Highgate & Morden Line passed to the **London Passenger Transport Board** in 1933, and in 1937 became the **Northern Line.**

The platforms at Hampstead remain the deepest on the **London** tube network at 192 ft below ground level, while the tunnel between East Finchley and Morden via the CLSR line at 17$^1/4$ miles was for many years the longest railway tunnel in the world.

Chartered Institute of Transport

Created in 1919, the same year that the **Ministry of Transport** was formed, the first president was the first minister, Sir Eric **Geddes,** and he was followed by Lord **Ashfield.** Initially simply the Institute of Transport, it received its Royal Charter in 1926. At first it offered either full membership, MInstT, or associate membership, AMInstT, but later fellows were added and the grades became FCIT, MCIT, AMCIT. It provided education and examinations in transport subjects, as well as meeting and lectures, and its branch network spread throughout the British Commonwealth and the Irish Republic. Its *Journal* for many years published papers, but became a review of developments in transport during the 1980s.

Membership of the Institute has never been spread evenly throughout transport, and the railways were always the strongest supporters, followed by road transport and then shipping. The decline of the railways was accompanied by a decline in membership, and it merged with the Institute of Logistics to form the Institute of Transport and Logistics.

Cheshire Lines Committee

Despite the name, most of the 143 route miles of this railway were in Lancashire, as well as the largest of its seventy stations, including Liverpool Central and Manchester Central, connected by punctual expresses taking just forty minutes, while most of its revenue came from the same county. In 1865-66, the **Manchester, Sheffield & Lincolnshire Railway,** (see **Great Central**), the **Great Northern** and the **Midland Railways** formed a committee with the intention of breaking the **London & North Western Railway's** monopoly in **Manchester.** Companies were formed to build lines in the Manchester and Stockport areas that linked to the MSLR, while the company also gained access to **Liverpool** docks, and reached Birkenhead docks over the **Wirral Railway.** A line was built to Chester Northgate to connect with the GCR lines to Bidston and North Wales. Highly profitable, it was estimated that at one time the CLC took almost a fifth of the trade of the port of **Liverpool.** Locomotives were provided by the member companies, and after grouping in 1923 mainly by the LNER, but the CLC had its own rolling stock, including four Sentinel **railcars.**

Chester & Holyhead Railway

Authorised in 1844, the Chester &

Holyhead Railway was supported by the **London & Birmingham Railway**, which provided £1 million towards its capital and half the directors, while Robert **Stephenson** was the engineer for the 84 route miles intended for traffic to Dublin. The line opened as far as Bangor in 1848, running along the coast, with a tubular bridge at Conway and another, but much larger over the Menai Strait, the Britannia Bridge, and opened to Holyhead in 1850. By this time, the CHR had taken over and opened the Mold Railway from Chester in 1849. In 1852, it leased the Bangor and Carnarvon Railway. A branch was opened to Llandudno in 1858, the year before the company was acquired by the **London & North Western Railway**. The inner harbour at Holyhead was built by the CHR, developing it as a packet port, from which the LNWR operated services to Ireland. Branches were later opened to Bethesda, Bettws-y-Coed, Blaenau Festiniog, Denbigh, Dyserth and Holywell, and on Anglesey, while between 1852 and 1867 the line from Carnarvon was extended to meet the **Cambrian Railway** near Pwllheli, with a branch to Llanberis.

In addition to developing the Irish traffic and opening up the resorts of the North Wales coast to holidaymakers, the company also stimulated commuter traffic with a daily Llandudno-Manchester service launched during the 1880s and from 1908 this included a **club** carriage. The following year, the summer express from Euston to Rhyl was the LNWR's longest non-stop run, and was later named *The Welshman* by the **London, Midland & Scottish**.

Churchill, Viscount

Taking over the **Great Western** in 1908, Churchill has been described as 'one of the greatest railway chairmen of the twentieth century'. When he arrived the railway was entering its most prosperous period, but then had to face the difficulties imposed by the First World War, and while these were as nothing compared with those encountered during the Second World War, state intervention meant that the railway could not be run as it needed to be, while there were manpower shortages and even locomotives and rolling stock were requisitioned to help with the war effort. Postwar came the challenge of the grouping, the miners' strike of 1926 and the related national strike, and the years of the great depression.

Not everything was as wonderful at the GWR in 1908 as it might have seemed to outsiders. Churchill arrived to find a fierce internal battle between the general manager James **Inglis** and the highly respected chief mechanical engineer George **Churchward**. This was not simply a question of a senior officer of the company seeking to resist interference with his area of responsibility; it was nothing less than a question of who ran the company. Churchill sided with Inglis, himself formerly in charge of the GWR's engineering, and eventually persuaded his fellow directors to do the same. Sadly, the death of Inglis in 1911, and the demands of the First World War, meant that not much was done by Inglis's successor, and it was not until Felix **Pole** took over in 1921 that the way ahead seemed assured.

Inglis and Pole were the two greatest out of the five general managers serving under Churchill's chairmanship, which also covered the industrial unrest of the 1920s before retiring from the board in 1934.

Churchward, George Jackson, 1837-1933

Trained by John Wright on the **South Devon Railway** and William **Dean** of the **Great Western Railway**, in 1882 he became assistant to the carriage works manager at **Swindon**, producing an improved vacuum-brake and also improved axle bearings to reduce overhauls. He became carriage works manager in 1885, and a decade later was appointed locomotive works manager, also becoming Dean's principal assistant in 1897, and his successor as chief mechanical engineer in 1902.

To ensure that locomotive efficiency was properly tested and understood, in 1904 he built Europe's first locomotive testing plant at Swindon. A believer in standardisation, he introduced nine standard locomotive classes between 1903 and 1911, making maximum use of standardised components and using the latest in US and European design features. His elegant locomotives had free-steaming tapered boilers and long-travel valve gear. He adapted divided drive and other features from three imported French locomotives for his four-cylinder express locomotives, and was an advocate of superheating to increase power and improve efficiency. So influential was he that not only did his successors at the GWR continue his philosophy, but it also influenced the post-grouping CMEs on other railways. He introduced 70-ft main line carriages that gave a significant advance in comfort.

Churchward built Britain's first Pacific locomotive, 4-6-2 *Great Bear*, but is reputed never to have liked the locomotive as built, although it was a matter of some pride to the GWR's management, and it was later converted to a standard 4-6-0 Castle-class. He was criticized for the high capital cost of his locomotives, but defended this by maintaining that they were amongst the cheapest to maintain.

Circle Line – see Underground

City & South London Railway

Opened in 1890, this was the world's first deep-level electric railway, running from King William Street in the City of **London** 1¼ miles to Stockwell. It was built using the Greathead Shield, which enabled tunnels to be bored through soft soil. Originally, it was planned to use cable haulage, but before opening it was decided to use electric engines using the third and fourth rail system for current. Because of the depth of the line, each station had two hydraulically-operated lifts.

The line was an instant success, carrying 15,000 passengers daily, but it was overwhelmed by the traffic. The King William Street terminus was too small and congested, the two-car trains were inadequate and even so, the locomotives were under-powered and the current supply unreliable, while the 10ft 2-in diameter of the tunnels was too restrictive. Despite these problems, the CSLR was extended north and south, reaching Moorgate and Clapham Common in 1900 and then Angel in 1901, before reaching **Euston** in 1907. It was acquired by the **Underground Group** in 1913 and then linked to the Hampstead Line, predecessor of the **Northern Line**. Between 1922 and 1924, it was completely reconstructed with standard diameter tunnels and standard Underground equipment, although a few single island platform stations, the only ones on the deep level tube network, survived. This enabled through running of Northern Line trains, which became the only tube line to have two routes through the centre of London, with the CSLR line becoming the 'City Branch'. In 1926, it was given its final southern extension to Morden, where the London County Council built a large housing estate.

Clarence & Hartlepool Junction Railway

Named after the Duke of Clarence, later King William IV, as a compliment, the Clarence Railway was the first promoted specifically to compete with an existing railway, the **Stockton & Darlington**, which was being extended to Middlesbrough. Authorised in 1828, it was intended to serve a new port on the north bank and branched out of the S&D at Simpasture. The line opened in 1833-34, three years after the S&D's extension, and undercut the earlier railway's freight charges. While it attracted its share of the rapidly growing coal traffic, it struggled to pay its way, and was nearly closed in 1842, but was leased in 1844, and in 1853 the lessees merged with the Hartlepool West Harbour & Dock Company, purchasing the railway outright and changing its name. It was acquired by the **North Eastern Railway** in 1865.

Cleobury Mortimer & Ditton Priors Light Railway

Built under a light railway order of 1901, this was a light railway that retained its independence until taken over by the **Great Western Railway** in 1922. It ran for twelve miles from Cleobury Mortimer, to the west of Kidderminster in Shropshire, to serve quarries at Ditton Priors, but it also carried agricultural traffic. It opened to goods traffic in July 1908, and to passengers the following November, with halts at Cleobury Town, Stottesdon and Burwarton. Over its short length, there were no less than thirteen level crossings and many gradients. In common with many light railways, there were no signals and it was usually worked on the basis of 'a single engine in steam'.

There were only a few four-wheeled passenger carriages, and the GWR withdrew the passenger service on 26 September 1938, although the line remained open for goods traffic.

Club trains

Apart from the Royal trains, grandest of the trains on Britain's railways were the 'club' trains, and as the term implies, not everyone could travel in such comfort. Club trains had their origin in passenger demand. During the 1890s, first class season ticket holders commuting from **Blackpool** to **Manchester** approached the **Lancashire &** Yorkshire Railway seeking a special carriage for their exclusive use in return both for a guarantee that a minimum number of annual season tickets be purchased and for payment of a supplementary fare. This was to be a genuine club, not to be compared with the so-called airline 'club class'. Members had to be elected by a committee – initially the founding members – and the members once elected had to abide by the club rules. In 1895, the L&Y introduced the first club car operating from Blackpool in the morning and home again in the evening. The members had their own reserved seats and were served cups of tea from a small galley. Amongst the rules was one that stipulated that the windows of the club car had to be kept closed while the train was in motion. This venture was so successful that by 1902, a second club car had been added to the main Blackpool-Manchester commuter express, and eventually a third class club car was also provided. The club carriages were carefully marshalled in the train so that on arrival at **Manchester** they would stop close to the exit barriers.

The **London & North Western Railway** was the next to adopt the concept, introducing club cars on the main morning and evening trains on services between Llandudno and other coastal towns in North Wales, and between **Liverpool** and Manchester, all before the outbreak of the First World War, by which time a further club car was in service between Windermere and Manchester. The **North Eastern Railway** was next, with a club car on the service from Bridlington into **Hull**.

Grouping did not disturb the concept, despite the doubtful economics of a specially-built or adapted carriage that made just one return journey daily, but no doubt on occasion such rolling stock found other uses, as when railway company directors ventured out to view their empire. Certainly, in 1935 the **London, Midland**

Scottish commissioned a specially-built club car, but this, and all the other club cars, fell victim to the drastic reductions in service and catering introduced as an austerity measure during the Second World War, and unlike the Pullman services, club cars were not reinstated after the war, although apparently a few were used for trains on 'rail cruises' in the 1950s. Despite this, the Blackpool to Manchester commuter trains continued to be loosely described as 'club trains' for several decades after the war had ended, so that the title survived into a more egalitarian age.

Cockermouth, Keswick & Penrith Railway
Opened in 1864 and 1865, the Cockermouth Keswick & Penrith Railway was worked by the **London & North Western Railway** and the **North Eastern Railway**, before becoming part of the **London, Midland & Scottish Railway** in 1923.

Collett, Charles, 1871-1952
Originally trained as a marine engineer, Charles Collett joined the **Great Western Railway** at Swindon as a draughtsman in 1893 when he was twenty-two years of age. He became assistant works manager in 1900 and works manager in 1912, and became deputy to **Churchward** in 1920.

Collett took over as chief mechanical engineer in 1922, and his arrival coincided with that of Felix **Pole** as general manager. A protégée of Churchward, one can only assume that Collett was far easier for others to work with, and he was also an inspired CME. It was Collett who designed the Castle and King-class 4-6-0 locomotives that for many were the finest examples of Great Western locomotives. Both these classes continued to follow Churchward's principles of locomotive design, since the Castle was a development of the earlier Star-class. Collett also introduced further standard types, notably the Hall and

Grange-class mixed traffic locomotives, again these were based on earlier locomotives, in these examples the progenitor being the Saint-class express locomotives. When they entered service, the members of the King-class were Britain's heaviest and most powerful 4-6-0 locomotives, and their operation only made possible by a relaxation in permitted axle-loadings on the company's main lines, but even so, they were not permitted to operate west of **Plymouth**.

Less obvious but perhaps even more important, Collett continued and developed Churchward's work on the standardisation of locomotive boilers and fittings which must have reduced costs considerably and also shortened repair times. One of his achievements was to extend this work to the locomotives absorbed from the many smaller companies that passed into Great Western control. High degree precision construction and repair work became the standard at Swindon, Wolverhampton and Caerphilly works, greatly extending the intervals between workshop visits, while the stationary testing plant was modernised, as was the company's dynamometer car. As a result, Collett set the accepted British standards for locomotive testing and research.

Safety was much improved by Collett's extension of the GWR's automatic train control system to all of the company's main routes, and in 1927 he became a member of the Pringle Committee that studied the use of such systems in Britain. Some have criticised Collett's later locomotive designs as being too conservative, perhaps owing too much to his mentor Churchward, but he was the first to consider complete dieselisation of the fleet, electrification being a less attractive option for the GWR as little of its route mileage experienced the heavy traffic flows and high frequency services that made this option so worthwhile for the **Southern Railway**. It was also the case that Collett worked on a railway that no longer enjoyed the prosperity of earlier years: In addition to the desperate international economic situation, all of the railway companies were already suffering from the impact of road and even air competition. He retired in 1941.

Colne Valley & Halstead Railway

Opened between 1860 and 1863, the Colne Valley & Halstead Railway linked Chappel Cone & Wakes Cone to Halstead and Haverhill, becoming part of the **London & North Eastern Railway** in 1923. A short section at Castle Hedingham is now preserved as the Colne Valley Railway.

Commuting

A fact of life for so many today, commuting in fact pre-dates the railways as during the era of the stagecoach, regular travellers would catch the 'short stages' from dormitory towns such as Esher into **London**. In the UK, the term itself did not become normal usage until well after the Second World War, being of American origin. In the USA, the term 'commute' was used to recognise the change between being a resident and a worker, or the payment for journeys in advance. Before the term became widely accepted in the UK, the term was 'season-ticket holder', although in the north the term 'contract' was more widely used. A season ticket came to provide unlimited travel between two points, often including the use of intermediate stations, for a period of a week, a month, a quarter or a year, and regular travellers came to expect substantial discounts, even in excess of 60 per cent of the standard single or return fares on longer distances, despite putting railways, and other public transport operators, to considerable extra expense in providing extra rolling stock and personnel just for the daily peak periods.

The first recorded example of season tickets on Britain's railways was in March 1834 on the **Canterbury & Whitstable Railway**, providing 'Family and Personal Tickets from Lady Day [25 March] to 1 November', adopting a facility offered on the River Thames steamboats. It is clear from this that these were not intended for workers, but for pleasure-seekers. A variant were the subscriptions offered on the Dublin & Kingstown Railway from 1834. In 1836, the **London & Greenwich** offered 'Free Tickets' for a quarter's travel at £5 first-class, £4 second-class and £3 third-class. The **Leeds & Selby Railway** rejected proposals for 'composition' tickets in 1834, but the idea was adopted by the **Hull & Selby** in 1841, and the **Liverpool & Manchester** the following year. The London & Brighton introduced first-class season tickets between the two towns for £100 in 1843, but by 1914, its successor, the **London, Brighton & South Coast** was offering this facility for just £43.

Many railways also offered special tickets for shareholders, while railway directors received a gold pass guaranteeing them free first-class travel anywhere.

Some railways resisted the trend, and it was not until 1851 that the Great Western introduced season tickets, and then only as far from London as Windsor and Maidenhead. Others, such as the London & North Western and the Eastern Counties, provided heavily discounted tickets at outer suburban stations to encourage new housing development, but were largely unsuccessful. On the other hand, the pressures on housing in central London meant that the Metropolitan in particular found that there was a movement away from the centre to the cheaper housing of the outer suburbs, for which the term 'Metroland' was coined. The trend towards longer journeys to work really became significant with the dawn of the twentieth century, helped by a combination of electric trams and the electric trains that were the railways' response, but the lack of electrification in itself was no deterrent to the Diaspora of urban dwellers, and both Liverpool Street and **Fenchurch Street** soon became busy commuter stations. Initially, only first and second-class season tickets were offered, but soon all classes were available.

The First World War saw a dramatic increase in the sale of season tickets as, to cut unnecessary travel, ordinary fares were increased, but not season ticket rates. Between the wars, the **Southern Railway** in particular sought to encourage season ticket holders to its newly electrified lines and ran advertising campaigns such as 'Live in Surrey, Far from Worry', and 'Live in Kent and be Content'. Working hours were longer at the time and Saturday morning working was normal, so the morning and especially the evening peaks were longer than became the case post-war.

To further encourage longer-distance commuting, special trains were run. The most famous of these were the **club** trains in the North-West, but the Southern after electrification of the **Portsmouth Direct** had one train that ran non-stop from Haslemere to **Waterloo** each morning, known appropriately enough as the 'Stockbrokers' Express', albeit informally. An all-first-class train ran every morning from **Bournemouth**, stopping only at Southampton, to Waterloo, but this ended with the end of steam as standardised electric multiple-units meant that this facility was no longer available. The advent of the **High Speed Train** meant that even longer distance commuting became attractive, again urged on by higher property prices in London and the South East, but it also meant that attractive cities such as Bath, **Bristol** and **York** could be home to **London's** commuters.

The shortening of the evening peaks has meant that railway managers no longer seek commuter traffic as it demands personnel, infrastructure and rolling stock that is not needed for most of the day, with expensive trains making just one return journey daily. Nevertheless, the market is now so large and politically powerful that they have no alternative but to accommodate it, and this is written into the contracts for the train operating companies on the mainland. Lines with a good variety of traffic can cope well: The Portsmouth Direct could balance its daily peaks by using the same rolling stock for its intensive summer Saturday and Sunday service, while before defence cuts began to bite deeply, the crowds flooding to the coast and then home again were balanced by naval personnel returning to their ships. It is rare to see trains busy in both directions other than on the congested underground lines in Central London.

Even today, especially over longer distances, season tickets provide bargain travel and the passenger does not need to commute every day to enjoy worthwhile savings.

Competition
Until the late 1860s, competition between railway companies, or the interests anxious to sponsor a new railway, could be intense. In some cases, such competition could be ruinous for the companies involved, with perhaps the best example, which continued until almost the end of the century, being that between the **London, Chatham and Dover**, and the **South Eastern Railways**, which was not resolved until the creation of what became known as the **South Eastern & Chatham Railway**. In some cases, the competition was so fierce that battles broke out, including the famous Battle of Havant in 1859 when the **London & South Western** attempted to send its first through train from **Waterloo** down the Portsmouth Direct, only to find that the **London, Brighton & South Coast** had chained a locomotive to the rails!

Attempts were made to reduce competition, with the Scotch Railways Agreement being one example, that between 1860 and 1870 attempted to divide traffic for Scotland between the **London & North Western**, and its partners, at **Euston**, for **Glasgow**, and the **Great Northern** at **King's Cross**, and its partners amongst the East Coast Group, for **Edinburgh**. At **Portsmouth**, the LSWR and LBSCR eventually worked the line from Havant to Portsmouth Harbour jointly, along with the Portsmouth-Ryde **ferries** and the line on the **Isle of Wight** from Ryde Pierhead to Ryde St John's, which was interesting since neither company actually operated trains on the island. The LSWR and the **Great Western** also pooled their Channel Islands' ferries, not only to safeguard the business, but also because overtly competitive masters had ensured that safety was often compromised in difficult waters.

Even late in the final quarter of the nineteenth century, the urge to compete remained. The most dramatic was that of the **Midland Railway**, with its new route between Settle and Carlisle so that it could send its trains from **St Pancras** in **London** to St Enoch in **Glasgow**. The route was longer and slower than those of its two competitors, but it ensured that its rolling stock was more comfortable, and, of course, passengers paying the third-class fare were accommodated in what had been second-class carriages.

The mergers of the mid and late nineteenth century produced many much stronger companies, and many of them were described by commentators as being 'strong local monopolies', with just limited competition at their boundaries. Travel between London and Exeter was competed for by the LSWR and the Great Western, for example, with the latter competing with the LNWR between London and **Birmingham**.

A reduction in competition was one of the objectives of the **Grouping**, but in many

ways this failed. It left the **London Midland & Scottish** competing between London and Southend with the **London & North Eastern**. Competition remained between London and Birmingham, as before. The LMS and LNER, both hard-pressed financially for much of their existence, managed to invest considerable sums in strong competition and excellent trains with high-stepping locomotives for passenger traffic between London and Scotland.

Post-nationalisation, even before **Beeching**, attempts were made to rationalise the network. Many might consider that this was not so much an elimination of competition as an end to choice, and an end to diversionary routes when one line needed engineering work or was blocked by a mishap.

Cook, Thomas, 1808-1902

Originally a wood-turner by trade, Thomas Cook was an active Baptist and a strong supporter of the Temperance movement. His first venture was in conjunction with the **Midland Counties Railway** in July 1841, when he took a party from Leicester to Loughborough to a Temperance fair. He moved to Leicester and appears to have become a printer. He organised excursions every summer and soon went beyond the simple day trip and sent what had become his customers as far afield as North Wales and Scotland by 1846, but this was the year that he became bankrupt. He was back in business by 1851 and with his son John, 1834-99, became the **Midland Railway's** agent for its heavy excursion traffic to the Great Exhibition in **London**, later claiming that he handled 165,000 people for this one event alone. He developed connections with other railways, including the **Eastern Counties** and **London, Brighton & South Coast**, and started sending travellers to France. His next move was to issue vouchers for hotel accommodation, which he redeemed, and which was the precursor of the package holiday. While he continued to acquire the business of other railway companies, in 1863, the Scottish companies decided to run their own excursion business. Nevertheless, he opened his first office in London in 1865, in Fleet Street, and made his son its manager. That same year, he visited the United States, and in 1866, he sent a tour across the Atlantic. In 1868, he sent tours to Egypt and Palestine, and during 1872-73, he made a circumnavigation of the globe, offering this to clients from then on until interrupted by the two world wars.

Throughout his life, Thomas Cook saw his role as an offshoot of his faith and his advocacy of temperance, while his son saw it as a straightforward commercial enterprise. The son was the businessman and no doubt the saviour of the business which his father had bankrupted earlier. After the relationship had become very heated and strained, with John objecting to his father's philanthropy, Thomas Cook retired in 1879, returning to Leicester. It was John Cook's vision that made the company world famous and a leader in its field, despite the jealousy of railway companies and shipping lines anxious to save his commission. By 1890, it had offices in Australia and New Zealand, with the British, French and German governments as customers. John even made the arrangements for Kaiser Wilhelm II to visit Palestine in 1898, accompanying him to ensure that all went well, but he caught dysentery and died in 1899.

His two sons did not inherit their father's business acumen, and were unable to fend off the new rival, American Express that emerged early in the twentieth century. After much of their business had to be suspended during the First World War, they revived the operation post-war and in 1926 moved into a purpose-built headquarters in Berkeley Street. Just two years' later they sold the business to Wagons-Lits, the sleeping car company and the business moved to Brussels. Post-war, the business passed to the **British Transport Commission**, which eventually sold it to the Midland Bank in 1971, the first privatisation, after which it was sold to German interests and, finally, to its old rival, American Express in 1996.

Coras Iompair Eireann, CIE

More usually known simply as *CIE*, *Coras Iompair Eireann* means Transport Company of Ireland and was formed in 1945 specifically for the nationalisation of railways in the Republic of Ireland, formerly the Irish Free State. It also acquired the railways' extensive bus networks and later Dublin Corporation bus services. The mainstay of the nationalised railway was the **Great Southern Railways**, while the cross-border lines remained private enterprise until the collapse of the largest, the **Great Northern Railway of Ireland** in 1951, when control passed to *CIE* south of the border, and to the **Ulster Transport Authority** in Northern Ireland. *CIE* itself rationalised its railway network, but when UTA ceased operating freight trains, *CIE* continued to do so and operated into Northern Ireland.

In 1986, the railways came under their own management as *Iarnrod Eireann*, more usually known as *IE*, Republic of Ireland Railways, although that in turn remains a subsidiary of *CIE*.

Cork & Macroom Direct Railway

Opened in 1866, this became part of the **Great Southern Railways** in 1925, but passenger services were withdrawn in 1935. After **nationalisation** in 1945, it closed completely in 1953.

Cork & Muskerry (Light) Railway

A 3ft gauge line incorporated in 1883 and opened in stages in 1887 and 1888, connecting Cork with Blarney, Donoughmore and Coachford, and which in 1893 took over the line from Donoughmore to St Anne's which had been built and worked by another company. It became part of the **Great Southern Railways** in 1925, and closed in 1934.

Cork, Blackrock & Passage Railway

Incorporated in 1846 as the Cork Blackrock Passage & Monkstown Railway, it opened between Cork and Passage in 1850 using the Irish standard gauge of 5ft 3 in. It was converted to 3ft gauge between 1900 and 1904 and at the same time an extension was built to Crosshaven. It was absorbed by the **Great Southern Railways** in 1925, but closed in 1932.

Cork, Brandon & South Coast Railway

Incorporated in 1845 as the Cork & Brandon Railway, the first section opened in 1851 between Cork and Bantry. Later, branches were built to Baltimore, Clonakilty, Courtmacsherry and Kinsale. It was absorbed by the **Great Southern Railways** in 1925 and passed into state control when that was nationalised in 1945.

Cornwall Railway

Sponsored by the **Great Western, Bristol & Exeter** and **South Devon Railways**, who provided a fifth of the capital when the company was incorporated in 1846, and which became known as the 'Associated Companies', the Cornwall was to build a 66-mile line that would link Falmouth with the SDR at Plymouth, and also connect with the **West Cornwall** at Truro. Originally, W S Moorsom was appointed engineer, but Isambard **Brunel** took over. The line opened to Truro in 1859 and to Falmouth in 1863. The grandeur of Brunel's Royal Albert Bridge at Saltash contrasting with the wooden bridges and viaducts used for the rest of the line which crossed many deep valleys.

The line was also supported by landowners and business interests anxious to reduce the transport costs of Cornish tin and copper, which had previously been shipped by sea and had become uncompetitive. The railway also assisted the china clay industry, but it was to be many years before it made an impact. The main beneficiary from the railway at first was to be agriculture, with Cornish produce able to be transported fresh to the major markets in London and the Midlands. The mild climate meant that Cornish growers were first with the new season's produce. The CR also made Cornwall easily accessible to visitors.

The CR was managed jointly by the Associated Companies and the WCR. It did not make an operating profit until 1882, but the number of passengers grew by 68 per cent between 1860 and 1888, and turnover by 144 per cent. The following year, it was absorbed by the GWR. The new owner doubled much of the track, and post-**Grouping** replaced many of the wooden structures with stone or steel.

Corris Railway

Authorised in 1858 as the Corris, Machynlleth and River Dovey Tramroad to carry slate from the quarries at Corris to the River Dovey, the line was built to a gauge of 2ft 3in and operations started in 1859 with horses pulling the slate wagons. The section between Machynlleth and Derwenlas was closed once the Cambrian opened its line from Machynlleth to Borg in 1863, while the title was shortened to Corris Railway in 1865. Steam locomotives were not introduced until 1879. Four years later, the first passenger services were introduced between Corris and Machynlleth, and in 1887 these were extended to Aberllefeni.

The Bristol Tramways and Carriage Company obtained a controlling interest in the CR and so the company did not pass into the **Great Western** sphere of influence until the late 1920s, after the GWR had obtained powers to operate bus services and taken a majority holding in Bristol Tramways. The GWR absorbed the CR completely under an act of 1930, and in 1931 replaced the passenger service with buses. The slate traffic continued, although in decline, and the line was finally closed after nationalisation in 1948.

County Donegal Railways Joint Committee
Formed in 1892 as the Donegal Railway when the Finn Valley Railway, originally opened in 1861, and used the Irish standard gauge of 5ft 3ins and ran between Strabane and Stranlorlar, merged with the 3ft gauge West Donegal railway opened in 1889 which ran between Stranorlar and Donegal. The system underwent further work between 1893 and 1905, including conversion of the former Finn Valley line to 3ft gauge and construction of branches to Killybegs, opened in 1893; Glenties, 1895; and Ballyshannon, 1905. The County Donegal Railways Joint Committee was formed when the railway was taken over by the **Great Northern Railway of Ireland** and the **Midland Railway** in 1906, and while the line from Londonderry to Strabane was actually owned by the MR, all services were worked by the Joint Committee. The CDRJC also worked the Strabane & Letterkenny Railway, which opened in 1909. In all, the system amounted to around 125 miles of narrow gauge railway, the largest such system in the British Isles.

On **Grouping**, the MR's interest passed to the **London, Midland & Scottish Railway**. The company worked through a sparsely populated area of Ireland, with Donegal being one of the three counties of Ulster left out of Northern Ireland in 1922, so that the line ran mainly in what became the Irish Free State but had its terminus just over the border in Londonderry. To economise, it was one of the pioneers of petrol and diesel **railcars**. On **nationalisation** of the GNR(I) in 1953, the company became jointly owned by the nationalised transport undertakings of the two parts of Ireland, but closures had already started in 1947, and by 1959, the company was a bus operator, with its services and vehicles eventually transferred to *Coras Iompair Eireann, CIE*.

Crewe
Originally a small hamlet, in 1837 Crewe found itself at the junction of three important railway lines, with the newly authorised Chester & Crewe and Manchester & Birmingham Railways, and newly completed **Grand Junction Railway**, all predecessors of the **London & North Western Railway**, meeting. In 1840, the GJR acquired the CCR, and acquired large areas of land to which it moved its locomotive and carriage works from **Birmingham's** Edge Hill. When the MBR opened in 1842, it was worked by the GJR. Crewe's expansion was rapid, for by 1843, the GJR had built 200 houses and was moving workers into these and the rapidly expanding works. The LNWR continued the expansion of Crewe, although carriage building was moved several times, eventually finding a permanent home at Wolverhampton. The town's role as a junction was no less important, and both the **North Staffordshire Railway** in 1848 and the **Great Western Railway** in 1863 and 1867 sent new lines into Crewe. Meanwhile, the LNWR had to rebuild the station twice, in 1849 and again in 1867, to accommodate growth. By 1900, the LNWR employed 10,000 people in the town, where it had provided utilities and its first police force, while more than a thousand trains a day passed through and additional land had had to be purchased to the south to accommodate expansion. After **Grouping**, the **London, Midland & Scottish**

moved its locomotive department from **Derby** to Crewe in 1932.

In 1938, with war in Europe looming, Rolls-Royce built an aero-engine factory, so that Crewe was no longer exclusively a railway town. Post-war, RR moved its car production to Crewe.

The years after the war also brought nationalisation and contraction, with the works eventually slimming down to a quarter of its peak size. Nevertheless, the town remained important to the railways and benefited from the **electrification** of first the lines to the Midlands from **Euston**, and then those to the North-West and, ultimately, to Scotland.

Cubitt, Sir William, 1785-1861, **Benjamin**, 1795-1848, and **Joseph**, 1811-1872

William trained as a millwright before moving to Ransomes of Ipswich, agricultural engineers, where he rose to become a partner, before becoming a civil engineer in 1826. His early work included improvements to the Oxford Canal; before being appointed engineer to the Birmingham & Liverpool Junction Canal in 1835, after which he became engineer to the South Eastern Railway (see South Eastern & Chatham) in 1843, which included the section through the cliffs between Folkestone and Dover, while his brother Benjamin worked on the company's locomotives. He then acted as consulting engineer on the **Great Northern Railway**, again working with his brother before being knighted for his work supervising the erection of the Crystal Palace for the Great Exhibition of 1851.

William's son Joseph trained under Benjamin before becoming chief engineer on the GNR under his father, and then worked on his own as engineer to the **London, Chatham & Dover Railway** (see SECR) in 1861.

There appears to be no direct family connection with Thomas, William and Lewis Cubitt, three brothers who nevertheless also undertook work on the **London & Birmingham Railway**, including the famous Doric Arch at **Euston**.

D

Dean, William, 1840-1905

Apprenticed to Joseph Armstrong, the northern division locomotive superintendent of the **Great Western Railway**, he was given charge of the Wolverhampton works when just 24. He then became Armstrong's successor at Swindon at the age of 37. Dean had the unusual task of modifying standard gauge locomotives to run on the surviving broad gauge lines, and then reverse the modifications after the change in 1892. From 1877 onwards, he built passenger carriages intended to be converted from broad gauge to standard gauge, while from 1880 he worked on improving vacuum brakes achieving a higher degree of vacuum than hitherto.

His locomotives were generally regarded as simple and robust, leaving his successor **Churchward** to make significant improvements in performance and economy. Nevertheless, the range of locomotives built by Dean varied from 0-6-0 freight locomotives, of which 280 were built between 1883 and 1898, and 4-2-2 express locomotives, one of which ran at an average speed of 72 mph between Paddington and Bristol in 1904. His most famous locomotives, however, were the Duke-class 4-4-0s that first appeared in 1895, which proved their worth on the more arduous routes in Devon and Cornwall. He built the prototype of the modern sleeping car, but less successful were his larger carriages, using his own design of centre-less, pendulum-suspended truck, which although lighter than a true bogie was also far less satisfactory.

An enduring legacy was the establishment of a materials and chemical testing laboratory at Swindon.

Dearne Valley Railway

Opened in 1909, although incorporated in 1897, initially this line between Black Carr Junction, south of **Doncaster**, and Brierley Junction, east of Barnsley, running via Cadeby and Grimethorpe, was freight only and intended to serve the collieries in the area. Passenger services were introduced in 1912. Throughout its life it was worked by the **Lancashire & Yorkshire Railway**, but it passed into the control of the **London & North Western** on the eve of grouping and then became part of the **London, Midland & Scottish** in 1923.

Derby

Unlike **Crewe**, Derby was an important county and market town with a long-established silk manufacturing industry before the railways came. It was well-located as a centre for the new railways, but also an important traffic generator in its own right. During 1839 and 1840, three railway lines met at Derby, the **Midland Counties**, the **Birmingham & Derby Junction** and the **North Midland**. Nevertheless, they could only accept an offer from the council of land on the outskirts if they agreed to a joint station with reluctance. Each company built its own engine sheds and workshops, but in 1844 they merged to form the **Midland Railway**. The railway area of Derby remained just outside the town, rather than the town springing up around the railway, as at Crewe and Swindon.

There was no need to build more lines into Derby, but the expansion of the MR to London increased the company's and the town's importance, and the company based its headquarters in the town, refusing to move to London even after **St Pancras** opened. An impressive station was built and a large marshalling yard just outside the town at Chaddesden eventually coped with 2,500 wagons daily. The MR combined the works of its main constituent companies, and the total area occupied quadrupled over the next three decades. It was not until 1851 that locomotive building began, and by the turn of the century almost 5,000 were employed in this activity, aided by the relocation of the carriage works, eventually, by 1900, the MR employed 12,000 people, 12 per cent of the local population, in every kind of railway activity. After **grouping**, Derby played an important role in the **London, Midland & Scottish Railway's** development of diesel traction, but in 1932, the steam locomotive department was moved to Crewe. Nevertheless, the LMS located its School of Transport in the town.

The railway works provided a skills base that attracted Rolls-Royce to Derby as early as 1907, and by 1945, the company was Derby's largest employer. The presence of RR and its skills base then attracted the **British Railways'** technical centre to the town in 1964.

District Line – see Metropolitan District Railway

Docklands Light Railway

After many years of speculation over the best form of railway for regeneration of the London docklands, the Docklands Light Railway was authorised in 1985 to run from the Minories, with the station named Tower Gateway to Island Gardens in North Greenwich and from Poplar to Stratford, giving $7^1/_2$ route miles initially. For those advocating monorail or rubber-tyred solutions, the end result was surprisingly conventional, with steel wheel on steel rail, and although **London Transport** acted as a consultant initially, the line was independent until later absorbed by Transport for London, and while using standard gauge track, used third rail electrification in contrast to the third and fourth rail of the **London Underground** network.

Built as a light railway with two car multiple units often working in pairs, the line offers fine views over the former docklands and Canary Wharf, but suffers from tight curves. The trains are completely automatic, but an attendant can take control if necessary. Initially, the line proved both unreliable and inadequate for peak period loads, and substantial rebuilding proved necessary. The line was extended to Bank, with transfers to the tube lines, in 1991, and later to serve the City Airport. It now runs under the Thames to serve Lewisham and plans are afoot to lengthen platforms and convert the trains to three-car units.

Doncaster

Even before the advent of the railway, Doncaster was an important coaching town on the long journey from London to the North of England and Scotland, but it was not until 1849 that the **Great Northern Railway** reached the town and made a connection four miles to the north with the **Lancashire & Yorkshire Railway**. Nevertheless, Doncaster soon became one of the greatest British railway towns, with the GNR opening its works in 1853, adding 3,000 to the local population within a very short time, for which the company built two schools and its shareholders subscribed to the building of a church. Within half-a-century, the works was employing 4,500 men and had 60 miles of sidings, which were largely cleared every September to allow space for the St Leger race meeting, which was transformed into a popular event in the racing calendar.

Doncaster became an important junction with direct lines to both **Sheffield** and **Hull**, while it was also the main centre for marshalling the coal trains from the South Yorkshire collieries, brought by the South

Yorkshire Railway which also connected the town with the steelworks at Scunthorpe. **Grouping** led to the town becoming the main works for the **London & North Eastern Railway**.

Donegal Railway – see **County Donegal Railways Joint Committee**

Double-Deck Trains

The restricted loading gauge of Britain's railways have precluded the widespread use of double deck trains, or bi-levels as they are more usually known, which are commonplace in Europe and in North America. As an alternative to the cost of lengthening trains and therefore also the even more costly platform lengthening, which usually requires repositioning of points and signals, and sometimes work on bridges or tunnels, the **British Railways** Southern Region Chief mechanical Engineer, Oliver **Bulleid**, proposed a novel design of double deck train. Two four-car electric multiple units were built with interleaved upper and lower compartment, with the upper reached through the lower compartment which had slam doors.

The emus worked as a pair and the resulting eight-car train had 1,104 seats, a 30 per cent increase in capacity over the 4-SUB and 4-EPB units then handling the suburban services on the Southern Region. They operated in the suburban services from **Charing Cross** to North Kent. Nevertheless, ventilation in the upper compartments was poor, as was headroom in both compartments, and loading was slow. Eventually, they were withdrawn and suburban trains extended to ten carriages with the addition of two-car emus.

The aircraft manufacturer BAC at one stage advocated a double-deck design for airport to city centre use, with the upper deck having a side-gangway similar to that on the older-style of lowbridge bus, but this never advanced beyond the design stage. More recently, variations on the continental concept have been suggested as being suitable for use in Britain, but at present the sole double-deck trains in the British Isles are 'Le Shuttle' carriages, in which cars and their passengers are conveyed across the Channel.

Dover

At first, the influence of the railways on sea traffic was not always fully appreciated, and a factor in this was the unsuitability of many of the older facilities for railway use, with narrow quays and piers rather than the long quaysides, as in the Western Docks at **Southampton**, that allowed the railways easy access. The construction of warehouses close to the dock sides and the congested residential areas close to the older port areas also contributed to the problems.

It soon became apparent that the railways could combine with shipping to produce new and more direct routes, saving time and often by-passing significant areas of danger. A good example of this was the way in which travel to the continent through Dover or Folkestone (qv) avoided the hazards of the North Foreland, and also enabled the traveller to take the shortest route between England and France.

The SER invested heavily in Dover, where the older part of the harbour was owned by the Admiralty, especially after railways were allowed to operate their own shipping. The transfer of passengers, their luggage and mail between train and ship was eased considerably by the new Dover Marine station that was sufficiently far forward as to be useable by the military during the First World War, and was completed for civilian traffic after the war, shortly before **grouping**. Dover and Folkestone were completely taken over by the military during the war years, while during the Second World War, played an important role in the evacuation

from Dunkirk, but were then used only by the Royal Navy until after the Normandy Landings. For those left behind in the town during the Second World War, life was uncomfortable with heavy shelling by German artillery across the Channel.

Under Southern ownership, Dover became the main port for the short cross-Channel services, including such up-market operations as the famous *Golden Arrow* Pullman express, which in more prosperous times had the luxury of its own ship, and the now virtually forgotten *Night Ferry* through night sleeper service between **London** and Paris. Southern backwardness in developing drive-on car ferries, for which the train ferry configuration pointed the way forward, allowed a certain Captain Townsend to develop competition.

Drummond, Dugald, 1840-1912

Initially trained on the Caledonian & Dumbartonshire Junction Railway, where his father was a permanent way inspector, Drummond later trained with several contractors, including **Brassey**, before becoming manager of the **Highland Railway** workshops at Inverness under the company's chief engineer, William **Stroudley**. When his mentor left to join the **London, Brighton & South Coast Railway**, Drummond followed him in 1870.

He returned north in 1875 as locomotive superintendent on the **North British Railway**, introducing a successful range of locomotives including 4-4-0s well-suited to the tight bends of the line, and modernising Cowlairs workshops. Joining the rival **Caledonian Railway** in 1882, he produced similar designs, but also sought to improve locomotive efficiency. He moved to industry in 1890, but was lured back to railways as chief mechanical engineer on the **London & South Western Railway** in 1895, where he stayed until his death in 1912. He replaced the inadequate workshops at Nine Elms, between Clapham Junction and **Waterloo**, with a modern, purpose-built establishment at Eastleigh, near **Southampton**. He continued to produce 4-4-0 locomotives based on his earlier work, but his 4-6-0s were regarded as less successful and notorious for their oscillation at speed. Amongst his innovations were feedwater heating, firebox water-tubes, smokebox steam driers.

Dublin & Belfast Junction Railway

Opened in stages between 1849 and 1852, the line connected the port of Drogheda to Portadown, and became part of the **Great Northern Railway of Ireland** in 1876.

Dublin & South Eastern Railway

Originating as the Waterford, Wexford, Wicklow & Dublin Railway in 1846, it incorporated the Dublin & Kingstown Railway, which dated from 1834, and itself opened in stages between 1854 and 1904. The railway ran south from Dublin close to Ireland's east coast as far south as Wicklow and on to a junction at Macmine, where it divided with one line running south-east to Wexford and the other south-east to Waterford, a total route mileage of 160 miles. In 1907 it changed its name to the Dublin & South Eastern Railway, but after home rule in 1922, the railways in the Free State were grouped in 1925, and the DESR became part of the **Great Southern Railways**.

Dundalk, Newry & Greenore Railway

Originally incorporated in 1863 to run from Dundalk to Greenore, while in 1873, the year that the line was opened, an extension was authorised to Newry, giving a total route mileage of around 26 miles of Irish standard gauge line when this opened in 1876. The driving force behind this short line was the **London & North Western Railway**, which operated a steam packet service between Holyhead and Greenore,

and which supplied locomotives and carriages of its own standard design but modified for the 5 ft 3 in gauge, and also appointed six out of the eight directors. On **grouping** in 1923, it became part of the **London Midland & Scottish Railway**, and from 1933, the LMS, while retaining ownership, passed management and operation to the **Great Northern Railway of Ireland.**

When Britain's railways were nationalised, ownership passed first to the **British Transport Commission** in 1948, and the following year to the **Ulster Transport Authority**. Under both new owners, the line continued to be managed and operated by the GNR(I), but even before that company was nationalised in 1953, the line was closed in 1951 and the company dissolved in 1957.

Dundee & Arbroath Railway

Opened in 1840, the line's engineer, Thomas Grainger, adopted the 5ft 6in gauge and the line had to be relaid as standard gauge in 1847 to integrate with the Dundee & Perth Railway, a predecessor of the Caledonian Railway.

Dundee & Newtyle Railway

Opened in 1831, the line climbed steeply over the Sidlaw Hills with three inclines operated by stationary engines with ropes, with the incline at Law having a gradient of 1 in 10. A more circuitous and conventional route was opened in 1861 running via Lochee. Meanwhile, the railway had integrated with the Dundee & Perth in 1847.

E

East & West Yorkshire Junction Railway

Opened in 1848 between Knaresborough and Poppleton Junction, it was worked by the York, Newcastle & Berwick Railway before being absorbed by the **York & North Midland Railway** in 1851.

East & West Yorkshire Union Railway

Opened between Stourton Junction, **Leeds**, and the Lofthouse and Newmarket Colleries in 1891, it remained independent until absorbed by the **London & North Eastern Railway** in 1923.

East Coast Main Line/ECML

Even before grouping, the railway companies on the East Coast, the **Great Northern, North Eastern** and **North British** collaborated as the 'East Coast Group of Companies' to provide a through service from Aberdeen, reached over the **Caledonian Railway**, and **Edinburgh** to London King's Cross. Through running to Edinburgh was achieved in 1862, and until 1870, the Scotch Railways Agreement meant that Edinburgh was the preserve of King's Cross and **Glasgow** of **Euston**. Until 1877, trains had to reverse at **York**, and until 1906, at **Newcastle**, making high speed through services more difficult. To ensure a uniformly high standard, the three companies commissioned special rolling stock for the through trains between London and Scotland, including elliptical roofed carriages designed by Sir Nigel **Gresley** in 1905.

After the **Forth Bridge** opened in 1890, through running between **Aberdeen** and London was possible, and the line was shorter and more easily graded than the rival **West Coast** route. Between the two world wars, the Hertford Loop and the line between York and Darlington were quadrupled, but even today, much of the southern and northern section of the line remain double, with fast trains being hampered by suburban and goods services. In 1983, a 13-mile diversion opened near Selby to allow coal mining, and in 1991, electrification completed to **Leeds** and **Edinburgh**, although somewhat cheaply so that high winds affect reliable running.

The route saw Britain's first long-distance non-stop train, the *Flying Scotsman*, and in 1935, the **London & North Eastern Railway** introduced the first streamlined trains in the British Isles. Post-nationalisation, the line was home to the Deltic diesel-electric locomotives that provided a massive increase in traction power, and then to the Inter-City 125 or **High Speed Train**. When electrification was completed allowing running of the Inter-City 225 trains capable of 140 mph (225 kmph) in service, and much higher on test, the line became Britain's fastest until completion of the **Channel Tunnel** Rail Link in 2007.

East Lincolnshire Railway

Connecting Grimsby to Louth and Boston, the East Lincolnshire was incorporated in 1846, but even before it opened throughout in 1848, it was leased by the **Great Northern**, and on grouping passed to the **London & North Eastern Railway**.

Eastern Counties Railway

Authorised in 1836, the line was intended to run from an inconveniently-situated terminus at Bishopsgate in **London** to Great Yarmouth via Colchester, Ipswich, Diss and Norwich, but stopped at Colchester in 1843. In 1844, it was forced to change its gauge from 5ft to the standard gauge. The rest of the route was built by three separate companies and not completed until 1849. Although through running rights were maintained, relationships were uneasy until the three companies merged in 1862. The ECR was also threatened by the **Northern & Eastern** and the **Norfolk Railway**, which built a route from London to Norwich via Cambridge, but eventually an agreement was reached with these rivals. When George **Hudson** became chairman in 1845, he attempted to use the ECR to beat the **Great**

Northern in building a line to the north. When his empire collapsed, the company survived with difficulty.

The ECR failed to make the most of the traffic potential of its area and its attempts to establish packet steamer services from Harwich failed. In 1862 the various companies feeding into the ECR merged with it to form the **Great Eastern**, but it took more than a decade for the company's financial situation to improve.

East Kent Light Railway

Built under Light Railway Orders approved in 1911 and 1912, the East Kent Light Railway initially ran between Canterbury Road in Wingham and Sandwich Road in Shepherdswell and opened in 1912 to freight, with passenger services following in 1916. An extension from Shepherdswell to Richborough was built but not opened. It survived to become part of the Southern Region of **British Railways**, but was almost immediately closed. Nevertheless, part of the line is being preserved.

East Lancashire Railway

Formed in 1845 on the merger of two smaller companies, it soon acquired others, developing a network that was roughly 'T'-shaped, running northward from Clifton Junction on the Manchester-Bolton line of the **Lancashire & Yorkshire Railway** to Bury and Accrington, dividing eastward to Burnley and Colne, and westward to Balckburn, Preston and **Liverpool**. There were also a number of branches. Overall route mileage was 88 miles. Headquarters and workshops were at Bury.

While the ELR and the LYR shared Tithebarn Street station in Liverpool, and the ELR connected with it as eight points, including running powers from Clifton Junction in to **Manchester**, the two companies had an uneasy relationship. The situation worsened when the ELR established a through route via Colne and the **Midland Railway** into Yorkshire, with even a confrontation and the dispute was not resolved until the two companies placed the Clifton Junction-Salford line under joint ownership in 1854. In 1855, the ELR refused to allow services by the LYR-backed Blackburn Railway over its lines unless an exorbitant toll was paid, but again the two companies shared ownership of the Blackburn Railway. The difficult situation was finally resolved by a merger of the ELR and LYR in 1859.

The ELR had many of its lines on the slopes of the Pennines and these were marked by steep gradients. Although one of the first to introduce continuous braking, in 1860 an excursion train composed of former ELR carriages broke in two on the gradient from Bury to Haslingden, and the carriages ran downhill, crashing into another train with the deaths of ten people.

Many of its lines have been closed, although the Bury-Rawtenstall section remains as the preserved East Lancashire Railway, and the Radcliffe-Bury line, electrified by the LYR in 1916, is part of the Manchester Light Rapid Transit system.

East London Railway

The East London Railway was authorised in 1863 to connect all of the lines running into London from the north, east and south. It utilised the Thames Tunnel built by Sir Marc Brunel between 1825 and 1843. Opened between New Cross and Shoreditch, a distance of 5¼ miles, in 1876, it also provided access to **Liverpool Street**. At its southern end, it connected with the **London, Brighton & South Coast, London, Chatham & Dover** and **South Eastern Railways** at New Cross, but failed to provide any substantial link at the northern end. No rolling stock was owned by the ELR, and services were worked by other companies. It was leased in 1882 by a committee of five railways, the LBSCR, LCDR, SER, **Metropolitan** and **Metropolitan District Railways**, with the **Great Eastern** joining in 1885. It was electrified on the third and fourth rail system in 1913, after which the MR operated the trains, but ownership passed to the **Southern Railway** in 1925.

The line did not pass to **London Transport** until **nationalisation** in 1948. In 1955, it lost a wagon hoist at Spittalfields used by freight traffic, and in 1966 it lost the connection to **Liverpool Street**. It has since become part of the Transport for London Overground network and is being extended north to Dalston and south to East Dulwich.

Edinburgh

Scotland's capital was already a tightly built up area by the time the railways arrived, while the topography included high ridges running from east to west. There was substantial passenger traffic to be had from the affluent areas around the city centre, but goods traffic depended on being able to reach the port and industrial area of Leith to the north, and the coal mining areas to the south. The first railway was the horse-drawn **Edinburgh & Dalkeith**, which was extended to the docks at Leith, but which was effectively a tramroad. When the first steam railway, the **Edinburgh & Glasgow** reached the city, it stopped in the West End, then under construction, at Haymarket, with strong local opposition to any further advance eastwards, and it was not until the **North British Railway** arrived in 1846 that a short connecting line was built under the shadow of the Castle to a new joint station at Waverley, situated out of sight in a valley that divided the medieval Old Town from the Georgian New Town. The Edinburgh Leith & Granton Railway, next to be built, had its platforms at right angles to those of the NBY at Waverley and ran in tunnel under the New Town.

History repeated itself in 1848 when the **Caledonian Railway** reached Edinburgh, having to stop at the bottom of Lothian Road, close to the western end of Princes Street, which it named its terminus. Nevertheless, by 1850, the NBR provided a link to the north of England and eventually this became the **East Coast Main Line**, and the opening of a branch to Hawick later led the way through the Border Union Railway to Carlisle, giving the NBR a second route over the border and Edinburgh a second route to Carlisle, and south via the **Midland Railway**. The last major link in the network of railways in and around Edinburgh followed in 1890 with the completion of the **Forth Bridge**, which meant that the city sat astride the most direct route between **Aberdeen** and **London**.

Included in the Edinburgh network were a number of suburban and country branches, with lines opened to Polton and North Berwick in 1850, Peebles in 1855, Dolphinton in 1864, Penicuik in 1876 and Gullane in 1898. There was also a link line to Galashiels, while a light railway was opened to Gifford in 1901. Eventually, a number of routes of varying degrees of directness linked Edinburgh and Glasgow. In 1884, the NBR opened the Edinburgh & District Suburban Railway. The inner suburban railways soon suffered from competition from electric trams, and this was especially so of the EDSR, which was laid out as an oval and so often did not provide the most direct route between two points.

Most of these lines terminated at Waverley, which became every congested and needed rebuilding in 1890, and has been rebuilt again in 2007. A new station at Leith was opened to ease the pressure on Waverley, but Leith Central was not convenient for most of the passenger traffic, and especially not for the first-class traveller looking for an express. Both the NBR and the Caledonian built branches into the docks at Leith.

The NBR had two locomotive sheds in Edinburgh, at Haymarket and St Margaret's, but after merging with the Edinburgh & Glasgow, it transferred most of its heavy work to Cowlairs at **Glasgow**.

Edinburgh lost many of its country and suburban branches after nationalisation, starting in the 1950s, although there had been closures as early as the 1930s, including the station at Turnhouse, Edinburgh's Airport. Barton, Balerno and Leith all lost their branches, followed by the line to Bathgate, while the **Beeching** cuts resulted in the loss of the Waverley route from Carlisle, as well as the closure of Princes Street Station and the EDSR. Nevertheless, the Bathgate line was re-opened in 1986, and some new services have been opened on existing lines, sometimes for park and ride, but also to serve new developments such as that at South Gyle.

Electrification of the **East Coast Main Line** reached Edinburgh in 1991, and in 1993 the route from Carstairs to Edinburgh followed.

Edinburgh & Dalkeith Railway

Although authorised in 1826, the Edinburgh & Dalkeith did not open until 1831, and was worked by horses except for a short gradient at Edinburgh worked by a stationary engine. Built by Robert **Stephenson**, the main traffic over the $8^{1}/_{2}$ mile line, with a four mile branch to the docks at Leith, was coal, and customers provided their own wagons and horses. Passengers were carried, but tickets were never issued. It was acquired by the **North British** in 1845, with steam locomotives introduced the following year. Some claim that it was known as the 'Innocent Railway', but this is to confuse it with another railway that ran around Arthur's Seat.

Edinburgh & Glasgow Railway

After the failure of earlier plans for a railway between Scotland's two largest cities, the Edinburgh & Glasgow was approved in 1838 and opened in 1842. Designed by Grainger and Miller, it was designed for high speed running with gentle curves and easy gradients, which required extensive viaducts, cuttings and three long tunnels. At first, there was the possibility that it would have a 5ft 6in gauge, but it was eventually completed to standard gauge, while at **Glasgow**, a stationary engine hauled trains up to the terminus at Queen Street. Initially the railway competed with the Union Canal, but this was bought in 1847.

Such an important line soon attracted the attentions of other railway companies that saw it as providing a key link in their network, but it was not until 1865 that the **North British** succeeded in acquiring it. Meanwhile, the company took over the working of the Glasgow, Dumbarton & Helensburgh Railway in 1857, and constructed branches off its own line to Falkirk, Larbert and Lennoxtown. It connected with the Monklands Railways along its route, and acquired these the day before it passed into North British ownership.

Edinburgh, Perth & Dundee Railway

Originally formed as the Edinburgh & Northern Railway, opened in stages between Burntisland, on the Forth coast of Fife, to Tayport, across the **Tay** from Dundee, between 1847 and 1850. Despite the title, it depended on train **ferries** to connect with **Edinburgh** at one end and Dundee at the other. It built some magnificent stations, including the southern terminus at Burntisland, but the line itself suffered from tight curves, although there were no severe gradients. On the southern bank of the Firth of Forth, the Edinburgh, Leith & Granton Railway, acquired by the

ENR in 1847, provided a link between the **North British Railway** at Waverley, running through a steeply graded tunnel using cable-working to arrive at right angles to the NBR platforms. When the tunnel closed in 1868, traffic to and from Granton for the train ferries then used a route via Piershill Junction.

Isolation ended when a line was opened in 1848 from Ladybank to connect with the **Scottish Central Railway** at Hilton Junction, south of Perth. The following year, the name changed to the Edinburgh, Perth & Dundee Railway, but it was not merged into the **North British Railway** until 1862, and the train ferries survived until the bridges over the Tay and **Forth** were completed in 1878 and 1890 respectively. It was not until the Forth was bridged that trains could use the most direct route from Edinburgh and England to Aberdeen, which then gave the East Coast Group of Companies (see **East Coast Main Line**) a clear advantage.

Edmondson, Thomas, 1792-1851

Trained as a cabinet-maker, Edmondson's Carlisle business failed and he joined the **Newcastle & Carlisle Railway** in 1836. He became station master at Milton (since renamed Brampton), where he soon realised that there was little revenue control with the existing fare collection systems. He prepared card tickets, all numbered and initially hand-written, until he could produce a simple ticket printing frame which was used with a wooden press to date the tickets using an inked ribbon. This elementary system was improved with the help of John Blaylock, a local clockmaker, producing an improved dating press in iron and a ticket printing machine with automatic feed.

In 1839, Edmondson moved to the **Manchester & Leeds Railway**, where he again introduced his fare collection system,

before leaving to work with his son in Manchester in 1841 to set up his independent ticket production business. The business used the name of his son, John B Edmondson, and from the 1840s the system gradually spread over the whole British railway network. Companies paid a fixed annual royalty of 10s (50p) for every route mile. It did not disappear until **British Rail** switched to a new system in early 1990.

Electrification

While a full-sized battery-powered railway engine, *Galvani*, was demonstrated in London by Robert Davidson from Aberdeen in 1837, electrification in railway terms means trains powered by current picked up from either special rails or from overhead wires. Davidson's *Galvani* was also demonstrated on the **Edinburgh & Glasgow Railway**. A definite step towards the concept of electrification came in 1879, when Werner von Siemens demonstrated a locomotive drawing power from a third rail at the Berlin Exhibition of that year, and then brought his invention to London to demonstrate at the Crystal Palace in 1881-82. This was followed by three electric railways being built in the United Kingdom between 1883 and 1885: the **Giant's Causeway, Portrush & Bushmills** and the Bessbrook & Newry Tramway in Ulster (now Northern Ireland), and the **Volk's Railway** at **Brighton**, of which only the last survives.

Between 1890 and 1900, there were four more electric railways opened in Great Britain; the **City & South London; Central London Railway; Waterloo & City;** and the **Liverpool Overhead Railway**. Initially, these all used third rail electrification at 550-550 V dc. A significant advance was the invention in the United States by Frank Sprague of a system for controlling locomotives or self-propelled units, 'multiple units' in railway terms, operating in tandem or 'multiple', in 1898. This meant that two or more units could be coupled together and still need just one driver. The first trials of this system in Britain was on the Central London Railway in 1901, while the first to order electric multiple unit trains was the **Great Northern & City Railway** that same year, although by 1903, the CLR was first to actually put such trains into service. It was soon followed by the **Metropolitan District** and by the **Metropolitan Railway**, although the latter electrified only its underground or sub-surface sections, with trains steam hauled once in the open and electric engines used instead of multiple units. It was from this time that the London **Underground** railways began using a central insulated negative rail for return current to avoid leakage from the return rails that could cause electrolytic corrosion of tunnel linings. It became the practice for the 'live' rail to be position outside the running rails.

Competition from electric street tramways was beginning to make inroads into the traffic for suburban steam railways, and electrification was seen as an effective counter-measure. The first such conversion from steam to electricity was the **Mersey Railway** in 1903, and the following year the **Lancashire & Yorkshire Railway** electrified the first sections of its Liverpool-Southport line and the **North Eastern Railway** did the same with its North Tyneside system, which included the first electric goods trains on a British mainline.

The next stage was to consider using higher voltages, necessary if main line electrification was to be contemplated. The **Midland Railway** on its Lancaster-Morecambe-Heysham electrification in 1908, and from 1909 the **London, Brighton & South Coast Railway**, both favoured 6,600/6,700 V ac overhead electrification, but the latter's suburban plans were not completed until after the First World War. Meanwhile, the NER next used 1,500 dc

overhead wiring for its heavy mineral trains in the North East.

There were distinct advantages and disadvantages to the different systems. Third rail direct current required less infrastructure work as bridges and tunnels could remain unchanged, but needed many more additional sub-stations. Overhead alternating current required fewer sub-stations, but overbridges and tunnels needed higher headroom while the trains themselves lost space to transformers.

Grouping enabled rationalisation of the extensive electrification plans for the three operators in the south of England, and with the **London & South Western Railway** the dominant company with a third-rail inner suburban network, it was this system that was adopted, even though the LBSCR overhead continued to be installed until completed in 1925. By 1923, there were 363 miles of electrified surface railway. Between the two world wars, the **Southern Railway** completed its suburban electrification and by 1939 towns from Portsmouth to Hastings, reached via Eastbourne, enjoyed main line electrified railways. Only the **Great Western** did not electrify any of its track mileage between the wars, but the **London, Midland & Scottish** and **London & North Eastern** systems were minor compared to those of the SR.

Up to this time, the railway companies had usually electrified using their own power stations, but a Committee on Main Line Railway Electrification, the Weir Committee, advocated using power from the newly created Central Electricity Board's national grid. Nevertheless, the Weir Committee was lukewarm over electrification. It may have been influenced by the LMS and LNER, who felt that steam traction had still to exploit its full potential, and indeed, the electric trains of the day offered considerable improvement in running times on stopping and even on semi-fast services, but very little if any on fast non-stop services.

After **nationalisation**, electrification did not return to the agenda for some years as the railways struggled to overcome wartime arrears of maintenance. When it did, overhead electrification was decided upon, but because of the vast existing third-rail electrified network and the engineering costs, the new **British Railways** was happy to stick with third-rail for first the Kent Coast electrification schemes and then that to Bournemouth and, ultimately, Weymouth, as well as for some in-fill work such as the direct line to Hastings. The Modernisation Plan saw first electrification of the Eastern Region suburban services followed by the **West Coast** lines and the **Glasgow** suburban services, after which the longer-distance lines into Suffolk and Norfolk and the **East Coast Main Line** followed. All of this was completed by 1997, after which only a few isolated electrification schemes have been completed, of which the most important was that of the **Channel Tunnel Rail Link**, although the Heathrow Express route also bought the overhead wires to **Paddington**.

Environmental concerns and fears over the availability and cost of fossil fuels have prompted renewed pressure for electrification in the UK, but another matter of concern has to be the high proportion of diesel trains, mainly freight but including some passenger trains, that continue to run 'under the wires'.

Elliot, Sir John, 1898-1988
Elliot started life as a journalist, becoming assistant editor of the London *Evening Standard* after the First World War. Elliot was wooed away from journalism in 1925 to join the **Southern Railway** as public relations assistant to Sir Herbert **Walker**. In complete contrast to the career paths of modern PR people, he became assistant traffic manager in 1930 and in 1938 assis-

tant general manager to Gilbert **Szlumper**. Post-war, he became acting general manager when Sir Eustace **Missenden** was appointed to the Railway Executive, and after nationalisation he became chief regional officer of the new **British Railways** Southern Region. He took over from Missenden in 1951 as chairman of the Railway Executive, and when that body was abolished, filled a number of other roles in the nationalised transport industries.

Ellis, Cuthbert Hamilton, 1909-1987
Famous both as a writer on railways, especially their history, and as a railway artist, C Hamilton Ellis, as he was usually known, was educated at Westminster before going to Oxford, although he did not complete his studies. He travelled extensively and wrote around thirty-six books, of which his best has been regarded as *Railway Carriages in the British Isles, 1830-1914*, published in 1965. His *British Railway History*, published as two volumes in 1954 and 1959, has been criticised for some errors and for his failure to tackle an immense subject as a satisfactory narrative, but remains a rare attempt at the overall subject.

He has been criticised for the lack of references in his work, which makes validation difficult.

Ellis, John, 1789-1862
Originally a Leicestershire farmer and corn merchant, he was one of the supporters of a plan for a railway linking the collieries of northern Leicestershire with the city of Leicester itself. With George **Stephenson** as engineer, the **Leicester & Swannington Railway** opened between 1832 and 1833. Ellis later became a director of the **Midland Counties Railway**, and when the **Midland Railway** was formed in 1844, he became deputy chairman under George **Hudson**. He managed to avoid involvement in Hudson's

financial manipulations, and took the lead in the acquisition of the **Bristol & Gloucester** in 1846. In 1849, on Hudson's resignation, he became chairman of the Midland and was instrumental in rebuilding its fortunes and by building an extension to Hitchin in 1857, ensured that the company was able to reach **London**. He also found time to become Leicester's MP between 1848 and 1852.

Euston

London's first main line railway terminus, as with so many it was a joint effort between an engineer and an architect, in this case Robert **Stephenson** and Philip Hardwick. The station was built for what was then the London & Birmingham Railway, predecessor of the **London & North Western Railway**, and opened to the public on 20 July 1837. The station was built on the grand scale, unlike many other of London's termini, distinguished by Hardwick's famous Doric portico, while his son Philip Charles designed the Great Hall.

Originally, it had been intended that the terminus would have been at Islington, stopping close to the Regent's Canal, to allow easy trans-shipment of freight to the London docks. Stephenson proposed a site further west, close to Marble Arch, but this was regarded as unsuitable for freight. The third suggestions, a site near Maiden Lane, close to **King's Cross**, was rejected by the House of Lords. When the LBR board asked for economies to be made, Stephenson proposed a stop at Camden Town, again close to the Regent's Canal. This received Parliamentary approval in 1833, but in 1834, the LBR decided to go closer to **London** and sought approval for a 1¼ mile extension to Euston Grove. This was clearly the right idea, but after crossing the Canal, the new site for the terminus could only be reached by a severe gradient that varied between 1 in 68 and 1 in 77. This meant

that at first trains were intended to be hauled up by stationary engines, but in fact until the stationary engines were completed, locomotives had to move trains up the gradient with one locomotive at the head of the train and another as a 'banker' pushing from behind.

As was usual at the time, tickets were collected before the train reached the terminus, and in the case of LBR trains, this was at Camden Town, after which the trains were attached to the cable and descended the bank to Euston controlled by 'bankriders'. Cable working only lasted until 1844, and the stationary locomotives were then exported to Russia. Afterwards, steam locomotives often needed assistance in the climb out of Euston, but for some years a pilot locomotive was used and this was disconnected near the bridge over the Canal until the LNWR returned to having a banking engine at the rear of the train.

From the start, the line into Euston was quadrupled, with the two eastern lines used for trains working to and from the terminus, and only these were fitted with the cable. The most westerly of the four tracks was used for locomotive workings, while the remaining line was effectively a carriage siding. The station itself had four roads, but only two of these had platforms, known as the 'arrival stage' and the 'departure stage'. Railway offices were built on the eastern end of the large site that had been bought, for the western end was reserved for the **Great Western Railway's** London terminus, as the main line from Bristol was planned to meet the LBR at Kensal Green. The seemingly inevitable arguments between the two companies over tenancy at Euston were compounded by the GWR's insistence on the broad gauge, and it was as well that the GWR changed its mind and built its own terminus at **Paddington**. Although distinctly out of balance at first, the business at Euston eventually required all of the land to be used by the LNWR so having the GWR as a tenant, no matter how amicable, would have led to problems.

Another big 'first' for Euston was the first railway hotel, or indeed hotels, as two were built and opened in September 1839. Both four-storey buildings were designed by Hardwick; they were placed on either side of the portico and some way ahead of it. On the west, there was the Victoria Hotel, a 'dormitory and coffee room', unlicensed and cheerless. To the east, there was the more comfortable and up-market Euston Hotel, aimed at first-class passengers. In 1881, these were linked by a French-style hotel by another architect, which completely obscured the view of the portico, but compensated for the visual damage by earning itself a good reputation with travellers. Damaged by enemy action during the Second World War, the hotel was demolished in 1963 to enable work to start on reconstruction of the terminus.

The land that had been reserved for the GWR was soon taken over, in 1846, when growing traffic led the company to use it for trains to and from Yorkshire, leaving Lancashire trains with the original station. The change only lasted until the **Great Northern Railway** provided a more direct route to Yorkshire from 1850.

The enlarged hotel was not the only development in 1881, when further offices were found to be necessary, and so the steady development of Euston as a dark and dreary terminus with the architect's original vision increasingly dominated by mundane extensions began.

The LNWR was growing into one of Britain's leading railways, and Euston also had to expand further, even beyond the site that had been reserved for the GWR. Between 1887 and 1892, the station expanded westwards so that Cardington Street had to be diverted over a cemetery. Once completed, the enlarged Euston had

fifteen platforms and two booking offices reached from different entrances, effectively having a station within a station, which caused considerable confusion and even caused comparison with the old **Waterloo**. Eventually, a cab yard extension and a new booking office put matters right.

Fifteen platforms was the maximum extent of the old Euston. Main line arrivals used 1 to 3; suburban trains, 4, 5 and 7; 6 handled arrivals and departures, as well as Royal trains; while 8 to 10 were used for parcels and peak period local trains; 11 was used for parcels, fish and milk; 12 to 15 were used for main line departures. Inserted between platforms 5 and 6 was a road known as the 'horse box' line. Behind the Great Hall were reception sidings, known as 'the field', and at the outer end of 10 and 11 was a carriage dock and a locomotive siding. There were also sidings between 10 and 11, 13 and 14, and alongside 15; while an engine turntable was at the outer end of 15.

Eventually, the LNWR decided that this altogether unworthy mess should be rebuilt and obtained parliamentary approval in 1900, but the Boer War had unsettled financial markets and so Euston continued to develop piecemeal. Nevertheless, between 1901 and 1906, the cutting between Camden and Euston was widened to allow an additional down line, and carriage sheds were built, eliminating the $5\frac{1}{2}$ mile trip to Willesden depot. This meant that there were two up and two down lines in and out of the terminus. Before the outbreak of the First World War, the LNWR built a new booking concourse south of the Great Hall and the old booking offices converted to refreshment rooms.

Earlier quadrupling of the line north of Camden enabled Euston to start its first suburban service in 1879, running to Watford. The station was, and remains, predominantly a main line terminus. The connection with the London Underground that commuters find so convenient did not come until May 1907, when the **City & South London** tube was extended from the Angel, and a little over a month later the **Charing Cross, Euston & Hampstead Railway** also provided a link. Earlier plans to extend the surface railway from **Charing Cross** to Euston had never come to fruition, but the tube was a workable substitute. The **Metropolitan Railway** responded in 1909 by renaming its nearest station Euston Square, even though it was at the northern end of Gower Street, but this was, and remains, some distance away, a good five minutes brisk walk without heavy luggage!

Meanwhile, the LNWR clearly decided that there was value in suburban traffic. In 1906, it announced plans to build a new electrified line alongside the existing lines between Euston and Watford. In 1909, the LNWR assumed the management of the **North London Railway**, and agreed with the Underground companies that the new outer suburban line would include LNWR electric trains to Euston and **Broad Street**, and **Bakerloo** tube trains running from Watford to the West End and Waterloo through a new tube connection from Queen's Park to Paddington. Plans for the LNWR electric trains to use an underground loop at Euston to reverse were dropped, and instead these would run into the existing station where platforms 4, 5 and 7 were electrified on the third and fourth rail dc system. To avoid interference with main line traffic, the new electric lines would run in twin tubes at Primrose Hill and through borrowing junctions at Chalk Farm. A new single track tunnel would also be provided for a new line for empty carriage workings. The First World War delayed completion of these plans until 1922, the eve of **grouping**.

The LNWR was absorbed into the **London, Midland & Scottish Railway** in

1923. On 26 April the following year, a serious accident occurred when, at 7.53 am, a six-car electric train ran into the back of a Cup Final excursion train from Coventry, waiting at the up slow home signal. Five passengers in the excursion train were killed, and the motorman of the electric train was trapped in his cab for five hours. The inspecting officer found that the signalman had intended giving train out of section for an up Glasgow express standing on the fast line next to the excursion train, but had instead used his up slow instrument, so that the electric train was cleared to enter the section. The hapless motorman on the electric train did not see the waiting excursion train until he was within sixteen yards of it because smoke and steam under Park Street Bridge had obscured his view.

No major changes or improvements were made to the terminus by the new company until 1935, when it proposed to demolish the entire station and build a new one using low-cost government loans. It was to take another three decades with another war and nationalisation before this dream was realised. Some limited installation of colour light signalling was introduced, but overall, signalling, as with so much else at Euston, remained inadequate for such a great terminus.

The Second World War left Euston comparatively unscathed compared to other major London termini. In 1940 at the height of the Blitz, a bomb damaged the roof of the Great Hall, while another bomb landed between platforms 2 and 3 and wrecked offices and damaged part of the hotel.

Nationalisation saw no immediate change in the muddle that was Euston. **British Railways** spent a substantial sum on make do and mend, patching up as necessary, but lacking the means to completely rebuild the station. A large train arrival bureau was provided at the London end of platforms 1 to 3 in June 1951, with seats for

92 people to watch train information back-projected onto a 12-panel screen. The Great Hall and the shareholders' meeting room were restored to Hardwick's original designs between 1951 and 1953. Of more practical use, changes to the approaches were made in 1952 so that long trains in the arrival platforms did not obstruct the approaches to the other platforms. The track layout was simplified and the number of diamond crossings reduced from eighteen to five. Platforms 1 to 3, 6, 7 and 15 were lengthened by between 40ft and 190ft. In 1954 and 1955, platforms 12 to 15 were repositioned and widened.

The late 1950s saw changes to the booking offices, which were modernised with new suburban and main line booking offices, barely necessary with reconstruction looming, and London's first fully-mechanised ticket-issuing machines. A 'Continental Refreshment Terrace' was opened on the concourse at the southern end of the departure platforms in 1958 – a feature that could only have appealed to the most determined enthusiasts as there was little appealing about the noise coupled with the aromatic blend of smoke, steam and diesel fumes.

On 6 August 1949, the new owners were reminded of Euston's deficiencies by another accident. That morning, empty stock was being pushed into platform 12 when it was misdirected into platform 13, occupied by the carriages for the 8.37 am express to Manchester, running into it at around 5mph. The absence of track circuits meant that signalmen had nothing to show them which platforms were occupied, other than a slate in No2 box on which they were supposed to chalk up details of trains on platforms. It was not until 1952 that new signalling came, and this all had to be replaced when the new Euston was built, after just fifteen years.

When reconstruction came, it was for a new all-electric railway, with the initial electrification planned for Birmingham, Manchester and Liverpool services, with those to Carlisle and Glasgow in the distant future. It marked the end of the old Euston, hardly loved by the passenger, but it also meant the end of the Great Hall which could not be accommodated in the new terminus, and of the portico, although the demolition contractor had the foresight to carefully number the stones. The cost of preserving the portico and re-erecting was considered too high, and the lack of a suitable site for its reconstruction was another factor, despite widespread public protest.

During rebuilding, services continued to run. The work moved across the station from east to west. Temporary structures were built, including ticket offices and the amenities expected by passengers. Some services were diverted to other stations at times, but Euston never completely closed. The new station accommodated no less than twenty platforms, of which fifteen were for passengers, while platforms 8 to 10 had both conductor rails and overhead ac wires. No longer were there arrival and departure platforms for main line trains, all, except the overnight sleepers from Scotland were turned around in the same platform, adopting a practice that almost all other termini had adopted many years before. The first main line electric trains started operating in November 1965, and the full electric service began early the following January. It was not until late 1968 that the new passenger areas were completed.

Exeter

If **Bristol** was the gateway to the West Country, Exeter was the gateway to the South-West, and as such was to be served by both the **Great Western Railway** from **Paddington** and Bristol, and by the **London & South Western Railway** from **Waterloo** and Salisbury. The broad gauge **Bristol &**

Exeter Railway reached the city in 1844, and the GWR reached the city over its tracks and then continued through the city's main station at St David's, on a riverside location on the outskirts, to **Plymouth** using the lines of the **South Devon Railway**. From Exeter, the South Devon lines also reached Kingswear, across the river from Dartmouth, while the rival L&SWR headed north to North Devon, although it also built and operated the branch to Exmouth, which rapidly became what almost amounted to a suburban line.

By 1862, St David's had become an important junction and, for the next thirty years, interchange point between broad and standard gauge, which did little to expedite traffic through the city, although it was spared the worst of the problems that afflicted Gloucester, possibly because there was less interchange traffic given the overlap of the LSWR and GWR networks in the area.

While the LSWR station at Queen Street, later renamed Exeter Central, was in the centre of the city, it entailed a steep descent to St David's, and in the opposite direction a steep climb away from the GWR station. The opening of a competing LSWR line inland via Okehampton to Plymouth in 1876 produced the oddity of London-Plymouth trains through St David's travelling in opposite directions, with the GWR insisting on a compulsory stop for its rival's services.

St David's was rebuilt twice, once in 1864 and again between 1911 and 1914. The LSWR attempted to build a line by-passing the station in 1905, but was successfully opposed by the GWR, but the **Southern Railway** did obtain Parliamentary approval for a new route in 1935, but the Second World War and then **nationalisation** prevented this being built.

Express trains

The term 'express' pre-dates the railways and applied to a fast messenger or message being sent urgently. It was first adopted by the railways for a train chartered for the 'express' use of an individual or party. It was not until 1844 that the current meaning of the word first applied, when used by the London & Brighton Railway, predecessor of the **London, Brighton & South Coast Railway** for public services by fast trains between **Victoria** and Brighton. The **Great Western** was next, with **Paddington** to **Exeter** trains running at an average speed of 43mph from May 1845.

The higher speeds of express trains raised objections that they were more expensive to operate than ordinary trains and, given the state of technology at the time, more dangerous. They certainly clashed with ordinary trains given primitive signal technology and the paucity of multiple lines on the early railways. The GWR expresses ran without speed-related accidents throughout the late 1840s and 1850s, while the **Great Northern**, which introduced them in 1852, was less successful. While the concept faded and speeds were reduced, a resurgence of competition ensured that expresses returned to Britain's railways, and supplements were charged in return for the convenience of shorter journey times and to meet the higher costs of operation. The **Midland Railway** led the way by abolishing supplements in 1859, and by 1870, all of the companies north of London had followed suit. In Europe, supplements continued to be charged, often at quite high rates, well into the twentieth century. The British definition of an express was set initially as a train running at an average speed of 40mph or higher, while that for Europe was set at 29mph or higher, until in the early 1900s the concept gained acceptance in France with a number of trains running at 50mph plus.

Between the wars, the GWR's Cheltenham Spa express, popularly known as the 'Cheltenham Flyer', set a record for a daily service of 66.2mph between Swindon and Paddington in 1929, but increasingly the fastest expresses were to be found in the United States and Germany, with the latter having the diesel 'Flying Hamburger' running between Berlin and Hamburg. Both the **London, Midland Scottish** and the **London & North Eastern** produced fast streamlined luxury expresses on their main routes and especially those to Glasgow and Edinburgh. Elsewhere, express goods trains became widespread, especially for perishable traffic. Not all British expresses ran to and from London, with one of the most famous cross-country expresses being the 'Pines Express' between Bournemouth and **Manchester**, running partly over the **Somerset & Dorset**.

Under nationalisation, the concept of Inter-City largely took over the express network, while with standardised clock face departures, individual named trains have also become a rarity. The concept has also been overtaken by such services as the French TGV, for example, and in the UK, by Eurostar, running at speeds far higher than those on Britain's historic network.

F

Fairbairn, Sir William, 1789-1874

A native of Kelso in the Scottish borders, he trained as a millwright and then an engineer, before entering manufacturing as a partner of James Lillie in 1817, although the partnership was dissolved in 1832. Meanwhile, he built the famous iron-hulled canal boat *Lord Dundas* in 1831, and worked on wrought-iron shipbuilding in both **Manchester** and **London**, and his patents included a riveting machine in 1839. His work on cast-iron beams and testing led to Robert **Stephenson** taking his advice on both the Britannia and Conway tubular bridges. In 1846, he took out a patent on wrought-iron beams. He became president of the Institute of Mechanical Engineers in 1854, and his later life included many honours and medals, including being created baronet in 1869.

Fairbairn, Charles Edward, 1887-1945

Apprenticed to Henry **Fowler** at the **Derby** locomotive works of the **Midland Railway** in 1910, he joined Siemens in 1912, working on the overhead line **electrification** of the **North Eastern Railway** freight line between Newport and Shilden. In 1919, he created the English Electric traction department and was appointed manager of its works at Preston and Stafford. He returned to the railways in 1934 when he was appointed chief electric engineer on the **London, Midland & Scottish Railway** under Sir William **Stanier**, whom he succeeded as CME in 1944. He oversaw large scale introduction of diesel-electric shunting locomotives and proposed 1,500-hp main line diesel-electric locomotives before his sudden death in 1945.

Fairlie, Robert Francis, 1831-1885

Trained on the **London & North Western Railway** before becoming locomotive superintendent on the Londonderry & Coleraine Railway, after which he worked in India. He objected to the trend to increase locomotive power by increasing the size of the locomotive, which put additional wear on the track, and as a result in 1864 he patented a double-ended steam locomotive mounted on two powered bogies. His first practical 'Fairlie' was the 2ft gauge *Little Wonder*, which performed so well on its trails on the **Festiniog Railway** in 1869 that it gained publicity throughout the world.

He advocated 3ft gauge articulated 'Fairlie' locomotives as a means of providing railways in the undeveloped countries, but while visiting Venezuela to promote a project; he caught a fever and became an invalid.

Fay, Sir Sam, 1856-1953
Fay joined the **London & South Western Railway** in 1872 and by 1881 was an assistant storekeeper. He launched the *South Western Gazette* with two colleagues and in 1881 published a short history of the company, *A Royal Road*. He was seconded to the **Midland & South Western Junction Railway** on its bankruptcy in 1892, and by 1897, the company was restored to solvency, with one contemporary observer noting that he had 'made an empty sack sit upright'.

On returning to the LSWR, he was appointed superintendent of the line in 1899, but in 1902, he moved to the **Great Central Railway**, which was in a parlous financial position. Fay once again developed the railway, using its central position for through cross-country traffic while working with the **Metropolitan** and **Great Western Railways** to develop suburban traffic in London. Fay was a pioneer of conciliation boards to reduce the problem of industrial disputes. He was largely responsible for the GCR's new port at Immingham on the Humber. He was knighted in 1912. During the First World War, he worked at the War Office from 1917 to 1919. He left the railways on grouping in 1923 and moved into locomotive manufacturing with Beyer Peacock at **Manchester**.

Fenchurch Street
The smallest railway terminus in London, it was originally built for the **London & Blackwall Railway** in 1841, but rebuilt in 1854 by George Berkeley. Originally it had four platforms, but after the railway was acquired by the **Great Eastern**, a fifth was added. The **London & North Eastern**

Railway remodelled the station between 1932 and 1935, but most of the trains were operated by the **London, Midland & Scottish Railway**, which had acquired the **London, Tilbury & Southern Railway** under the 1923 grouping. The line was electrified in 1967, and in 1987, a large office block was built over the station. The **Docklands Light Railway** now occupies two of the platforms.

Fenton, Sir Myles, 1830-1918
Appointed as a clerk on the Kendal & Windermere Railway at the age of 15, Fenton moved through posts at four other railways before becoming secretary of the **East Lancashire Railway** at just 24. This surprising mobility and the experience gained enabled him to become operating superintendent of the **Metropolitan Railway** when just 32 in 1862, and general manager a year later. One of his achievements came in 1866, when he introduced the first feeder bus services to a **London** underground line. When the chairman, John Parson, was forced to resign and Sir Edward **Watkin** took over, Fenton became involved in his plans to use the MR as the link between the **Manchester, Sheffield & Lincolnshire** (predecessor of the **Great Central**) and the South Eastern to form a through service between **Manchester** and **Dover**, and possibly beyond as Watkin was an advocate of the **Channel Tunnel**, and also in the eternal disputes between the MR and the **Metropolitan District Railway**.

His next task was as general manager of the SER where he found himself embroiled in that company's uneasy relationship with the **London, Chatham & Dover Railway**, as well as having to improve the performance and reputation of the SER itself. He managed to win the support of the King of the Belgians to stop the Dover-Ostend ferry service being switched to Harwich, a **Great Eastern Railway** port.

Fenton played a major role in planning for the use of the railways and their ports for wartime troop movements and was a Lieutenant-Colonel in the Engineer & Railway Volunteer Staff Corps, but retired in 1896, before the Boer War or the First World War, in both of which the railways played a major role. In 1889, he was the first serving senior railwayman to be knighted.

Ferries and Shipping Services

Railway involvement with 'ferries' took two forms: the first being the operation of ferries across rivers and estuaries; the second shipping services between the mainland of Great Britain and the **Isle of Wight**, Ireland, the **Isle of Man**, the Channel Islands or the near Continent. These latter operations are sometimes referred to as shipping services. The railways, as owners and operators of ports, also became owners of tugs and dredgers, amongst other vessels necessary for the efficient functioning of a port.

At first, the railway companies were not allowed to operate ferries for fear that they might compete unfairly with the established operators. The attraction of a connecting shipping service for operations to Ireland and across the English Channel nevertheless were such that the railway companies merely sought to by-pass the law through subsidiary or associated shipping companies. The **London & South Western Railway** was involved with the South Western Steam Navigation Company, founded in 1842, and the **London, Brighton & South Coast Railway** went further, with a wholly-owned subsidiary, the Brighton & Continental Steam Packet Company, in 1847. The LBSCR's duplicity was exposed by its rivals and within two years the steam packet operation ceased trading. Meanwhile, the railway companies were allowed to seek parliamentary approval for steamer services provided that they were for specific routes. So in 1848, the LSWR gained authority to operate to Le Havre in Normandy and to the Channel Islands. In 1863, all railway companies could operate passenger steamers provided that they sought authorisation for specific routes. Slightly different conditions applied to cargo services.

Rivers and estuaries

Ferries across the rivers and great estuaries were important because of the delay in building bridges and tunnels. Indeed, on the River Dart, the railway never reached Dartmouth, although the **Great Western** did maintain the ferry terminus as a 'station'.

At first, the railway companies did not have powers to operate ferry services, and those across the Mersey at Birkenhead and at **Hull** for the Humber were acquired without the necessary authority and had to be sold to independent contractors. It was not until 1847 that parliamentary powers were gained for ferries across the Severn, Forth and Tay. That across the Forth was the world's first train ferry and started operations in 1850 by the Edinburgh & Northern Railway, predecessor of the **Edinburgh, Perth & Dundee Railway**. Designed by Thomas **Bouch**, the ferry took wagons from Granton, just outside **Edinburgh**, to Burntisland on the southern coast of Fife. Next was the ferry across the Tay, and after the **Tay Bridge** disaster of 1879, it had to be reinstated until the replacement bridge was completed in 1887.

The early train ferries across the Firth of Forth in 1850, and the Tay the following year, had carriages and wagons loading using moving ramps onto wagon decks fitted with rails. Other train ferries included one by the LBSCR from Langstone to Bembridge on the Isle of Wight. The Scottish train ferries were abandoned as soon as the bridges were opened, while the Bembridge route also had a short life span.

On the Severn, the ferry from the New

Passage at Portskewett operated in conjunction with the railway to offer a fast journey between **Bristol** and **Cardiff**, but was closed as soon as the **Severn Tunnel** opened in 1886.

By the late nineteenth century, the remaining railway ferries were across the Humber to New Holland; from Kingswear to Dartmouth, opened in 1864; and from Tilbury to Gravesend, opened in 1875. The last two continue to run, although no longer in railway ownership.

The railway companies also became involved with ferries on the River Clyde and to the islands, building an extensive network. For some reason, there was delay in allowing the railway companies to operate their own ships, so here the companies used contracted operators until the **Caledonian Railway**, refused powers to operate ships in 1889, established the Caledonian Steam Packet Company, predecessor of today's Caledonian MacBrayne, which operated most of the services to the Western Isles. Elsewhere in Scotland, to encourage tourism the railways operated steamers on Loch Lomond and other lochs.

Cross-Channel and Irish Sea operations
One major difference appeared as the railways became involved in ferries across the English Channel, the Irish Sea and the North Sea. The traditional shipping lines serving these routes had tried to operate between the major cities at either end. For example, Burns & Laird operated between **Glasgow** and Belfast, while the Belfast Steamship Company operated between **Liverpool** and Belfast: both later became subsidiaries of Coast Lines and, eventually, of P&O. By contrast, the railways looked for the shortest possible sea crossing and provided railway connections at either end, if necessary with a company on the other side, as the **Great Western** did with its services to the south of Ireland. Few of the old shipping company routes have survived as the emphasis has been for the shortest possible crossing, and while many of the railway routes have, but today passengers with their cars are the main market rather than rail-borne traffic.

Once allowed the necessary powers, the railways wasted little time in using them. The first official railway ferry service was that of the Great Grimsby & Sheffield Junction Railway, a predecessor of the **Great Central**, in 1846, between **Hull** and New Holland, although the latter did not get its railway connection until 1847. In 1848, the **Chester & Holyhead Railway** obtained powers for a service from Holyhead to Kingstown (now renamed Dun Laoghaire) in Ireland. The **South Eastern Railway** obtained powers in 1853 for a service between Folkestone and Boulogne.

During the First World War, the British Army started a train ferry service across the English Channel, from Richborough in Kent, but this port was rejected when the Southern Railway decided to introduce through sleeping car services between London and Paris with the 'Night Ferry' train from **Victoria**, which started in 1936: goods wagons were also carried on the three ships. Before this, the **London & North Eastern Railway** introduced a goods train ferry between Harwich and Zeebrugge in 1924.

Given the means of loading and unloading railway rolling stock, it is hard to believe that the early arrangements for loading motor cars consisted of the cars being craned aboard the ship while the driver had to board along with other foot passengers. When the **Southern Railway** damaged his car, a certain Captain Townsend was so incensed that he set up his own company, which later became Townsend Thoresen and ultimately European Ferries. The first roll-on/roll-off ferry, as they are known to shipping companies (but drive-on, to the travelling public) was the *Princess Victoria*, introduced to the Larne-Stranraer route of the **London, Midland & Scottish Railway** in 1939, but it was not until 1952 that such a vessel entered service on the Channel services when the *Lord Warden* started to ploy between Dover and Boulogne, and even then, she could not operate as such until a linkspan was completed at Dover the following year.

In both world wars, the railway ferries were taken up by the Royal Navy for a variety of duties. Many, railway and otherwise, were converted into seaplane carriers in the earlier conflict, while in the Second World War, some were used as minesweepers. Only on the Irish Sea and Isle of Wight services was any kind of service maintained during the Second World War, and in the First World War the main ports and routes were closed to civilian traffic. Especially during the Second World War, many former railway ferries were lost whilst acting as troopships or hospital ships. Early in the war, many ferries, especially those of the Southern Railway, assisted in the evacuation at Dunkirk, and in bringing civilians away from the Channel Islands.

While the ferries were standardised as far as possible, there was a considerable difference between the small ferries used on the half-hour crossing between **Portsmouth** and Ryde, and the overnight ferries across the North Sea and the Irish Sea, and on some of the longer Channel crossings, such as **Southampton** to Le Havre, which had overnight accommodation. Day and night ferries had accommodation divided into classes, although this practice was abandoned on the shorter crossings much earlier and was withdrawn on the longer crossings in the 1960s. As a rule, railway ferries were fast ships, with speeds of 18 to 21 knots, and on some routes, such as Holyhead-Dun Laoghaire, 25 knots was usual.

It was usual for the railway companies to combine their ferry services. This was done on the Channel Island services to avoid dangerous competition at first, but the practice also occurred elsewhere. In any event, shipping practice was often to operate regular services as a 'conference'; in railway terminology this meant a joint service.

Nationalisation saw the shipping services passed to **British Railways**, which continued their development, especially as while the railway's fortunes declined, those of the shipping services improved with the growth in paid holidays and of continental travel. The North Sea services were an exception to this, once North Sea Ferries introduced a new service from **Hull**. BR entered into collaborative operations with European railways, especially SNCF or France. The British Railways Act 1967 authorised the nationalised railway to operate any kind of shipping service anywhere, while in 1970, the ferry services were rebranded as Sealink, as were those of the French and Belgian railways. A hovercraft operating subsidiary was established at Dover as Seaspeed. When non-core businesses of **British Rail** started to be sold off, the ferry services were amongst the first to go, with Sealink being sold in 1984 to the US-based Sea Containers.

Festiniog Railway

Authorised by Parliament in 1832 to construct a line from the harbour at Portmadoc to the slate quarries at Blaenau Festiniog, the 13¼ mile Festiniog Railway was the first of the narrow gauge lines and was built to a gauge of 1ft 11½ inches. Work started in 1833 and the line was opened in 1836. The line required extensive engineering works and costs would almost certainly have been prohibitive had it been built to standard gauge, with the line running for some distance on a narrow shelf cut into a hillside, and spanning deep ravines on narrow stone embankments 600 feet high in some places, and with two tunnels.

At first, the line was worked by horses and gravity working, with the first steam locomotives not introduced until 1863, and passenger traffic started as early as 1850, possibly earlier. Between the two world wars, growing competition from road transport saw passenger services suspended in winter. The company remained independent, but operations were suspended in 1946, and not restarted until taken over by a preservation society in 1954.

Forth Railway Bridge
Often simply referred to as the 'Forth Bridge', the bridge was needed to enable trains from the south to run through to Dundee and Aberdeen, replacing the train ferry introduced in 1850. Throughout the 1860s and 1870s, a succession of proposals were made for bridges across the Firth of Forth, and it was not until 1878 that William Arrol started work on Bouch's stiffened suspension bridge. Work stopped immediately after the Tay Bridge disaster in 1879, although the Forth Bridge was not officially abandoned until 1881.

With Bouch discredited, it was not surprising that Sir John Fowler and Benjamin Baker were commissioned in 1881 to build their design consisting of three double cantilevers with suspended spans in between. This design was refined into the present bridge, with main spans of 1,700ft, which at the time made it the greatest bridge in the world. In reacting to the Tay disaster, the new bridge was designed to resist a wind force of 56 lbs per square foot, and is widely regarded as being over-cautious in design, but it can safely accommodate trains many times heavier than those running at the time it was completed. William Arrol remained as contractor.

With the North British Railway crippled by the loss of the Tay Bridge, it was joined by the Great Northern, North Eastern and Midland Railways in building the bridge as joint shareholders in the Forth Bridge Company, although the NBR worked the trains once the project was completed in 1890.

Famous for many years for the team of painters who had to start re-painting the bridge whenever they had just finished, in recent years more modern paint technology has been applied and there will be periods when painting is not being done at all. Unfortunately, modern health and safety conditions mean that whenever painting is necessary, the parts being worked on are cocooned, spoiling the visual impact of the bridge.

Fowler, Sir Henry, 1870-1938
After serving an apprenticeship at the Lancashire & Yorkshire Railway's Horwich works under John Aspinall, Fowler joined the Midland Railway in 1900, and was promoted to assistant works manager at Derby in 1905, before becoming works manager in 1907. He became chief mechanical engineer in 1909 and retained this position until grouping, being knighted for his services to the railways during the First World War. In 1923, he became deputy CME for the London, Midland & Scottish Railway and became their CME from 1925 until he retired in 1930.

At the LMS, he struggled to integrate the design, locomotive and carriage construction and repair policies of six major companies. Nevertheless, he had considerable experience in workshop management and in improving productivity in both railway and government workshops. He had already organised line production for locomotive overhauls, reducing the time needed, while standardising components and eliminating small locomotive classes or those that offered reliability or maintenance problems, also boosted productivity and reduced costs. His plans for 4-6-2 passenger and 2-

8-2 freight locomotives were overruled by train operators because of the need for larger turntables. Nevertheless, he was responsible for the Royal Scot 4-6-0s built between 1927 and 1930, although Sir William **Stanier**, his successor, had them rebuilt.

In retirement, he was a consultant to the LMS vice-president (research) and authorised the introduction of prototype diesel shunting locomotives, with the LMS introducing these on a large scale by the time the Second World War broke out in 1939.

Fowler, Sir John, 1817-1898

After early experience with J T Leather and J U Rastrick, the engineers, he became engineer for the Stockton & Hartlepool Railway in 1841, and was then appointed the company's general manager, becoming one of the few Victorian engineers with operational experience.

He then worked on lines in Yorkshire and Lincolnshire, including those which later became part of the **Great Central Railway's** predecessor, the **Manchester, Sheffield & Lincolnshire**, and the **Great Northern**. After moving to **London** in 1844, in 1852 he became engineer for the Oxford Worcester & Wolverhampton, later a component part of the **West Midland Railway**. He was engineer for both the **Metropolitan** and **Metropolitan District Railways** from 1853, and then became engineer or consultant for most of the London Underground railways under construction before his death, as well as for the **Great Western** after **Brunel** died, and for the GNR, **Cheshire Lines** and the **Highland Railway**, as well as a number of railways abroad. His advice was sought for a number of major termini, including Glasgow St Enoch, Liverpool Central, London **Victoria**, including Grosvenor Bridge, and for many bridges, including the first concrete bridge at Torksey. His most famous work was with Sir Benjamin **Baker**, the **Forth Bridge**. He was knighted in 1885.

Fox, Sir Charles, 1810-1874; Sir Charles Douglas, 1840-1921; Sir Francis, 1844-1927.

Turning his back on the medical profession, Charles Fox was apprenticed to John Ericsson in 1829 and worked on the locomotive *Novelty*, for the **Rainhill** trials, after which he joined Robert **Stephenson**. In 1838, he became a partner of Joseph Bramah at his Smethwick iron foundry, which became Fox Henderson & Co from 1841. He invented and patented a switch. His company became a leading contractor on structural ironwork, providing the structure of the Crystal Palace as well as station roofs at **Paddington** and **Birmingham** New Street, and many iron bridges, as well as becoming railway contractors, building the East Kent, which became part of the **London, Chatham & Dover** (see **South Eastern & Chatham Railway**), and lines in Denmark, France and Germany.

Despite this activity and a sound reputation, the company went bankrupt in 1856, after which Fox became a consultant, being joined by his sons Douglas in 1860 and Francis in 1861. Together, they worked on the **Liverpool Overhead Railway**, the **Great Central** extension to **London**, the Mersey railway tunnel and the Battersea railway approach, and were engineers for both the **Charing Cross, Euston & Hampstead** and the **Great Northern & City** underground railways in London. Abroad, they designed lines in Australia, Canada, Africa and South America.

Freshwater, Yarmouth & Newport Railway – see Isle of Wight

Furness Railway

This had its origins in an isolated line built in 1846 to move iron ore and slate from the Furness peninsula to the docks at Barrow-in-Furness, but a series of take-overs and extensions resulted in a line from Carnforth to Whitehaven, opened in 1857, with branches into the Lake District and connecting steamer services on Lake Windermere and Coniston Water. In 1862, it acquired the Ulverston & Lancaster Railway. The company initially prospered with the steel and shipbuilding industry, but during the late nineteenth and early twentieth century, its promotion of tourism brought it great benefits until it became part of the **London, Midland & Scottish** in 1923.

G

Galbraith, William Robert, 1829-1914
Apprenticed to John Errington at 17, he worked on the **Aberdeen** and **Scottish Central Railways**, before becoming resident engineer on the **London & South Western Railway's** Yeovil-**Exeter** extension between 1856 and 1860. He became the LSWR's new works engineer in 1862, and was responsible for the lines from Yeoford Junction to Bude, on which he built one of the first concrete railway viaducts in England, Padstow and **Plymouth** as well as the Barnstaple-Ilfracombe line. He returned to Scotland to become a consultant, and with R F Church worked on the northern approach to the **Forth Bridge** and the rebuilding of **Edinburgh's** Waverley Station, as well as working on the **Bakerloo** and **Hampstead** tubes, and worked with J H **Greathead** on the **Waterloo & City Line**.

Galt, William, 1809-1874
A solicitor, Galt was the first recorded advocate of **nationalisation** of the British railway system, arguing his case and the organisation of the resulting business in a book *Railway Reform*, of which there were four editions in 1843-1844, the year of **Gladstone's Act**, which it may well have

influenced. The book was re-published, updated and enlarged, in 1865, the year that Galt gave evidence to the Royal Commission on the Railways. There was no political force behind Galt's advocacy of nationalisation, but instead he desired the best solution for the country, in effect seeing the railway as a new form of public highway. Many of the early arguments in favour of nationalisation saw the railways being similar in structure and operation to the Post Office.

Geddes, Sir Eric Campbell, 1875-1937
Indian-born Eric Geddes joined the **North Eastern Railway** in 1904, specialising in management techniques and by 1914 was general manager. He became a civil servant during the First World War; he had a succession of posts including munitions production, transport organisation and naval supply, eventually becoming the first **Minister of Transport** post-war. The concept of **grouping** was his idea, and he had similar plans for the electricity supply industry. As Minister, he pushed the Railways Act 1921 through Parliament, but before it could take effect, he left politics and joined Dunlop, the tyre and rubber manufacturer, becoming chairman. His final task in politics was to push through dramatic cuts in national expenditure, known to this day as the 'Geddes Axe'. In 1924, he was made part-time chairman of the new state-sponsored airline, Imperial Airways, whilst retaining his position at Dunlop. His final service to the state was to organise the delivery of essential supplies during the 1926 General Strike.

Giant's Causeway, Portrush & Bush Valley Railway & Tramway
Opened between 1883 and 1887, this was the first railway to use hydro-electric power, but closed in 1949.

Gladstone, William Ewart, 1809-1898

Gladstone became an MP in 1832, but more significant, and, apart from Eric **Geddes**, he was one of the better informed members as far as railways were concerned, since his father, Sir John, had been an enthusiastic promoter of the early railways in Scotland, and by 1843 had accumulated £170,000 (£9.4 million today) of railway investments. The only real question had to be just how impartial did this make his son who, early in 1844, chaired a House of Commons Committee on Railways? On the one hand, it could account for the watering down of the early provisions of the Railway Bill that resulted from the committee's deliberations, but on the other, shortly after the measure was enacted, Gladstone resigned, largely because he was aware of the conflict of interest between his own family's involvement in railways and his powers as their parliamentary overlord. He maintained this distance between himself and railway regulation for the remainder of his life, attending only two sessions of Cardwell's Committee on Railways which sat in 1852-53, even though he was nominally a member, and avoiding service altogether on the 1865 Royal Commission on Railways.

On the other hand, in later life Gladstone did not maintain a physical distance between himself and the railway, as the only prominent British politician to use the railways during electioneering, often addressing crowds at railway stations and even from carriage windows, a style more usually associated with the United States than the United Kingdom, and probably possible because at the time it was still a practical proposition for an individual to hire a train.

Gladstone's Act, 1844

The Railway Regulation Act 1844 has become more commonly known as 'Gladstone's Act'. It was significant as much as for what it didn't do as for what it did, as no attempt was made to enforce gauge standardisation, which would have been a practical measure. The most significant provisions were for cheap railway travel, a predecessor of the later 'Cheap Trains Act', while telegraph companies were enabled to compel railway companies to allow their wires to be carried alongside their lines and, for the first time, the possibility of the **nationalisation** of the railways was enshrined in British law. Gladstone himself felt that the Act had been an opportunity missed, and that the powers contained within the Act were far too weak, largely due to the power of the railway companies who had many members of both Houses of Parliament amongst their shareholders and directors.

The importance of the Act should not be underestimated as it authorised the purchase of railway companies by a British government in the future, although it applied only to those companies established after 1 January 1845, and the powers could not be exercised before 1866. The price to the government of a railway company was to be the profits for a 25 year period, averaged out over the preceding three years. As we shall see, by the mid-1860s, many railway companies were passing through a bleak period and no doubt the cost of acquisition at the time would have been low, but the railway system was still incomplete. One cannot help speculate that, had nationalisation occurred at this early stage, would the total mileage have ever reached its ultimate grand total of more than 20,000 miles? Given post-nationalisation experience of the attitude of the Treasury to investment in the railways, one may be excused for doubting it.

Glasgow

Variously known as the 'Workshop of the British Empire', Glasgow, the largest city in

Scotland with twice **Edinburgh's** population, was one of the world's leading industrial cities during the nineteenth-century, with a substantial proportion of the world's merchant shipping built on the Clyde. This was not a one industry city, however, and its engineering activities included several major railway locomotive works, some of which were independent, and later commercial vehicles were also built, while lighter engineering included the Singer sewing machine factory and there were also cotton mills and breweries. These industries and the surrounding coal mines were served by a rudimentary network of tramroads developed during the eighteenth century.

Glasgow's first railway was the Glasgow & Garnkirk, opened in 1831, which soon built an extension to a temporary wooden terminus at Buchanan Street, which was taken over by the **Caledonian Railway**, initially for its services to **Aberdeen**, but it later also became the terminus for services to **London Euston**. The city soon became a focal point for a growing number of railways, with the next being the Glasgow, Paisley, Kilmarnock & Ayr, which shared a terminus at Bridge Street, south of the Clyde, with the Glasgow, Paisley & Greenock. North of the river was the **Edinburgh & Glasgow's** Queen Street Station, initially reached by a cable-working from Cowlairs.

Initially, the Clyde proved to be a major barrier with the north and the south of the city kept separate, partly because of Admiralty objections to a fixed bridge. The river was not bridged until 1876 when the **Glasgow & South Western** sent its line into St Enoch, also the terminus for **Midland Railway** services from London **St Pancras**. In 1879, the CR opened Glasgow Central Station. The **North British Railway** was able to use land vacated by the University as it sought more suitable premises, and also had the support of the City council in demolishing some particularly bad slums, in building its sidings and sheds, while it used Queen Street, acquired with the EGR. Between 1885 and 1910, the rival companies each built their own competing lines into the docks and many industrial areas. Suburban and even urban routes proliferated, and included the **Glasgow Subway,** a circular route initially worked by cable.

Glasgow was the only city outside **London** to have a Royal Commission on its railways, but unlike that in London, which imposed an inner limit on construction of new surface lines and termini, that in Glasgow had no effect. The city's industry contributed much, and the CR in particular was predominantly a freight railway, but even so passenger numbers at Central Station rose from 4.75 million in 1880 to reach 15.75 million in 1897. The termini included hotels, such as the St Enoch Hotel, which when opened was the largest hotel in Scotland. Suburban lines developed on a scale second only to London, including the famous 'Cathcart Circle', albeit never a true circle, which operated out of Glasgow Central. The expansion of Central between 1901 and 1905 took it over Argyll Street, which famously became a meeting place for exiled Highlanders, known as the Highlandman's Umbrella, or *Hielanman's Umbrella.*

As with other major cities, passenger numbers began to fall as the urban and inner suburban networks soon proved vulnerable to competition first from the electric tram, and then after the First World War, from the motor bus. Cathcart Circle or not, traffic at Central began to decline from 1905 onwards. Glasgow also began to lose its competitive edge, with heavy industry beginning a slow decline, while the 1926 miners' strike hit demand for coal particularly hard. To counter this, new stations were opened close to new residential or industrial developments. The Glasgow

Subway was taken over by the City and electrified between the wars.

Grouping had little impact on the pattern of railway services. There was some rationalisation of the networks to the south-west, mainly favouring the former GSWR lines than those of the rival CR, but plans to rationalise the four termini, Buchanan Street, which would have been enlarged, Central, Queen Street and St Enoch, into two failed, for regardless of the economies that could have been achieved and the greater convenience of passengers, the money was simply not available. Another plan never implemented was to expand the Glasgow Subway.

Nationalisation could also not stem the decline, and after the Second World War freight traffic went into serious decline, despite a Freightliner terminal being opened at Gushetfaulds, but even this closed in 1993, with termini outside the city, including Eurocentral at Mossend, taking over the traffic. The one big achievement was the electrification of much of the suburban network, initially with the famous 'Blue Trains', named after their livery, which operated to destinations along the Clyde and as far south-west as Ayr. A number of services were cut back, and finally some rationalisation occurred, with services from Buchanan Street and St Enoch diverted to Central and Queen Street.

The formation of Passenger Transport Authorities and local government reform saw the new Strathclyde Region take over responsibility for buses and suburban trains, which soon appeared in orange and black. When further local government reform reversed much of this, Strathclyde continued as a transport authority, with trains painted in carmine and cream, not dissimilar to the original **British Railways** 'strawberry and cream' or 'blood and custard'. The other difference is that instead of the trains being operated under contract

to Strathclyde by British Rail, they were operated by Scotrail, now a train operating company and passenger franchise.

Glasgow & South Western Railway

Formed in 1850 when the Glasgow, Paisley, Kilmarnock & Ayr Railway, authorised in 1837, acquired the Glasgow Dumfries & Carlisle Railway. The line to Ayr had been completed in 1840, and was followed in 1843 by a branch from Dalry to Kilmarnock, but this eventually became the main line to Carlisle via Dumfries. It had less severe gradients than the rival Caledonian line to Carlisle via Beattock, but was eighteen miles longer. For the remainder of the nineteenth century, the company acquired other lines in its area, including Scotland's first railway, the Kilmarnock & Troon, dating from 1811. It built the first railway hotel for golfers at Turnberry in 1906. The main works were at Kilmarnock, completed in 1856, but a new workshop at Barassie, near Troon, was completed in 1901.

The main business of the railway was the movement of coal, and tourist and commuter traffic to the resorts on the Ayrshire coast, while it also handled a substantial volume of traffic to Ireland. It was forced to operate the 'Port Road', the lines from Dumfries to Portpatrick, and later Stranraer when that became the main Scottish port for Ireland, in partnership with the **Caledonian, London & North Western** and **Midland Railways**. Financial and operational difficulties delayed completion of the Glasgow-Stranraer route until 1877 and it was not fully incorporated into the GSWR until 1892. The problems were caused partly by competition for Irish traffic by ports in Ayrshire, and the fact that at the time it was also possible to sail directly from Glasgow to Belfast and other Irish ports.

In Glasgow, through running to the **North British** became possible when the

City Union railway was completed in 1870, and through running to the Midland Railway's Settle and Carlisle started once this route was completed. Parliament rejected plans for a merger with the Midland, but the two companies collaborated on express services from **St Pancras** to St Enoch, completed in 1876. Strong competition developed with the Caledonian in Ayrshire, and joint operation of a new direct Glasgow-Kilmarnock line was forced on the companies when it opened in 1873. A bid for the GSWR by the CR was rejected by Parliament in 1890. Quadrupling of the thirty miles from Glasgow to Kilwinning was largely completed by 1914.

The company was merged into the **London, Midland, Scottish Railway** in 1923, and while Caledonian management policies and rationalisation of the GSWR's locomotives followed, it was often the GSWR routes that survived when duplication was tackled. Since nationalisation, the 'Port Road' has closed, but the Glasgow-Stranraer route survives, as does that via Dumfries to Carlisle.

Glasgow, Paisley, Kilmarnock & Ayr Railway – see **Glasgow & South Western Railway**

Glasgow Subway
Alone outside of London, **Glasgow** has a deep level tube railway, originally authorised as the Glasgow District Subway in 1889. A circular line in twin tubes with an unusual 4ft gauge, it serves districts on both sides of the River Clyde. Initially it was worked by continuous cable haulage powered by stationary steam engines based in Scotland Street. The company was badly affected by tramway electrification and from 1919 onwards it lost money, but was bought by the City Corporation in 1922. The line was electrified between 1932 and 1935, and officially renamed Glasgow Underground, but the name 'Subway' has stuck, although at one period in its history, when the carriages were all painted orange, it was known as the 'Clockwork Orange'. Under municipal ownership, plans existed during the 1930s to expand the system, but these were never implemented. It was modernised during the 1970s and the carriages had a complete rebuild, reopening in 1978. Two of the line's original cars can be seen in Glasgow Transport Museum.

Gloucester
Although not a major centre, Gloucester achieved considerable importance to the **Great Western** as its first uninterrupted route into Wales and as a vital objective in its progress from **Bristol** to **Birmingham**, until foiled by the intervention of the **Midland Railway**. It became notorious in railway circles for the problems of transhipment between broad gauge and standard gauge. The city's significance in railway terms fell considerably after the opening of the **Severn Tunnel** and the conversion of the broad gauge to standard gauge, both of which meant that trains could run directly, with by-passing Gloucester altogether.

Glyn, George Carr/Lord Wolverton, 1797-1873
A partner in Glyn Mills & Co, bankers and a predecessor company of the Royal Bank of Scotland, he was one of the first directors of the **London & Birmingham Railway**, eventually becoming its last chairman and first chairman of the **London & North Western Railway** until 1852. He recognised the need for cooperation between railway companies and was a founder-member of the **Railway Clearing House** in 1842, doubtless because of his banking experience, and was its first chairman until his death. Known for being an effective chairman and capable of differen-

tiating between the responsibilities of the directors and the company officers, he also recognised that Mark **Huish**, despite, or because of, his talents, did not work well with his colleagues and had difficulty in establishing sound relationships with other companies, and was instrumental in his departure.

He was Liberal MP for Kendal for more than twenty years until 1868, and was created Lord Wolverton the following year.

Glyn Valley Tramway

Built to the unusual gauge of 2ft 4½ inches, the Glyn Valley Tramway was a roadside line running for 8¼ miles from Chirk in Denbighshire to Glyn Ceirog and Pandy. Its main traffic was slate, granite and silica from local quarries and instead of running to a harbour, its destination was the Welsh section of the Shropshire Union Canal. Authorised in 1870, the line used a combination of horse traction and gravity working when it opened in 1873. Powers were obtained in 1885 to withdraw services from the Pontfaen-Chirk section in favour of a new line from Pontfaen to the **Great Western** station at Chirk, while powers were also taken to extend the line from Glyn to Pandy and use steam locomotives. The line remained independent until its closure in 1935, while passenger services had been withdrawn in 1933.

Golden Valley Railway

This nineteen mile long railway was completed between 1881 and 1889 and ran through sparsely populated farmland between Hay-on-Wye and Pontrilas. It failed to cover its cost, carrying around just 125 passengers each weekday, and was subsidised by local landowners until closed in 1898. It was sold to the **Great Western Railway** which reopened it in 1901, but passenger services were withdrawn in 1941.

Gooch, Sir Daniel, 1816-1889

The middle Gooch brother, after training and working in ironworks and mechanical engineering, he was appointed as the **Great Western Railway's** first locomotive superintendent in 1837, under Isambard **Brunel**, whose early locomotives were generally disappointing except for the **Stephenson**-designed Star-class. The Stars were the basis of the first Gooch locomotives which appeared from 1840 onwards.

Swindon works was completed in 1841, and from 1846, started to build locomotives to Gooch's own designs. His most significant design as the *Great Western*, an immediate success on expresses between **Paddington** and **Exeter**, and which provided the basis for his Iron Duke-class. Gooch's 4-4-0 saddle-tank locomotives performed well on the steep gradients of the GWR lines in Devon and Cornwall.

Disillusioned with internal disagreements at the GWR, Gooch left in 1864, and was largely responsible for the laying of the transatlantic telegraph cable, for which he was knighted. He returned to the GWR as chairman in 1865, and provided a steady hand until his death. He found the GWR in a poor financial condition, and kept the company alive through strict and sometimes over-zealous economy, which eventually had an adverse effect on the company's reputation. One exception to the policy of economy was the **Severn Tunnel**, completed in 1886. He was also Conservative MP for Cricklade for twenty years until 1885.

Gooch found time for other interests, including coalmining, but also assisted the management of a number of smaller railways.

Gooch, Thomas Longridge, 1816-1889

Apprenticed to George **Stephenson** at Newcastle when 15, he became a draughtsman and surveyor, working with Joseph **Locke** on the **Newcastle & Carlisle Railway**, then returned to Stephenson as secretary in 1826, working on the **Liverpool & Manchester**, until he succeeded Locke in 1830 as resident engineer on the Liverpool end of the line. He then moved to the **Manchester & Leeds Railway**, which established his reputation firmly. He worked on the **London & Birmingham** before returning to re-survey the MLR and, after helping to obtain parliamentary approval for it, supervised its construction from 1837 to 1844, working under Stephenson: he was responsible for the Summit Tunnel at Littleborough.

Gooch left the MLR in 1844 to work on the Trent Valley Railway between Rugby and Stafford, which opened in 1847. He retired in 1851, exhausted by constant work, but remained a friend of Stephenson's son **Robert** and many other of the leading engineers of the day.

He was an elder brother of Daniel **Gooch**, while a third brother, John Gooch, 1812-1900, was locomotive superintendent of the **London & South Western** and **Eastern Counties** railways.

Graham, George, 1822-1899

Apprenticed to the marine engineer, Robert Napier, under whom he worked on the steam engines for the first Cunard steamship, *Britannia*, after a spell of ill health he moved to work for Joseph **Locke** on the survey for the **Caledonian Railway** and was then involved in its construction. In 1853, he was appointed engineer-in-chief and remained with the company until he died, seeing the company's route mileage rise from 195 to 1,116. He wrote a history of the CR which was published privately in 1888.

Grand Junction Railway

Europe's first trunk railway, the Grand Junction was authorised in 1833 and completed in 1837, providing an important link between the **London & Birmingham** Railway's terminus at Curzon Street, **Birmingham**, and the **Liverpool & Manchester Railway** at Newton (later renamed Earlestown) in Lancashire. In 1834, it absorbed the Warrington & Newton Railway, which had opened in 1831, and incorporated its lines into its last 4½ miles of route, giving a route mileage of 82½ miles. Once opened, the GJR provided a continuous route from **London** to **Liverpool** and **Manchester** via Birmingham. In 1840, the Chester & Crewe railway was acquired, and the GJR's works were moved from Edge Hill to **Crewe**.

Engineered by George **Stephenson** and Joseph **Locke**, who is credited with most of the work, especially after 1834. Unusually, it was completed on time and within budget. Throughout its history, it was consistently profitable, with dividends of 10 per cent or more.

The pivotal position enjoyed by the GJR encouraged it to support the **North Union Railway**, designed to extend the West Coast trunk route as far north as Preston, and it also invested in both the **Lancaster & Carlisle** and **Caledonian** railways. In 1845, the GJR and LMR merged and acquired two branch lines around Bolton before they joined the **Manchester & Leeds Railway** in acquiring the NUR in 1846.

Meanwhile, rivalry between the Liverpool and London financial interests involved with the GJR and the LBR resulted in an uneasy relationship between the two companies, especially after the Manchester & Birmingham Railway proposed a shorter route to the LBR running through the Potteries, but was persuaded by the GJR to run to **Crewe** instead, before the GJR reneged on the agreement. The MBR then sided with the LBR. When the GJR discovered that the LBR was planning to acquire the MBR, it tried an alliance with the **Great Western**, but this alarmed the LBR sufficiently for the three companies to develop a new Trent Valley line in 1846, before all three combined to form the **London & North Western Railway**. The GJR's general manager, Mark **Huish**, became the LNWR's first gm.

Great Central Railway

The last mainline railway to reach **London**, the Great Central Railway was the new name coined for the **Manchester, Sheffield & Lincolnshire Railway** to celebrate its transition from a trans-Pennine railway when it opened its new line to London in 1899 with a new terminus at **Marylebone**. The company had its origins in the Sheffield Ashton-under-Lyne & Manchester Railway, opened in 1845 and which had required construction of the Woodhead tunnel, three miles long and at the time the longest in the UK, through the Pennines. The SAMR acquired three railway companies and the Grimsby Docks Company in 1847 to form the Manchester Sheffield & Lincolnshire Railway. The company continued to prosper, and in 1863 it entered the south Yorkshire coalfield through the acquisition of the South Yorkshire Railway. Expansion westward lay in the creation of the **Cheshire Lines Committee** with the **Great Northern Railway** and the **Midland Railway**. This gave the MSLR access to North Wales and to the port of **Liverpool**. Earlier alliances involved the **London & North Western, Lancashire & Yorkshire** and **East Lancashire**, as well as the Midland, in what was known as the Euston Square Confederacy, but this was dissolved in 1857 and replaced with a fifty year agreement with the **Great Northern Railway**, hitherto viewed as a rival.

In 1864, a new chairman, Sir Edward **Watkin**, was appointed. This was just one of his railway chairmanships and he was an early advocate of a **Channel Tunnel**. His other ambitions included taking the MSLR to **London**, and the company embarked on a period of expansion at the cost of its profitability, with no ordinary dividends paid after 1889. The London expansion was widely regarded as wasteful, with centres such as Nottingham, Leicester and Rugby already having good links to London, and was achieved by building a new line from Annesley in Nottinghamshire to Quainton in Buckinghamshire, and then running over a joint line with another Watkin company, the **Metropolitan Railway**, and from that a short line to the new terminus at **Marylebone**, to which the headquarters was moved from Manchester in 1905.

A new chairman in 1899, Alexander Henderson (later Lord Faringdon) appointed Sir Sam **Fay** as general manager in 1902, and he was joined that year by John G **Robinson**, who had trained at Swindon. Robinson started to equip the GCR with powerful new locomotives, built at the company's Gorton, Manchester, works, as well as comfortable new carriages. It was amongst the first railways to use bogie goods vehicles, and in 1907, one of the first hump marshalling yards at Wath-upon-Dearne in the South Yorkshire coalfield proved capable of sorting 5,000 goods wagons in 24 hours. A new port was built at Immingham, which allowed expansion of the company's Humber shipping serices, and when opened by King George V in 1912, Fay was publicly knighted. Power signalling was also introduced. Under Fay, the company expanded its through passenger services. There were also trials of steam and petrol-electric railcars, while a second route to London via High Wycombe was built jointly with the GWR. Nevertheless, despite the work on passenger services, 67 per cent of its turnover came from goods traffic and just 22 per cent from passengers.

The First World War ended expansion, and while three ships were seized in continental ports by the Germans, the rest were requisitioned for the Royal Navy. Robinson saw his 2-8-0 heavy goods locomotive adopted as the standard for War Office use overseas, while Fay became director of movements at the War Office from 1916 until the end of the war.

On grouping, the company was merged into the **London & North Eastern Railway**.

Great Eastern Railway
Formed in 1862 on the amalgamation of the **Eastern Counties Railway** with the East Anglian, Eastern Union, East Suffolk and the Norfolk railways, which had been worked by the ECR. The arrangement was long overdue, and gave East Anglia a single unified railway network east of Cambridge, but even so, relations between the companies were such that it took four years before the finances could be rationalised, and by that time, 1866, during the banking and railway finance crisis, the new company was forced briefly into liquidation. Nevertheless, the company had already purchased land in the City of London for a new terminus to replace the inconveniently sited Bishopsgate.

Lord Cranbourne, who later became Marquess of Salisbury, became chairman in 1868, and the GER began to move forward. The new **Liverpool Street** station opened during 1874-75, the last terminus to open in the City and only permitted because it was approached in tunnel. By this time the GER also had a dense network of suburban lines in the north-eastern suburbs.

The GER inherited a broad spread of business, with extensive commuter traffic, albeit working class and less prosperous than that of the lines to the south; goods and passenger traffic to five ports, Felixstowe, Harwich, King's Lynn, Lowestoft and Yarmouth, with the last two providing heavy fish traffic for **London** and the Midlands; holiday traffic, especially Clacton, Lowestoft, Southend and Yarmouth; race traffic to and from Newmarket; and agricultural traffic, although this declined during the 1870s and 1880s with a crisis in Britain's arable farming. Later, it develop coal traffic from Yorkshire to East Anglia when a line was opened in 1882 jointly with the **Great Northern** from south of **Doncaster** through Lincoln and Spalding to March. Although mishandled at first, from 1883 onwards the GER also operated steam packet services, mainly to the Netherlands.

Despite the race and continental traffic, the company suffered from a mass of low fare business, and because of this, in 1872 it followed the **Midland Railway** by providing third-class accommodation on all passenger trains. In 1891, it was the first to provide restaurant car accommodation for third-class passengers. The company gained a reputation for punctuality and efficiency, although it struggled to cope with its peak period commuter traffic. The pressure on peak traffic declined sharply from 1901 after electric trams appeared in the East End of London, and the cost of electrification meant that it was rejected. For goods traffic, in 1899, its goods yard at Spitalfields, London, was the first in the UK to have electro-pneumatic power operation. Mainline services were recast in 1914 by a new general manager, the American Henry Thornton, and after the First World War he did the same for the suburban services. The company was amongst the first to use distinctive stripes to identify classes, with first having yellow lines and second blue, which earned them the title of the 'Jazz Trains'.

In the meantime, a number of independent branch lines had been built in GER territory, while west of King's Lynn a number of lines had been built with the support of the Great Northern and the **Midland**, which then continued across Norfolk to Cromer, Norwich and Yarmouth before being merged to form the **Midland &**

Great Northern Joint Railway in 1893. Competition ensued for the goods traffic, especially fish, from the Norfolk ports to the Midlands, and for holiday traffic from the Midlands. Nevertheless, the continental traffic grew unabated and in 1883 a massive extension to Harwich was opened at Parkeston Quay, named after the then chairman. A complementary development at the Hook of Holland that opened in 1893 encouraged further growth in traffic across the North Sea. During the First World War, Harwich became an important naval base.

While a number of its locomotive engineers were with the company for a short time, others lasted far longer, notably James Holden, who was amongst the first to experiment with oil-fired steam locomotives, with considerable success. The GER's locomotives from 1878 onwards were mainly built at its Stratford, East London, works.

The early problems meant that the dividend was low before 1882, but by the turn of the century, it was an attractive 6 per cent, before the marked decline in its London suburban traffic depressed revenue so that by 1913, a good year for many of Britain's railways, it was just 2 per cent.

Great North of England Railway

An ambitious plan to provide a link from **York** and **Leeds** to **Newcastle** and create a trunk route from **London**, the line as completed only ran for the forty-three miles between York and Darlington, with the former terminus shared with the **York & North Midland Railway**. It was almost level throughout with just one short and gentle incline. The original engineer, Thomas Storey, was replaced by Robert **Stephenson** after difficulty with a number of smaller structures, while the two main viaducts were designed by other engineers.

The GNER was leased by George **Hudson** in 1845 and some of its statutory authority was transferred to the Newcastle & Darlington Junction Railway, authorised in 1842. The plan was to use these railways and the YNMR for a line from London to **Edinburgh** via Rugby and **Derby** and spoil plans for a direct line from London to York. In 1846, the NDJR acquired the GNER, and the combined company became the York & Newcastle, before changing again in 1847 to the **York, Newcastle & Berwick**.

Great North of Scotland Railway

Sometimes described as 'neither Great nor North of Scotland', this opened in stages between **Aberdeen** and Keith between 1853 and 1856, along the alignment of the Aberdeenshire Canal as far as Inverurie, the Great North of Scotland Railway was built to link with the Inverness & Aberdeen Junction Railway, completed two years later, as well as extend services that reached Aberdeen over the Aberdeen Railway, forerunner of the **Caledonian Railway**. There were disagreements with the IAJR, including payment for a bridge over the River Spey, and these continued even after the IAJR changed its name to the **Highland Railway** in 1865, when the HR tried to block running powers to Inverness, while the GNSR was refused approval for a rival line to Inverness. Relationships between the two companies improved considerably during the last two decades of the nineteenth century, with pooling of receipts and through running, while in 1905, an amalgamation was proposed. An alternative, amalgamation with the Caledonian was rejected.

Despite the logic of through connections with the Caledonian at Aberdeen, the GNSR maintained its own station and did little to ensure connections for passengers arriving from the south. It even delayed becoming a member of the **Railway Clearing House**. Nevertheless, a new joint station opened in Aberdeen in 1867. The main line was doubled between 1861 and 1900 and lines opened to Elgin via Duftown and a new coast route opened, all incorporating lines that had started as local projects. Significant branches were opened to Peterhead in 1862, Fraserburgh in 1865, Ballater, for Balmoral, in 1866, Macduff in 1872, Boddam in 1897 and St Combs in 1903, as well as a number of minor branches. A suburban line was developed between Aberdeen and Dyce in 1887, and extended to Culter in 1894. Much of the goods traffic was provided by the fishing ports which thrived following the arrival of the railway, as did the distilleries on Speyside, while another major traffic was cattle. Resorts on the Moray Firth were promoted as the Scottish Riviera. A hotel was built at Cruden Bay, with an electric tramway to the local railway station.

The main locomotive depot was at Kittybrewster, Aberdeen, but moved to Inverurie in 1903. Despite its small size, the GNSR experimented with single line tablet exchange, equipment for dropping and collecting mail bags while the train was moving, and also was amongst the first to provide electric lighting at its stations.

In 1923, it became part of the **London & North Eastern Railway**.

Great Northern & City Railway
Originally supported in 1892 by the **Great Northern Railway** which needed relief from the congestion at **King's Cross**, the line was left in limbo by the GNR switching its support to the **Piccadilly Line**, although even without a connection to the surface railways, its tunnels were built to a 16ft diameter, suitable for mainline rolling stock. The contractor, Pearson & Sons, nevertheless persevered with the project and the GNCR opened in 1904. Despite an awkward interchange at Finsbury Park, the line was carrying 16 million passengers by 1907, but with bus and electric tram compe-

tition, it fell to 12.8 million by 1912, before being bought by the **Metropolitan Railway** the following year, intending to extend it northwards to connect with the GNR and also southwards as well. The Metropolitan's ambitions came to nothing, except that it closed the GNCR's generating system and introduced the only first-class accommodation on a deep level tube.

The line passed to the **London Passenger Transport Board** in 1933, which introduced standard tube rolling stock, scrapped first-class, and proposed extending the line to High Barnett, Edgware and Alexandra Palace over the lines of the **London & North Eastern Railway**, but in the event, these destinations were reached by the **Northern Line**. Part of the line was taken over by the **Victoria Line** in 1968, and it was decided to hand the remainder to **British Railways** to provide a city terminus for its Great Northern electric services. Before this could happen, on 28 February 1975, the London Underground's worst train **accident** occurred, with a train running through Moorgate at full speed to crash into the tunnel headwall with the loss of forty-three lives and more than seventy injured. The true cause of the accident remains a mystery.

LT stopped using the line in October 1975, and BR services commenced the following year.

Great Northern & Western Railway
Opened between 1860 and 1866, this line like Athlone and Westport, and a branch to Ballina from Manulla was opened in 1873. In 1890, the line was acquired by the **Midland Great Western Railway**.

Great Northern Railway
Originating as the London & York Railway, authorised in 1846 in the face of heavy opposition, the GNR title was adopted by the following year. The first services used a

leased section of line between Louth and Grimsby from 1848, but the main line opened between a temporary station at Maiden Lane, **London**, and Peterborough, and between **Doncaster** and **York**, in 1850, by which time it was also able to serve all of the important centres in the West Riding. It was in 1852 that the through line between London and Doncaster was completed along with **King's Cross**. Other smaller companies were acquired or running powers taken so that the GNR served Bradford, Cambridge, Halifax, Leeds and Nottingham, and with an agreement with the Manchester, Sheffield & Lincolnshire Railway (see **Great Central**), express services from London to **Manchester** started in 1857. The following year, the **Midland Railway** ran over the GNR line south of Hitchin to London, helping to undermine the 'Euston Square Confederacy' sponsored by the **London & North Western Railway**.

The revenue from the Yorkshire coal traffic attracted the jealous attention of the **Great Eastern** and the **Lancashire & Yorkshire**, who twice attempted unsuccessfully to promote a bill through Parliament for a trunk line from Doncaster through Lincolnshire. In the meantime, the GNR improved its position by joining the MSLR in buying the West Riding & Grimsby Railway, linking Doncaster with Wakefield. In 1865, with the MSLR, both companies promoted a Manchester-Liverpool line, and expanded into Lancashire and Cheshire through the **Cheshire Lines Committee** with the **Midland**. In 1879, it joined the GER in the Great Northern & Great Eastern Joint lines between Huntingdon and Doncaster, a route that required some new construction.

GNR main line services were reliable and punctual, especially after Henry **Oakley** became general manager in 1870. It was soon running more expresses than either the LNWR or MR, including some of the world's fastest, hauled by Patrick **Stirling's**

famous single driving-wheel locomotives. The intensity of service required block signalling and interlocking, while stations and goods sidings had to be enlarged and working improved. By 1873, it had reached a peak of profitability, but for the rest of the decade, investment grew more quickly than revenue and especially in the extension of the **Cheshire Lines** network, the company risked over-extending itself. In the East Midlands, it constructed new lines jointly with the LNWR, to some extent spurred by an earlier rates war with the Midland, but, in 1889, with the MR, it acquired the Eastern & Midlands railway, creating the **Midland & Great Northern Joint Railway**.

Earlier, the creation of the **East Coast** main line was helped in 1860 when the East Coast Joint Stock, a common pool of passenger vehicles, was created by the GNR, **North Eastern** and **North British**. In 1862, the first through services from **King's Cross** to Edinburgh Waverley started, with the 10am departure in each direction being named the *Flying Scotsman* from the 1870s. The first regular restaurant cars appeared in 1879 and continuous vacuum braking from 1881. The company later introduced the first fully-fitted goods trains. As traffic and the weight of trains increased, the entire route had to be relaid with heavier rails from the mid-1890s, with widening at the southern end of the route, while heavier trains were worked by H A **Ivatt's** new locomotives, while from 1905, Nigel **Gresley** designed new carriages, including some using articulation to improve the ride and reduce weight.

The company also expanded its London suburban traffic, using **Broad Street** as a City terminus in conjunction with the **North London Railway**.

On grouping in 1923, the GNR became part of the **London & North Eastern Railway**.

Great Northern Railway of Ireland

Usually referred to as the GNR (I), it was incorporated in 1876 as the Great Northern of Ireland Railway, but more usually known as the Great Northern Railway (Ireland). It began operations in 1877. The company consisted of a merger of the Dublin & Drogheda Railway, opened 1844, with the Dublin & Belfast Junction, the **Irish North-Western** and the Ulster Railway, opened 1839 and which had a 6ft 2in gauge, as well as a number of branch lines. It operated from both Dublin and Belfast to Londonderry, the latter in competition with the **Belfast & Northern Counties**, as well as to Bundoran and Enniskillen and a branch to Newcastle, Co, Down, eventually creating some 616 route miles built, and rebuilt, to the Irish broad gauge of 5ft 3in. It became one of Britain's first international railways with the creation of the Irish Free State in 1922, and customs posts were established at Dundalk and Goraghwood, while a police presence was maintained at many stations close to the frontier. During the Second World War, locomotive crews working from Northern Ireland would often pass coal to their Dublin-based counterparts to help the steaming of their locomotives forced to burn peat, because of the shortage of coal in Eire. The main line was 112¹/₂ miles between Dublin Amiens Street and Belfast Victoria Great Victoria Street, although the secondary main line from Dublin to Londonderry Foyle Road was slightly longer at 121¹/₂ miles.

The international nature of the operation ensured that it avoided nationalisation in 1948, but this followed the bankruptcy of the company in 1953, when was initially managed in liquidation by the Great Northern Railway Board before its rolling stock and route mileage was divided between the **Ulster Transport Authority** and *Coras Iompair Eireann*, the Irish transport authority, in 1958. Its main line between Belfast and Dublin remains in use today, but the lines to Londonderry and Newcastle have been long closed.

Great Southern & Western Railway (Ireland)

Incorporated in 1844 seeking authorisation for a line from Dublin to Cashel and later extended to Cork, reaching Penrose Quay at Cork in 1855. It absorbed a number of smaller lines until its route mileage reached 1,030 miles by 1914, making it Ireland's largest railway. Most of its track mileage was south of Dublin, and apart from the narrow coastal strip reached by the **Dublin & South Eastern Railway**, it was the predominant railway south of a line from Dublin to Galway. The main line linked Dublin and Cork, but there were other important lines to Limerick, Valentia Harbour in the extreme west, and to Tralee, while a solitary northward line ran through sparsely-populated country from Limerick to Ennis and Athenry to terminate at Sligo, on Donegal Bay.

Despite the sparse population served by the company, it was generally regarded as efficient and it was profitable, paying good dividends. On the grouping of the Irish Railways, it was the main company in the **Great Southern Railways**. With the **Great Western Railway**, it collaborated on Anglo-Irish packet services from Cork to Fishguard.

Great Southern Railways

Formed on the grouping of the then Irish Free State's railways in 1925 from the merger of the **Great Southern & Western Railway**, the largest constituent company and completed in 1855; the **Cork, Blackrock & Passage Railway**, opened in 1850; the **Cork, Brandon & South Coast Railway**, first opened in 1851 as the Cork & Brandon Railway; the **Midland Great Western Railway**, opened in 1847; and the **Dublin & South Eastern Railway**, first opened in

1854, as well as a number of smaller railways, giving it a total route mileage of 2,187 miles. Almost half of the route mileage came from the GSWR.

Most of the route mileage was Irish standard gauge of 5ft 3in, but an important exception was that of the CB&PR, which had been built to standard gauge but converted to 3ft gauge between 1900 and 1904, when it was also extended to Crosshaven. The latter was closed early, in 1932, as the break in gauge meant that through running was not possible with the rest of the system and bus operation was more economical and even, at times, faster.

On **nationalisation** of railways in what later became the Irish Republic, the GSR became the major constituent company of the new *Coras Iompair Eireann*, *CIE*.

The Great Southern Railways Preservation Society maintains a line between Tralee and Fenit on the former GS&WR branch to Fenit.

Great Western Railway (1): 1837-1922

A number of proposals for a railway between **London** and **Bristol** were promoted from 1824 onwards. The first of these to succeed was the Great Western Railway, authorised in 1835 after an early refusal. The GWR was able to raise capital of £2.5 million, equal to about £140 million today, and a further £0.83 million (£45 million today) in loans. The new company had as its engineer the young Isambard Kingdom **Brunel**, who convinced the directors of the merits of his scheme for a 7ft gauge railway, which he judged, rightly, to offer the prospect of higher speeds. To the objection that this would result in difficulties in through operation with other companies, he suggested that in areas where company boundaries met, the issue could be resolved through laying mixed gauge track, something that did not work easily or effectively in practice.

The GWR and Brunel wasted little time, and in 1838, operations began between the London terminus at **Paddington** and a station near Maidenhead, Berks. Locomotives became the responsibility of the first locomotive superintendent, Daniel **Gooch**. The entire 116 mile line from London to Bristol via Bath was opened in 1841, but costs had risen from a projected £3.3 million to more than £6 million. Many shareholders blamed Brunel for the slow completion and the high price, regarding his broad gauge as a mistake, and had even tried to get rid of him in 1839.

From its trunk route, the GWR expanded with branches to Basingstoke, **Gloucester**, Hungerford, Oxford and Windsor opened by 1849, while other companies supported by the GWR had also extended the line from Bristol to Plymouth using the broad gauge. When Gloucester was reached, the worst nightmares of the sceptics came true as the GWR met the standard gauge **Birmingham & Gloucester Railway**. The confusion only became worse when the **Midland Railway** leased the broad gauge **Bristol & Gloucester** intending to link it into the standard gauge, so that in 1854, standard gauge trains were able to reach Bristol using mixed gauge track.

Meanwhile, the GWR was racing ahead of its competitors, almost literally, with the introduction of express trains between London and Exeter in 1845 that covered the 194 miles of the route via Bristol at 43mph, including three stops, the world's fastest expresses at the time. Expansion included the opening of a mixed gauge line from **London** to **Birmingham** in 1852, bringing the GWR into direct competition with the **London & North Western Railway**. Two years later, the GWR purchased the Shrewsbury & Birmingham and Shrewsbury & Chester companies, and with running powers to Birkenhead found itself with a route network that extended as far north as

Merseyside. When the **Cornwall Railway** opened in 1859, this proved to be a satellite of the GWR and its allies, who had subscribed a fifth of its capital, and by 1867, through trains were running from London to Penzance.

Not content with the west, the Great Western had already ventured into Wales well before this time. In 1845, the GWR's satellite **South Wales Railway** obtained parliamentary approval for a broad gauge line from the GWR near Gloucester through to the coast at Fishguard. It opened to Carmarthen in 1852, but never reached Fishguard, being diverted instead to Milford Haven, which it reached in 1856, and from which steamers plied across to Waterford in Ireland. The broad gauge of the SWR meant that through trains could run from South Wales to London and the Midlands, but all of the valley lines were built to standard gauge, requiring costly transhipment of coal and iron ore, making the GWR unpopular in South Wales. The SWR and the **West Midland Railway** were both absorbed into the Great Western in 1865, giving it a total route mileage of 1,105 miles. By this time, the mixed gauge had been extended from Oxford to London, the work being carried out between 1856 and 1861. It took strong pressure from industrialists and mine owners to persuade the GWR to convert the SWR to standard gauge, but once the argument was won and the decision taken, the entire 300 miles was switched with completion taking just one weekend in 1872. By 1876, the only substantial remaining broad gauge operation was that from Penzance to London.

The railway insolvency crisis of 1866 had forced considerable economy on the company, by this time under the chairmanship of Gooch. Nevertheless, investors had considerable confidence in the GWR, even though the average dividend between 1841 and 1879 amounted to just 3.8 per cent.

There were also heavy investments, of which the most significant by far was the **Severn Tunnel**, built between 1873 and 1886, at the time the longest underwater tunnel in the world. The need for economy and the demands of the Severn Tunnel may have been behind the lack of further significant route extensions during the years up to 1900, although the system grew by the absorption of other companies to reach 2,526 route miles, the longest of any of Britain's pre-grouping railways. Financial difficulty certainly lay behind the limitations on investment in rolling stock, although innovation was not completely lacking, with the first refrigerated vans for frozen meat being introduced during the 1870s. To its credit, the company also operated safely, having just one fatal accident between 1874 and 1936.

Gooch died in office in 1889 at the age of 73 years, being given the credit for saving the company, but blamed for economies that were excessive and counter-productive. His successors returned to developing the company, re-shaping the passenger services, while first William **Dean** and then later, after 1902, George **Churchward**, started to produce a line of worthy locomotives.

Abolition of the broad gauge was completed in 1892, so that through carriages could be offered between **Liverpool**, **Manchester** and **Leeds** to the fast growing resort of Torquay. Restaurant cars were introduced in 1896, ending the compulsory refreshment stop at Swindon in 1895 by paying the refreshment rooms £100,000 (around £9m at today's prices) in compensation. By 1899, there were quadruple tracks over the entire 53 miles between London and Didcot.

The early years of the twentieth century saw a renewed vigour in the GWR. Much traffic had passed to competitors offering more direct services, so much so that many wags described the GWR as the 'Great Way

Round' so 'cut off' routes were built between 1903 and 1910, with the most significant the new direct route from London to Cardiff, by-passing Bath and Bristol, and at a distance of 145 miles saving 10 miles over the route via Bath and 35 miles compared with that by Gloucester. London to Exeter received a new direct route of 174 miles, instead of the previous 194 miles that had compared so badly with the **London & South Western's** 172 miles. Jointly with the **Great Central**, a more direct route was opened between London and Birmingham, cutting the distance from 129 miles to 111 miles, making it more competitive with the London & North Western's 113 miles. These routes required considerable new construction.

The new routes were accompanied by new carriages hauled by Churchward's excellent new locomotives, so that journey times started to fall considerably, while from 1906 onwards the company became the pioneer of automatic train protection. That same year, the company built a large new harbour at Fishguard and introduced three turbine-powered packet steamers for the Irish market, while between 1909 and 1914, it provided boat trains for passengers off Cunard transatlantic liners, taking them to London from Fishguard (261 miles) in 4½ hours. With the **Great Southern & Western Railway**, it collaborated on Anglo-Irish packet services from Fishguard to Cork.

The quest for economy did not end at the turn of the century. Up to the 1860s, carriages had been chocolate brown and only then were cream upper panels introduced. In 1908, all-over chocolate was reintroduced as an economy measure, but dark red was introduced for passenger carriages in 1912, while goods wagons were either dark red or grey.

The GWR had a relatively quiet First World War, and afterwards tried first to fight off the proposed **grouping**, and then

fought to have the six other constituent companies regarded as subsidiary companies so as not to have to provide a seat for a representative of each on the parent board, but was unsuccessful.

Great Western Railway (2): 1923-1947

The 1921 Act created a 'Western Group' of railway companies, and the Great Western was just one of those companies, but in fact **Paddington** predominated. As we have already seen, the new company might have been different, but it was the only substantial company amongst those grouped, the only one with access to **London**, and while companies such as the **Cambrian** had a substantial network, it had neither the balance sheet nor the reputation to influence events. The Great Western was spared the in-fighting that did so much damage to the **London, Midland & Scottish**, and unlike the **Southern**, which sometimes seemed to pretend that grouping hadn't happened, there was no doubt that this was an integrated railway with a management structure that could easily absorb the other companies.

The Great Western Railway had as its constituent companies the original GWR itself, plus the **Barry Railway**; Cambrian Railway; the **Rhymney Railway**; the **Taff Vale Railway** and the **Alexandra (Newport and South Wales) Docks & Railway**; with, as subsidiary companies, the **Brecon & Merthyr Tydfil Junction Railway**; **Burry Port & Gwendraeth Valley Railway**; **Cleobury Mortimer & Ditton Priors Light Railway**; **Didcot, Newbury & Southampton Railway**; **Exeter Railway**; **Forest of Dean Central Railway**; **Gwendraeth Valleys Railway**; **Lampeter, Aberayron & New Quay Light Railway**; **Liskeard & Looe Railway**; **Llanelly & Mynydd Mawr Railway**; **Mawddwy Railway**; **Midland & South Western Junction Railway**; **Neath & Brecon Railway**; **Penarth Extension**

Railway; Penarth Harbour Dock & Railway; Port Talbot Railway & Docks; Princetown Railway; Rhondda & Swansea Bay Railway; Ross & Monmouth Railway; South Wales Mineral Railway; Teign Valley; Van Railway; Welshpool & Llanfair Light Railway; West Somerset Railway, and the Wrexham & Ellesmere Railway.

There was a sense of triumph emanating from the GWR that may well have irritated many of those from the smaller railways. The GWR had started its own employee publication, *The Great Western Railway Magazine*, as early as 1888, and the issue for January 1923 showed a cartoon, titled 'A Survival of Title', of an explosion, with 'amalgamation' and 'upheaval' at its heart and railwaymen being thrown around, except for a man in GWR uniform saying: 'Hoorey! Never even blew me cap off!'

The 'new' GWR emphasised its identity by reverting to the 'old' GWR livery. Chocolate brown with cream upper panels were reintroduced in 1923, with white roofs. The company's coat of arms, a simple device showing simply the arms of London and of Bristol, did not reflect any of the companies taken over, just as it had never reflected the GWR's own expansion. The sole change was that the original coat of arms was encircled by a garter, and this was dropped during the 1930s.

The GWR of 1923 took everything in its stride, with most of the real work carried out during 1922 when the new management team led by Felix **Pole** settled down in anticipation of the formal transfer on 1 January 1923. Yet, for the Great Western its inheritance was a mixed blessing. It had some of the best railway lines in the country and linked London with **Birmingham** and **Bristol**, and these two cities together. But, the start of the South Wales coal industry's decline coincided with grouping, with output declining steadily from 1923 onwards, aided by recession and a miners'

strike. The small companies that had fed coal to the South Wales ports from the valleys were to be a liability rather than an asset, and it is likely that had these companies with their short haul and hugely local business not been absorbed, some might not have survived. As it was, the GWR had to withdraw passenger services from some 25 miles of railway.

A highly profitable railway before the grouping, the GWR was to remain profitable overall between the wars, the most profitable of the four grouped companies and the third largest. Route mileage grew from 3,005 miles to 3,712 miles, while staff had grown from 87,000 to 108,000, and shareholders from 95,000 to 120,000. The GWR was always concerned about the quality of service on its branch lines, and was also the line least dependent on a heavy London commuter traffic. When the **London Passenger Transport Board** was established in 1933, the receipts of all the suburban railway services within the area, less operational costs, were pooled with those of London Transport, that had taken over most of the underground system, the GWR's share of the pool was just over 1 per cent.

It was the only one of the major railway companies to continue the old tradition of allowing the chief mechanical engineer to retain control of locomotive operation, so that engine crews were on his payroll.

Concern about rising costs meant that economy once more became important, with engine firemen reminded that keeping full steam up after a locomotive had finished its work and was ready to be taken to the yard was wasteful, as the fires would have to be doused and coal thrown out. There was government pressure to cut charges, with passenger fares reduced from 75 per cent to 50 per cent above pre-war levels, while goods rates were to be cut from 112 per cent to 75 per cent above.

Nevertheless, traffic receipts started to decline alarmingly in 1924, although those for passengers recovered during the summer months. Part of the problem was simply the uncertain state of the economy, but this was compounded by increasing competition from road transport. While the Railway Rates Tribunal kept a strict control over what the railways could charge, one of the first acts of the Great Western's management on grouping was to bring the season ticket rates on the many lines in South Wales into line with its own charges. For most of the commuters affected, this actually meant a reduction in the cost of their tickets.

On 3 May 1926, many GWR personnel joined the General Strike in support of the mineworkers, and volunteers were sought, many of them from the general public, to help run the railway, but the dispute had cost the company £1.8 million. Even after the return to work, the industrial situation remained uncertain, with losses as the mines remained closed.

In 1929, the then Chancellor of the Exchequer, Winston Churchill, finally abolished the Railway Passenger Duty, a tax that had replaced that on stage coaches and yielded the Treasury £400 million annually, about £25 billion by today's prices, and dated from 1832. Churchill was not so much concerned about the railway companies or the traveller, but wanted to help ease unemployment. It was a condition of the abolition of the duty that the railways spent the money thus saved on modernisation. The GWR decided on a programme of improvements to its stations and goods yards, while also doubling single track stretches and quadrupling double track stretches to ease points of congestion. It was already engaged in replacing many old wooden viaducts, and this extended not only to work on the main lines, but also to branches as well, including that to Falmouth in Cornwall. New goods wagons were introduced.

Sir Felix Pole was replaced by Sir James **Milne** in 1928. At this time the company started major investment in road transport, acquiring bus companies such as the Bristol Omnibus Company and Western National, as well as taking a substantial stake in others, sometimes with other railway companies, and the 'Big Four' moved into road haulage jointly rather than independently. The GWR was one of the pioneers of internal air services, with one of the first routes being form Cardiff to Plymouth, a lengthy journey by rail or road, and became a member of **Railway Air Services**, although most of its efforts went into Southern & Western Air Services, operated with the Southern Railway.

During the 1930s, the struggle to attract passengers saw the bargain rates, of return fares just a third above the single fare, offered to third-class passengers extended to those in first-class, who paid 60 per cent more than the third-class fare. In each case, the minimum fare for the attractive new return rates to take effect was 2s 6d third-class, 4s first-class. Meanwhile, to enhance earnings from freight traffic, on those routes where there was competition with the LMS or the LNER, freight receipts were pooled. It was not until just before the outbreak of the Second World War that the company commissioned consultants to look more closely at electrification. Meanwhile, it had considerable success with diesel rail cars, used both for local services and for some cross-country expresses, such as between Birmingham and Cardiff.

On the outbreak of the Second World War, negotiations took place with the government over the compensation for its virtual take-over of the system. There were also the other uncertainties, a pay rise had been agreed and there were still further claims forthcoming as prices began to rise under wartime pressures. From the operational point of view, 1940 got off to a bad start, with what was described as the 'worst winter on record' with heavy snow in January and February. Early in 1943, an attempt to cope with the growing demand for freight wagons, saw the 'Q' campaign started earlier in the war to turn wagons around more quickly followed by 'up-plating' of wagons, so that they could carry a heavier load, although everyone was assured that the rolling stock and track engineers had examined the issue and found the increased weights to be safe. For the Great Western's locomotives, there was a two year backlog for repairs and renewals, but passenger traffic in 1944 was 64 per cent up on 1938, and even 28 per cent up on 1923, which had been the busiest year for passenger traffic between the wars. All of this was carried on trains that travelled 23 per cent fewer miles than in 1938. Freight traffic in 1944 was double that of 1938.

Greathead, James Henry, 1844-1896
South African-born James Greathead was apprenticed to Peter **Barlow** and his assistant on the **Midland Railway** extension from Bedford to **London** in 1867. He also became involved in a number of unsuccessful projects before working with Douglas Fox on the **Liverpool Overhead Railway** between 1888 and 1893.

His most significant contribution to railway civil engineering was the invention of the Greathead shield which made construction of tunnels easier in clay and wet soils, for which he also advocated the use of compressed air during construction. His invention, which improved the original shield first devised by Sir Marc Brunel, father of Isambard Kingdom **Brunel**, was first used on construction of the Tower Subway in London in 1870.

Gresley, Herbert Nigel, later Sir, 1876-1941
Initially apprenticed at **Crewe** on the

London & North Western Railway, he moved to the **Lancashire & Yorkshire Railway**. In 1905, he became carriage and wagon superintendent on the **Great Northern Railway**, where he succeeded Henry **Ivatt** as chief mechanical engineer in 1922. On **grouping**, he became CME of the **London & North Eastern Railway**. He was knighted in 1936, the same year that he was elected president of the Institute of Mechanical Engineers.

Gresley was initially best known for his introduction of elliptical roofed carriages on the GNR, which was also adopted for the East Coast Joint Stock in 1905. He gave the GNR a modern 2-6-0 locomotive in 1912, and followed this with 2-8-0s, initially with two cylinders but later with three. His first A1-class Pacific was the *Great Northern*, which appeared in 1922. His Pacific locomotives saw steady improvement from 1926, with long-lap valves and higher pressure boilers, and included the famous A3 *Flying Scotsman*. The peak of his locomotive design and performance was the streamlined A4-class, first introduced in 1935 and used for high speed trains such as the 'Silver Jubilee' and 'Coronation'. One of the class, *Mallard*, set a speed record of 126 mph in July 1938, which has never been beaten for steam locomotives. At the other end of the scale, his V2 2-6-2 mixed traffic locomotives were in volume production from 1936 and many were taken up for use by the War Office during the Second World War.

Gresley design teak-panelled carriages for the GNR, and these were adopted by the LNER. He was famous for his advocacy of articulation as a means of improving the riding of passenger rolling stock and also of increasing the number of seats within a given train length, as well as saving cost and weight. He applied the concept to improve the riding of six-wheel carriages inherited on grouping from the **Great Eastern**, but earlier, in 1921, he introduced the first articulated five-car dining set, also the first to use electric cooking, followed by an articulated sleeping twin-car set in 1922, and four and five-car suburban sets between 1923 and 1930. He applied pressure ventilation and even air conditioning to his prestige passenger carriages during the 1930s. He introduced welded underframes in 1934, and used aluminum and plywood for body panels.

Grouping (Great Britain) 1923

One of the major events in the history of Britain's railways was the grouping that took effect on 1 January 1923, authorised by the Railways Act 1921. The changes required in merging more than a hundred railway companies, many of them substantial, required a whole year of negotiation and appointments. Many mergers that had failed to reached fruition were in fact completed during 1922, most notably that of the **Lancashire & Yorkshire** with the **London & North Western**. Elsewhere, the **Great Western** took over operation of the **Taff Vale's** passenger services. The legislation could be seen as a means of side-stepping the issue of nationalisation, which had resurfaced again prior to the outbreak of the First World War. The original scheme foresaw seven large companies rather than four, which could have made better sense. In attempting to reduce competition, the grouping ignored the continuation of direct competition on a number of busy routes, such as **London** to Southend, London to **Birmingham** and London to **Exeter**, while there were still three trunk routes to Scotland.

The railways were under state control from the outbreak of the First World War until just before grouping. Little freedom was accorded the railways before or after the grouping, with charges and fares controlled. The grouping foresaw a target revenue for each railway company, but this was never achieved and added to the years

of recession and the crippling miners' strike, which saw many export markets for British coal lost forever, the railway companies struggled through the inter-war years. The heavier their reliance on freight traffic, the more they suffered. It was a matter of considerable duty and, for the shareholders, sacrifice that so much money and effort was paid to keeping the system in good working order despite the poor revenues.

The legislation did not specify the names of the railway companies after the grouping, but simply specified that there should be 'Southern', 'Western', North Western, Midland and West Scottish' and 'North Eastern, Eastern and East Scottish' Groups. These resulted in the **Southern Railway, Great Western Railway, London Midland & Scottish Railway** and **London & North Eastern Railway**. The pre-grouping companies were classified either as 'constituent companies', in which case they were entitled to board representation on the post-grouping company, or 'subsidiary companies', which were simply absorbed. The constituent and subsidiary companies of each of the group companies, usually known as the 'Big Four', are given early in their entries. The company least affected by the grouping was the Great Western, which so dominated its group that it retained its title and policies intact. All of the others brought together a number of large companies, and on the Southern, the dominance of the **London & South Western Railway** over the other major companies within its area was the least marked, but the **South Eastern & Chatham Railway** was impoverished by years of excessive competition between its two member railways, while the **London, Brighton & South Coast** was basically operating just one main line.

Grouping (Irish Free State) 1925

The counterpart of the grouping of the railways in the mainland of Great Britain was that in the then Irish Free State, as the south of Ireland became known after partition in 1922. The grouping was incomplete as no action was taken on those companies that ran across the border into Northern Ireland, and this included the **Great Northern Railway of Ireland**, the **County Donegal Railways** Joint Committee and the **Londonderry & Lough Swilly Railway**, the last two being 3ft gauge lines. There was no similar grouping north of the border.

The most significant company to emerge from the grouping was the **Great Southern Railways**, which included the former **Great Southern & Western Railway**; the **Cork, Blackrock & Passage Railway**; the **Cork, Brandon & South Coast Railway**; the **Midland Great Western Railway**; and the **Dublin & South Eastern Railway**.

Guernsey Railways & Tramways

Early proposals for a railway in Guernsey had come to nothing, although ideas were mooted as early as 1845 for a line from L'Ancresse to St Peter Port, the island's capital, via St Sampson's, and continuing to Perelle. Later attempts to start a street tramway were rejected because of fears over Sunday operation. The States of Guernsey (the island's Parliament) authorised the construction of a tramway in 1877, and the following year the Guernsey Steam Tramway was registered in **London** after some difficulty in raising funds locally. Steam locomotives fitted with the necessary guards to protect pedestrians and animals pulled one or two single deck carriages, although a double deck trailer was added in 1881. Technical difficulties with locomotives coupled with competition from horse bus services and licensed hackney carriages meant that after an initial good start, traffic gradually fell away and the company went bankrupt in 1883.

The Guernsey Railway Company was formed in 1888, registered in Guernsey and acquiring the assets of the GST from the liquidators. The tramway operations resumed in 1889, and approval sought from the States to convert the system to electric operation, which was granted in 1891. Guernsey became the first operator of electric trams in the British Isles, using an unusual side-mounted overhead current collection trolley. The electric service started in 1892 and plans were made to convert the larger and more modern of the steam trailers to electric operation, but the equipment was unreliable and the steam trams were back within three days. Nevertheless, a change of contractor and duplication of generating equipment meant that services were soon resumed, and in 1895, the original electric cars had their onboard equipment up-dated.

The trams soldiered on until 1934, when they were withdrawn and the GRC became one of the island's two main bus operators. It never operated a railway service, and the main route, St Peter Port to St Samson's, being just two miles long, would hardly have been viable as a railway. Plans were laid for freight-only branches to the north of the island, but passengers from the trams, and had it been built from the trains as well, had to change at St Samson's onto buses.

H

Hackworth, Timothy, 1786-1850

Trained as a colliery engineer and blacksmith, Hackworth was working as foreman blacksmith at Wylam Colliery in 1813 when William **Hedley** started work on his three locomotives, including the famous *Puffing Billy*. After helping Hedley, Hackworth was recruited by George **Stephenson** to manage his locomotive workshops in Newcastle. Stephenson offered Hackworth a partnership, which was turned down, but instead became resident engineer on the **Stockton & Darlington Railway** where he remained until 1840, developing the company's Shildon Works. The early steam locomotives were incapable of the longer journeys and at one time, even on the SDR, replacement by horses was considered. Hackworth's contribution was to improve the performance of these primitive locomotives by improving the blast pipe and inventing a return flue boiler, thus improving the fire and increasing the heating surface without sacrificing economy.

Hackworth put his developments into a locomotive, the *Sans Pareil*, which performed well at the **Rainhill** trials in 1829, but even so was still beaten by Stephenson's *Rocket*. The weakness of *Sans Pareil* was that it retained a vertical cylinder which hindered higher speed running, but it was sold to the Bolton & Leigh Railway and saw several years' service. Hackworth next started to use multi-tube boilers, and also developed his own Soho Works near Shildon, but despite his own success at improving the steam locomotive, his designs steadily fell behind those of the rising generation of engineers.

Hammersmith & City Railway

Opened in 1864, the Hammersmith & City Railway initially ran from Green Lane Junction (later re-named Westbourne Park) via Shepherd's Bush to Hammersmith, a distance of three miles. At Latimer Road, there was a connection to the **West London Railway**. The line was built mainly on viaduct and until 1868-1869, it was mixed gauge. In 1867, the line was acquired jointly by the **Great Western Railway** and the **Metropolitan Railway**, with both companies providing locomotives and rolling stock until the line was electrified during 1906-07, when new jointly-owned rolling stock was provided. That the line was a success was despite the fact that the two

shareholders had suffered severe differences when the original Metropolitan Railway had been built, but by 1867 relations had improved considerably.

Meanwhile, under the joint owners, Hammersmith & City Railway trains were extended eastwards in stages using the Inner Circle Line and then over the **East London Line** to reach New Cross in 1884. Although through electric working between Hammersmith and New Cross began in 1914, it was discontinued in 1941, never to resume.

When the **London Passenger Transport Board** was established in 1933, it took the Metropolitan Railway interest in what became the Hammersmith & City Line, but not that of the Great Western Railway, which in retrospect seems strange. The line continued to be operated jointly and did not pass completely into **London Transport** control until railway **nationalisation** in 1948.

Hampstead Line/Hampstead & Highgate –
see **Charing Cross, Euston & Hampstead Railway**

Harrison, Sir Frederick, 1844-1914

Originally joining the **London & North Western Railway** as a clerk at Shrewsbury, Harrison was identified by Sir George Findlay, the then general manager, as having potential and by 1875, he was appointed assistant superintendent of the line. He became assistant goods manager in 1884, goods manager in 1876, and when Findlay died in 1893, he became general manager.

He inherited a policy of continual modernisation from Findlay, and paid particular attention to the needs of the travelling public. He completely rebuilt both the station and the junction at **Crewe** and improved train services and rolling stock. On retirement in 1909, he was deputy chairman of the **South Eastern & Chatham**

Managing Committee for a while, and remained a board member until his death.

Hawksworth, Frederick

Hawksworth spent his entire working life on the **Great Western Railway**, starting during the **Churchward** era when he worked in the drawing office, and became chief draughtsman under **Collett**. His drawings were used for the *Great Bear*, the GWR Pacific locomotive, and he supervised all of the design work for the King-class locomotives.

Taking over from Collett in 1941, he kept the GWR rolling stock on the move in wartime when stations, works and lines were subjected to intense enemy aerial attack, while locomotives had to struggle to haul trains of extended length often while using inferior quality coal. Later, despite resenting the interference of the **British Transport Commission** and the loss of much autonomy, he adapted the GWR's locomotives and practice to meet the new conditions, and introduced higher degrees of superheating to improve performance. Hawksworth conducted successful trials on oil-firing of steam locomotives and also was responsible for the introduction of the first gas turbine locomotive to operate in the UK.

Headcodes

Growth in traffic meant that it became necessary to identifying different classes of train and different routings by using headcodes. Initially, this was done by varying the position of the headlamps, and often by using different coloured lights, while in daytime large white discs occupied the positions of the lamps. In 1905, the **Railway Clearing House** started to establish a standard set of headcodes and coloured lights were dropped, but local variations on headcodes remained until 1950.

The system underwent changes with the introduction of electric trains, with localised headcodes giving signalmen and waiting passengers the route and sometimes the stopping pattern of a train using either illuminated letters or numbers. The **Great Western** between the wars introduced headcodes that gave an approximation of the route, and whether the trains was the first or second portion of a major express, operated in portions during a busy summer Saturday.

Hedley, William, 1779-1843

Trained as a Northumberland colliery manager, he nevertheless moved into locomotive design and construction, combining the work of **Trevithick** and George **Stephenson**. He moved to Wylam Colliery in 1805, finding that a locomotive had been ordered from Trevithick, but this could not run on the wooden rails laid in the colliery. When Trevithick refused to supply another locomotive after the colliery lines had been laid with iron plate rails, Hedley, with the assistance of Timothy **Hackworth**, built three successful steam locomotives. He later modified these as eight-wheelers to reduce the wear on the track.

High Speed Trains

From the earliest days, speed was an important factor in railway operation, and from the beginning, high speed and speed records made the news. Speed was predominantly a characteristic of passenger expresses, but not exclusively so. While the railways marked a massive change in the speed at which people travelled, and in the beginning this was an increased from the 12mph or so of a stage coach to more than 30mph, it also affected some types of freight, including newspaper traffic and, of course, the **mails**. Overnight fast goods trains sped perishable produce, especially milk, from the country to the towns, and fresh fish traffic from the ports also became important. The opening up of a through route from **Aberdeen** and

Peterhead to the markets of **London** and other major cities with the bridging of the **Forth** and the **Tay** had an important bearing on the prosperity of the fishing trade.

The famous **Rainhill trials** were intended to satisfy the directors of the **Liverpool & Manchester Railway** over whether steam or horse traction would be most suitable, but while speeds of around 30mph were achieved, even better was the 36mph achieved by *Rocket* on the opening day, speeding the injured George Huskisson to Eccles in a vain attempt to save his life.

In theory, the **Great Western Railway** should have offered the highest speeds given the greater stability not just of its broad gauge, but of the gentler curves that were a result of widening the gauge. While the Gauge Commission did indeed find that average speeds of 54.6mph were achieved on the GWR between **Paddington** and Didcot, it was also the case that the company did not exploit this advantage to the fullest extent, especially in later years, just as it failed to make the most of the greater carriage widths that the broad gauge made possible. In any event, speeds for normal passenger trains were given a boost not on the GWR but on the rival **East** and **West Coast** Main Lines during the **races** to Scotland during the late 1880s.

One problem in assessing the early speed records was that the recorders used stop watches for many years, and this was a far from accurate means of measurement, even though it became popular with enthusiasts riding on trains and observing the mile posts. While **Brunel** and **Gooch** experimented with what was known as a 'measuring van', the twentieth century saw the introduction of the dynamometer car for precise recording of speeds, and this became the most important carriage in the race behind a record-setting locomotive.

The lack of precise measurement meant that the first locomotive to exceed 100mph,

the GWR's *City of Truro*, set an unofficial speed record in 1904. Nevertheless, the claim that the locomotive was the first to reach 100mph, and in fact may have achieved 102.3mph, has been borne out by later analysis to the extent that she certainly did exceed 100mph. That was the same year that the GWR introduced a 7 hr timing between **Paddington** and **Penzance**, a distant of 312 miles, which proved that speed was a commercial asset.

Generally, speed records belonged to special trains that were specially prepared, not least because they were 'short-formed', that is that they had less than the usual number of carriages. Nevertheless, there were serious attempts to produce fast, regular, passenger trains that offered a speed record of a different kind; that is the fastest regular scheduled run. Unofficially known as the 'Cheltenham Flyer', and first introduced in 1923, the GWR ensured that its afternoon express from Cheltenham to Paddington was the fastest express in Britain, and after successive accelerations, the train eventually managed the world's first 70mph timings, albeit only between Swindon and Paddington, and on one occasion achieved a record of 81.6mph. The accolade was short-lived, as for prestige Nazi Germany ensured that the Berlin-Hamburg express, the 'Flying Hamburger', became the world's fastest.

Prestige streamlined trains on the East and West Coast Main Lines also vied for records. The **London & North Eastern Railway** ran trials that achieved 100 mph and then 108mph, before introducing the 'Silver Jubilee' in 1935 with an average 70.4mph between Darlington and London, but on the press launch of the service, it managed to exceed 100mph for twenty-five miles and twice reached 112mph. Not to be outdone, the **London, Midland & Scottish Railway** also managed an average 70mph between **Glasgow** and London non-stop that year. In June 1937, the press launch of the first Princess-class locomotive set a new record of 113mph. All of this has been overlooked because, in 1938, the Gresley A4 Pacific *Mallard* set an unbeaten speed record for steam of 126mph running down Stoke Bank on the ECML. This was a greater achievement than generally realised, not just because it has never been beaten anywhere, but because far from being specially prepared, *Mallard* had worn valves and was driven hard by a driver known for thrashing his locomotives. Had she been properly prepared and all valve clearances correct, the record might have been set even higher.

Post-war, it took time to get the railway back into shape for high speed operations. The emphasis switched from steam to diesel and electric propulsion, but it was not until the arrival of the English Electric 'Deltic' diesel-electric locomotives on the East Coast Main Line that speeds once again matched the best of those achieved pre-war. By 1977, infrastructure improvements and the Deltics combined to produce a 5hr 27min schedule between **King's Cross** and **Edinburgh**, compared with that of 6hr before the war. To be fair, the 1977 schedule included a stop at **Newcastle** rather than a non-stop run. Many timings showed averages over 80mph in the years that followed, and this became even more commonplace once the West Coast Main Line was electrified.

Truly high speeds required specially built railways with few stops, generous curves and easy gradients, and these were being built in Europe, with the French leading the way. In an attempt to avoid this cost and upheaval, as well as delay, **British Railways** looked at the trains themselves. The experimental Advanced Passenger Train, APT, used tilt to enable it to operate at high speeds on existing track, and in 1979 set a British record of 162.2mph. Despite running between **Euston** and **Glasgow** in 1984 at an average of 103.4mph, problems with passenger comfort and the tilting mechanism meant that the project was cancelled. Had development continued until the problems were ironed out, Britain could have truly high speed trains many years earlier and not have had to import Italian Pendolinos for its West Coast modernisation early in the twenty-first century.

Anticipating the need for an interim diesel-electric while further **electrification** and the APT arrived; BR developed the train known variously as the High Speed Train, HST, or the Inter-City 125, IC125, meaning a service speed of 125mph. In 1973, a prototype set a world record for diesel traction of 143.2mph between **York** and Darlington, and a number of service trains managed speeds in excess of 100mph. In 1983, an HST set a new diesel record of 144mph, which was later raised to 148.5mph during trials of bogies for the HST's electrified successor, the 'Electra' or IC225 (which referred not to *miles per hour*, but *kilometers per hour*, so the new trains were really IC140s!). Even so, the new InterCity 225s managed a new British speed record pf 161.7mph on test, but in service were limited to 125mph due to problems with the track, but on the press launch, Edinburgh was reached in September 1991 in 3 hr 29 min from **King's Cross**, an average of 112.5mph.

These speeds have been exceeded by the trains on the **Channel Tunnel** Rail Link between the tunnel and **St Pancras**, but this is a continental-style special line, built for high speed.

Highland Railway

Formed in 1865 from the merger of the Aberdeen & Perth Junction Railway with the Inverness & Aberdeen Junction Railway, initially with main lines to Keith, opened in 1858, and Dunkeld, 1863. A line was built north, reaching Wick and Thurso in 1874, albeit taking an extremely circuitous route around the Beauly Firth via Dingwall, while another went to Kyle of Lochalsh, reached in 1897. These lines included steep gradients of as much as 1 in 70, while there was a swing bridge over the Caledonian Canal at Clachnaharry, and viaduct over the Kyle of Sutherland between Culrain and Invershin. It acquired the Duke of Sutherland's Railway in 1884. A plan for a direct Inverness-**Glasgow** line through the Great Glen, promoted in 1883, proved fruitless, but a direct line was opened to Aviemore in 1898.

The HR planned a number of branch lines, but by this time road transport was emerging as a serious competitor, especially in remote areas. Nevertheless, the **North British**-sponsored West Highland Railway, 1894, and the Invergarry & Fort Augustus Railway, 1903, threatened the HR's position.

Most of the network was single track, with passing loops and a double section between Clachnaharry and Clunes providing the total of 47 miles of double track, but efficiency improved when train staff and tablet instruments were introduced during the 1890s. The problems of heavy snowfall on isolated stretches of line led William **Stroudley**, the HR's first locomotive superintendent to design a range of snow ploughs. His successor, David **Jones**, designed Britain's first 4-6-0 locomotive.

The HR did much for the fishing industry, especially with fast goods trains running from Buckie on the Moray coast to **Liverpool** and **Manchester**, and from Wick and Thurso south. There were also significant movements of beef cattle and whisky distilleries were sited close to the railway. The company also attempted to boost tourism, even building a branch to the spa town of Strathpeffer in 1885 and building a hotel there in 1911. Nevertheless, given the low population, mixed trains were commonplace, and carriages could be behind loose-coupled goods wagons, but after a number of accidents, the Railway Regulation Act 1889 demanded continuous braking for passenger trains, although the HR was given an extended period until 1897 to adapt.

The system came under sustained heavy use during the First World War, with the famous 'Jellicoe Specials' carrying men and coal to Thurso for the fleet at Scapa Flow, while Invergordon was another major naval base along its route. Later in the war, Kyle of Lochalsh also became important, with mines for the Northern Barrage and also US naval personnel.

On **grouping**, the HR became a constituent company of the **London, Midland & Scottish**.

Historical Model Railway Society

Formed in 1950, this society caters mainly for those interested in Britain's railways prior to **nationalisation**. Amongst its assets is a superb collection of old railway photographs, ideal for modellers to work from.

Holborn Viaduct

By 1870, the congestion at Ludgate Hill was such that it was clear that another station needed to be built, and although the London, Chatham & Dover Railway (see **South Eastern & Chatham Railway**) was still in Chancery, the sale of its telegraph system to the Post Office for £100,000 provided the necessary funding, although to avoid possible problems with creditors, a front company, the Holborn Viaduct Station Company, was formed to raise the rest of the money. The use of small companies to achieve extensions to the railway network or to cover new projects such as termini or bridges, was not in any case uncommon at this time. Holborn Viaduct was reached by a 264yd spur of the through line and was intended for mainline trains, with just four short platforms, each of 400ft, serving six roads, with the idea being that all trains would be half length as they would have been split en route into City and West End portions. Sometimes described as a 'mini-terminus' Holborn Viaduct opened on 2 March 1874. It was used by boat trains for Dover and Sheerness, the latter having a service to Flushing, as well as trains to Maidstone and Ashford.

A few local trains used Holborn Viaduct, but most were relegated to a low level station with two platforms used by trains running through to Farringdon, and known initially when it opened on 1 August 1874 as Snow Hill, but changed to Holborn Viaduct (Low Level) on 1 May 1912.

Despite the cramped accommodation, a hotel was built and leased to the LCDR's caterers, Spiers & Pond, for 6 per cent of its capital cost and 10 per cent of its profits. The hotel was requisitioned by the government during the First World War, afterwards becoming offices, and never being reinstated as a hotel. It was destroyed during the blitz in 1941.

Holborn Viaduct was not a popular station for the City, being criticised by the Corporation as 'the great useless station called Holborn Viaduct' at a time when Ludgate Hill was also suffering criticism as being dangerous for the great number of people using it. It was not until 1907 that reconstruction of Ludgate Hill was started, removing the main line island platform, whose trains now used Holborn Viaduct, and slewing the tracks to provide a much larger platform for local trains. The staircases were also widened to help passengers clear the platforms more quickly. This took until 1912 to complete, by which time the local traffic had slumped dramatically as passengers switched to electric trams and to the developing network of underground services. Even before work had really

started in 1907, the **Great Northern Railway** removed its trains, and the **Midland Railway** followed in 1908. Wartime demands on the only north-south link through the centre of **London** meant that SECR trains stopped running through to Moorgate and Farringdon in April, 1916.

Electrification came to Holborn Viaduct in 1925 with services to Shortlands and Orpington via Herne Hill, but because of the constraints on space, only two platforms, 4 and 5, could be lengthened to take eight-car trains. Further **electrification** followed up to 2 July 1939, when services to Gillingham and Maidstone were electrified. The old hotel building was bombed on 26 October 1940. Services were badly affected following the collapse of the bridge over Southwark Street during the heavy raid on the night of 16/17 April 1941, and while services were reinstated when a temporary bridge was erected, more was to follow. On the night of 10/11 May, the old hotel building was hit again, and completely gutted by fire, with the damage to the station itself so extensive that it could not be used by trains until 1 June, and a temporary booking office had to be provided.

Post-war, the services withdrawn as wartime austerity measures were gradually reinstated, but the station remained a gutted mess for many years after **nationalisation**. It was not until the late 1950s that rebuilding started, and completed in 1963.

Horncastle Railway

Opened in 1855 between Horncastle and Kirkstead Junction, the line was worked by the **Great Northern Railway** and under grouping was incorporated into the **London & North Eastern Railway**.

Hudson, George (1800-1871)

George Hudson was born in 1800 in the small Yorkshire village of Howsham, he moved to **York**, working in a draper's shop, marrying the owner's daughter and later, in 1827, received the then considerable inheritance of £30,000 (about £1.38 million today), from a distant relative. The inheritance enabled him to become active in local politics, becoming Mayor of York three times, and also to invest in local railway schemes. In 1836, he was elected chairman of the **York & North Midland Railway**, linking his adopted city with **London**, albeit by a circuitous route via **Derby** and Rugby, taking 217 miles, but offering four through trains a day, with the journey from York to London taking ten hours as against around 20 hours by stage coach. The company leased and then later absorbed adjoining lines, as well as building a number of extensions itself. Hudson pressed for a major trunk route up the East Coast to Scotland, but the line being built by the North of England Railway from York to **Newcastle** was in difficulties and by 1841, it had exhausted its capital, but still had only managed to reach as far north as Darlington. Hudson was dismayed by this situation, as not only was his vision of a line to Newcastle and beyond compromised, but the Board of Trade had finally started to take an interest in creating strategic routes, and wanting to link London with Scotland, had opted for a route from Carlisle to **Edinburgh** using a competing route that had already reached as far north as Lancaster. It was left to Hudson to bring the various assorted railway interests involved together.

Believing that the finance needed was unlikely to be raised on the open market, Hudson suggested that each of the companies present should offer shares in the

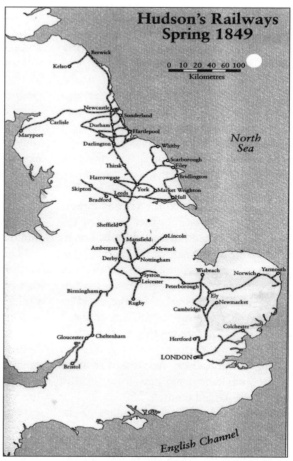

This shows just how much of Britain's railway network was in the hands of George Hudson, earning him the title, the 'Railway King'.

proposed line to their own shareholders with a guaranteed dividend of 6 per cent. A new company was formed, the Newcastle & Darlington Junction Railway, with Hudson as chairman. It was not until 1842 that the necessary legislation was passed through Parliament, undoubtedly a factor in Hudson deciding to become an MP.

Meanwhile, the YNMR had been doing well, paying a ten per cent dividend at a time of recession, but the North Midland, over which much of its traffic proceeded, was suffering. Hudson headed a committee enquiring into the affairs of this company, and within a week proposed a dramatic reduction in expenses, cutting these from £44,000 weekly to £27,000. This decisive action saved the company, but its neighbours, the **Midland Counties** and the **Birmingham & Derby Junction**, were also suffering difficulties. With remarkable clarity of purpose, Hudson proposed a merger of all three companies, one that would achieve still further savings, with the new **Midland Railway** formed in September 1843.

Hudson forecast that the railway bubble was about to burst and that many of the new and proposed lines would turn out to be unviable, but staunchly maintaining that '...the public would rather (the railways) be in the hands of companies than... government'. Hudson was asked by the directors of the other railway companies to head resistance to **Gladstone's Bill**, and so it was that when the parliamentary process was complete, the Railway Act 1844 saw most of the troublesome and unwelcome clauses of the original bill omitted.

On 18 June 1844, the 39 miles of the Newcastle & Darlington Junction Railway opened. The railway journey from York to London had taken ten hours in 1837, but by 1844 the much longer journey from Gateshead to London took just eight hours, a clear indication of progress. Hudson became Conservative MP for Sunderland in 1845, largely because his railway ambitions could be helped by a seat in the House of Commons. While he did much to improve the town's docks, he was also driven by a desire to sabotage the plans for a direct line between York and London, which later became the **Great Northern Railway**, and in 1846 this drew him into taking over the **Eastern Counties Railway**. Hudson won over the ECR shareholders by trebling dividends and it soon became clear that he was paying dividends out of capital: unacceptable but a fairly commonplace practice at the time. This raised questions amongst those concerned with his other companies, and it was soon found that the same practice was being applied, so that by the end of 1849, he was forced to resign all of his chairmanships. By this time, the Great Northern route was open and pragmatic to the end, Hudson decided to use the new route and abandoned his own plans to extend the Eastern Counties line, with the result that simultaneously, Hudson was under pressure from angry Midland Railway shareholders who objected to the diversion of traffic away from their route and on to the more direct route.

Had the railway boom continued, Hudson could have avoided the problems that beset him over paying dividends out of capital. It was not to be. Claim after claim was lodged against Hudson, who continued to the end to attract warm local support in both Sunderland and Whitby, as the inhabitants of both towns saw him as a local benefactor. Initially, Hudson was able to fight off the threat of bankruptcy by selling his extensive estates, which he had acquired to leave to his sons, and afterwards because as a sitting MP he could not be arrested for bankruptcy. When he lost his parliamentary seat, he was forced to flee to France, and spent many years in and out of exile.

Hughes, George, 1865-1945
Apprenticed to F W Webb at **Crewe** on the **London & North Western Railway** in 1882, he joined the **Lancashire & Yorkshire Railway** in 1895, where he was principal assistant for carriages and wagons before being appointed works manager at Horwich in 1899, and then chief mechanical engineer from 1904 until 1921. At the LYR, he was one of the pioneers of fire tube superheaters, along with the **Great Western's Churchward**, which he introduced on 0-6-0s in 1906 and to 4-4-0s in 1908, which were also fitted with long-lap, long-travel

piston valves. While his four-cylinder 4-6-0s introduced in 1908 were initially costly, fuel consumption improved by 25 per cent once rebuilt with super-heated boilers and long-lap valves. Amongst his other locomotives were 0-8-0 goods engines and 2-4-2 tanks.

When the LYR and LNWR merged in 1922, he became CME, and was the first CME of the **London, Midland & Scottish** in 1923, staying until 1925. Inheriting a large fleet of smaller locomotives from the **Midland Railway**, he immediately identified a need for 4-6-2 Pacific express passenger locomotives and 2-8-2 goods engines, but financial constraints meant that construction could not go ahead. Even after retirement, 245 of his 2-6-0 mixed traffic locomotives were built for the LMS.

Huish, Mark, 1808-1867

After service in the East India Company's army, he returned home and was appointed secretary to the Glasgow Paisley & Greenock Railway in 1837, before joining the **Grand Junction Railway** as secretary and general manager in 1841, retaining this position after the merger with the **Liverpool & Manchester Railway** in 1845. He was largely responsible for the merger with the **London & Birmingham Railway** to form the **London & North Western Railway** in 1846, of which he also became GM.

It was Huish who established some of the early railway cartels, sometimes known as the 'Euston Square Confederacy', which allocated traffic between the major companies from 1850, but he was also active in debates about safety, financial management, traffic management and telegraphic communication. He was to resign in 1858 after his agreements had collapsed the previous year. He retired to the **Isle of Wight**, where he became a director of the Isle of Wight Railway, and also became part-time chairman of the Clifton Suspension Bridge Company and the

Electric & International Telegraph Company. He was also sought after as an arbitrator in inter-company railway disputes and gave evidence to the Royal Commission on Railways in 1866,

Hull

Unlike **Southampton**, which owes its importance as port to the railways, Hull was already an important port attracting traffic from a large area to the east of the Pennines. By the late eighteenth century, the port was already inadequate and three further docks were built between 1778 and 1829. The railway first reached Hull in 1840, when the Hull & Selby (see **Leeds & Selby**) ran along the banks of the Humber to its terminus at Manor House, close to the docks. Further lines were sent into the town, with the next being the **York & North Midland Railway**'s line to Bridlington in 1846, which leased the Hull & Selby before itself becoming part of the **North Eastern Railway**. Paragon Station opened in 1848, closer to the city centre, while Manor House became a goods station. The docks were further extended in 1850, with a railway connection into the new Victoria Dock.

By this time, Hull also had a railway connection from the south, but by ferry, when the Manchester Sheffield & Lincolnshire railway, predecessor of the **Great Central**, provided a service across the Humber from New Holland. As with the **London & South Western** at Southampton, the NER's monopoly made it unpopular in Hull, but a rival emerged in 1885 in the form of the **Hull & Barnsley Railway**, but before long both companies collaborated in the building of the King George V Dock, and amalgamated almost on the eve of **grouping** in 1922.

Little changed after grouping, but post-**nationalisation** the railway network around and in the town was rationalised, starting in 1955 and accelerated after **Beeching** with the closure of many branch lines, while the Victoria Dock branch closed in 1968. Freight traffic dropped between the wars with increased competition from road haulage, but after nationalisation, this dropped still further, the situation made more difficult by the loss of fish traffic which at one time required eleven fast goods trains daily. Through trains remained to cities in the north, but services to London were slashed dramatically until after privatisation and the appearance of an open access operator, Hull Trains.

Hull & Barnsley Railway
More correctly, the Hull Barnsley and West Riding Junction Railway & Dock Company, was authorised in 1880 as a deliberate attempt to break the monopoly held by the **North Eastern Railway** and the Hull Dock Company, and enjoyed the backing of Hull Corporation. The 53 mile long line opened in 1885 at the same time as the associated Alexandra Dock, having overcome both engineering and financial difficulties, running from Hull's Cannon Street Station to join the **Midland Railway** at Cudworth, two miles from Barnsley. In an attempt to avoid level crossings, it ran on an embankment near Hull and used thirty-four bridges, while further west, there were severe gradients as it crossed the Yorkshire Wolds, with 1 in 100 westbound and 1 in 150 eastbound, compared with the easier gradients of the NER along the Humber.

The excellent facilities of the Alexandra Dock enabled the line to make a significant impact, and after initial competition on freight rates, the situation eased so that during the 1890s, the relationship with the NER became close and the two companies jointly built the King George V Dock, which opened in 1914. Both companies merged in 1922, and the NER then passed into the **London & North Eastern Railway** the following year. Despite the sharp downturn

in coal traffic after the miners' strike, the line and the docks continued to handle export coal traffic throughout the 1930s, but failed to survive the post-war years, with passenger traffic ending in 1955 and through freight in 1958, except for some local freight to Little Weighton until 1964. Nevertheless, part of the line serves Drax power station and the high level section still carries freight to Saltend and Hull's eastern docks.

Hull & Selby Railway – see **Leeds & Selby Railway**

Humber Commercial Railway & Dock
Opened between Ulceby and Immingham Docks in 1910 and leased by the **Great Central Railway**, it was opened throughout in 1912, when it also acquired the Barton & Immingham Light Railway, also leased to the GCR. The entire operation passed to the **London & North Eastern Railway** in 1923.

Hurcomb, Cyril William/Baron Hurcomb of Campden Hill, 1883-1975
After a career in the Civil Service, including the Post Office and Ministry of Shipping, as well as being Permanent Secretary of the **Ministry of Transport** between 1927 and 1937, and Director-General of the Ministry of War Transport from 1941 to 1947, he became the first chairman of the **British Transport Commission** in 1947, ready for **nationalisation** of the railways, canals and much of road transport the following year. Although the mind behind the nationalisation programme implemented in 1948, he was opposed to the nationalisation of all inland transport. His strength lay in administration, his weakness in a failure to communicate well and fully appreciate operational matters. He was also a strong believer in centralised control, which did little to endear him to the executives set up to administer the railways, docks, canals

and **London Transport,** for example, and also subservient to politicians.

I

Iarnrod Eireann, IE

Republic of Ireland Railways was formed in 1986 to take over the railway operations of *Coras Iompair Eireann,* or *CIE,* although it remains a subsidiary of *CIE.* Although Ireland had a number of 3ft gauge lines, all of today's railways in Ireland run on the 5ft 3in Irish standard gauge, of which *IE* has just over 1,200 route miles. It also operates freight services into and from Northern Ireland, and a regular Dublin-Belfast express, 'The Enterprise' is operated jointly with **Northern Ireland Railways.**

Inglis, Sir James Charles, 1851-1911

Aberdeen-born Inglis worked under James Abernethy in the construction of the Alexandra Docks at Newport, before becoming assistant engineer on the **South Devon** and **Cornwall Railways** in 1875. When these companies were absorbed by the **Great Western** in 1878, he joined that company and worked on the development of its docks at **Plymouth.** Between 1881 and 1883, he was the GWR's resident engineer building the **Princeton Railway.** He became the GWR's assistant engineer in 1892, but was almost immediately promoted to chief engineer.

While he improved the GWR routes between **London** and both South Wales and the West Country, as well as between **Birmingham** and **Bristol,** his main achievement was the construction of the new harbour at Fishguard and the railway connection to it for the Irish Sea and transatlantic services. He became the GWR's general manager in 1903, planning to centralise management, but despite board approval he encountered fierce oppo-

sition from George **Churchward** and his reforms were left to a later generation. He was knighted in 1911.

Inverness & Perth Junction Railway

One of the predecessors of the **Highland Railway,** the line opened in 1863 between Dunkeld and Forres, using the Pass of Drumochter, hitherto regarded as too difficult for earlier locomotives. At Forres, a junction with the Inverness & Aberdeen Junction Railway enabled Moray to be reached. Crossing largely open country with many streams, the line needed eight viaducts, 126 bridges over streams and rivers, and another 119 over roads, and at first many of these were built of wood, both for quickness and economy. There were a number of steep gradients, and the summit at Druimuachdar remains the highest on any British main line.

Irish North Western Railway

Formed in 1862 on the merger of the Dundalk & Enniskillen Railway with the Londonderry & Enniskillen Railway, both of which were incorporated in 1845, the Irish North Western was itself taken over by the **Great Northern Railway of Ireland** in 1876.

Irish Railway Clearing House

The development of a railway network throughout Ireland created the same problems as in Great Britain, and in 1848, an Irish Railway Clearing House was established with a function similar to that of the **Railway Clearing House.** Despite nationalisation of railways in the Republic in 1945 and in Northern Ireland in 1948-49, with the **Great Northern Railway of Ireland** following in 1953, the IRCH continued in existence until 1974.

Isle of Man

The railways in the Isle of Man at no time

presented a coherent whole, although the Isle of Man Railway presented a network that reached much of the island. Other railways included the **Manx Electric Railway**, originally known as the Douglas & Laxey Coast Electric Tramway and the **Snaefell Mountain Railway**, but there were also horse trams in Douglas, the capital, and a 2ft Groudle Glen Railway.

Isle of Man Railway

Tourism to the Isle of Man started during the early nineteenth century, but because of poor roads, most of the visitors remained in Douglas. A number of schemes for railways were put forward after 1847, but it was not until 1873 that the Isle of Man Railway opened a line between Douglas and Peel via St John's using a 3ft gauge. The following year, a second line opened between Douglas and Port Erin via Castletown. Locomotives were built by Beyer Peacock in Manchester, which produced a class of outside cylinder 2-4-0 tank engines, which remained in production, much improved, until delivery of No16, *Mannin*, in 1926. The railway initially used four-wheel carriages produced by the Metropolitan Railway & Carriage Company, but later the bodies were removed and paired to fit on new bogie underframes.

A further line was opened by the Manx Northern Railway in 1879, linking St John's with Ramsay, and when the Foxdale Railway between St John's and Foxdale opened in 1886, it was operated by the MNR. In 1904, the MNR and the FR were taken over by the IOMR giving a total of 46^1/$_2$ route miles.

The railways were a great success, and tourism boomed, with most visitors from the north-west of England, **Glasgow**, Belfast and Dublin. In 1913, the number of visitors peaked at 615,000. The First World War saw the holidaymakers disappear, but military personnel, prisoners of war and internees were sent to the island. The internment camp at Knockaloe had a short branch built off the Peel line, paid for by the British government and worked by the IOMR; post-war the track was lifted.

Post-war, the number of visitors fell far below the level of 1913, with 1925 having just 534,000 visitors. Perhaps more serious, bus competition began to make an impact, so that between 1925 and 1937, the number of passengers fell from 1,344,620 to 775,000. Freight was also badly affected by road haulage – better suited to the short distances on the island.

The Second World War once again saw the end of the holiday market, and for the first time government assistance was given to the IOMR to compensate for the loss of traffic. Even so, the line to Foxdale, always the most marginal of the IOMR network, closed for good in 1942. Because the Isle of Man is not part of the United Kingdom, operations were not taken over by the Railways Executive Committee in either war.

Post-war, the Isle of Man suffered a further fall in tourism, and railway services began to be pruned, especially during the winter months. As an economy measure, a diesel locomotive was introduced and two railcars bought from the **County Donegal Railway**, but these were seldom used. By 1964, the only line with a year-round service was between Ramsay and Port Erin. In 1965, after all of the remaining lines were operated during the summer, the IOMR announced that it would close for the winter, followed by the announcement in January 1966 that the railway would not re-open for the summer. It was leased by the Marquess of Ailsa for the summers of 1967 and 1968, then closed again. The lines to Peel and Ramsay were lifted, and while some services were operated between Douglas and Port Erin, it was not until the IOMR was nationalised in 1978, and operated as part of the Manx Electric Railway

Board, which subsequently became the Isle of Man Passenger Transport Board in 1983, and more recently the Department of Tourism, Leisure and Transport. Services continue through spring, summer and autumn between Douglas and Port Erin.

Isle of Wight

It is worth considering the railways of this small island as a whole because, unlike those in Jersey or the Isle of Man, they interconnected and after **grouping** could be operated as a cohesive while. The railways of the Isle of Wight were small companies, but they were fiercely independent, with three operating 56 miles of railway in an area with a population of around 85,000 and an area of just 127 square miles. The ambitions of the **LSWR** and **LBSCR** had not ignored the island, with the line from Ryde Pier Head to St John's owned jointly by the two companies, even though neither ran any trains on the island.

Of the three companies, the only one with a reasonable level of traffic and capable of producing adequate returns was the Isle of Wight Railway, whose main line from Ryde to Ventnor opened as far as Shanklin in 1864, and then reached Ventnor through a tunnel cut under St Boniface Down in 1866, a distance of 12½ miles including the section along the pier at Ryde, essential so that ferries from Portsmouth could come alongside at all states of the tide. The IWR also operated the short 2¾ mile branch from Brading to Bembridge Harbour, opened in 1882, which was initially operated in conjunction with a wagon ferry from Langston on Hayling Island provided by the LBSCR, but abandoned in 1888. In 1898, the IWR took over the branch.

The Isle of Wight Central Railway had opened as the Cowes & Newport Railway in 1862, and this remained an isolated operation until the opening of the Ryde &

Newport Railway in 1875. The two companies did not amalgamate until 1887 to create the IWC, which also took over the struggling Isle of Wight (Newport Junction) Railway which operated from Newport to Sandown, where it shared the station with the IWR. When a branch was built from Merstone, on the Newport-Sandown line, to Ventnor West between 1897 and 1900, that also became part of the IWCR. Traffic even on the line from Ryde to Newport and Cowes was never substantial, although there was some freight at Medina Wharf between Newport and Cowes. Altogether, it is not surprising that no dividend was paid until 1913.

Between them, these two railways did at least link major centres of population on the Isle of Wight, but the third company, the Freshwater, Yarmouth and Newport used a 12 mile route to reach places no bigger than a village. The ferry from Yarmouth to Lymington was the least well placed of the three main ferry routes for traffic from **London** and the main south coast cities. Opened during 1888-9, the Freshwater, Yarmouth and Newport Railway was initially worked by the IWCR until 1913, when it decided to work on its own, purchasing and hiring three tank engines. To be fair, there were schemes to provide a tunnel to link the line to the LSWR just north of Lymington, but these never came to fruition. Even if they had, there would have been a major bottleneck at Newport, where trains to West Wight had to reverse out of the station before making their way through remotely populated countryside. Space at Newport, the island's principal town, would also have been a problem.

Although a plan was mooted for the island railways to evade grouping by uniting into a single railway, this came to nothing and in 1923, the **Southern Railway** took over the island lines and also the ferries from Portsmouth and Lymington. The SR moved quickly to up-date rolling stock and locomotives, largely standardising on 0-4-4T locomotives, but even so, all rolling stock was late Victorian. In 1929, the main island bus operator, Vectis, was acquired and became Southern Vectis. After **nationalisation**, the island lines passed to the Southern Region of **British Railways**, and before long, closures were being made. The first line to close was the branch from Merstone Junction to Ventnor West in 1952, followed in 1953 by the lines to Yarmouth and Freshwater, and the branch from Brading to Bembridge. The line between Newport and Sandown survived until 1956. As a result of the **Beeching** report, complete closure of the two remaining lines was mooted, albeit with a shuttle service from Ryde Pierhead to Ryde St John's Road, where a large bus-railway interchange was mooted. In the end, the line from Ryde to Newport and Cowes was closed in 1966 along with the line between Shanklin and Ventnor. The line between Ryde and Shanklin was electrified on the Southern third-rail dc system and ex-**Bakerloo Line** tube trains modified to run on the island, later being replaced by **Northern Line** 1938 stock. The 'Island Line' survives today, but receives the largest subsidy per passenger of any line on Britain's railways.

Isle of Wight Central Railway – see **Isle of Wight**

Isle of Wight Railway – see **Isle of Wight**

J

Jersey Eastern Railway

The initial success of the **Jersey Railway** led to three other schemes being promoted within months of the JR opening. The most promising of these was the Jersey Eastern Railway, and after the JR had overcome the various obstacles in getting approval from the States of Jersey, the approval for the JER was much quicker. Unlike the easy seafront line of the JR, the JER had to cut across country with cuttings, embankments and bridges, and its terminus in St Helier was at Snow Hill, reached through a cutting, although initially a temporary terminus was used at Green Street. It opened in August 1873 to Grouville, but after a few weeks the line was extended to Gorey Village. The line reached the Snow Hill terminus in May 1874. At the other end, the line was extended to Gorey Pier, giving a route mileage of 6¼ miles. The initial rolling stock consisted of two 0-4-2T locomotives and fourteen carriages.

In contrast to the JR, the JER enjoyed reasonable prosperity from the start. It even ran special boat trains to connect with the packet ship to France from Gorey. A third locomotive was acquired from the JR when that line abandoned standard gauge, while another two locomotives were acquired new in 1886 and 1889. In 1927, the JER bought standard gauge Sentinel railcars, and like its western neighbour, opened new halts. The bus service operated by a Mr Thullier was also acquired. Nevertheless, by this time the JER was also suffering from road competition, and services finally ended on 21 June 1929.

In common with the JR, lines were relaid and services started by the Germans during the occupation of the Channel Islands during the Second World War, but these services were not available to the public. Snow Hill became a bus terminus for services to the eastern end of the island, with the rare feature of the turntable being used to turn buses. Later, when all bus services were concentrated on the Weighbridge, it became a car park. The old Gorey Village station remains, sitting on the sea front, while the Gorey Pier terminus is used by the island's buses.

Jersey Railway

A railway for Jersey was considered as early as 1845, initially with English backing at the height of 'Railway Mania', but none of these plans came to anything. This was a shame in hindsight as one scheme proposed a line running across the island from St Aubin to Gorey through St Helier, and would have avoided the lost opportunity that resulted when two different unconnected railways were built. Eventually, a proposal was submitted to the States of Jersey (the island Parliament) for a line from St Aubin to St Helier, and which was finally approved in 1869, resulting in the Jersey Railway.

Work progressed quickly on the $3^3/4$ mile standard gauge line running along the sea front, much of it on trestles at first, and services between a station close to the Weighbridge at St Helier and St Aubin commenced in October 1870. Initially, trains ran hourly on weekdays and Sunday afternoons, but half-hourly on Saturdays. There were two 2-4-0T locomotives, four open and four closed carriages, but a third locomotive was added in 1871, and frequencies increased. The carriages were unusual in having a veranda on either side, so despite the standard gauge, they had a width of 13ft 9ins. The early success of the railway encouraged no less than three other ventures to be promoted, but the only one of these to make any progress was the Jersey Eastern Railway linking St Helier with Gorey.

Despite a promising start, the JR soon encountered financial difficulties as there was insufficient business between St Helier and St Aubin, and at the end of 1874 it was declared *en desastre*, effectively bankrupt. It was bought in 1875 by a Louis Maire, although sold on in 1878 to a Mr F Nalder,

before being acquired in 1883 by an English company, the Jersey Railways.

Meanwhile, progress had been made on a line between St Aubins and La Moye, and unlike the JR this was intended to be primarily a goods line carrying stone from the quarries, with work starting in 1873, but ending in 1876 with bankruptcy. Work resumed with a change of gauge to 3ft 6ins, but little progress was made until 1883 when the line was acquired by the JR, and the line opened from St Aubin's to La Moye in 1884. This was the signal for the JR also to convert to 3ft 6ins to allow through running, and at the same time rebuild much of its structure. La Moye Station was renamed la Corbiere after the lighthouse nearby, and with two new locomotives and rolling stock, through running between St Helier and Corbiere started in August 1885. In 1893, despite a third locomotive arriving, the company went into voluntary liquidation, but was rescued by a local syndicate in 1896, the Jersey Railways & Tramways, which intended to electrify the railway. While electrification did not come, a fourth locomotive did, and a tunnel was cut at St Aubin which made working the line easier. The railway then embarked on a period of modest prosperity.

After the First World War, the arrival of the motor bus seriously affected the railway, especially with the foundation of Jersey Motor Transport in 1923, which brought an organised and professional approach to public transport on the island. To counter the competition, the JR introduced railway bus services, additional halts and steam-driven railcars, which proved successful. It then acquired Jersey Motor Transport, and reached an operating agreement with another bus company, SCS. The result was that the JR soon found that running buses was more profitable and better suited to small island distances, so in 1931, the winter train service was discontinued. In

October 1936, just before that season's summer service ended, a fire at St Aubin's station destroyed most of the passenger carriages, and the closure of the line was announced.

During the German occupation of the Channel Islands during the Second World War, the line was reinstated and extended with a number of other new lines, to supply German bases and artillery emplacements, but it was not reopened to public service.

The track between St Aubin's and Corbiere is now a public footpath, while Corbiere station remains.

Jubilee Line

Authorised in 1969 as the Fleet Line to run 2¹/₂ miles from **Charing Cross** to Baker Street to ease pressure on the **Bakerloo Line** in central **London**, and then take over the Stanmore branch. In 1972, an extension was authorised along the line of Fleet Street through the City of London and south to Lewisham. It was renamed in 1977 by the then Great London Council, after opening in 1979 between Stanmore and Charing Cross, the eventual extension ran to **Waterloo**, then to the new developments in London's Docklands, and finally north to Stratford.

Originally planned to have moving block signalling, this was found to be impractical and conventional signalling is used. On the new stretches of line, it is the first London tube line to have platform doors.

K

Kent & East Sussex Railway

A light railway authorised by a Light Railway Order in 1896, originally as the Rother Valley Railway, with the line between Tenterden and Robertsbridge opened in 1900. A further LRO allowed an extension from Tenterden and Headcorn in

1902, which opened in 1903, and the Kent & East Sussex title was adopted in 1904. The company passed to the **Southern Railway** on **grouping**, and was eventually **nationalised**. It closed to passengers in 1954, and to freight in 1961, but part of it reopened as a preserved line using the KESR title in 1974.

Kilmarnock & Troon Railway

Authorised in 1808, the first railway in Scotland to have Parliamentary sanction, and opened as a 4ft gauge double track in 1811, initially horse drawn and mainly handling coal, although there were two passenger carriages, *Caledonia* and *The Boat*. George **Stephenson** was invited to demonstrate a steam locomotive on the line in 1817, but this was too heavy for the track. The railway was consistently profitable, dividends averaging 14 per cent throughout the 1840s. After being leased to the Glasgow Paisley Kilmarnock & Ayr Railway in 1846, it was converted to standard gauge and steam locomotives were introduced. The **Glasgow & South Western Railway** acquired the line in 1899.

Kilsyth & Bonnybridge Railway

An extension of the Kelvin Valley Railway, which opened in 1879, the Kilsyth & Bonnybridge opened in 1888. While the KVR was operated by the **North British Railway**, the KBR was operated jointly by the NBR and the **Caledonian Railway**, and although it passed to the **London & North Eastern Railway** in 1923, joint working with the **London, Midland & Scottish Railway** continued until **nationalisation**.

King's Cross

King's Cross was built for the **Great Northern Railway** to replace its temporary station, used since 1850 and located next to Maiden Lane, now renamed York Way. To reach King's Cross, the line had to be buried under the Regent's Canal and then through the 528 yard Gas Works tunnel. The temporary facilities at Maiden Lane were named 'King's Cross' in the timetable, and consisted of two timber platforms, which had to cope with the Great Exhibition traffic of 1851, and also were used by Queen Victoria and Prince Albert for their trip to Scotland that August.

The real King's Cross was built on a ten-acre site which had been occupied by the smallpox and fever hospitals, while a number of houses were also demolished. It opened on 14 October 1852. Initially, the daily service consisted of twelve trains in each direction, with just three of them expresses, with departures starting at 7am and ending at 8pm, while the last arrival was at 10pm. Passengers were met by horse-buses which for 6d (2½p) would convey them to **London Bridge**, **Waterloo** or **Paddington**.

Lewis **Cubitt** designed a simple, yet practical, station, with two 800ft long, 105ft wide, train sheds which were joined at the southern end by a 216ft façade of London stock bricks with two arches, but with little ornament. The lack of pretension was spoiled somewhat by a central square clock tower, 112ft high, with an Italianate turret with a clock with three faces, as the north-facing one was blocked off as it could not be seen from the ground. The clock's chimes were silenced at the outbreak of the First World War and not reinstated until 1924, then silenced again in 1927. The west side of the station had a departure platform, now No10, while on the east was an arrival platform, now No1, with fourteen carriage roads in between them. A carriage road ran alongside the arrival platform, while between the departure platform and an external carriage road were refreshment rooms and first and second-class waiting rooms and ladies' rooms, as well as the station offices. As was the custom at the

time, a hotel was also built, opening in 1854, but the Great Northern Hotel was set apart from the station to the south-west.

Around three-quarters of the roof was glazed, supported by arches and laminated wood girders, which had to be replaced on the east side during 1869-70, and on the west during 1886-87.

Once finished, King's Cross was for the time the largest terminus in the British Isles, but the GNR was accused of extravagance, which was denied by the Board, who pointed out that they had obtained good value. In fact, the portico and Great Hall at **Euston** had cost as much.

At the start, King's Cross was a mainline station, with just four stations between London and Hatfield, 17¾ miles away, but intermediate stations were opened over the next decade or so. In February 1858, the GNR trains were joined by those of the **Midland Railway**, although these were later removed when **St Pancras** was opened in September 1868. Shortly after the **Metropolitan Railway** opened in 1863, a station was opened at King's Cross slightly to the east of the terminus, and in October of that year, all GNR suburban trains were diverted to Farringdon Street, with up suburban trains having to back into the terminus, using the departure platform: up trains had to stop at a platform outside the terminus named York Road, before descending to the Metropolitan.

The station was marred from the outset by the difficult approach. In 1860, an excursion train from **Manchester** mounted the buffers after the guard, who was drunk, had forgotten that he needed to provide addition assistance with his brake as the train descended into the station. No one was killed, but the damage was considerable. On 2 November 1865, a coal train running through one of the tunnels broke in two, leaving one portion to run away down into King's Cross itself. The guard jumped clear, while the wagons hit the buffers and overturned, losing their loads. Frantically, rescue parties dug at the coal for fear of finding casualties, but no one was hurt.

The Growing Station

In 1862, a further arrival platform was inserted, replacing some of the carriage roads, with one face, later No 2, of full length, while the other presented a short bay, but long enough for a short train. Meanwhile, a connection between the Metropolitan and the London Chatham & Dover Railway (see **South Eastern & Chatham Railway**) in 1866 meant that the approaches to King's Cross carried a heavy goods traffic, mainly of coal trains, having run south on the GNR and then diverted onto the Metropolitan for Kent. Suburban services were introduced by the GNR with the opening of branches to Edgware and Finchley in 1867, which later became part of the **Northern Line**. Cross-London trains were introduced, initially by the GNR, running from Hatfield to Herne Hill in 1866, but diverted to **Victoria** in 1868. In 1878, an Enfield to Muswell Hill service was introduced, but this passed to the South Eastern Railway in 1880. In the meantime, the City Widened Lines had been constructed alongside the Metropolitan, new junctions had to be built outside King's Cross, which were opened in 1868. Further suburban branches opened during the early 1870s, to Enfield, High Barnet and Alexandra Palace. These branches and the traffic they generated as well as the coal and other trains resulted in heavy congestion, so that it could take thirty minutes in the rush hour to cover the 1½ miles between Holloway and King's Cross during the mid-1870s. Temporary relief came when the **North London Railway** took over much of the traffic running over GNR tracks and diverted them to **Broad Street**. Nevertheless,

it was essential to undertake substantial works to improve the approaches, with additional tunnels and a skew bridge to separate trains for the goods yard from passenger services, and much of this work was done between 1875 and 1877, but further works were needed and completed in mid-1886, while a third tunnel under the Regent's Canal was finished in 1892, allowing separate tunnels for up and down trains. Nevertheless, the approaches were congested and confused, while the run down into the tunnels and then up again placed a strain on many a heavily loaded train, with runbacks a real danger, while the tunnels and the yard could flood in heavy rain: on 25 July 1901, traffic had to be suspended completely for 4½ hours after a flood.

The growing suburban traffic initially used the sole departure platform, which was also backed into by trains coming from the Metropolitan. In 1875, three short platforms and two tracks just outside the western wall were opened, with the clumsy title of 'King's Cross Main Line (Local) Station', with three platform faces. This replaced a carriage repair shop, but was used only for departures. In 1878, the Metropolitan connecting trains no longer had to back into the terminus, but instead used the new King's Cross (Suburban) platform, but it suffered from a steeply graded and curving platform that became an embarrassment for fully-loaded trains, while the tunnel from the Metropolitan, known as 'Hotel Curve', was also steeply graded and curving, and shrouded in smoke that required repeater signals *and* hand held lamps for safety. Double-heading was not an option as the pilot locomotive would smother the crew of that behind with smoke and fumes. In this dense and unwelcoming, not to say unhealthy, atmosphere, the GNR provided a man whose job it was to spread sand on the track after each train had passed. In July 1932, a train slipped so badly on the climb from the Metropolitan that it ran into the train running behind. The report on the accident noted that in the darkness, enginemen could only judge if the train was moving forward by reaching out and touching the tunnel walls, while breathing was difficult and drivers had 'little or no chance of rectifying an error'. Lights were fitted in the tunnel to help them judge their speed.

Between 1867 and 1881, the number of season ticket holders using King's Cross rose from 2,500 to 14,400. The passenger business was growing overall, but as with most of the London termini, trains were stopped and tickets checked before the station was reached. For King's Cross, the checks were conducted at Holloway until this was abandoned in 1896. In the meantime, with no checks at King's Cross, 'The Cross' in railway jargon, or at York Road, many a youngster enjoyed a free ride between the two.

The two train sheds were separated by a central wall, which incorporated arches, and in 1893, new platforms, which eventually became 5 and 6, were built on either side, with the westernmost becoming the long-awaited second departure platform. An iron girder footbridge came into use at the same time, located about half-way down the platforms and allowing easy access across the station. Next, in 1895, an additional track and a new island platform, 500-ft long, were added to the local station. This required the locomotive yard, coaling stage and turntable to be moved westwards, while the curve to the Metropolitan was flattened to some extent and the platform for the connection rebuilt, with a short bay also built. New milk and horse and carriage docks filled the remaining space between Cheney Street and the back of Culross Buildings. To avoid confusion with the main line station, the local platforms were designated A to E from west to east, with A and B designated as suburban platforms to

distinguish them from C to E, the local platforms. The arrival and departure platforms in the main station were confusingly numbered 1 and 2 departures and 1 to 5 arrivals, until a more logical station-wide system was introduced in 1921. In addition, there was separate access from the terminus to the Metropolitan, and from 1906 this also gave access to the **Piccadilly** tube platforms, and access was provided to a separate booking hall for the **City & South London** tube, which reached King's Cross in 1907. The arrival of the underground trains and electric trams caused many of the suburban through workings across London to be reduced, and they were withdrawn finally in 1907.

Despite these changes, the station itself continued to develop piecemeal, and nowhere was this more evident than outside where the empty space, left after the diversion of the St Pancras Old Road in the 1870s to run alongside St Pancras station, was occupied by sellers of garden furniture and sheds, hoping to interest the homeward bound commuter. Later shops appeared at the front of the station, with the hard-pressed LNER doubtless anxious for some rental income.

Major changes were made during 1922-24 to impose a more consistent approach to the station, while the off-peak through workings to the Metropolitan had been ended in 1915 and were never reinstated. Changes were made to the approaches, including turning the up carriage road in the centre of the three Gas Works tunnels into an up relief running line. Other changes saw arrivals able to use all platforms other than 16 and 17, while up suburban trains used 11 and 13. The new **Gresley** Pacific locomotives were catered for by a 70ft turntable at King's Cross which reduced light engine working in the approaches and eased congestion.

The difficulty of operating the complicated track layout on the approaches, and the fact that not all of it was visible from either the East or West boxes, meant that a primitive form of track circuiting was in use on some of the lines in the tunnels from 1894. Full track circuiting was completed by 1923, while power-operated upper quadrant signals had started to appear the previous year. On 3 October 1932, colour light signalling replaced all of the semaphore signals at King's Cross, and a new box replaced the separate East and West, centrally situated at the ends of platforms 5 and 6.

Wartime and Beyond

For safety's sake, during the First World War, mainline trains were drawn into the tunnels whenever enemy airships or bombers were overhead, but King's Cross remained unscathed. This was fortunate, as not only did the terminus and its immediate surrounding lines carry much coal and many passenger trains, explosives also passed through the station, often on passenger trains.

Post-war, by the time the railways were freed from state control, it was almost time for grouping, with the GNR becoming part of the **London & North Eastern Railway**. While the GNR's management had encouraged people to buy houses in 'Bracing Barnet' and on the 'Northern Heights' before the war to stimulate suburban traffic, post-war relief came when the Northern Line took over the High Barnet and Mill Hill branches in 1939, while before this the northern extension of the **Piccadilly Line** also reduced suburban traffic into King's Cross. While the LNER imposed logic on platform numbering, it was not adverse to creating fresh mysteries of its own, as when platform 4 was extended to full length, and in so doing platform 3 disappeared.

The Second World War once again saw King's Cross extremely busy. Many trains carried as much as 2,000 passengers, and to cope with the demands of wartime, were often as long as twenty or more carriages. Locomotives would pull one portion out of the platform, and then reverse on to the second portion. This imposed risks of its own. On 4 February 1945, the 6pm to Leeds stalled in the tunnel and then ran backwards into the front of the 7pm 'Aberdonian' standing in platform 10. Despite the low speed, the moving carriages rose into the air and demolished the signal gantry, while two passengers were killed. It took two weeks before a new gantry could be installed, causing the termination of all up suburban services at Finsbury Park.

King's Cross did not escape the impact of enemy action. Two 1,000-lb bombs, chained together, fell on the west side during the Blitz early on Sunday 11 May 1941, destroying much of the general offices, the grill room and bar, and wrecking the booking hall, killing twelve men. Fortunately, the station was quiet at the time. Temporary booking and refreshment facilities were organised quickly, and no trains were cancelled. Elsewhere, bombing on the Metropolitan lines meant that services to Moorgate were suspended from 30 December 1940, and not reinstated until after the war.

Plans to combine King's Cross with **St Pancras** as a terminus for **Channel Tunnel** trains were abandoned and instead these now use St Pancras. Much of the clutter outside the station has now been removed, but complete rebuilding of King's Cross is as far away as ever.

Kirtley, Matthew, 1813-1873

Trained by Timothy **Hackworth** on the **Stockton & Darlington Railway**, he became an engine driver on the **Liverpool & Manchester**, Hull & Selby (predecessor of the **Leeds & Selby**) and **London & Birmingham Railways**, driving the first train into Euston for the last-mentioned. He joined the **Birmingham & Derby Junction Railway** in 1839 and in 1841 became its locomotive superintendent. When the **Midland Railway** was formed in 1844, he became its locomotive and carriage superintendent, a post he held until his death. He developed the works at **Derby**, which produced its first new locomotives in 1851. His 0-6-0 goods and 2-4-0 passenger locomotives were simple, yet effective and elegant, but Kirtley's contribution to locomotive design was the introduction of brick arches and deflector plates to fireboxes so that coal could be burned instead of coke.

L

Laing, Samuel, 1812-1897

Having trained as a lawyer, initially he worked as a law clerk in the Railway Department of the **Board of Trade** from 1840, becoming law secretary in 1844, in which role he worked on **Gladstone's Act** and was a member of Dalhousie's Railway Board in 1844-45, after which he left the civil service. He had the distinction of twice being chairman of the **London, Brighton & South Coast Railway**, between 1848 and 1855 and again between 1867 and 1894: in both cases he was appointed at a time of poor financial performance and boardroom quarrelling. He was a member of parliament between 1852 and 1885, although he did not hold his seat continuously, and during one spell out of office, 1860-65, he was finance member of the government of India.

Lancashire & Yorkshire Railway

The **Manchester**-based Lancashire & Yorkshire Railway played a pivotal role in the British railway network, with its 600 route miles, which made it 11th largest amongst mainland railways, belying its importance – far more impressive and reflective of its status was the locomotive fleet, which made it the fourth largest, while its fleet of thirty ships was the largest of any pre-grouping railway.

Much of its infrastructure was built by Sir John **Hawkshaw**, and the trans-Pennine routes featured steep gradients, tall viaducts and tunnels, while on the western side, much of the route mileage was relatively flat. The company emerged in 1847 on the renaming of the **Manchester & Leeds Railway** as it acquired the Wakefield Pontefract & Goole, which opened the following year. Later, it joined the **London & North Western** in acquiring the **North Union** and **Preston & Wyre**, as well as the docks at Preston and Fleetwood, and also gained access to **Blackpool** and Lytham St Annes. Further lines were added to the system on both sides of the Pennines, before absorbing the **East Lancashire Railway** in 1859, and the **West Lancashire**, which had opened a line between Preston and Southport in 1882, followed in 1897. Nevertheless, the main LCR system was complete by 1880.

Despite its strategic importance and the wealth of the major cities on its network, as well as the tourist and commuter potential of many destinations, the LYR was for many years notorious for trains that were dirty, slow and unpunctual. This began to change in 1883 when John Parsons replaced Thomas Barnes as chairman, and when he died in 1887, his work was continued by George Armytage, who remained in office for more than thirty years. A new locomotive works at Horwich, near Manchester, replaced the two old and cramped sites at Miles Platting and Bury. A new locomotive superintendent took over in 1886, J A F **Aspinall**, and he began a major programme of producing modern steam locomotives to replace the aging fleet, with many elderly engines having been kept in service to meet rapidly growing traffic. The most significant of the new locomotives were 2-4-2 tank engines, which took over all passenger services other than the main line expresses, with 332 built between 1889 and 1911. Aspinall became general manager in 1899, with similar success in his new role. Many of the LCR's routes were lengthier than those of the rival **London & North Western**, but in 1888-89, new lines by-passed Bolton and Wigan, allowing many services to be accelerated. Early in the new century, the best expresses took just 65 minutes for the run from Manchester to Blackpool, on which the famous **club** trains were introduced, while through workings with other companies saw trains run from Colne to **Euston** and from both **Liverpool** and Manchester to Scotland, and from major cities in Yorkshire to the South Coast. Prominent in through running was the **Midland Railway**, which used running powers to reach the Seattle & Carlisle Line, and from 1888 provided Scottish services from the LCR.

The main passenger and goods stations were also developed during this period, with new marshalling yards, while the busiest parts of the main-line were quadrupled, as were many lines around Manchester and near Liverpool. Freight traffic included coal, cotton, wool, finished manufactured goods, timber, grain and fish. Jointly with the LNWR, shipping services were operated to Belfast, while the company had its own service from Liverpool to Drogheda. In the east, the company was the major railway at Goole, and ran packet and cargo ships to Denmark, Germany, the Low Countries and France.

Nevertheless, these developments were not without cost, and as a result of the heavy capital investment, and the earlier neglect of the system and the customers, dividends during the early years of the twentieth century were around 3-4 per cent.

In 1903, the LYR introduced Britain's first electro-pneumatic signalling, initially at Bolton, and then on lines near Manchester and Stockport. The signalling school at Manchester Victoria used a model layout for training. Electrification was introduced by Aspinall for the growing suburban traffic around Liverpool and Southport, using third-rail 600 volts dc power and electric multiple units, with the first sections operational in March 1904. The network was extended to Liverpool-Aintree in 1906. Instead of sticking with the original system, experiments followed with overhead electrification on a branch line running from Bury to Holcombe Brook in 1913, and in 1916 with 1,200 volts dc third-rail between Manchester, Whitefield and Bury, which must have pleased as the Holcombe Brook branch was converted to this system in 1917.

With **grouping** looming, the LYR merged with the LNWR in 1922, with both companies passing into the **London, Midland & Scottish** the following year. Several LYR senior officers were given senior posts with the LNWR and then with the LMS.

Lancashire, Derby & East Coast Railway – see **Great Central Railway**

Lancaster & Carlisle Railway

Supported by the four companies involved in plans for a West Coast route to Scotland, the route for the Lancaster & Carlisle was the most easterly of three considered, although amended to pass close to Kendal and avoid the need for a tunnel. Joseph **Locke** was the engineer and Thomas **Brassey** his contractor, for the 69 mile route, which was built through difficult terrain in just 30 months, despite fighting between English and Irish navvies at Penrith in 1846. When finished, the LCR was worked by the **London & North Western**, which by this time owned the entire line south from Lancaster to London. The LCR itself had also tried to acquire the Lancaster & Preston Junction Railway, believing that its lease to the Lancaster Canal in 1842 had been defective, and a serious situation then arose when both companies tried running trains over this line, which resulted in a collision. The LCR took over management of the LPJR in 1849.

The LCR acquired its own rolling stock in 1857, intending to become independent of the LNWR, but in 1859 leased itself to the LNWR, and in 1879 the LNWR bought it. In its turn, the LCR was an investor in the South Durham & Lancashire Union Railway, which reached Tebay in 1861 and carried Durham coke to the Furness peninsula.

Lauder Light Railway

Authorised by a Light Railway order in 1898, the Lauder Light railway opened between Fountainhall and Lauder in 1901, and was known to the locals as 'Auld La'der Licht'. It was worked by the **North British Railway**, with through trains from Edinburgh Waverley, and became part of the London & North Eastern Railway in 1923. It closed to passengers in 1932, and complete closure followed in 1958.

Leeds

A centre both of industry and, from the days of the canals, transport, Leeds had its first railway as early as 1758, when the first parliamentary authority for a railway was obtained by Charles Brandling, for a double track 4ft 1in gauge wooden wagonway from his colliery at Middleton to Leeds Bridge. Worked by horses, the line opened that year and for a while gave Brandling a monopoly over the coal supply to industry in Leeds. The **Middleton Railway** later became the first on which a steam locomotive ran commercially on rails, but this was in 1812.

The railway age can truly be said to have reached Leeds as early as 1834 when the **Leeds & Selby Railway** opened linking the city from its station at Marsh Lane with the Rivers Ouse and Humber, where passengers could catch a steam packet to Hull. The LSR was soon followed by two more significant railways, the **North Midland Railway** linking the city with **Derby** to the south, opened in 1840, and the following year it provided access to Leeds for the **Manchester & Leeds Railway**, giving a strategic link through the Pennines. None of these railways managed to get closer than a mile from the town centre, until, in 1846, the Leeds & Bradford Railway ran into the Central Station. This was originally intended to be an imposing structure that could be used by all of the city's railways, but in the end, the only other users were the **Great Northern** and the **Lancashire & Yorkshire**. Meanwhile, the NMR had become part of the **Midland Railway** and its Wellington terminus was becoming congested as it was also used by the **London & North Western** and **North Eastern Railways**. The solution was to build the New Station, a collection of dark arches that straddled the River Aire and the canal, but unlike many city centre stations lacked a frontage. All three railways used New Station, and the NER built a connection through the LSR's terminus at Marsh Lane providing a through route from Leeds to **York** and **Hull**.

The improved communications provided by this network of railways benefited industry in Leeds, which rapidly became the major centre of the textile trade, while several steam locomotive builders, amongst whom were Hunslet and Manning Wardle, also based themselves in the city. It was not until 1938 that the scheme for a single station was realised, when Wellington and New connected to provide Leeds City, but even this was a makeshift solution and it was not until 1967 that a new Leeds City was completed and Central Station could close. The line from **King's Cross** was electrified in 1990, and **electrification** was continued to Bradford in 1995.

Leeds & Selby Railway

A seventeen mile line authorised in 1830 to link Leeds with Selby, a transhipment point for the river craft that used the Ouse to get to the port of **Hull**, through which the Leeds textile industry imported much of its wool and exported its finished cloth. Built by James **Walker**, the line opened in 1834 and was unusual in that enough land was taken to allow for eventual quadrupling, although this was never needed. It was the first railway on which passengers were drawn through a tunnel by a steam locomotive, and to allay their fears, the walls were painted white and copper plates fitted at the bottom of the air shafts to reflect the light: today the former tunnel has been replaced by a deep cutting. In 1836, the Hull & Selby received approval, a thirty-one mile long line again engineered by Walker. While the lines remained independent, through working to Hull meant that transhipment at Selby onto river vessels and then again at Hull onto ships was reduced to a single transhipment at Hull.

The Leeds & Selby was leased to the **York & North Midland Railway** in 1840, and purchased in 1844, while the Hull & Selby was also leased by the YNMR from 1845, and eventually bought by the **North Eastern Railway** in 1874.

Leeds Northern Railway

Authorised in 1845 as the Leeds & Thirsk Railway and completed in 1849 by Thomas **Grainger**, it was routed via **York** and was designed to end George **Hudson**'s monopoly on traffic from Leeds to the north-east. It was a costly project requiring tunnels and viaducts, with the most spectacular being a 23-arch viaduct across the River Aire followed by a tunnel of more than two miles

at Bramthorpe and then by a 21-arch viaduct across the River Wharfe. A branch from Starbeck, the station for Harrogate, to Knaresborough should have opened with the main line, but the viaduct over the River Nidd collapsed, and could not be opened until 1851. New routes followed, with an extension from Northallerton to Stockton and then a line from Melmerby to Northallerton, again with Grainger as engineer, both of which opened in 1852, a year after the Leeds Northern title was adopted.

A connection was established with the **London & North Western Railway** at Leeds and to Hartlepool Docks, and these enabled the company to challenge the combined **York & North Midland** and **York, Newcastle & Berwick Railways**. The initial prosperity of the LNR and its rivals was undermined by the reckless competition that followed, and eventually they merged in 1854 to form the **North Eastern Railway**.

Leek & Manifold Valley Light Railway

A 2ft 6in gauge railway authorised by a Light Railway Order in 1899 and opened in 1904, the Leek & Manifold Valley Light Railway linked Waterhouses with Hulme End. It was worked and maintained by the **North Staffordshire Railway**, and under **Grouping** became part of the **London, Midland & Scottish Railway**.

Leicester & Swannington Railway

The first railway worked by steam in the Midlands, authorised in 1830, engineered by Robert **Stephenson**, and its sixteen miles were opened during 1832-33. Passengers were carried as well as freight, but the priority was the coal traffic and the Leicestershire mine-owners saw the line as a route to the canal at Leicester and onwards to **London**. A stationary steam engine, part of which is now at the National Railway Museum, was used to work the 1 in 17 incline at Swannington. The railway prospered and managed to pay a dividend of 5 per cent between its opening and 1845, when it was acquired by the **Midland Railway**, offering a £100 Midland share for each LSR one of £50.

Letterkenny & Burtonport Extension Railway

Authorised by a Light Railway Order of 1898, the line opened in 1903 and was worked by the **Londonderry & Lough Swilly Railway**.

Liddell, Charles H, 1812-1894

A civil engineer who worked under George **Stephenson** on the **North Midland Railway**, Charles Liddell also worked on the Syston-Peterborough line of the **Midland Railway**, where he was caught up in the battle at Saxby in 1844, when the local landowner's men fought railway prize fighters in an attempt to stop a survey going ahead. He worked with Robert **Stephenson** on other schemes in the Midlands, before working on the Newport, Abergavenny & Hereford Railway in 1851, followed by the Worcester & Hereford Railway in 1853, while in 1857 he was appointed chief engineer on the Leicester-Hitchin line of the MR, and then the Bedford-Radlett section of the extension to **London** in 1868. During this time he also worked on the development of wire ropes and was for a period a director of a railway in the north of Italy.

Between 1873 and 1893, he was consulting engineer on the Manchester Sheffield & Lincoln Railway, predecessor of the **Great Central**, and the **Metropolitan Railway** under Edward **Watkin**, before resigning over the terms for the post of chief engineer.

Light railways

The high cost of railway construction, but the value of a railway connection, meant that efforts were always made to reduce costs. One means of doing this was by using a narrower than standard track gauge as the cost of engineering works and equipment rose with broader gauges. Another was to retain the standard gauge and use lighter methods of construction and also allow tighter curves and steeper gradients. It was also possible to combine both means to produce a really low-cost railway. Such methods were important given that road transport at the time was horse-drawn, slow and expensive. There was also some linking with light railways in some areas with tram networks, and others ran alongside roads. They were often unfenced.

There was another heavy cost in building a railway, that of obtaining parliamentary sanction. On the mainland of Great Britain, this was resolved by a measure included in the Regulation of Railways Act 1868 and then later the Light Railways Act 1896, which enabled such railways to be authorised by an order under the Act rather than by full scale parliamentary legislation. There were a number of restrictions on light railways, including such matters as a maximum speed of 25mph.

In Ireland, at the time still undivided and part of the United Kingdom, the authorising measure was the Tramways and Public Companies (Ireland) Act 1883.

Limited Expresses

A number of **named** trains had the word 'limited' in their titles, mainly on the **Great Western Railway**. This meant that seating was limited to those with seat reservations in an attempt to end overcrowding and standing on long distance services. Often, the normal seat reservation fee was waived for such trains.

Liskeard & Looe Railway

An extension of the Liskeard & Caradon Railway opened from Moorswater, where it joined the Liskeard & Looe Union Canal, to

South Caradon in November 1844, and extended to Cheesewring Quarries in 1846. Gravity working was used for the loaded wagons carrying tin ore and granite, which were returned to the head of the line using horses. The extension to Looe running alongside the banks of the canal opened at the end of 1860, and from 1862 the line throughout was worked by the Caradon railway, which shortly afterwards introduced locomotives. Initially passengers on the Caradon could travel on mineral wagons by the expedient of paying for the transport of a parcel, and receiving a 'free' pass! Passenger carriages were introduced on the Caradon line from 1860, and on the line to Looe from 1879.

The connection with the main line using a steeply graded and tight loop from Coombe Junction was opened in May 1901, and passenger traffic trebled almost immediately, but the ore and stone traffic was in sharp decline by this time. The **Great Western Railway** took over working of the Looe and Caradon lines in 1909, but the latter system was abandoned in 1916. The Liskeard & Looe Railway survived to be absorbed into the GWR in 1923. As late as 1935, a scheme was mooted for a new direct line from St Germans, which would have been easier to work, but this was not built.

Listowel & Ballybunnion Railway

Incorporated in 1886, the Listowel & Ballybunnion Railway opened in 1888, operating through a remote part of Co. Kerry between the two small towns. It was unique in that its 9¼ route miles were of Lartigue monorail, one of the most extensive of this kind anywhere. Lartigue monorail, named after Charles Lartigue who patented the system in 1883, consisted of a single rail mounted on trestles about 3ft above ground level, augmented by a light guide and stabilising rail on either side

about a foot below the main rail. This left the locomotives and rolling stock straddling the line, and indeed the LBR's locomotives were almost 'Siamese twins' with a boiler on each side of the track, while the carriages were also double-sided.

The line ran through compromising territory which was also remote from the main centres in Ireland, and was closed in 1924, which must be a cause of regret for enthusiasts everywhere.

Liverpool

At the dawn of the railway age, Liverpool was already one of Britain's major ports, and the fact that the **Liverpool & Manchester** was amongst the country's first railways was simply a reflection of this. The city's ocean trade expanded rapidly throughout the nineteenth century and the railway age naturally coincided with that of the steamship and the firm establishment of the British Empire. The LMR opened in 1830, while in 1840; Samuel Cunard introduced regular steamship sailings to the United States and Canada. Even before this, with a grant of £2,000 (worth £150,000 today) from the City, Lime Street replaced the original LMR Crown Street terminus in 1836, and in 1838, the city had good railway links to both **Birmingham** and **London**. Initially Lime Street had to have its approaches worked by a cable, while the station was rebuilt and expanded in 1849 and again between 1867 and 1874. The LMR and the **London & North Western Railway**, which absorbed it, had reached the docks through long tunnels opened in 1839 and 1849.

The LNWR did not have a monopoly in Liverpool for long, for the **Lancashire & Yorkshire Railway** reached the city, initially stopping at Great Howard Street, but had a new terminus, Exchange, close to the docks. By 1859, the LCRY connected Liverpool with **Manchester**, **Preston**, what was then the small village of Southport, and Wigan. Nevertheless, a duopoly was soon established which other railways could not break, although the **Great Northern, Manchester, Sheffield & Lincolnshire** (see **Great Central Railway**) and **Midland Railway** formed the **Cheshire Lines** committee in 1865 and in 1874 opened a third line between Manchester and Liverpool. Meanwhile, the LNWR had shortened its approach to the city by building the Runcorn Bridge and opening a direct line in 1869, prompted by competition for traffic to and from the Midlands following the arrival of the **Great Western** across the Mersey at Birkenhead in 1854.

Other developments that followed before the end of the nineteenth century included the **Liverpool Overhead Railway**, completely opened in 1896, running more than six miles between Dingle to Seaforth. The world's first elevated electric railway, it used third rail DC electrification.

The Mersey Docks & Harbour Board built an extensive network of lines serving 38 miles of quays.

While the railway network changed little after **grouping**, although third-rail dc **electrification** of the lines to Ormskirk, Southport and the Wirral was completed, and integrated with the **Mersey Railway**, **nationalisation** saw electrification of services to **Euston** in 1962 and services concentrated on Lime Street, with Exchange finally closing in 1977. Before this, the LOR had closed because repairs and modernisation was considered too expensive. By this time, the Merseyside Passenger Transport Authority had been established in 1971, taking over the electrified lines and branding these as Merseyrail. During 1977-78, the different parts of Merseyrail were joined by two underground lines with three interchange stations, including Lime Street, and an extension to Garston. The Merseyrail network provides cross-city routes of up to 20 miles and stretches as far as Chester and Southport.

Liverpool & Manchester Railway

Authorised in 1826 and one of the first railway companies to receive parliamentary approval, after earlier attempts had failed and two engineers, William James and then his successor, George **Stephenson** had been sacked for failing to pursue the project quickly enough. After authorisation, Stephenson was reappointed, although later criticised by Robert **Telford**, both for his methods and for acting as engineer and contractor. The line required heavy engineering works, including the marshes at Chat Moss, a 1$^1/_4$ mile tunnel under Liverpool to reach the docks, and other works at Olive Mount. In addition to the company's own capital, of £510,000 it had authorisation to raise £127,500 in loans, finding this from the Exchequer Loan Commissioners in what were still pre-railway mania days.

The famous **Rainhill trials** in 1829 proved that steam rather than horse power was the way forward, and Robert Stephenson built eighteen locomotives for the company. Opened by the Prime Minister, the Duke of Wellington, in 1830, the event was better known for the first railway fatality, when the Liverpool MP William Huskisson was killed by a train.

Within weeks of opening, the LMR was carrying excursion passengers, followed by mail and road-rail containers. In 1836, it probably was the first railway to suffer a strike by footplate men, after which it guaranteed them minimum wages, possibly also persuaded by poaching of experienced men by other new railways. By 1841, it had its own locomotive works, but in 1845 merged with the **Grand Junction Railway**, and the following year both were absorbed into the **London & North Western**.

Liverpool Overhead Railway

Running 16ft above street level for the 6½ miles from Dingle to Seaforth, the Liverpool Overhead Railway was built during 1893-96 and was the world's first elevated electric railway. Third rail DC electrification was used. Elevated construction kept the line clear of the entrances to the many docks along its route, and it was nicknamed the 'Dockers' Umbrella'. In 1905, it was connected to the **Lancashire & Yorkshire Railway's** Ormskirk and Southport electrified lines. Notable firsts also included Britain's automatic semaphore signals and, in 1921, colour light signalling.

It was closed in 1956 because the heavy cost, c. £2 million, of replacing the steel decking could not be justified in the light of declining traffic.

Liverpool Street

The largest terminus within the City of **London**, Liverpool Street was built to replace the Shoreditch terminus of the **Eastern Counties Railway**. When the ECR was absorbed into the **Great Eastern Railway** in 1862, the question arose again of terminus in central London, coupled with the building of additional suburban lines and the conversion of Shoreditch to a goods station. A number of locations were considered, including Finsbury Circus, and for the track to continue from Bishopsgate on viaduct. Parliament approved the scheme in 1864, mainly because the line approached Liverpool Street in tunnel so that the demolition of London's housing stock would be kept to the minimum, but also because it was beside the terminus of the **North London Railway** then being built at **Broad Street**.

The plan was that the lines should leave the existing high level route at Tapp Street, just west of Bethnal Green, and fall to below street level, and then run in tunnel under Commercial Street and Shoreditch High Street before turning to enter the terminus, which would be built on what had been the gardens of the Bethlehem Hospital. Some demolition was inevitable, including the City of London Theatre and the City of London Gasworks, and 450 tenement dwellings housing around 7,000 people. The GER was bound under the terms of the Act to run a 2d daily return train between Edmonton and Liverpool Street, and another between the terminus and Walthamstow. Later claims by the GER to have paid between 30 and 50 shillings as compensation to displaced tenants can be discounted as the payments at the time would have been much lower.

The terminus was built below street level, much to the consternation of many of the directors, but Samuel Swarbrick, the GER's general manager, was concerned to cut costs, despite the fact that departing trains would be faced with a tunnel through which the track climbed steeply. The new station opened in stages, with the first being on 2 February 1874, handling just the suburban services to Enfield and Walthamstow, and the station was not fully open until 1 November 1875, when the old Bishopsgate terminus was handed over to be converted for goods traffic, reopening in 1881 and remaining in use until it was destroyed by fire in December 1964.

Liverpool Street occupied ten acres in the heart of the City and had ten platforms, numbered from west to east. Platforms 1 and 2 ran under the station building and the street to a junction with the **Metropolitan Railway**, to the west of its Liverpool Street underground station, known until 1909 as Bishopsgate. Until its own station was completed in July 1875, the MR trains used platforms 1 and 2 of the terminus. In fact, debate over charges for through workings completely defeated the exercise, and the connecting tunnel was in the end used only for special workings, the last being a MR working from Rickmansworth to Yarmouth in 1904, and the junction was removed in 1907. The main line arrival and departure platforms were 9 and 10, and were 900ft long. The street front of the new station consisted of three blocks, with the main one 90 feet high and running along Liverpool Street itself, and a second running from its western then running into one at its northern end set at right angles to it, 67ft high. In the space left by the blocks were four roadways for pedestrians and vehicles. The roof was perhaps the best feature of the building, set high and with a delicate appearance, with four glazed spans. There was a clock tower on the outside of the building, on the roof of the north block: inside, the train shed the roof later had two four-faced clocks suspended from it.

Behind the north block, was the suburban station with eight tracks and ten platform faces, while the mainline platforms were to the east of the middle block. Later, the suburban platforms were numbered 1 to 8, with platform 9 used by both suburban and long distance services.

Costs for building a terminus in the heart of the City of London were high, and while compensation for the displaced tenants was poor, the landowners received far higher compensation, so that the cost of Liverpool Street eventually mounted to £2 million (£120 million by today's prices), and to allow for this, an Act of 1869 allowed the GER to charge the two-mile fare for the 1¼ mile extension.

The opening of Liverpool Street encouraged the GER to build a set of three suburban branch lines north of Bethnal Green, serving Hackney Downs and Tottenham, Edmonton, with a junction with the original Enfield branch, and from Hackney Downs through Clapton to a junction with the Cambridge line and the still new branch to Walthamstow. The latter was extended to Chingford in 1873, and the line to Tottenham and Edmonton was extended to Palace Gates at Wood Green in 1878. Some of these lines were open before Liverpool Street was ready, so a new station, Bishopsgate Low Level, was opened on the new extension to Liverpool Street in November 1872. The low level station was under the existing terminus, and with no room for smoke and steam to escape, the tank engines used were equipped with condensing apparatus, which was also seen as necessary for the projected through running onto the MR. The low level station was eventually closed as a wartime economy measure in 1916.

Added to the GER's own branches were services running from the **East London Railway**, completed in April 1876. In July of that year, the **London, Brighton & South Coast Railway** introduced a service from East Croydon, while the South Eastern Railway (see **South Eastern & Chatham**) started a service from Addiscombe in April 1880, which lasted until March 1884. At the beginning of 1886, the GER took over the LBSCR services, although from 1911 they terminated at New Cross and were withdrawn when the ELR was electrified in 1913.

The Growing Station

The new suburban lines, the continued growth on the earlier lines and a growing business to and from the holiday resorts and market towns of East Anglia, meant that by 1884 it was realised that the traffic at Liverpool Street itself would soon outgrow the station. Fortunately, the GER had been steadily acquiring land to the east of the station, and had eventually land up to Bishopsgate 188-ft wide and six acres in extent. Clearance began and on 1890 work began on what was to become the East Side Station. A sign of social change was that Parliament insisted that alternative accommodation be found for the tenants in the properties cleared away, and indeed that they be rehoused at low rents. Accommodation could only be found for 137 tenants in existing property, so another 600 were housed in tenements built by the GER.

It was not enough simply to expand the station: the approach lines had to be expanded as well to avoid congestion. A third pair of approach tracks was built between Bethnal Green and Liverpool Street, enabling the westernmost set of tracks to be reserved entirely for the Enfield and Walthamstow services, so from 1891, these were known as the suburban lines, the middle set became the local lines and the easternmost, the through lines. The four tracks continued as far as Romford. Inside the terminus, platforms 1 to 5 became West Side Suburban, handling suburban and local services, while 6 also handled Cambridge trains; platforms 7 to 14 handled both local and through services, and 15 to 18 handled through services only. The services to and from the ELR used platform 14, or if this was not available, 18.

The new Liverpool Street was the largest London terminus until **Victoria** opened, rebuilt, in 1908. By the number of passengers handled daily, it remained the busiest terminus even after 1908. In a typical day, it handled 851 passenger arrivals and departures, as well as 224 empty carriage trains, ten goods trains and five light engine movements.

The new East Side frontage was taken by the Great Eastern Hotel, completed in May 1884, and the largest hotel in the City. Designed by C E Barry, the hotel presented a far more impressive face to the world than the original station buildings. Beneath the hotel, an area known as the 'backs' included an extension of the tracks from platforms 9 and 10. This was used by a nightly goods train that brought in coal for the hotel and the engine docks, as well as small consign-

ments for the offices and the hotel, while taking away the hotel's refuse and ashes from the engine docks. The eastward extension also meant that these two platforms split the station in two, and so a footbridge was built right across the station, although on two levels and too narrow to accommodate the numbers needing to use it at peak times. Relief came when the **Central London Railway** reached the terminus in 1912, with the tube station under the west side, but the subway to the booking office ran the full width of the station. It was not until after **nationalisation** that the extension into the 'backs' was ended and level access provided around the ends of 9 and 10.

Meanwhile, other suburban branch lines had been added to the GER network, although the first of these, the line to Southend, completed in 1889, would not have been regarded as even outer suburban at the time. It was joined by a line from Edmonton to Cheshunt, known as the Churchbury Loop, in 1891, and between Ilford and Woodford, known as the Hainault Loop, in 1903. The former closed in 1909 due to disappointing traffic, and that to Hainault was not much more successful, so it must have been a relief when an eastwards extension of the Central Line took it over some years later.

Despite these disappointments, overall traffic continued to grow, so that by 1912, Liverpool Street was handling a thousand trains daily. These included Britain's first all-night service, half-hourly between the terminus and Walthamstow, introduced in 1897. Walthamstow's population had grown from 11,092 in 1871 to 95, 131 in 1901. This was not unusual and other suburbs saw similar growth.

Of all the London termini, Liverpool Street had the most difficult First World War. Several bombs fell on the approach lines on the night of 8/9 September 1915, wrecking the suburban and through lines, while the local lines were flooded by a burst water main. Repairs were completed and normal services resumed by 11 am on the morning of 9 September. Worse was to follow. A daylight raid on 13 June 1917 saw three bombs hit the outer end of the station, wrecking carriages on the noon train for Hunstanton, standing at platform 9, as well as destroying two carriages in the dock between platforms 8 and 9 which were being used for medical examinations. In all, sixteen people were killed and another thirty-six wounded.

Competition from the expanding London **Underground** and the electric trams meant that electrification was considered as early as 1903. Nevertheless, the Underground seemed to have stopped expanding and while Parliamentary approval was obtained, nothing was done, even though daily passenger numbers rose from around 200,000 in 1912 to 229,073 in 1921, but just fourteen trains had been added to the timetable. The cost was enormous, however, estimated in 1919 at £3.5 million (equivalent to more than £70 million today), with little prospect of achieving a worthwhile return. The alternative, a stop-gap measure, costing £80,000, was to change the layout of the approaches, the station arrangements and signalling, so that steam trains could continue to operate, but at the maximum efficiency.

The new service was officially described as the 'Intensive Service', but was named the 'Jazz Service' by one evening newspaper, partly because jazz music was the rage at then time and also because to speed loading, second-class carriages had a blue line painted above the windows, and first-class had yellow lines, while third remained unmarked. Sixteen-carriage trains of four-wheeled carriages operated with twenty-four per hour at peak periods on just one line between Liverpool Street and Bethnal Green, still using manual signalling and 0-6-0 tank locomotives that had first appeared in 1886. Trains spent just four minutes in a platform, while platforms 1 to 4 had their own engine docks and layouts that enabled locomotives to be shunted without going beyond platform limits. At peak periods, trains started every two minutes in sequence from platforms 4 to 1, followed by a four minute gap for arrivals.

A miners' strike in 1921 meant that the intensive service had to be suspended to save coal, and again during the General Strike and prolonged miners' strike of 1926. Nevertheless, the pressure began to ease not just because of the additional trains but because commuters were moving further out into the country. **Gresley** improved the standard of the rolling stock by producing five-car articulated units with a much improved ride. Nevertheless, traffic continued to fall, with the daily number of passengers peaking at 244,000 in 1923, but dropping to 209,000 in 1938, and eventually to 171,000 in 1959.

Grouping and Beyond

The **London & North Eastern Railway** took over the GER and Liverpool Street on 1 January 1923. The company, impoverished by the collapse of its hitherto heavy coal traffic as a result of the 1926 strike, could do little to implement electrification and concentrated on its more glamorous expresses to Yorkshire and Scotland from **King's Cross**. The East Side booking office was modernised in 1935 and equipped with ticket issue and accounting machines, while during 1938 and 1939, an attempt was made to clean up to the station and improve its general appearance.

The Second World War was even harsher to the station than the earlier conflict. When bombs fell on Platforms 1 and 4 during the blitz, a train was wrecked and this took some days to remove. The East Side booking office was also damaged as was platform 18, while a delayed action bomb exploded in the engine sidings beyond platform 10 and killed two men, despite being surrounded by four trucks of ballast. A bomb that fell on Broad Street threw a wagon onto the roof of Liverpool Street. The station buildings also suffered heavy damage, with the clock tower burnt out, and it took British Railways until 1961 to replace the clock.

The war also disrupted plans for electrification once government-sponsored loans became available, and the extension of the Central Line to Loughton and Hainault did not take place until 1947, when services from Liverpool Street to these towns ended. The LNER plans for overhead electrification of the line to Shenfield were not completed until after nationalisation, starting in late September 1949. To make the best of these developments and allow easier transfer between surface trains and the tube at Stratford, the through and local lines on the approaches were swapped, with the result that platforms 13 to 18 were used by electric trains, although 11 and 12 were also wired.

Electrification was extended to Chelmsford and Southend in 1956, while the 1955 Modernisation Plan called for further electrification of the suburban network, using the 25kv overhead system, and the existing overhead electrification on what had now become the Eastern Region of **British Railways** was also converted. Steam suburban services ended in late November 1960, and by late 1962, the remaining steam services had been replaced by diesel multiple units on local and non-electrified suburban services, and diesel-electric locomotives for the mainline or 'through' services. In 1963, Liverpool Street received its first fast electric service, to and from Clacton. While traffic on the inner suburban services was less than at its peak, a sign of the times was that platforms 11 to

15 were lengthened to accommodate 12-carriage trains on the Southend line. Concurrent with electrification, a programme of installing colour light signalling got under way.

Sadly, electrification ended a long run of accident-free operation. On 13 December 1963, the last car of a departing electric suburban train was derailed near the former Bishopsgate Low Level station by a broken axle, killing a young woman when the carriage overturned.

Under British Railways, Liverpool Street became a cleaner, brighter place, and not just because of the end of steam. The terminus was cleaned and fluorescent lighting installed, the backs were closed and the concourse continued right across the station, albeit with a small detour, and the mainline booking hall was modernised. In 1975, it was announced that the station would be rebuilt to accommodate an office complex, but a more conservative scheme actually occurred between 1985 and 1991, when the old roof was replaced by an office block overhead, but the integrity of the trainshed was maintained, even while being extended.

Llanelly & Mynydd Mawr Railway

This was a small privately-owned railway built by an Edinburgh railway contractor on the route of an old tramway, the Carmarthenshire Railway, which dated from 1804 or 1805, in return for a share of the receipts. He also provided the rolling stock. Although authorised in 1875, the line was not opened until 1883. It ran for twelve miles from Llanelly. Unusually, the locomotives all carried names without numbers.

Lloyd George, David, Earl, 1863-1945

As a young solicitor in Criccieth, David Lloyd George battled for five years from 1890 with the **London & North Western Railway** for alleged discrimination against

Welsh-speakers in its employ. Elected to Parliament, he was MP for the Caernarfon boroughs from 1890 until his death in 1945 without a break. Appointed President of the **Board of Trade**, he became involved in negotiations between the railway companies and the trade unions when a national strike was threatened in 1906, and took the political lead in establishing conciliation boards, as advocated by Sir Sam **Fay**, so that industrial disputes could be resolved without strike action. Despite this progress, a national strike did arise in 1911.

Locke, Joseph, 1805-1860
Apprenticed to George **Stephenson** in 1823, he later worked for him on the **Liverpool & Manchester Railway** and on his tunnels, but his discovery of alignment problems in both the Wapping Tunnel in 1827 and then, in 1832, Lime Street Tunnel, resulted in estrangement, especially when Locke replaced Stephenson on the **Grand Junction Railway** in 1835. His achievements included the design of the works at **Crewe** and the railway town. Afterwards, in 1837, he took over from Francis Giles on the London & Southampton Railway, predecessor of the **London & South Western Railway**, and then in 1839, from C B Vignoles on the Sheffield Ashton & Manchester, one of the predecessors of the **Great Central Railway**.

Locke was one of that rare breed of engineers who completed his assignments on time and within budget, keeping careful control over contractors and on expenditure. Working with **Brassey** and **Mackenzie**, his work went beyond the British Isles and included lines in France, the Netherlands and Spain. In Great Britain, his work included most of the separate lines that together formed much of the route between **Birmingham** and **Aberdeen**, foreseeing the **West Coast Main Line**, but his preference to avoid tunnels to cut costs also meant that there were steep gradients, especially at Beattock and Shap.

He became MP for Honiton between 1847 and 1860, when he died from overwork.

London
In 1801, London already had a population of 1,110,000 and was by far the largest city in Europe, already heavily built-up and with congested streets. Over the next forty years, the population more than doubled, and by 1901, it was 6,581,000. The topography varied, but around the Thames it was flat, often marshy, with much property built on reclaimed land, while to the north, the land began to rise, as it did to the south. Beneath the surface, there was thick, heavy clay. While the earliest railways were built away from London and between pairs of towns with local trading interests, it was inevitable that lines would be sent into London at an early date. London presented both opportunities and problems for those entrepreneurs anxious to develop the railways. The opportunities included its size and the congestion, the fact that it was a political, legal and financial capital, the largest port, and that it needed fresh food and coal brought to it in vast quantities; the problems were the congestion and the sheer impossibility of fitting anything else easily into this dense mass of humanity, housing and industry, and the poor drainage of such low-lying terrain.

The first railway in London was the **Surrey Iron Railway**, a horse-drawn tramroad built to carry freight from the Thames, it had no potential for the future, and it was not until the **London & Greenwich** and **London & Blackwall Railways** were built in the 1830s that railways as we know them arrived in London, and these were both short distance, local lines. The first railways were of minor importance and built largely on viaducts in poor areas, so that there were few objections even though they displaced many slum dwellers and no doubt added to their misery. When the **London & Birmingham** approached from the north-west and the **Great Western** approached from the west, they had to battle through prosperous areas with well-educated landowners able to resist the railway or fight for compensation, and both terminated outside the central area at **Euston** and **Paddington** respectively. In 1846, Parliament decided that no new termini should be built in the centre of London, with the southern boundary of the 'centre' being the Thames, which is why **Charing Cross, Blackfriars** and **Cannon Street** all cling to the north banks of the river. An example of the impact that railways had as they approached the centre of London was the **London & South Western Railway**, which had terminated at Nine Elms because of the difficulty and cost of getting closer. To extend to **Waterloo** in 1854 required the demolition of 700 houses for a much narrower spread of tracks than exists today. The **Great Eastern** extension to **Liverpool Street** built during 1861-64 was passed by Parliament on condition that it ran workmen's trains from Edmonton and Walthamstow at a return fare of 2d (0.8p) per day for the journey of 6-8 miles, and was one of the few to pierce what almost amounted to a surface railway exclusion zone because the final leg of the extension was in tunnel.

Meanwhile, in 1863, at the height of a renewed, and very short-lived, railway boom, the House of Lords Select Committee on Metropolitan Railway Communications looked once again at the concept of a large central terminus for all of the railways, and once again reported against it. The Committee concluded that any new lines within the central area would have to be underground, with the limits placed by the original Royal Commission of 1846 being extended still further out. The concept of an 'inner circle' north of the Thames to link the termini was first mooted, and this was endorsed by the Parliamentary Joint Committee on Railway Schemes (Metropolis). Thus the basis of the **Circle Line** were laid and assured of political support. It might have been even better if the line had managed to touch Euston rather than simply dump passengers with heavy luggage nearby, and also stray south of the Thames to include Waterloo, whose passengers at the time were the most inconvenienced, stuck south of the River Thames. The last terminus in London, the **Great Central Railway's** station at **Marylebone**, had an especially difficult time as the company's extension to London ran through St John's Wood, the residents of which objected, and past Lords, the cricket ground, having burrowed under Hampstead.

The railways undoubtedly contributed much to the further growth and prosperity of London, and without them, the capital would not have been able to expand to its present extent, and by the end of the nineteenth century London was pulling in workers from as far afield as the Sussex Coast. The history of the individual stations, main line railway and underground lines is dealt with separately. Nevertheless, as the century drew to a close, the railway suburban services were suffering from growing competition from the electric street tramways, and it was this that forced the railways to consider **electrification**, initially in the London area this was on the South London line, linking **Victoria** with **London Bridge**, the two termini of the **London, Brighton & South Coast Railway**. It was an instant success and encouraged the railways south of the river to start a rolling programme of electrification, although the **South Eastern & Chatham** plans were delayed by the First World War and not implemented until after **grouping**, when they were changed considerably by the **Southern Railway**. The widespread electrification of first the inner suburban lines and then the outer suburban may well have been the reason why London south of the Thames has been so badly served by the tube network, with only the **Northern Line and District** (see **Metropolitan District**) penetrating to any extent.

The formation of the **London Passenger Transport Board** in 1933 not only brought together all of the underground lines and the capital's bus, tram and trolleybus operations, it also embraced the railways whose suburban revenue within the LPTB area was pooled. Intended from the outset as an integrated road and rail transport organisation for London, the London Passenger Transport Area stretched out as far as Windsor, Guildford, Horsham, Gravesend, Tilbury, Hertford, Luton and Dunstable. Within this area, all suburban railway services were to be coordinated by a Standing Joint Committee consisting of four LPTB members and the four main line railway general managers, and all receipts from the area, less operating costs were to be apportioned between the LPTB and the railways. The **Southern Railway's** share of these receipts was fixed at $25\frac{1}{2}$ per cent, a tribute to the traffic growth generated by its investment in suburban electrification, by this time completed, while at the other end of the scale, with very little suburban traffic, was the Great Western Railway, with just over 1 per cent.

As the tube network grew, the Northern Line in particular took over stretches of suburban branch line for its expansion, but there was no wholesale handover of surface railway until the recent transfer of the London area operations of the train operating company, Silverlink, to Transport for London which is branding the services as 'Overground'. The first completely new tube line to be opened since 1907 did not appear until 1968, with the **Victoria Line**, although this has since been joined by the **Jubilee Line** and the surface **Docklands Light Railway**. Not all of the capital's surface railways were fully utilised over the years, and it has taken privatisation to inject worthwhile services into the **West London Line**.

London & Birmingham Railway

The first major trunk route out of **London**, after several attempts failed, the line was finally authorised in 1833. The initial share capital was £2.5 million for the 112-mile route, with Robert **Stephenson** as engineer. While the original intention was for the line's London terminus to be at Camden, this was later changed to **Euston**. Opened in stages during 1837-38, the line had eight tunnels, of which the most difficult was at Kilsby, south of Rugby and almost $1\frac{1}{2}$-miles long, which suffered from running sand, and deep cuttings at Roade and Tring, but these works avoided any steep gradients other than that between Euston and Camden. Between Euston and Camden, a stationary steam engine hauled trains up the gradient, as steep as 1 in 70 in places, until 1844. A locomotive and carriage works was completed at Wolverton in 1838.

The **Birmingham** terminus was at Curzon Street, where the LBR connected to the **Grand Junction Railway**, providing a through route from London to both **Liverpool** and **Manchester**. In addition to the LBR's own line from Blisworth to Northampton and Peterborough, completed in 1845, there were five branches constructed by companies supported by the LBR: Cheddington-Aylesbury, opened in 1839; Coventry-Warwick, 1844; Bletchley-Bedford, 1846; Leighton Buzzard-Dunstable, 1848; and Rugby-Leamington Spa, 1851.

Meanwhile, the line connected with other

railways. As early as 1839, there was a junction with the **Birmingham & Derby Junction Railway** at Hampton, between Birmingham and Coventry; and in 1840 a junction at Rugby with the **Midland Counties Railway** route from Derby and Leicester. In 1844, these companies merged to form the Midland Railway, and used the LBR for traffic from the East Midlands and the North-East to reach London until the **Great Northern Railway** opened in 1850.

Not all railway relationships were harmonious, and those with the GJR were damaged by the proposed Manchester & Birmingham Railway to provide a shorter route to the LBR. There was also growing competition as the **Great Western** extended its broad gauge lines into the Midlands, gaining an ally in the GJR. Nevertheless, when the LBR invested in the Trent Valley Railway, connecting Rugby with Stafford, the GJR took a 50 per cent stake. Eventually, the GJR and LBR, and the Manchester & Birmingham, all merged to form the **London & North Western Railway** in 1846.

London & Blackwall Railway

Originally authorised in 1836 as the Commercial Railway, the 5ft gauge line linked the Minories, to the east of the City of **London** with Blackwall, with the first 2½ miles of the 3½ mile route being on a viaduct 18ft above street level. An extension to Fenchurch Street was authorised in 1839, the company adopting the London & Blackwall title, and the following year the line opened. The line was worked by cable powered by stationary steam engines to reduce the risk of fire to shipping and cargo in the docks. Each carriage had a brakeman and carriages were slipped and picked up at intermediate stations. It was the first to adopt an even headway service with a train every fifteen minutes. In 1849, the line was converted to standard gauge and steam trac-

tion adopted, while the company connected with the Blackwall Extension Railway, which ran from Stepney Junction to Bow, then the **Eastern Counties Railway**, and in 1856, the line was linked with the **London, Tilbury & Southend Railway** at Gas Factory Junction.

The **Great Eastern Railway** leased the London & Blackwall in 1866 for 999-years.

London & Croydon Railway

Running from **London Bridge** to what is now West Croydon, the line was authorised in 1835 and opened in 1839. Although it had its own terminus at London Bridge, the company used the **London & Greenwich Railway** as far as Corbetts Lane Junction before running along its own lines for the remaining 8¾ miles to Croydon. Originally, it had been intended to use the alignment of the disused Croydon Canal, but this was not suitable.

The LCR lines were used in turn by both the London & Brighton, predecessor of the **London, Brighton & South Coast Railway**, and the South Eastern Railway from 1842. The LCR coped with the growing congestion on its line by installing the first flying junction near Norwood to carry its own trains, by this time using the atmospheric system, over the lines used by the other two companies. Although an extension was authorised to Epsom in 1844 using the atmospheric system, this proved unreliable and was abandoned in 1847, the year after the company amalgamated with the London & Brighton to form the **London, Brighton & South Coast Railway**.

London & Greenwich Railway

Authorised in 1833, the line ran on a brick viaduct 22 ft above street level, partly because of the existing pattern of streets around its terminus at **London Bridge** but also to avoid periodic flooding around Bermondsey. As London's first railway, initially raising the necessary capital proved difficult. Like many lines, it opened in stages between early 1836 and late 1838. An unusual feature was the use of low centre of gravity carriages, with frames just 4in above the track, to avoid carriages falling off the viaduct, which had 4ft 6in walls, while as a further safety measure, the line was gas lit at night. Also unusual, and impractical, initially granite sleepers were set into concrete.

Once opened, this costly 3³/₄ mile line was used first by the **London & Croydon,** then by the London & Brighton and the South Eastern, initially for a toll of 3d per passenger, although this was increased to 4¹/₂d once the viaduct was widened in 1842, over the 1³/₄ miles between Corbetts Lane Junction and London Bridge. Three years later, the line was leased by the SER.

London & North Eastern Railway

Second largest of the 'Big Four' railway companies created by the Railways Act 1921, the London & North Eastern Railway's constituent companies were the **Great Central Railway; Great Eastern Railway; Great North of Scotland Railway; Great Northern Railway; Hull & Barnsley Railway; North Eastern Railway** and the **North British Railway;** while as subsidiaries there were the Brackenhill Light Railway; **Colne Valley & Halstead Railway; East & West Yorkshire Union Railway; East Lincolnshire Railway;** Edinburgh & Bathgate Railway; Forcett Railway; Forth & Clyde Junction Railway; Gifford & Garvald Railway; **Great North of England Railway;** Clarence & Hartlepool Junction Railway; Horncastle Railway; **Humber Commercial Railway & Dock; Kilsyth & Bonnybridge Railway; Lauder Light Railway; London & Blackwall Railway; Mansfield Railway;** Mid-Suffolk Light Railway; Newburgh & North Fife Railway; **North Lindsey Light Railway; Nottingham**

& Grantham Railway; Nottingham Joint Station Committee; **Nottingham Suburban Railway;** Seaforth & Sefton Junction Railway; Stamford & Essendine Railway and the West Riding Railway Committee. Many of the smaller companies were already worked by their larger neighbours, while others had been absorbed during the final year of independence. Before the First World War, the Great Central, Great Northern and Great Eastern had been refused permission to merge.

The LNER was the most heavily dependent on freight traffic of any of the railway companies, and from the outset its markets in the industrial areas of the north and Scotland were in decline, but the miners' strike of 1926 and the accompanying General Strike had a massive impact on coal traffic, not only at the time but afterwards as export markets for British coal were lost for good. Added to this, the chairman, William Whitelaw, was from the NBR, a railway that was notorious for its economy. The net result was that the LNER board and management were cautious, and the company gained a reputation for being 'poor but honest'. The shareholders saw little for their investment in the company, which also suffered from being over-capitalised, and the company paid its management less than did the other companies, even though productivity did improve with employee numbers falling from 207,500 in 1924 to 175,800 in 1937, while more trains were running a higher mileage. One distinct advantage of working for the LNER was that it inherited the NER's Traffic Apprenticeship Scheme, brought by the first chief general manager, Sir Ralph **Wedgwood.**

The LNER board overruled Wedgwood's proposed departmental organisation in favour of strong decentralisation with three areas, **London, York** and **Edinburgh,** each of which had its own divisional general manager and area board. There remained a small cadre of 'all-line' officers, including the chief mechanical engineer, the former GNR Sir Nigel **Gresley**, and chief general manager, whose role was largely one of advising the board, handling policy issues and adjudicating in disputes between divisional general managers.

There was a considerable difference between the operations out of **King's Cross** and those from **Liverpool Street**, and this was also reflected in the difference in treatment between the company's long distance high speed trains and the suburban services. Despite some **electrification** in the north of England, the LNER was primarily a steam railway. A series of attractive high speed locomotives were built for the main services, including the non-stop London-Edinburgh *Flying Scotsman*, *Silver Jubilee*, *Coronation* and *West Riding Limited*, culminating in setting a still unbeaten world speed record for steam of 126mph in 1938. The company served the suburbs of north and east London, which became renowned for being overcrowded and slow, as well as dirty, but nevertheless the LNER achieved much in operating such a high intensity service worked entirely by steam, and with the restrictions on the approaches to Liverpool Street in particular.

Famous for the use of articulation, with adjoining carriages sharing a bogie, on both its expresses and on the suburban services, Gresley initially applied this as a remedy for the poor riding of inherited six-wheel suburban carriages, while it also enabled the maximum number of seats to be included in any given train length. On the high speed expresses, articulation reduced train weight as well as improving the ride.

The LNER competed head on with the **London, Midland & Scottish** for traffic to both **Edinburgh** and **Glasgow**, although it had the advantage on traffic to **Aberdeen**, but it also competed with the LMS on traf-

fic between London and Southend.

Despite the poor prospects for freight traffic, the LNER invested heavily in modern mechanized yards, including Whitemoor in Cambridgeshire and at **Hull**, while fast overnight goods trains were also introduced to counter growing competition from the road haulage industry and to enable perishable goods to get to their markets. Reluctant to borrow and instead heavily dependent on revenue for any investment in new equipment, the company found the ending of the Railway Passenger Duty useful, but it was not until 1933 and the availability of low interest loans from the Treasury that substantial modernisation was planned. Electrification was at last started for the London suburban services into Liverpool Street, and for the heavily used and steeply graded line between Manchester and Sheffield, mainly used for freight, but these schemes were suspended during the Second World War and for the most part were not completed until after **nationalisation**. One reason for the slow completion of these schemes was the decision to use overhead electrification with added engineering works especially with tunnels and overbridges. The inner London suburban services were in the area of the new **London Passenger Transport Board**, which became operational in 1933, with receipts being apportioned between the '**Big Four**' and the LPTB's own railway services.

The company's V2 and V4 locomotives were amongst the best mixed traffic engines available, and ordered by the War Office for service overseas during the Second World War.

Despite the inroad beings made into the railways' continental traffic during the 1930s, the LNER was the only one of the grouped companies not to take an active interest in the development of air transport. It joined the other companies in buying Pickfords and Carter Paterson, while also investing heavily in buying bus companies once the railways were allowed to do so, including United, United Counties, Eastern Counties and Eastern National. It inherited hotels, docks and shipping services from its predecessor companies, and continued to develop these, with modern vessels on its services to the Netherlands.

The LNER suffered badly from enemy action during the Second World War, although not quite as badly as the **Southern**, and was also put under additional pressure to move bulk freight, and especially coal, as the coastal convoys came under attack. Recognising the courage of railwaymen working through the blackout and the blitz, the LNER founded its own medal for acts of heroism. In one case, a burning wagon on an ammunition train was uncoupled from the rest of the train and taken to safety by an engine crew before it blew up, saving the village of Soham in Cambridgeshire from almost certain destruction.

Post-war, the LNER was nationalised, despite offering a 'landlord and tenant' deal, somewhat similar to the current franchising system, to the government. On nationalisation, it was divided amongst the Eastern, North-Eastern and Scottish Regions of the new **British Railways**, the only company to be divided into three.

London & North Western Railway

Formed in 1846 by an amalgamation of the **London & Birmingham, Grand Junction and Manchester & Birmingham** railways, initially it consisted of 247 trunk route miles stretching as far north as Preston, with through running over other lines to Carlisle, while also serving **Liverpool** and **Manchester**. Lacking a regional base and vulnerable to competition, the LNWR immediately set about establishing alliances and also acquiring other lines along its route. The first major alliance was known as the Euston Square Confederacy, formed in 1850, and was a defensive measure against the **Great Northern**. This was followed by the Octuple Agreement, pooling receipts for traffic between London and points north of **York**, which in turn was replaced by the English & Scotch Traffic Agreement which ran from 1859 to 1869, and which gave **Glasgow** traffic to the LNWR's **West Coast** route and that to **Edinburgh** to the **East Coast**.

In the meantime, by 1859 the LNWR had added Cambridge, **Leeds**, Oxford and Peterborough to its network, while also leasing the **Lancaster & Carlisle Railway**, and concluded an alliance with the **Caledonian Railway**, so that the **West Coast Main Line** served not just Glasgow, but also Edinburgh and **Aberdeen**. It had also acquired the **Chester & Holyhead Railway** and the major share of the traffic to Ireland through both Holyhead and Liverpool, where in 1864, the company acquired the dock at Garston, which was enlarged in 1896, mainly for coal to Ireland. Later, it reached the Cumberland coast and started running through mid-Wales and established a cross-country service from Shrewsbury to Swansea and Carmarthen, largely run over its own lines. This was followed by a further cross-country service from Hereford to **Cardiff** and Newport, and acquiring a number of branch lines in South Wales. In the London area, it acquired the **North London Railway** which retained its identity as a subsidiary, and used a number of lines in west London operated jointly with the **Great Western** that enabled it to by-pass the capital and operate through to the south. In 1847, the Trent Valley line opened, by-passing Birmingham, and this was followed by another line in 1864 that by-passed major junctions at Winwick and Golborne, and in 1869, a direct line was opened to Liverpool through Runcorn.

From 1861, all locomotive building was concentrated on **Crewe**, while the works at

Wolverton that had built locomotives for the Southern Division before it was merged with the Northern Division, concentrated on carriage building. Crewe also included a steelworks and produced the company's rails, at the time longer than any other railway in the British Isles at 60ft, helping to provide the smoother ride and high quality permanent way in which the company took such pride. Eventually, almost everything from soap and tickets to signalling equipment was produced 'in-house'.

Crewe became the ultimate company town, with the LNWR providing the services that would normally be provided by a local authority. The chief mechanical engineer from 1871 to 1903, F W Webb, took the existing stock of 2-2-2 and 2-4-0 locomotives, added many more of the latter, and then started to build compound locomotives, and the first 0-8-0 freight locomotives in Britain.

Despite collaboration with the GWR in London, competition developed on traffic to Birmingham and Liverpool. In an attempt to secure its position, the LNWR proposed a merger with the **Midland Railway**, but this failed and further competition resulted when the Midland managed to reach London over the GNR. A planned merger with the **North Staffordshire Railway** also failed. By 1869, there was heavy competition with the MR and later the **Great Central** for Manchester business. This extended to Anglo-Scottish traffic once the Midland completed its **Settle and Carlisle** line in 1875.

A far happier relationship flourished with the **Lancashire & Yorkshire Railway**, despite competition between Liverpool and Manchester, and in 1863 the two companies established a series of traffic pooling agreements. Parliament rejected a merger in 1872, but in 1908 the two companies and the MR agreed to send freight consignments by the shortest route. Freight was important

to the LNWR, and at Liverpool, it operated no less than six goods depots. In 1882, it pioneered gravity-operated marshalling yards at Edge Hill. The mixture of slow freight traffic and fast expresses led the company to quadruple its tracks and when this was not possible provide a double-track alternative, so that by 1914, 89 per cent of the 209 miles between **Euston** and **Preston** was covered in this way, as well as much of the route to Holyhead and to **Leeds**. Flying junctions, of which the first was at Weaver Junction, north of Crewe, also accelerated traffic and reduced conflicting movements.

While the company invested in shipping as well as railways and ports, it did not acquire the mail contract from Holyhead to Ireland until 1920, while previously political considerations had left this with the City of Dublin Steam Packet Company. The LNWR had worked hard for the previous forty years to gain this business, building a new harbour and quays at North Wall, Dublin, as well as building faster ships. The reward in the interval was a major share of cattle and freight traffic across the Irish Sea. Earlier, in an attempt to gain the traffic between Great Britain and Belfast, the company took a majority shareholding in the **Dundalk, Newry & Greenore Railway**, and in 1873 had started a shipping service to Greenore. Perhaps more successful was the joint operation with the LYR from Fleetwood to Belfast and from Stranraer in Scotland to Larne with the Midland, Caledonian and **Glasgow & South Western**.

Despite the length of its trunk route to Scotland, the chairman between 1861 and 1891, Sir Richard Moon, believed that excessive speed used too much coal and argued that 45mph was sufficient. Nevertheless, a step forward in comfort came with bogied carriages in the late 1880s, and these were followed by all-corridor trains for the Scottish services in 1893. With Liverpool the major port for transatlantic traffic at the time, special twelve-wheel carriages were built for the boat trains, but eventually most of the traffic transferred to **Southampton**. Between 1914 and 1922, it electrified, using the fourth rail system favoured by the **Underground Group of Companies**, its suburban services from Euston and Broad Street to Watford, and after **grouping**, these were extended to Rickmansworth.

In the year before the grouping, the LNWR finally merged with the LYR, using the LNWR name, a move intended to strengthen its influence in the eventual grouping in 1923, when the LNWR was one of the three largest railways in the British Isles and contributed 2,066 route miles to the **London Midland & Scottish.**

London & South Western Railway

Largest of the constituent companies that formed the **Southern Railway**, the LSWR had its origins in the London & Southampton Railway, which received Parliamentary approval in 1834, and was opened from Nine Elms to **Southampton** in 1840, by which time the name had been changed to the London & South Western Railway. The new railway set about a vigorous programme of expansion, doubtless anxious to get as far west as possible before any rival appeared. It reached Dorchester in 1847, **Portsmouth** from Eastleigh in 1848, the same year as it also reached Salisbury, and then secured its position as one of the two main routes to the West Country when it reached **Exeter** in 1860. The LSWR had already acquired the Bodmin & Wadebridge Railway in 1847, giving a clear indication of its ambitions, but did not reach **Plymouth** until 1876 and Padstow, the end of the line, until 1899. The London terminus was moved from Nine Elms to **Waterloo** in 1848, recognising that the former was too remote. In the light of the town's subsequent growth, it seems strange that the orig-

inal line westward from **Southampton** to Poole and Dorchester avoided Bournemouth, and it was not until 1888 that the town was served by a direct route.

The variety of services operated by the LSWR was greater than that of the other ancestor companies of the Southern. Like the others, it had its London suburban network, in this case covering the western end of Surrey, part of Middlesex and much of Berkshire, and had a longer distance mainline network extending from Portsmouth to Exeter, but it also had the sprawling network to the west of Exeter which ensured that it was the main railway to serve North Devon and part of North Cornwall. Essentially, after Woking, the Southern split into three main lines, the Portsmouth Direct which branched off at Woking, the Exeter line that branched off at Basingstoke, and then the original Southampton line that eventually went all the way to Weymouth. An important secondary main line served Aldershot and Farnham, and for many years provided an alternative route to Winchester, while the network of lines serving the Thames Valley centred around the Waterloo to Reading line as its core.

Military and naval traffic was important from the start, with the LSWR area including Portsmouth, Portland, Aldershot and also running through Salisbury Plain. The importance of this first became apparent during the Boer War, when all of the traffic for South Africa was shipped through Southampton, where the docks had been acquired in 1892, and again during the First World War, although in this conflict the railways were effectively taken over by the government. In peacetime, it did mean that on the Portsmouth line, for example, heavy weekend and holiday traffic was balanced by a reverse flow of servicemen travelling home on leave or for the weekend, and in later years this was to become one of the most profitable routes in the south. In fact, in retrospect, it seems strange that the LSWR never seemed to accord the Portsmouth line the heavy service that it seemed to deserve, and did not spend more providing easier gradients, leaving the line difficult to work with steam traction and prone to earth slips.

The LSWR had competed with the **London, Brighton & South Coast Railway** for the important London-Portsmouth traffic, with the line through Eastleigh competing with that through Arundel, but the extension of the line from Guildford to create the Portsmouth Direct placed Portsmouth firmly in LSWR territory, but only just in time as the South Eastern had planned a branch to Portsmouth off the line from Redhill to Guildford – the embankment can still be seen to this day just south of the junction for Shalford, but it never carried track. There was competition with the **Great Western** for although the LSWR route to Plymouth was circuitous, as far as Exeter the route was the most direct. The LSWR route to Reading was never as fast as that of the GWR from **Paddington**, although it could be a better bet for those with the City as their ultimate destination. Windsor was another destination served by both companies.

The suburban network was completed in 1885 with what has become known as the 'New Guildford Line', running through Cobham.

One of the greatest achievements of the LSWR, and one for which many passengers have had cause to be grateful over the years, was the construction of flying and borrowing junctions, with a total of seven on the 42 miles west of Raynes Park, although the last of these, Worting Junction, was a Southern achievement. The major omission from this programme, and one that would have saved many conflicting train movements, was the flat junction at Woking, almost certainly

due to space constraints as the town quickly coalesced around the station, and this has always been the Achilles Heel of the South Western main line, with as many as six trains an hour coming off the Portsmouth Direct in addition to those starting from Guildford.

At one time, it was the practice for transatlantic liners to put passengers and mail ashore at Plymouth, saving a day in the journey to London, and the LSWR was spurred on by this to provide fast boat trains to Waterloo. Timings were eased considerably after one of these trains derailed at Salisbury in 1906 in the LSWR's worst **accident**, killing 24 of the 43 passengers on the train.

Shipping services were an important feature of the LSWR's expansion, and here too at first it competed with the GWR, with the LSWR's Channel Island services from Southampton competing with the GWR services from Weymouth, although the LSWR line to the town was the more direct. Eventually, the two companies operated a combined service to the Channel Islands. Southampton also proved the base for a network of ferry services to Le Havre and St Malo, while a Lymington to Yarmouth, **Isle of Wight**, ferry service was also started. At first, because legislation barred the railway companies from operating shipping services directly, services were developed at arm's length through shareholdings in shipping companies, in this case the South Western Steam Navigation Company, formed in 1842, but before the end of the decade railways were allowed to operate shipping services provided that they specified the route, and by 1863 complete freedom was granted.

The LSWR was a profitable railway, paying a dividend of $5\frac{1}{2}$ per cent or more from 1871 onwards. Surprisingly, while mainly a passenger railway, freight, docks and shipping business provided almost 40

Under Midland Railway ownership, the Belfast & Northern Counties Railway became the Northern Counties Committee, an arrangement continued by the LMS after grouping. This 2-6-4T locomotive was built by the LMS for the NCC in 1947, and is in working preservation today. (Irish Steam Railway Preservation Society)

Oliver Bulleid is remembered for his wide-bodied passenger carriages and for his air-smoothed Merchant Navy, Battle of Britain and West Country locomotive classes, but he left after nationalisation, angered by the rebuilding of his locomotives. (NRM 119/97)

When first opened in 1900, the Central London Railway, predecessor of today's Central Line, used electric locomotives to haul its trains, as well as overhead wires in the sidings, but the locomotives caused vibration in buildings along the route. (London Transport Museum)

They were replaced by Britain's first multiple unit trains in 1903, the ancestor of the modern tube train, using the third rail system in the tunnels until modernised and converted to the standard London third and fourth rail system in the late 1930s. (London Transport Museum)

Churchward was chief mechanical engineer for the Great Western before and after grouping and built Britain's first Pacific locomotive, *The Great Bear*, although he is supposed never to have liked it and later converted it to a Castle-class 4-6-0. He also built 70-ft long carriages renowned for their comfort. (NRM 2086/76)

Double-deck trains seem an obvious way to carry more passengers without lengthening platforms, but the British loading gauge imposes limitations of its own. This is one of Bulleid's two experimental double-deck electric multiple units, showing how upper and lower deck compartments were interleaved. (NRM 548/83)

An interior shot shows just how passenger accommodation was compromised with low headroom: in the foreground the steps to the upper level can just be seen. Ventilation on the upper deck was another problem. (NRM 58/98)

The East Coast Main Line was developed by three different companies, the Great Northern, North Eastern and the North British, later joined by the Midland, but collaboration ensured seamless end to end running and later its own dedicated passenger rolling stock. This is a 1922 advertisement. (Bradshaw)

SCOTLAND and CORNWALL

calling at Principal Towns in the NORTH, MIDLANDS and SOUTH WEST.

RESTAURANT AND SLEEPING CARS.

	Page	a.m.	p.m.			a.m.
ABERDEEN	784 dep.	9 45	12 50	PENZANCE ...... dep.		11 0
Dundee	784 "	11 41	2 53			p.m.
		noon		Truro	"	12 6
Glasgow (Queen St.)	791 "	12 0	4 0	Par	"	12 47
Edinburgh	778, 779 "	1 30	5 15	Plymouth (North Rd)	"	2 0
Newcastle	732 "	4 20	8 3	Newton Abbot	"	2 55
Sunderland	732 "	3 39	7 10	Exeter (St. David's)	"	3 27
West Hartlepool	732 "	3 20	6 50	Taunton	"	4 12
Middlesboro'	732 "	4 33	8 13	Bristol (Temple M'ds)	"	5 00
Darlington	732 "	5 15	8 59	Swindon	"	6 15
Scarboro'	758 "	4 50	8 5	Oxford	"	7 7
York	669 "	6 25	10 3	Banbury	"	7 42
Hull	698, 700 "	5 5	3 8*40	Rugby	arr.	8 15
Sheffield (G. C.)	698, 700 "	7 36	10§25	Leicester (Cen.)	"	8 38
			a.m.	Nottingham (Vic.)	"	9 11
Nottingham (Vic.)	698, 700 "	8 31	12 33	Sheffield (G.C.)	"	10 4
Leicester (Cen.)	698, 700 "	9 4	1 28	Hull	"	1 36
Rugby	698, 700 "	9 20	1 56	York	"	11 13
Banbury	699, 701 arr.	10 0	2 33			
Oxford	82, 80 "	10 33	3 25			a.m. a.m.
Swindon	15, 12 "	11 30	4 35	Scarboro'	"	5 55 10 7
		a.m.		Darlington	"	2 3 2 3
Bath	15, 12 "	12 35	5 26	Middlesboro'	"	5 45 5 49
Bristol (Temple M.)	15, 12 "	12 57	5 52	West Hartlepool	"	5 35 5 35
Taunton	15, 12 "	2 0	7 42	Sunderland	"	5 28 6 11
Exeter (St. David's)	22 "	2 46	8 38	Newcastle	"	1 9 3 59
Newton Abbot	22 "	3 23	9 52	Edinburgh	"	3 50 6 6
Plymouth (North Rd.)	22 "	4 25	10 40	Glasgow (Queen St.)	"	5 30 9 35
Par	22 "	5 40	11§27	Dundee	"	5 31 9 16
Truro	22 "	6 18	12 43	ABERDEEN	"	7 30 11 22
PENZANCE	22 "	7 40	1 20			

A Arrives later on Sundays. B Sundays excepted. D By slip carriage to Swindon.
* Via Selby and Pontefract. ‡ Via Newcastle. § Via Rotherham and Masboro.

EDINBURGH & NEWCASTLE AND SOUTHAMPTON & BOURNEMOUTH

RESTAURANT CAR SERVICE.

	Page	a.m.	a.m.			a.m.
EDINBURGH	778 dep.	....	10 15	BOURNEMOUTH (W.) dep.		11 50
Newcastle	731 "	8 0	1 6	" (Cen.)	"	12 3
Sunderland	731 "	7 20	12 30	Southampton (Town)	"	7 35 p.m.
Durham	731 "	8 24	12 37	" (West)	"	12 53
West Hartlepool	731 "	7 40	12 5	Eastleigh	"	7 54 1 8
Middlesboro'	731 "	7 52	12 22	Winchester (L.&S.W.)	"	8 16 1 24
Darlington	731 "	9 0	1 38	Oxford	"	10 50 3 15
Scarboro'	758 "	8 20	1 55	Banbury	"	11 25 3 48
York	669 "	10 13	3 0	Rugby	arr.	11 57 4 23
Hull	696, 698 "	9 0	1 55	Leicester (Cen.)	"	12 21 4 45
Sheffield (G.C.)	696, 698 "	11 45	4 17	Nottingham (Vic.)	"	12 57 5 19
Nottingham (Vic.)	696, 698 "	12 39	5 15	Sheffield (G.C.)	"	1 51 6 15
Leicester (Cen.)	696, 698 "	1 16	5 58	Hull	"	3 50 8 11
Rugby	696, 698 "	1 41	6 35	York	"	3 24 7 45
Banbury	697, 699 arr.	2 12	7 24	Scarboro'	"	4 37 9 2
Oxford	81, 82 "	2 48	8 0	Darlington	"	5 10 9 40
Winchester (LSW)	127, 128 "	4 39	10 7	Middlesboro'	"	6 9 10 4
Eastleigh	127, 128 "	4 52	10 23	West Hartlepool	"	5 9 9 39
Southampton (West)	127 "	5 10	....	Durham	"	6 5 10 21
" (Town)	128 "	....	10 46	Newcastle	"	5 35 10 5
BOURNEMOUTH (C.)	135, 136 "	6 13	2 0	EDINBURGH	"	8 45

C In connection at Southampton with Steamers to Havre and Channel Islands.
e Through Carriage, Southampton and Glasgow. Restaurant Car Express, Oxford and Scarborough. F Winchester (Cheesehill).

NEWCASTLE, &c., AND CARDIFF, SWANSEA, AND PRINCIPAL TOWNS IN MIDLANDS AND WEST OF ENGLAND.

RESTAURANT CAR SERVICE.

NEWCASTLE	Page 731 dep.	9 30 a.m.	SWANSEA (High St.) dep.		7 30 a.m.
Sunderland	731 "	9 13 "	Neath	"	7 48 "
Durham	731 "	9 57 "	PortTalbot&Aberavon	"	7 59 "
West Hartlepool	731 "	9 25 "	Bridgend	"	8 23 "
Middlesboro'	731 "	9 48 "	Barry Docks	"	9 2 "
Darlington	731 "	10 35 "	Cardiff (General)	"	9 35 "
York	669 "	11 45 "	Newport	"	9 55 "
Hull	696 "	10 50 "	Chepstow	"	10 24 "
Sheffield (G.C.)	696 "	1 0 p.m.	Gloucester	"	11 2 "
Nottingham (Vic.)	696 "	1 55 "	Cheltenham (South)	"	11 16 "
Leicester (Cen.)	696 "	2 28 "	Banbury	"	12 43 p.m.
Rugby	696 "	2 53 "	Rugby	arr.	1 16 "
Banbury	697 arr.	3 26 "	Leicester (Cen.)	"	1 33 "
Cheltenham (South)	104 "	4 53 "	Nottingham (Vic.)	"	2 9 "
Gloucester	104 "	5 4 "	Sheffield (G.C.)	"	5 4 "
Chepstow	70 "	5 50 "	Hull	"	5 31 "
Newport	70 "	6 16 "	York	"	4 15 "
Cardiff (General)	70 "	6 40 "	Darlington	"	5 45 "
Barry Docks	113 "	7 15 "	Middlesboro'	"	6 34 "
Bridgend	62 "	7 55 "	West Hartlepool	"	7 46 "
PortTalbot&Aberavon	62 "	8 16 "	Durham	"	6 20 "
Neath	62 "	8 28 "	Sunderland	"	7 39 "
SWANSEA (High St.)	62 "	8 45 "	NEWCASTLE	"	6 45 "

Nor were services between London and Scotland the sole aim, as Edinburgh and Newcastle were linked to the South Coast and South Wales, and with Truro and Penzance in Cornwall, something which later saw close collaboration between the LNER and the GWR. (Bradshaw)

Although the speed record was unofficial, later verification suggests that the GWR 4-4-0 locomotive, *City of Truro*, really was the first to run at more than 100 mph. She was also amongst the first to be preserved at York, seen there in 1938. (HMRS ACW234)

The supreme accolade for any locomotive designer must be to have one of his creations named after him, and this is Sir Nigel Gresley with the eponymous A4 locomotive. (NRM DON/313)

Even during the 1930s, Britain's railways were being challenged by their European, and especially German, counterparts in terms of high speed scheduled services, but the speed record of 126 mph set by Gresley's famous A4 Pacific *Mallard*, remains unbroken by a steam engine. (HMRS AEU 528)

Many years later, the Inter-City 125 or High Speed Train, also set a world speed record for diesel traction, which remains unbroken. (GNER/Rail Images)

An engraving showing the London & Blackwall Railway shortly after its opening. It reputedly ran over 700 arches. The carriages were low-slung to prevent them toppling over the viaduct. (London Transport Museum)

'Lynton for Lynmouth', the country-end of the Lynton & Barnstaple narrow gauge railway, one of the very few lines to be closed by the Southern Railway. (HMRS AAC127)

Sir James Milne guided the Great Western through the difficult years of the Second World War, and afterwards wisely decided to retire rather than work for the nationalised railway. (NRM 446/62)

...parse population has always made railway operation in Ireland less profitable than in ...Britain, which is one reason why this Great Southern & Western Railway locomotive ...ned in service from 1879 until 1964, serving the GSWR's successor, the Great Southern ...ays after Irish grouping in 1925, and finally, CIE. (Irish Steam Railway Preservation Society)

...e many railways, the Great Western was very concerned about branch line service, and ...attempt to improve their appeal and their economics, introduced a fleet of diesel ...rs, such as this. These were also expected to improve competition with local bus ...es. (HMRS M20002)

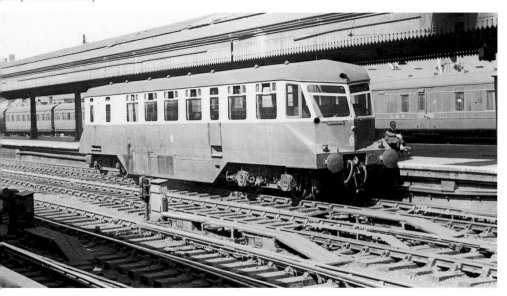

The most obvious aspect to the public of the railways involvement in shipping was their ferry services. At the top end of these was the Southern Railway's ferry *Canterbury*, an all first-class ship devoted solely to the passengers of the 'Golden Arrow' Pullman train and its French counterpart, the *Fleche d'Or*. (NRM BTC collection 305/59)

The Southern Railway created the world's largest electrified system, with most of the work completed between grouping and the outbreak of the Second World War. This is Guildford in August 1939, with trains running to London Waterloo, left via Cobham, centre, on the direct line with an up fast from Portsmouth Harbour running via Woking, and right, via Aldershot and Ascot. (NRM Box 512)

Sir William Stanier standing beside his locomotive No.10000, an early attempt at streamlining, in 1930. Later, this number was used for the prototype LMS diesel-electric locomotive. (SCM 11502/74)

Train Ferry to the Continent
LONDON—PARIS

THROUGH SLEEPING CARS
(1st and 2nd Class)
WITHOUT CHANGE EN ROUTE
via
DOVER — DUNKERQUE
EVERY NIGHT IN EACH DIRECTION.

TRAIN FERRY STEAMERS:—

"TWICKENHAM FERRY," "HAMPTON FERRY," "SHEPPERTON FERRY"

		p.m.				p.m.
LONDON (Victoria)	dep.	10 0	PARIS (Nord)	dep.	9.50	
						a.m.
Dover Marine	arr.	11 36	Dunkerque (Ferry Berth) ... { arr.	1.30		
		a.m.	{ dep.	2.0		
Dover (Ferry Berth)	dep.	12 35	Dover (Ferry Berth)	arr.	6 15	
Dunkerque (Ferry Berth) ... { arr.	4.30	Dover Marine	dep.	7 20		
{ dep.	5.15					
PARIS (Nord)	arr.	9.0	LONDON (Victoria)	arr.	9 10	

Restaurant Car, London to Dover and vice versa.   Buffet Car, Dunkerque to Paris and back.

Customs and Passport Examinations in the Train.

For Tickets and full information apply to :—
CONTINENTAL ENQUIRY OFFICE
VICTORIA STATION, LONDON, S.W. 1, or to any S.R. Travel Agency.
SOUTHERN RAILWAY

The most ambitious of the ferries were the train ferries that carried the Southern Railway's through sleeping car service from London Victoria to Paris Nord, 'without change en route' as the advertisement in *Bradshaw* states. (Bradshaw)

One of the greatest father and son partnerships ever was that of George Stephenson, pictured, and his son Robert, but the working relationship came under strain as the father failed to keep in step with developments. (NRM BTC 643/56)

Like his father, Robert Stephenson worked closely with Hudson, the 'Railway King'. (NRM BTC 255/69)

LONDON AND NORTH WESTERN AND CALEDONIAN RAILWAYS.

WEST COAST ROUTE TO and FROM

SCOTLAND.

Shortest Route to and from GLASGOW.

CORRIDOR, LUNCHEON, DINING, AND SLEEPING CARS.

COMMENCING JULY 10th, 1922. Week Days. | **Sun. ngt & Mon. mrn.**

STATIONS.	h mrn	g mrn	mrn	mrn	aft	a aft	a att	b aft	b aft	aft	mrn	b aft	d aft	d aft	a aft	aft	aft	aft	aft
London (Euston) ......dep		5 0	6 45	10 0		1 30		7 30	9 20	11 0		11 0	11 0	1140	11 45	7 40	9 30	11 0	1140
Birmingham (New St.) "	3 j 0	7 15	9 10	11 0	12 15	2 50		8 20	10 50			12 25	6 50	10 15					
Liverpool { Lime Street "			h					1040		12 45	12 45	1245			9 V 0	12 45			
{ Exchange.. "	9 47	9 47	12 40		3 20		5 8			1750	1 50				1 40		1 50		
Manchester { Exchange "							5 0	1055		1 10	1 10	1 10			1115	1 10			
{ Victoria. "	9 40	9 40	12 30	aft	aft	3 0		mrn	mrn				mrn		2 55			mrn	mrn
Carlisle..............arr.	1245	1 19	3 25	3 58	4 9	6 25	7 44	8 27	1 40	2 14	4 0	5 0	5 16	5 33	6 40	6 20	2 14	4 46	5 16	6 40
	aft																		
Edinburgh (Princes St.)arr.	3 20	4 5	6 0		6 30	9X18	10 10	11 0				8 0	8 15		9 0		8 0		
Glasgow (Central)..... "	3 20	4 22	6 5	6 30		9X15	10 10	11 0	6 55	7 40		8 0	9 35	9 0		7 16		9 35
Greenock (Central)..... "	4Q38	5 28	7 25	7 25		10 37	11Y31		7?55	8R48		9 15	1030		8 48			1030
Gourock................ "	4Q52	5 41	7 39	7 39		10 51	11Y45		8F10	9 H 0		9 20	1042		9 0			1042
Oban .... "	9 55				4 44	4 44		9 55	9 55		2 50			9 55		2 50			
Perth .... "	5 37		8 10		12 35	1235	5 55	5 35		9 12	9 37		5 35		9 12			
Dundee (West)........ "	7 22		8 58				C6 50	6 30		10 5	1022		6 50		10 5			
Dunkeld............... "	8 6				2F42	F4	6 21	6 21		10 6			6 21		10 6			
Inverness via Dunk'ld "				6F0	6F0	9 25	1015		4 42			9 40		4 42				
ABERDEEN .... "	9 5		10 35		3 0	3 0	7 40	7 40		11 50	1155		7 40		11 50			
Ballater............... "							9 45	9 45		5 0			9 45		5 0			
Inverness via Aberd'n "					8F56	8F5	1155	1155		6 21			1155		6 21			

Week Days. | Sun. from Scotland.

STATIONS	mrn	mrn	mrn	mrn	mrn a	aft	aft	mrn	aft	aft	aft	b	d	aft	aft	mrn	aft	aft
Inverness via Aberd'n dep.							7 40	b	b	1250	1250	b	d					
Ballater............... "					6 50		9 55			3 35	3 35					1 10		
ABERDEEN .... "			6 30	9 30		12 30	aft			7 30	7 45							
Inverness via Dunk'ld "	h	b	h	1120	aft 8 10	a	a	10 30	mrn		4 30		4 30		a			
Dunkeld............... "			7 51	mrn 10 6			1 10	aft		T								
Dundee (West)........ "			8 0	mrn 1110			2 25	mrn	7 5	9 0	9 15				3 0			
Perth .... "			7 51	mrn 1150			3 25		9 10	9 45	10 0				3 50			
Oban .... "			5 40	mrn 8 45			11 45	mrn	5 30		5 30							
Gourock............... "	8 20	8 20			1145	2 50	3 50	aft 8 0		9 5	9 59	59 5			3 15			
Greenock (Central)..... "	8 32	8 32			1155	2 59	4 1	8 11		9 15	9 15	9 15	9 15		3 24			
Glasgow (Central)..... "	10 0	1010			1 30	4 10	5 30	9 30		1030	1110	1110	1110	10 0	5 30		1030	
Edinburgh (Princes St.) "	10 0			1010	1 30	4 10	5 30	9 20		1030		mrn	10 0	5 30		1030	
Carlisle..............arr.	12 0	12 14	1232	1252	3 38	3 48	6 50	8 23	12 5	11 10	1 0	1 25	1 56	1 50	2 8	1235	8 20	1 0	mrn
	aft		aft	a		aft	aft	aft			mrn	mrn	mrn		mrn			mrn
Manchester { Exchange arr.					7 27	7 27	1036						5 50	6 5				
{ Victoria.. "	3 35		3 50	4 35	7 2		1035	12 18							4 15			
Liverpool { Lime St.... "								12 45										
{ Exchange.. "	3 25		3 45	4 43	7 5	7 5	1025						6 06	15	12 25			
Birmingham (New St.) "	5 17		6 40		9 45		2 15				6 52	7 11		7 23	2 15	6 13		
London (Euston) .... "	6 30		7 30		1030		5 0	6 55	7 40	7 30	8 0	8 20		7 30	5 0	7 30		

SLEEPING SALOONS ON NIGHT TRAINS.

a CORRIDOR, DINING, AND REFRESHMENT CAR EXPRESS.   **b** Not on Saturday nights.   **d** Saturday night and Sunday morning.   **F** No connecting Trains to these Stations on Sunday mornings.   **g** Corridor, Luncheon, and Tea Car Express.   **h** Luncheon Car Express.   **j** Leaves Birmingham 3 10 mrn. on Mondays.   **q** On Saturdays arrives Greenock 5 31 aft. and Gourock 5 45 aft.   **R** On Sundays arrives Greenock 9 15 and Gourock 9 29 mrn.   **s** Saturdays only.   **T** Calls at Dunkeld when required to pick up passengers. Notice to be given at the Station.   **V** Via Newton-le-Willows.   **X** On Saturdays arrives Edinburgh 9 23 aft., and Glasgow 9 20 aft.   **Y** On Wednesdays and Saturdays arrives Greenock 11 42 aft. and Gourock 11 56 aft.   **Z** Sunday mornings excepted.

ARTHUR WATSON, General Manager, L. & N. W. Railway.
DONALD A. MATHESON, General Manager, Caledonian Railway.

July, 1922.

The West Coast Main Line was another joint venture, although just the London & North Western and the Caledonian Railways were involved in this 1922 timetable, when corridor carriages were still something to boast about. (Bradshaw) per cent of turnover by 1908. Innovation included the first track circuits between Woking and Basingstoke installed between 1902 and 1907. While not a fast railway overall, the LSWR did have some fine locomotives from 1878 onwards with a growing degree of standardisation under a succession of chief mechanical engineers, CMEs, including **Adams, Drummond** and **Urie.** Nevertheless, it was not until Herbert **Walker** was poached from the **London & North Western** to become the LSWR's last general manager in 1912, that suburban electrification started, including the rebuilding of Waterloo, until that time a collection of four stations built at different times to cope piecemeal with expansion, so that this had the distinction of becoming the first major railway terminus in the world built for an electric railway. In 1922, the LSWR completed a new marshalling yard at Feltham, with electrically-controlled points and hump shunting.

The LSWR operated a number of joint lines, but the most important of these was the **Somerset & Dorset Line,** which the company acquired in partnership with the **Midland Railway** in 1875, much to the anger of the GWR which had its eyes on this important cross-country route that linked the South Coast with the West Country and provided a good through route to the Midlands and North West. In 1907, it also acquired the **Waterloo & City Railway,** completed in 1898, helping to ease the isolation of Waterloo by giving a through non-stop direct link with the City of London, taking passengers to just outside the Bank of England. Waterloo's position was also helped by the completion of the **Bakerloo** and **Hampstead** (now the Northern Line) tubes in 1906 and 1926 respectively. One final acquisition before grouping was the **Lynton & Barnstaple Railway,** a 2ft narrow-gauge line providing an important link across a sparely popu-

lated part of North Devon, but which, ironically, was to be one of the few closures during the Southern's reign.

In 1922, the LSWR operated 862 miles, and was involved in joint ventures that covered a further 157 miles.

London Bridge

The oldest of the London termini, London Bridge grew in a haphazard way, a situation not helped by being used by two railway companies with an uneasy relationship since **Waterloo** also grew piece by piece, but benefited greatly from the massive rebuilding of 1910-1920 that created an elegant and functional station.

In 1832 a 3½ mile railway, the **London & Greenwich,** was planned between Greenwich and Tooley Street, close to London Bridge. This set the fashion for many of the railways in the area by being built on a brick viaduct with 878 arches, creating a valuable investment income from the business premises and stables developed within the arches, and allowing the line to travel easily over the roads in this built up area. The first section of the new line was ready on 8 February 1836 between Spa Road, Bermondsey, and Deptford, making the former London's first terminus although, of course, purely a temporary one. The line was opened to the first London Bridge Station on 14 December 1836, with a grand opening attended by the Lord Mayor of London, even though it was outside his jurisdiction, the Common Council and sheriffs and around 2,000 guests. The grandeur of the opening was in stark contrast to the reality of the station, which was basically little more than the end of the viaduct, with low platforms and with the railway offices and booking offices below. The railway only ran as far as Deptford and it was not to reach Greenwich until 1838. Plans for a triumphal arch at the entrance to this crude station were never fulfilled. Yet, the new railway was not short of ambition, and had bought more land than it needed with the London Bridge end of the viaduct able to take eight roads. The LGR saw potential in allowing other railway companies to reach London through using its terminus. The first of these was the **London & Croydon Railway**, authorised in 1835, which joined the Greenwich line at Corbett's Lane, Bermondsey, and then ran to London Bridge, paying the then not inconsiderable sum to the LGR of 3d (1.25p) per passenger carried. A similar arrangement was proposed for the South Eastern Railway which would effectively extend the London & Croydon to Redhill and **Dover**.

While the LCR had to operate over the LGR's tracks, it had its own three road platforms immediately to the north of the LGR's terminus at London Bridge when it opened on 5 June 1839. This station obviously had the SER's needs in mind as it was far beyond the needs of the initial service of twelve trains daily. The LCR station was a grander development than that of the LGR, with a train shed 170ft long and 48ft wide, but again the booking office was in the street below, with the unusual refinement of separate staircases for first and second class passengers. A small goods station was also provided.

The LCR facilities were also to be shared with the new **London, Brighton & South Coast Railway**, but Parliament insisted on additional tracks on the Greenwich viaduct, preferring widening of an existing route to a new construction. It also persuaded the LGR and LCR to swap stations so that the LCR, SER and LBSC would not have to cross its tracks.

The additional lines into London Bridge were ready on 10 May 1842, although the first sections of the Brighton line had been opened since 12 July 1841. On 26 May, 1842, SER trains began to operate into the new station from Tonbridge. The new joint station was not ready until February 1844, and was operated by the Brighton, Croydon & Dover Joint Station Committee. Had it not been overtaken by later expansion, it could have been an attractive station, with a two storey frontage with a booking office and waiting rooms on the ground floor while the station offices were in a separate building. There were three train sheds, one on the site of the old LGR station with another two, one for arrivals and the other for departures, each with two platforms and three tracks. Access to a four road carriage shed was by traversers. Platforms varied between 240ft in the old LGR station now intended for the North Kent Railway, to 338ft for the main departure platform and 531ft for the main arrival platform.

The LGR, ever keen to make an extra penny out of its strategic position, now demanded 4½d (1.875p) per passenger, forcing the LCR with its short journeys to refuse to carry third class passengers between New Cross and London Bridge, while also considering introducing a horse bus service between New Cross Station and London Bridge. A slightly more practical measure was the construction of a new terminus for the LCR and SER at Bricklayers' Arms, which opened on 1 May 1844. The new station had one big advantage in that there was enough room to expand the goods facilities and also introduce those for sheep and cattle. The new station meant that the LGR lost its toll revenue, while the LCR at last felt free to introduce an hourly service, and was able to charge less than it had for trains to London Bridge. This had the desired results, forcing the LGR to charge more reasonable tolls and at different levels to reflect the fare paid, while the LCR responded by standardising fares and frequencies to both termini until it realised that London Bridge was the more attractive destination for its customers and pulled passenger traffic out of Bricklayers' Arms, which became a goods-only station.

Named after a nearby coaching inn, Bricklayers' Arms was neat and compact rather than grand: it had greater potential as a goods terminus than as a passenger one, being even further from the West End and City than London Bridge.

The SER agreed to take over the running of the LGR on lease from 1 January 1845, and this arrangement continued so that the LGR was one of the companies acquired by the **Southern** in 1923.

London Bridge then became the focus of one of the many inter-company squabbles that so marred the early development of the railways. The joint station was far too small for the SER and LBSC, but no attempt was made to create an enlarged joint station that might have worked as a cohesive whole. The SER built a boundary wall and established a new terminus on the north side of the site, with a three storey building at the street end with a canopy supported by iron pillars to provide shelter for travellers boarding or alighting from cabs. The main building was joined by another stretching down the approach road and dividing it from Tooley Street, with shops on Tooley Street and further shops and refreshment rooms on the approach side.

Inside the main building, were separate booking offices for the Greenwich, North Kent and **Dover** lines, with the Greenwich lines using the narrow shed built for the LCR as their station, and immediately adjoining these to the south was the station for the North Kent lines, with two platforms providing an arrival and departure road which were separated by a road used as a siding for rolling stock. Then, to the south of this, was the 'Dover Station' of similar layout, with its own single span roof and actually sitting on the site of the original 1836 station. The SER and LBSC had

come to a truce, allowing each company toll free running rights over key sections of the other's territory, with occasional exceptions. The SER's willingness to accommodate the LBSC could not disguise the fact that the available facilities were inadequate, so the Brighton company built its own new station to the south of the boundary wall, and by 1854, a three storey building with an Italianate frontage was completed. It had a number of features in common with the SER building, including a flat roof and a canopy, although the latter was replaced in the mid-1880s by a glass shed extending over part of the station yard. It was only half complete when the Great Exhibition of 1851 produced a tremendous upsurge in traffic. In 1860, the LBSC had established a second London terminus at **Victoria**, and on 13 August 1866, the South London Line was opened via Denmark Hill to connect the two termini and also serve the densely populated area between them. This required three more approach roads into London Bridge, one for Victoria trains and two for inbound traffic. Three additional platforms were also added at this time, giving the LBSC station a total of nine.

Despite its location, London Bridge was a success commercially, with the Commons Select Committee on Metropolitan Communications reporting in 1855 that the number of passengers using the two stations had risen from 5.5 million in 1850 to 10 million in 1854. Nevertheless, all was not well, and certainly not good enough, for Sir Joseph Paxton told the committee that it took longer to travel from London Bridge to the GWR terminus at **Paddington** than to travel from London Bridge to **Brighton**.

The extensions to **Cannon Street** and **Charing Cross** required substantial changes to London Bridge, making it a through station with a route for the through roads on the north side of the SER station, but the shopping arcade on the approach road had to be demolished and replaced by a railway viaduct which led on to a girder bridge carrying the line over the station approach. The line then had almost immediately to swing south-west to avoid Southwark Cathedral, taking it into the grounds of St Thomas Hospital. In constructing the extension, the original Greenwich Station disappeared, and the lines leading to it were raised on a viaduct to provide a high level station with five platforms, two for down traffic and three for up traffic. The high level station started to handle Greenwich and Mid-Kent trains from 11 January 1864, and was opened for all lines on 1 May.

The two new termini satisfied the SER's traffic demands for the time-being. The LBSC meanwhile saw its traffic continue to increase and put pressure on its station, but expansion in the 1870s was rejected because of the cost. Instead, tracks were re-arranged and signalling improved to get the maximum capacity out of the limited space, and by re-arranging the approaches to the platforms, many of which were extended, so that these could be used both for arrivals and departures. The cab road was shortened to allow the construction of two more short platforms. To increase capacity at London Bridge for passengers, the Continental Goods depot was moved in 1899 to Ewer Street, Southwark, on the Charing Cross extension line, and four low level terminal platforms were constructed between the LBSCR station and the high level viaduct, with canopies replacing the old depot's wooden roof, and these platforms were ready for use from 2 June 1902, initially numbered separately as 1 to 4. A further benefit for passengers came with the **City & South London** tube on 25 February 1900, although it was not until 2 December 1901 that lifts were available, and this made London Bridge just a little less remote. There were further changes at the turn of the century following the joint working of

the SER and LCDR, with the new SECR providing two more tracks on the north side of the approach viaduct.

Even these arrangements were far from permanent, with the LBSCR up main resignalled for reversible working on 19 October 1909 ready for the **electrification** of the South London Line. This also relieved the congestion on the SECR down main, which in 1912 was carrying fourteen LBSCR and five SECR trains between 17.00 and 18.00. Meanwhile, electrification started on 1 December 1909 with the South London Line using the 6,600 V ac system with overhead wires, described somewhat confusingly by today's standards as the 'elevated electric', with the six most southerly platforms in the LBSC station electrified, a clear indication of the company's intention to proceed with electrification on a grand scale. The next phases of electrification were completed during 1912, with services to Crystal Palace Low Level via Tulse Hill on 1 March, and to Streatham and Victoria via Tulse Hill on 1 June. What today would be described as the 'sparks effect' showed a tremendous increase in activity, with the pre-electrification services into the Brighton station running at 663 trains a day, but rising to 901 in 1912.

London Bridge was spared any damage from air raids during the First World War. The bringing together of the companies operating trains across the whole length of Southern England resulted in the creation of an opening in the wall between the former LBSCR and SECR stations, but this had to wait until 1928 as did a second footbridge over the low level to expedite movement across the station as now more than ever, it was realised that many arriving off the Brighton trains needed to continue their journey to Cannon Street, Charing Cross or Waterloo. The platforms were re-numbered in a single consecutive sequence 1 to 22 from north to south, with the omission of any platform 5, although there was a fifth road for light engine movements between the tracks served by platforms 4 and 6. Platforms 1 and 2 are believed to have been the first in London to have had the benefit of a loudspeaker system when this was installed as an experiment in 1927.

The initial electrification of what was now the Eastern Section of the Southern Railway saw third-rail electrification of services running through London Bridge to Addiscombe, Beckenham Junction, Bromley North, Hayes and Orpington from 28 February 1926, with services to Dartford via Blackheath, Bexleyheath and Sidcup all electrified on 6 June, although full services were not operated until 19 July. Services to Caterham and Tattenham Corner on the Central Section were electrified from 25 March 1928, with a full service from 17 June. This was accompanied by conversion of the Brighton overhead to third rail, with the services to Crystal Palace (Low Level) switching on 25 March 1928, and those to Victoria via the South London Line, Crystal Palace via Tulse Hill, Coulsdon North, Epsom Downs via West Croydon, Streatham Hill, Selhurst and Sydenham, were also on the dc system from 17 June, while on 3 March, 1929, third rail also covered services to Dorking North and Effingham Junction via Mitcham.

These changes also necessitated changes to the working of the approach tracks, and in 1936, the locomotive turntable opposite the ends of what were by now platforms 15 and 16 was removed, leaving the few remaining steam locomotives working the Kent Coast and Hastings trains to turn at New Cross Gate sheds.

The Southern next turned its attention to the South Coast, where many of its longer distance trains operated at peak period frequencies that rivalled some suburban lines. Platforms 14 and 15 were lengthened to 800ft. As an interim measure, electric trains started to operate to Reigate and Three Bridges from 17 July 1932, but on 1 January 1933, main line electric trains operated from London Bridge to Brighton and West Worthing. Seaford and Hastings via Eastbourne services followed on 7 July 1935, and from 3 July 1938, those to Littlehampton and Bognor, the latter reached by the Portsmouth No2 Electrification Scheme.

As the Second World War approached, London Bridge handled 250,000 passengers daily, although of these, 80,000 were on the trains continuing through to the City and West End. The station handled 2,407 railway movements daily, and in the morning peak hour received 94 trains, of which 46 terminated while 29 continued to Cannon Street and another 19 to Charing Cross. The war brought air raids, and the railways were a prime target because of their strategic importance. On 9 December 1940, the signal box had a parachute mine settle against its wall with its parachute caught on a signal, and displaying great heroism, the three signalmen continued working while a naval officer and a rating defused the mine. On the night of 29/30 December 1940, the station, while not in the City shared in the massive raid using incendiary bombs, and at 00.27, the upper floors of the station buildings were gutted by fire, which also destroyed many station offices. In an attempt to get the station working again, a wooden temporary ticket office was sited on the main concourse.

Post-**nationalisation**, London Bridge was badly neglected by **British Railways** for several decades, even leaving the wooden ticket office functioning. The only substantial changes for some thirty years were those associated with the spread of electrification to the Kent Coast. It took **London Transport** until 1967 to replace the lifts for the underground station with escalators.

London, Brighton & South Coast Railway

Railways had come to the South of England early. The Surrey Iron Railway had been authorised by Parliament in 1801 as the world's first public railway running from the banks of the River Thames at Wandsworth to Croydon, some 8¼ miles, following the course of the River Wandle. The track consisted of cast-iron plates of L-section fixed to stone blocks, with a gauge of 4ft 2in. Traction was provided by horses, which because of the lack of any substantial gradient could move five or six wagons, each weighing 3½ tons fully loaded, at around 2½mph. The line was supported by the many mills and factories spread along its route, showing that some at least of London's urban sprawl pre-dated the arrival of the railways. The promoters of the line were keen to see it extended to Portsmouth, but only succeeded in extending the tracks as far as the quarry at Merstham, a further 8½ miles. Part of its route was later to be used by the London Brighton & South Coast Railway.

The LBSC, or the 'Brighton' as it was commonly known, first appeared in 1846 on the amalgamation of the **London & Croydon** and London & Brighton Railways, and already had a network that included **Brighton**, from which a line had opened to Shoreham in 1840, while the main line to London Bridge was opened throughout the following year. Having its main line to London, the company set about making the most of the 'South Coast' in its title, reaching Chichester to the west and St Leonards to the east in 1846, and then continuing to **Portsmouth** in 1847. Newhaven was also reached in 1847, with Horsham in 1848 and Eastbourne in 1849. A second terminus in London was achieved in 1860 with the opening of **Victoria**, so that the railway was reasonably well placed to serve the West End and the City, although not actually within either.

The company was not above making the most of circumstances to grow its business. It was no coincidence that when the Crystal Palace was demolished after the Great Exhibition of 1851 that it was moved from Hyde Park to Penge Park, sold by its owner, an LBSCR director to a company associated with the LBSC, who opened a new branch ready for the official re-opening of the re-erected building by Queen Victoria in 1854. That this was an astute move can be judged by the fact that a single day in 1859 produced 112,000 passengers visiting the Palace.

A problem arose when the Brighton & Continental Steam Packet Company was found to be a wholly-owned subsidiary of the LBSCR, as railways were barred at the time from running shipping, and had to be liquidated. Despite this setback, the railways were gradually allowed to operate shipping services and, as with all of the major companies in the South, shipping soon became very important, with the LBSCR introducing its first shipping services from Newhaven to Dieppe in 1867 in partnership with the Ouest Railway of France, and also operated shipping out of Littlehampton from 1867 until 1882. Nevertheless, all was not well, and by 1867, the line was in danger of bankruptcy, partly through having paid over-generous dividends for the day of 6 per cent (at a time when the standard rate of interest was around 2½ per cent). More prudent policies over the next seven years led to far healthier finances so that during the final quarter of the nineteenth century dividends could be afforded of 5 per cent or even higher.

The Brighton line was not always the fastest in the country, but still produced an acceptable performance for the time, with through non-stop journey times taking 90 minutes in 1844, reducing to 75 minutes in 1865 and 60 minutes by 1898, which made the twentieth century timings look fairly lame and unexciting by comparison. This of course marked one big difference between steam trains and the first generation of electric trains, with the former performing at speeds that electric trains found hard to match on longer distances, while the electric trains came into their own on services with many stops because of their far superior acceleration. Freight was reasonably important for the LBSCR, producing a quarter of the company's turnover by 1913.

To maintain high end to end speeds while not neglecting the needs of intermediate stations, the LBSCR introduced the first slip carriages in the British Isles, serving Haywards Heath from 1858. Pullman cars were introduced in 1875, and electric lighting started to be introduced from 1881, while the 'Brighton' also rated highly for braking and signalling practice. Yet, in common with the **Great Western**, the 'Brighton' was also criticised during the late nineteenth century for its poor provision for third class passengers.

The LBSCR enjoyed a monopoly on its main lines, although there had been competition with the **London & South Western Railway** for Portsmouth traffic prior to the opening of the Portsmouth 'Direct' in 1859, which settled the matter in the latter's favour once and for all. It cooperated with the LSWR at Portsmouth and at Ryde, where the two companies were responsible for the line from the Pierhead through to St Johns and jointly owned the Portsmouth-Ryde ferry service. It also sought a similar relationship with the **South Eastern Railway** at Redhill and **London Bridge**, but found working relations difficult, and eventually resolved this at Redhill through the construction of an avoiding line, a by-pass line, for fast traffic, known as the 'Quarry' line, in 1900. This would have been needed sooner or later to avoid the flat junction at Redhill with its branches off to Guildford and Tonbridge.

The monopoly only extended as far as competition from other railways was concerned. The LBSCR had built a substantial suburban network, dominating the suburbs between Dulwich and Purley. Yet, this extensive network was vulnerable to competition from the new electric tramways, which often provided a more direct route for travellers, with the advantage of passing closer to the doorstep and to the destination. This was the spur for early electrification. There was also the threat of a new **London & Brighton Electric Railway** shortly after the turn of the new century. The LBSCR struck back, quadrupling its main line as far as Balcombe Tunnel and obtaining Parliamentary powers for electrification in 1903. The first electric services were introduced on the London Bridge to Victoria South London Line in 1909 using a 6,700 volts ac overhead system, and after this proved successful, the lines to Crystal Palace and Selhurst were electrified in 1912.

Including joint lines, in 1922 the LBSCR had a total mileage of 457 miles.

London, Chatham & Dover Railway – see **South Eastern & Chatham Railways Managing Committee**

London Electric Railway
The title for the original Great Northern Piccadilly & Brompton Railway (or **Piccadilly Line**), it was renamed in 1910 and became the parent company for the **Bakerloo** and **Hampstead** tubes. In 1913, the organisation was acquired by the **Underground Group**, and all passed into the control of the **London Passenger Transport Board** in 1933.

London & Midland & Scottish Railway
Largest of the four grouped railway companies, and believed to be the largest private enterprise concern in the British Empire, the London, Midland & Scottish had as its

constituent companies the **Caledonian Railway; Lancashire & Yorkshire Railway,** which had already agreed to be purchased by the **London & North Western Railway; Glasgow & South Western Railway; Highland Railway;** the **Midland Railway; North Staffordshire Railway** and the **Furness Railway;** with subsidiaries including the Arbroath & Forfar Railway; Brechin & Edzell District Railway; **Callander & Oban Railway;** Cathcart District Railway; Charnwood Forest Railway; Cleator & Workington Junction Railway; Cockermouth Keswick & Penrith Railway; **Dearne Valley Railway;** Dornoch Light Railway; Dundee & Newtyle Railway; Harborne Railway; **Leek & Manifold Valley Light Railway; Maryport & Carlisle Railway;** Mold & Denbigh Junction Railway; **North & South Western Junction Railway; North London Railway; Portpatrick & Wigtownshire Joint Committee; Shropshire Union Railways & Canal; Solway Junction Railway; Stratford-upon-Avon & Midland Junction Railway; Tottenham & Forest Gate Railway;** Wick & Lynster Light Railway; **Wirral Railway** and the **Yorkshire Dales Railway.** Some of the smaller lines were already leased to or worked by the larger companies.

This was the only railway company to be operating in all four countries of the United Kingdom, and its network stretched from Thurso in the north of Scotland to Bournemouth on the South Coast, and from Londonderry to Essex. Organising such a disparate and widespread set of railway companies into a cohesive whole was a massive problem, not helped by the fact that from the start there were struggles for dominance between the senior managers of the former MR and their counterparts in the LNWR, while in Scotland, the CR established itself as the dominant force and policy setter. On the engineering side, there was also serious fractional fighting between the two major locomotive works at **Crewe,** ex-LNWR, and **Derby,** ex-MR. The MR owned the former **London, Tilbury & Southend Railway,** which meant that the LMS was in direct competition with the LNER and under pressure from local authorities to electrify this line. The company also owned the Northern Counties Committee, the former **Belfast & Northern Counties Railway,** which had a main line from Belfast to Londonderry, with an important branch to Portrush and a secondary mainline to Larne, operating on the Irish broad gauge of 5ft 3ins, and had a significant interest in the **County Donegal Railway,** a 3ft gauge line running across the border into the Irish Republic from Londonderry. It shared the **Somerset & Dorset Railway** with the **Southern Railway.** It was not until 1927 that the public began to notice the change of ownership.

The legacy of the pre-grouping companies was mixed to say the least. The MR was famous for its policy of small locomotives, and this contributed in no small part to the LMS having the lowest main line speeds of any of the 'Big Four', although an earlier belief on the LNWR that 45mph was good enough did not help! On the other hand, the LNWR had begun electrification of its London suburban network, while the MR's policy of centralised train control was adopted and proved successful. Both the LNWR and MR had a reputation for comfortable mainline rolling stock.

The LMS was second only to the LNER in its dependence on freight traffic, and this was to prove to be a weakness with the years of the Great Depression worsened by the 1926 miners' strike and the loss of major export markets for British coal. Nevertheless, rationalisation of freight handling and management meant that by 1939, the company's freight business was generally profitable. This was despite the failure to introduce large 20-ton mineral wagons, even though new 2-8-0 Stanier freight locomotives accelerated trains and new fast freight trains were introduced, so that by 1938, there were seven running daily more than 150 miles non-stop, and another 57 running more than 90 miles non-stop. It was also a major operator of London commuter services, which it could not afford to electrify beyond the original LNWR scheme and which can hardly have been profitable.

The first step towards organising the LMS into a cohesive whole came with the creation of three, later four, operating divisions. Sir Josiah (later Lord) **Stamp** was appointed president in 1926, heading a four man executive, later increased to seven, which fulfilled the role of general manager and an officers' committee. Stamp came from outside the industry, and his management practices were those currently in vogue in the United States, including such practices as work study. A year later, he also took on the role of chairman. Costs were analysed and working practices standardised, and as funds permitted, this soon extended to new equipment.

Sir Henry **Fowler** of the MR became the first Chief Mechanical Engineer, and was ordered to produce a more powerful steam locomotive to end double heading. This was a tall order for a CME accustomed to building small locomotives and the result was the Royal Scot 4-6-0, which still fell short of what was needed. When Fowler retired, Sir William **Stanier** was recruited from the **Great Western**. One of his first achievements was to end the Crewe-Derby battles, and then to start a massive locomotive rationalisation and building programme that saw the number of classes fall from 404 in 1932 to 132 by 1938, while the number of locomotives needed to operate the system fell by 26 per cent. Similar standardisation followed in carriage and wagon design, which with modernisation of the repair

shops also saw massive gains in productivity. For the main line services, corridor carriages were mass produced which have generally been regarded as the best in the British Isles for comfort, while the later versions provided the basis for the **British Railways** Mk1 rolling stock. His famous 'Black Fives', the Class 5 4-6-0 mixed traffic locomotives, also provided the basis for a British Railways standard design postnationalisation. Irish broad gauge versions of the locomotives and carriages were built for the Northern Counties line. At **Derby**, a research laboratory and testing facility was opened and in 1938, this was joined by the world's first School of Transport.

Such forward thinking and a penchant for excellent publicity material nevertheless could not disguise the fact that the entire railway did not stand up to critical appraisal. Stations reflected the company's poverty, seldom painted and often dirty, and generally unwelcoming. Its branch line trains were often slow and dirty, in contrast to the fast expresses such as the streamlined *Coronation Scot*, running between **Euston** and **Glasgow**. The **Wirral**, **Mersey** and **Manchester South Junction & Altrincham** lines were electrified, the latter jointly with the LNER, but many of the electrified lines were inherited from the LYR and the LNWR.

Like the other members of the 'Big Four', the LMS operated ports, shipping and hotels, with Europe's largest chain of hotels, and in 1938 operated 6,870 route miles on the mainland of Great Britain alone. Its ferry services from Heysham and Stranraer to Northern Ireland and from Holyhead to Dublin were successful, although it was less involved in port operation and management than the LNER or the Southern. Nevertheless, despite the progress made between grouping and the outbreak of the Second World War, it struggled to make a profit and dividends were scarce.

The Second World War probably affected the LMS less than the other members of the 'Big Four', although it suffered badly in the bombing of Coventry, **Birmingham**, **Manchester**, Glasgow and **Belfast**. Its regional control centres proved themselves more than adequate for crisis management. Nevertheless, the strain of wartime operations and the shortage of skilled manpower meant that the weaknesses of the LMS were accentuated, giving rise to the graffiti; 'The LMS, a hell of a mess'. There are anecdotal stories of passengers being unable to see station name signs because of the grime on the carriage windows.

On **nationalisation**, the LMS was divided between the London Midland Region and Scottish Region of **British Railways**, with the services to Southend from **Fenchurch Street** passing to the Eastern Region. Its interests in Northern Ireland eventually passed to the **Ulster Transport Authority** and the **County Donegal Railway** came under the control of the Irish State-owned C I E.

**London Passenger Transport Board/
London Transport/London Transport
Executive**

The first official attempt at an integrated passenger transport system in the United Kingdom, 'London Transport' was adopted as the operating title and fleet name for the London Passenger Transport Board, which came into being in 1933. The first **nationalised** transport concern, its Act required it to provide a completely coordinated system of public transport by road and rail over its area, which amounted to almost 2,000 square miles and, inconveniently, did not match the boundaries of the London County Council, the Metropolitan Police area or that of the Metropolitan Traffic Area, one of a number of regional traffic areas set up under the first Road Transport Act in 1931. It covered not only under-ground trains, but also trams, trolleybuses and motorbuses, including a large fleet of green country buses and the Greenline coach network pioneered by the London General Omnibus Company, as well as taking over depots, vehicles and services from other bus companies whose operations were caught in its area, such as Thames Valley, for example.

The Act also required the LPTB to operate in coordination with the 'Big Four' mainline railways. In practice, this meant that their suburban fares were pooled with the receipts of the London Underground, and each of the grouped companies received a share of the revenue. The large suburban network of the **Southern Railway** ensured that it received the largest share after the LPTB itself, while the **Great Western**, with virtually no suburban system, had the least.

The actual board was appointed by five ex-officio trustees, including the **Minister of Transport**.

In 1948, the LPTB was taken over by the newly formed **British Transport Commission**, which operated through a series of executives, so it became the London Transport Executive, but the name London Transport survived, although the circle and bar logo was steadily up-dated to keep pace with changing artistic taste. When the BTC was scrapped in 1963, a new London Transport Board emerged, directly responsible to the Minister of Transport. In 1970, control was passed to the new Greater London Council, and the name of London Transport Executive was resurrected. In 1984, control was taken from the GLC and given to London Regional Transport with separate companies operating buses and trains, but even this situation has now been reversed and control is vested in a new body, Transport for London. Expansion has continued with the acquisition of the Silverlink North London Line, which has become part of the new

'Overground', now a railway network, with the East London Line, while the London Transport Executive built, and its successors have continued to expand the **Docklands Light Railway**.

The LPTB and its successors up to and including the London Transport Board, became a huge monopoly. At its best, it co-ordinated bus and underground railway travel, but this was at the cost of fares that reflected railway operating costs rather than those of road transport. Even **British Railways** had to pool suburban revenue. No one could operate a bus service in London without its approval, while it trained and examined its own bus drivers, who could not use the resultant PSV licence if they left to work for another employer.

London, Tilbury & Southend Railway

Authorised in 1852 as a joint scheme by the **Eastern Counties** and **London & Blackwall Railways** running from Forest Gate Junction on the ECR to Tilbury and Southend, ending rivalry between the two companies to expand into the area. In many ways, this was a contractors' line as the impetus had come from G P Bidder, as engineer, and the contractor Samuel Morton Peto, who was joined by two others, Thomas **Brassey** and E L Betts, who built the line, which opened in stages between 1854 and 1856, and then worked it under lease until 1875, although rolling stock was supplied by the ECR. The sponsors' ambitions were to attract the excursion traffic from Tilbury to Gravesend, and only later did the holiday market for Southend become important.

At first, trains were divided at Stratford with portions for Bishopsgate and **Fenchurch Street**. A branch was opened to Thames Haven in 1855 by the Thames Haven Dock & Railway Company, and this was taken over by the LTSR on opening. Traffic grew quickly, and an avoiding line had to be built

to avoid Stratford, opening in 1858, which then became the main line while all trains ran to and from Fenchurch Street only. The LTSR became independent in 1862, although the main shareholders remained the LBR and the newly-created **Great Eastern**, and the LTSR started running the line in 1875, after which the line was modernised and received its own 4-4-2T locomotives and carriages, with the LTSR running its own trains from 1880. Full independence followed in 1882, with the other two railways no longer appointing directors. In 1884, an extension from Southend to Shoeburyness, long delayed by War Office objections, was opened, with a shorter line from Barking to Pitsea via Upminster opened between 1885 and 1888, and in 1893 a branch opened from Grays to Romford. Meanwhile, the opening of new docks at Tilbury in 1886 provided goods traffic and called for boat trains when liners called, while the line served the new housing developments in the east of London as well as a growing commuter market at Southend.

Although acquisition of this thriving line by the GER was widely expected, in 1912 the LTSR was acquired by the **Midland Railway**, and under grouping passed to the **London, Midland & Scottish**, a self-contained and isolated line away from the company's main area of operations.

Londonderry & Lough Swilly Railway

Authorised in 1853, initially the line was to be 14 route miles linking Londonderry and Letterkenny, with a branch to Buncrana. It was the Buncrana to Londonderry section that first opened in 1863, and initially this used Irish standard gauge of 5ft 3in, but it was converted to 3ft gauge in 1885 and all the subsequent lines were built to this gauge. It acquired the Letterkenny Railway, opened in 1883; the Cardonagh Railway, opened in 1901; and an extension opened to Burtonport in 1903, running 50 miles from

Letterkenny through sparsely-populated and mountainous country.

The company was unprofitable for much of its life, but before the First World war, efficiency improved and it even managed to pay a small dividend. Lough Swilly was a major anchorage and naval base for the Royal Navy and during the war years, traffic to the base at Buncrana was heavy. Postwar, traffic declined to its old level and the situation was made worse by growing competition from motor bus services and road haulage, so that the LLSR became heavily dependent on subsidies from the then Irish Free State to continue. After the Second World War, the line was not nationalised and eventually closed in 1953, but the company survived as a relatively small bus operator and road haulier for many years.

Longmoor Military Railway

A number of railways were built by the British Army which had often extensive training grounds and encampments in England. The value of railways had been learnt during the First World War when the military even built a network of narrow-gauge lines behind the Western Front to move supplies and troops. Post-war, even though funds were short, a small number of military railways were built, including one on Salisbury Plain.

The most important of these was the Longmoor Military Railway. This was one of the most significant military railways to survive between the two wars. Originally founded as the Woolmer Instructional Railway for training members of the Royal Engineers in railway operation and maintenance, the Longmoor Military Railway also had the potential to serve the large base area around Bordon in Hampshire. The LMR linked the **Waterloo** to **Portsmouth** main line, known in railways circles as the 'Portsmouth Direct', at Liss with a branch line at Bordon, and in between a substantial

network developed. The line was sufficiently important to have been kept open by the British Army, which by this time had created a Royal Corps of Transport, until 1970.

In its heyday, the LMR operated a stud of tender locomotives and a number of 0-6-0ST, or saddle tanks, with ex-civilian railway passenger carriages painted blue. All of the locomotives, no matter how humble, were named. Many of them were bargains, including 0-6-2T *Thisbe*, acquired by the Woolmer Instructional Railway in 1914 after its original owners, the Shropshire Light Railway, found it too heavy for their needs.

Lynton & Barnstaple Railway

Authorised in 1895, 1ft 11½in narrow gauge railway opened in May 1898 with almost 20 route miles. It was promoted by Sir George Newnes, Bt, and who also promoted a funicular railway linking Lynton and Lynmouth. This independent approach was because neither the **Great Western** nor the **London & South Western Railways**, who met at Barnstaple Junction, would commit to building a railway in a sparsely populated area with some difficult geographical features. The choice of narrow gauge was based on estimates that put construction of standard gauge at £8,000 per mile (almost £700,000 by today's values) as against £2,500 for narrow gauge, but in the end the cost per mile was double this sum. The rise in costs occurred when landowners who had supported the line demanded more money for their land, and because the contractor had not realised that much of the line would have to be cut through hard rock.

The heavy cost of construction and the need for additional capital to be raised, meant that the line was financially burdened from the start and only a dividend of ½ per cent could be paid, and then only between 1913 and 1921. One effect of these problems was that the line could not be extended at Lynmouth to a more suitable terminus, more convenient for passengers and with a better water supply that did not dry up during a hot summer: In the height of summer, water had to be brought by rail from Barnstaple, adding to costs, and water had to be taken on at Parracombe Halt, extending journey times.

To stimulate tourist traffic, the company built stables for road traffic at Blackmore so that passengers could reach Ilfracombe, but the time saved compared to a through journey by road between Lynton and Ilfracombe was insufficient to attract sufficient passengers. Later, in 1903, a second attempt was made to capture this trade by using motor coaches, but the vehicles were unreliable and the police and the local magistrates forced the ending of this service. On the other hand, freight traffic grew steadily until after the First World War, when competition from road haulage began to be felt.

Although not formally grouped in 1923, in March of that year, the LBR was bought by the **Southern Railway**. The new owners completely re-ballasted the line and replaced the sleepers, and also advertised the service. Nevertheless, the decline continued, aided by re-routing of the main road between the two towns to avoid two steep hills.

Eventually, the line was closed in September 1935. It was largely shunned by local people in its final years, although it remained a great favourite with visitors, and had the railway preservation movement started a couple of decades earlier, it might still be open today.

M

McAlpine, Sir Robert, 1847-1934
Having started work in the collieries at the age of seven, at sixteen McAlpine became a bricklayer and within five years was working as a contractor, owning two brickyards by 1874, but his fortunes took a sharp reversal in 1877 with the collapse of the City of Glasgow Bank. Nevertheless, he created his own company, McAlpine & Co, with his five sons, and moved into railway work in 1885 with a contract to build the Lanarkshire & Ayrshire Railway. This was followed by the Lanarkshire & Dumbartonshire Railway in 1892 and then completed the **Glasgow Subway** in 1896, the same year that he obtained the contract for the **North British Railway's** Yoker to Dalmuir extension. The following year, he began the **West Highland Railway's** line to Mallaig, a difficult line with much rock to be cut and removed, and many bridges and tunnels. By this time he had gained a reputation for fast and low cost completion of contracts, partly by planning a suitable use for the spoil and also by being one of the pioneers of the extensive use of concrete from 1892 onwards, and gradually extended the size of concrete bridge spans from 60ft to 127ft. He earned himself the titles of the 'Concrete King' or 'Concrete Bob'. His most famous concrete structure was the curved 21 arch Glenfinnan Viaduct, 100ft high.

He became a baronet in 1918, but meanwhile the company he founded had moved into general construction as the demand for new railways faded.

McIntosh, John Farquharson, 1846-1918.
After early experience with the Scottish North Eastern Railway which he joined in 1862, he became chief running superintendent of the **Caledonian Railway** in 1891, being promoted to locomotive superintendent in 1895. He adapted the 4-4-0 and 0-6-0 designs of Dugald **Drummond**, creating the highly successful 'Dunalastair' 4-4-0s of 1896, followed by an 0-8-0 heavy goods

class and then the 4-6-0 express locomotives in 1903 that were the predecessors of the Cardean-class of 1906. His work was adopted by Belgian State Railways between 1898 and 1910; an unusual tribute. He also produced twelve-wheeled passenger carriages and was amongst the first to build higher capacity bogie coal wagons, which improved railway productivity whenever colliery owners could lay down sidings without tight curves.

Mail

The connection between the Post Office and the railways dates back to 1830, when the Superintendent of Mail Coaches met the board of the **Liverpool & Manchester Railway** to examine the possibility of mail being carried twice daily between the two cities. The LMR agreed to do so at a cost of 1d a mile, or 2s 6d per single trip, and this was accepted by the Post Office. Not all of the early arrangements were between cities served by the railway, with, for example, the **Grand Junction Railway**, acting as the railway link in carrying mail between Birmingham, that had arrived by road from **London**, onwards to **Liverpool** and **Manchester**.

It was clear that this was going to be an important traffic, and anxious to impose some uniformity on arrangements, the Post Office pressed for legislation and this resulted in the Railways (Conveyance of Mails) Act 1838, which gave the Postmaster-General power to require all railways, both existing and any that would be authorised in the future, to carry mail at such hours of the day that the Post Office might require. Mail carriages and trucks would be carried on flat wagons provided by the railway companies, and, if necessary, special carriages were to be provided exclusively for the carriage of mail and for sorting, and if necessary special trains were to be provided. Wisely, the charges for these

services were left to negotiation. That was the same year that the first exchange apparatus, devised by Nathaniel Worsdell, the LMR's carriage superintendent, appeared, but this was rejected by the PO.

The Post Office was quick to take advantage of new routes almost as soon as they were opened. When the **Great Western Railway** opened the first section of its line in 1838 between London and Maidenhead, after just two weeks of operation it was carrying mail coaches on flat trucks. Again, it became part of the railway/road combination used to serve destinations not yet reached by the railway, with the Cheltenham mail coach carried from late 1839, while those for Bath, **Bristol**, **Gloucester** and Stroud followed early in 1840. Other similar arrangements were made with other companies. Mail coach practice was followed to the extent of the mails being accompanied by a guard provided by the Post Office, while the mail had its own compartment or van, or could be carried on the roof in a container known as an 'Imperial'. On first the GJR, using a converted horsebox, and then the **London & Birmingham** and **North Union Railways**, travelling post offices, TPO, with sorters were in use by 1842.

It was not until 1855 that the first all-mail trains started, running between **Paddington** and Bristol on the GWR, the same year as the GWR's first TPO. Between 1869 and 1902, the GWR mail between London and Penzance carried passengers, but reverted to mail only service in the latter year. Posting boxes were installed on all TPO trains from 1882, but letters so posted had to have an extra $\frac{1}{2}$d stamp. The TPOs used mail exchange equipment invented by a PO employee, John Ramsay, adopted after successful trials at Boxmoor on the LBR in 1838. When corridor connections were provided, on TPOs the connection was offset to one side away from the sorters, who worked on one side of the carriage while mail bags were moved and readied to be dropped on the other, but eventually centre connections were provided to ease problems when connected to passenger carriages.

Further legislation was necessary for parcel post, introduced in 1883. To enable the same arrangements to be made with the railway companies, the Post Office (Parcels) Act 1882, enforced the carriage of parcels by train, with the main difference being that the railway companies received 55 per cent of the gross receipts of the PO for the parcels carried by train. To make calculation of this figure easier, each half-year the PO conducted a week-long audit of the parcels carried by rail and sent from the post towns, rather doing this on a nightly train-by-train means. In 1922, the railway companies agreed to the share of gross receipts being cut to 40 per cent in exchange for the PO agreeing not to send more than 10 per cent of parcels by road. While some sorting of parcels did take place on trains, there was no late posting facility and no exchange of parcels by trains on the move.

Nevertheless, an increasing volume of mail started to be moved by road, and also by air. All parcels were transferred to road by the early 1990s and in May 1993, the Anglo-Scottish TPOs were withdrawn. **British Railways** set up Rail Express Systems and the PO created Railnet, a streamlined mail network with a ten year contract with RES, with much mail being containerised, and new multiple unit TPOs were also introduced. Nevertheless, the early twenty-first century has seen most mail transferred to road haulage, mainly overnight.

Mallard – see **High Speed Trains**

Manchester

The opening of the **Liverpool & Manchester Railway** in 1830 was a reflec-

tion of the city's importance as an important centre for the cotton industry in particular, for which it needed access to the docks at **Liverpool** both for the import of raw materials and the export of finished goods. Nevertheless, that not all was well in relations between the two cities was demonstrated by the opening of the Manchester Ship Canal in 1894 to avoid the high harbour dues at Liverpool. The railways that follow provide a history of the growth of Manchester's railway network, along with the **Lancashire & Yorkshire Railway,** the **Midland Railway** and the **Great Central Railway.**

Manchester & Birmingham Railway – see London & North-Western Railway

Manchester & Leeds Railway

Authorised in 1837, the MLR was 51 miles long running from Oldham Road, Manchester to Normanton, from where it would have running powers over the **North Midland Railway** to **Leeds**, and later to **Hull** and **York**. The engineer was George **Stephenson**, and the route across the Pennines required many viaducts and tunnels, of which the most difficult was Summit Tunnel, more than a mile and a half long. It was no mean achievement that the line opened during 1839-40. Branches opened to Heywood in 1841; Oldham, 1842; Halifax, 1844, and Stalybridge, 1846, followed by a connecting line across Manchester in 1848 to the **London & North Western Railway**. Meanwhile, the Oldham Road terminus was relegated to a goods depot after **Victoria** Station was opened in 1844, allowing easy interchange between the MLR and the **Liverpool & Manchester Railway**. In 1846, the MLR took over the Manchester Bolton & Bury Railway, which dated from 1838, and the Liverpool and Bury Railway, which was still under construction, as well as joining the

Grand Junction Railway in leasing the **North Union Railway**. The following year, the company changed its name to the **Lancashire & Yorkshire Railway**.

Manchester, Sheffield & Lincolnshire Railway – see **Great Central Railway**

Manchester South Junction & Altrincham Railway
Formed in 1845 to provide a link between its owners, the **Liverpool & Manchester Railway** and the Sheffield, Ashton & Manchester, a predecessor of the **Great Central**, running for its 1½ mile length on a brick viaduct on the south side of the city, but with an eight mile branch from Castlefield to Altrincham, which soon became far busier than the connecting line as it encouraged the development of suburbs. Both shareholding companies provided frequent suburban trains to Altrincham, initially from Oxford Road and then, in 1879, from London Road, by which time they had developed into the **London & North Western** and **Manchester Sheffield & Lincolnshire Railways**.
Despite having come together to build the MSJAR, the two proprietors had an increasingly unhappy relationship, to the extent that a further Act in 1858 ensured that an arbitrator should attend their meetings. The MSJAR had its own carriages and wagons, but most locomotives came from the MSLR. In 1931, by which time the owners had become the **London, Midland & Scottish** and **London & North Eastern Railways**, the line was electrified using a 1,500 V dc overhead system, converted in 1971 to 25k V ac system used for electrification of the main line services to London and enabling through services to be run onto other lines. In 1883, the Castlefield-Altrincham line was converted to become part of the Manchester Metrolink tramway system, but remains in use for trains to Chester.

Mania – see **Railway Mania**

Mansell, Richard C, 1848-1882
While carriage superintendent of the **South Eastern Railway**, Mansell designed, and in 1848, patented the wheel that carries his name. A disc is built up from an iron or steel centre boss using 16 teak segments, and the disc forced into the tyre under hydraulic pressure, and then secured by screw bolts and nuts. There was no recorded failure of these wheels, but manufacture stopped before the First World War.
Other work by Mansell included some of the first standard gauge bogie carriages, first built in 1878. He also designed the SER's royal saloon. He resigned in 1876 after a dispute with the SER's chairman, Sir Edward **Watkin**, whose son succeeded him for a short time, but Mansell returned as locomotive superintendent until 1878.

Mansfield Railway
Opened in stages between 1913 and 1917, linking the **Great Central** at Kirkby, via Mansfield, with the same company's Chesterfield-Lincoln line, originally the Lancashire, Derbyshire & East Coast Railway at Clipstone. The line was worked by the GCR and passed to the **London & North Eastern Railway** on **grouping**.

Manx Electric Railway
Originally opened between Douglas and Groundle as the Douglas & Laxey Coast Electric Railway in 1893, using a 3ft gauge, the line reached Laxey in 1894, by which time the original track had been relaid and doubled. The line had been built by Alexander Bruce. At Groudnle, an R M Broadbent built both a hotel and a 2ft gauge railway. The extension to Laxey coincided with Bruce reorganising his business interests into the Isle of Man Tramways and Electric Power Company, which had also purchased the Douglas horse-tramway. A further extension to Ramsay was opened in

1899, with a half-hourly service between Douglas and Ramsay.

Meanwhile, Bruce also built and opened the Snaefell Mountain Railway in 1895, another electrified line but at 3ft 6in gauge and using the 'Fell' safety system on which a horizontal centre rail was engaged by guide wheels.

Bruce's empire had been underwritten by a local bank, Dumbell's, and when this collapsed in 1900, the shock seems to have contributed to Bruce's death from heart failure six months later. The entire empire went into receivership and was broken up, with Douglas Corporation buying the horse tramway, and a syndicate of Manchester businessmen buying both the Douglas & Laxey and the Snaefell Mountain Railway. In 1902, the two railways were renamed the Manx Electric Railway.

Competition from bus services and a decline in tourism combined after the second World War to reduce the number of passengers, but the MER was rescued and nationalised by the Manx government during the 1950s because of its importance to the tourist industry. It eventually provided a convenient shelter for the remnants of the Isle of Man Railway when that too was nationalised.

Manx Northern Railway – see **Isle of Man Railways**

Marylebone
The last terminus to be built in **London**, and always resembling a small provincial terminus, Marylebone was built for the London extension of the **Great Central Railway**. Some would claim that it was built to fulfill the ambitions of one man, the GCR's chairman, Sir Edward **Watkin**, whose interests in railways were wide and varied. He was chairman of the **Metropolitan Railway** from 1872. Earlier he had become chairman of the **Manchester, Sheffield & Lincolnshire**

Railway, a cross-county operation whose main line ran from Grimsby to **Manchester**. Without a London route of its own, it lost this growing traffic to the **Great Northern Railway** and, later, the **Midland Railway**. Opposition to Parliamentary approval was strong, especially from the cricketing fraternity as the line would run close to Lords. There was also opposition from the artists of St John's Wood. Eventually, the extension from near Nottingham to London was authorised in 1893.

The MSLR was not allowed to use the Metropolitan lines, which had a new chairman after Watkin stood down due to a stroke, but was able to use the same alignment. This was not just spite on the part of the new chairman, John Bell: the Metropolitan was already very busy with its own suburban traffic. Fresh powers had to be obtained so that new lines could be laid. It was also considered expedient to change the company's somewhat provincial title to the more impressive Great Central Railway on 1 August 1897.

The GCR needed more than fifty acres for the terminus, coal and goods depots, and 4,448 persons were evicted during the slum clearance that followed, with many moved to homes nearby, but 2,690 were moved to six five-storey blocks of flats, known as Wharncliffe Gardens after the new chairman of the GCR, built by the company. This was despite much of the approach being in tunnel or cut and covered construction passing under the streets of St John's Wood. The gradient was kept to 1 in 100. The engineers for the difficult two mile approach were Sir Douglas and Francis Fox. To allow for possible future quadrupling, not one but two tunnels were excavated under Hampstead. Between the Hampstead tunnels and St John's Wood tunnel, the line crossed the **London & North Western Railway** main line on a bridge. Three further parallel tunnels took the line under Lords.

Approaching Marylebone, the seven tracks expanded to fourteen as the line passed over the Regent's Canal, which included a second span for the proposed and authorised, but never built, Regent's Canal, City & Docks Railway. Coal and goods depots were built on both sides of Lisson Grove. Finally, outside the terminus the lines became down slow, up slow, down main, and to the east of these, a siding road, carriage sheds, locomotive yard and a platform or wharf for fish and milk. Provision was made for sixteen tracks over Rossmore Road, with a terminus of five double faced platforms, but only part of this was built.

The feeble resources of the GCR were stretched almost to breaking point by its expansion southwards. In its best year, 1864, its predecessor, the MSLR had achieved a dividend of just 3.5 per cent. An architect for the station was beyond the company's resources, while the terminus was a modest affair, albeit conveniently at street level, and the Great Central Hotel was left to others to develop. The extension demanded extra locomotives and rolling stock, but these could only be afforded by creating a trust company which bought the necessary equipment, and then sold them to the GCR under a form of hire purchase. A three storey office block was provided, with provision for additional floors when required, but most of the accommodation remained unused until the GCR moved its headquarters from Manchester in 1905. The concourse, intended for a terminus twice the size with five double-faced platforms, stretched beyond the nine tracks and four built at its eastern end. At the eastern wall were two tracks, then arrival platforms 1 and 2, separated by a 30-ft wide roadway. Two more tracks followed, with departure platforms 3 and 4 beyond and then a single

track. Even the Great Central Hotel, with its 700 bedrooms, was over-ambitious, and in 1916 it was requisitioned by the government as a convalescent home for wounded officers. Its one oddity was a cycle track on the roof! In the end, after being purchased as offices by the **London & North Eastern Railway** after the Second World War, it became 222 Marylebone Road, headquarters of the **British Transport Commission**, and when that was dissolved, the **British Railways Board**.

Goods traffic on the London extension started in 1898 with coal trains. On 9 March 1899, a ceremonial opening was performed by the President of the **Board of Trade**. Public traffic started on 15 March. For the first month, only two platforms were used. By summer, there were eleven trains daily each way, of which seven were Manchester expresses, but while the track bedded in, running times were not fast, at five hours for the 212 mile journey. Where the GCR did score was in the comfort of its new carriages, all of which were corridor stock with electric lighting.

The problem was that the GCR route to Manchester was longer than that of the LNWR, and that to Sheffield longer than that of the **Great Northern**. The GCR was best for Leicester and Nottingham, neither of which matched the other cities for traffic. Even so, the Marylebone to Manchester journey time was down to 3hrs 50 min by 1904, and Sheffield was three hours.

Much of these improved timings were due to a new general manager, Sam (later Sir Sam) **Fay**, who understood the need for good publicity and high standards of service. Timings were reduced, through services introduced to Bradford and Huddersfield using the LCR, and to Stratford-upon-Avon using the **Stratford-upon-Avon & Midland Junction Railway**. Buses were laid on to carry arriving passengers to the West End, for which Marylebone was well placed, and to the City, for which it was not.

Before Fay joined the GCR, the MR had completed quadrupling its lines as far as Harrow, and later, in 1906, the MR lines to Chesham, Brill and Verney Junction were leased to a new joint operating company of the GCR and MR, with the companies taking turns every five years to manage and staff the line. The agreement was that the GCR should not take local traffic between Marylebone and Harrow, but it was allowed to develop suburban traffic on the joint lines. The GCR soon took advantage of this, introducing local trains to Chesham and Aylesbury from March 1906. A year later, the opening of the **Bakerloo** tube line meant that Marylebone had good quick connections throughout the West End and to **Waterloo** and **Charing Cross**.

Despite the new found alliance between the GCR and the MR, the former still wanted a new route of its own. The MR line was more steeply graded than the GCR wanted for its planned express network, and also the curves were too severe for high speed running, especially at Aylesbury, which had a severe reverse curve. The answer lay in using the **Great Western's** new line from **Paddington** to **Birmingham**, with a connecting line from near Quinton Road to Ashendon, and then from Neasden to Northolt. The shared section of the main line was managed jointly by a committee of the GCR and GWR. In return for its generosity, the GWR had the GCR abandon its own plans for a route to Birmingham. The new route also offered new local and suburban possibilities, and brought welcome new traffic to Marylebone.

There was one serious accident at Marylebone. During the afternoon of 28 March 1913, a train arriving from Leicester was crossing to platform 4 as a train left platform 3 for High Wycombe. The fireman on the High Wycombe train could not see the starter signal which was obscured by smoke from the Leicester train, but the driver could see that the intermediate starter was off and believed that his fireman could see the starter signal. Too late, the driver realised his mistake and braked, but his locomotive collided with the last carriage of the up train, killing one passenger and injuring twenty-three, while five passengers on his train suffered slight injuries.

The terminus was largely unaffected by the First World War, and by retaining restaurant cars and not reducing train speeds by too much, it actually increased its share of the market.

Grouping

The GCR passed into the **London & North Eastern Railway** under **Grouping**, giving the new company three termini in London. The LNER reduced the use of the joint line with the GWR, but suburban traffic continued to grow. When Wembley Stadium opened in 1923, sporting events ensured that Marylebone became busy, while the British Empire Exhibition at Wembley Park in 1924 and 1925, prompted modernisation of the signalling. During the first year of the exhibition, a ten minute frequency non-stop service was provided that was superior to the Metropolitan alternative.

The LNER was, if anything, even shorter of funds for investment than the GCR had been. The recession and the strikes of 1926 saw much of its coal traffic lost, and as the member of the 'Big Four' most dependent upon goods traffic, the years of the Depression had the worst effect.

Marylebone itself escaped unscathed during the Second World War, with a few incendiary bombs soon extinguished, but the tunnel approach through St John's Wood was badly damaged, forcing Marylebone to close between 5 October and 26 November 1940, with single line working until August 1942. The goods depot was destroyed by fire on 16 April 1941. Finally, towards the end of the war, the signal box was hit by a flying bomb, killing two men.

Nationalisation, and rationalisation

At first, **nationalisation** must have seemed like an improvement in Marylebone's station, with the High Wycombe and Princes Risborough services concentrated on the terminus from mid-1949. In 1951, however, the stopping service to West Ruislip was cut. On the other hand, when diesel multiple units were introduced in 1961, first-class accommodation, lost during the wartime reductions, was reinstated. Meanwhile, **British Railways** introduced two named expresses to Marylebone, reversing the reductions of the LNER years, with the 'Master Cutler' to Sheffield introduced in 1947, and the 'South Yorkshireman' to Bradford the following year. Nevertheless, the policy of BR was rationalisation and concentration, stopping competing services from different London termini, and from 1960, the station lost its services to Bradford, Manchester and Sheffield, and services to Leicester and Nottingham were reduced. Then all main line services were withdrawn in September 1966.

There was a temporary reprieve, when the Western Region's services to Birmingham were transferred to Marylebone while signalling and layout at **Paddington** were modernised during 1967-1968.

Nevertheless, the station was earmarked for closure and plans were laid for it to be converted into a coach station, being ideally placed for services coming off the new M1 motorway. It was not to be. Marylebone survived and was retained for suburban services, while post-privatisation, the new train operating company, Chiltern Trains, expanded services and extended them to Birmingham once again.

Maryport & Carlisle Railway

Authorised in 1837 to extend the **Newcastle & Carlisle Railway** westwards. Engineered by George **Stephenson**, the 28-mile line was opened in stages between 1840 and 1845. In 1848, it briefly became part of George **Hudson's** empire, but regained its independence in 1850. Traffic consisted mainly of coal from the northern part of the Cumberland coalfield, but there was also iron ore and passengers and grain. Two branches were built, one through Mealsgate in 1866 failed to capture the anticipated traffic, but the second, to Brigham and known as the 'Derwent branch', opened the following year, provided a link to Cockermouth and with it the company reached a total of 43 route miles. It was an early convert from coke to coal as a fuel, and one locomotive is believed to have had the first all-steel boiler in 1862. Another distinction was the absence of any serious accident throughout its history.

The line achieved an average dividend of 6.6 per cent between 1850 and 1922, while between 1870 and 1882, it reached 11.1 per cent. It remained independent from 1850 until absorbed by the **London Midland & Scottish Railway** in 1923.

Maunsell, Richard Edward Lloyd, 1868-1944

Richard Maunsell was the **Southern Railway's** chief mechanical engineer, and a contemporary of **Walker**. Maunsell started his career at the Inchicore Works of the **Great Southern & Western Railway of Ireland**. He moved in 1891 to the **Lancashire & Yorkshire Railway**, where his experience was broadened and three years later he became assistant locomotive superintendent of the East Indian Railway, before he returned to Inchicore as works manager in 1896.

Maunsell joined the **South Eastern & Chatham Railway** as its chief mechanical engineer in 1913, inheriting a mixture of locomotives of differing quality from its two cash-starved constituent companies. He immediately created a new engineering team which set about improving the existing 4-4-0 locomotives as well as introducing modern 2-6-0 and 2-6-4 tank engines ideally suited for the shorter distance expresses and commuter trains of the South East.

Maunsell became chief mechanical engineer for the **Southern Railway** in 1923, when he continued the improving work started at the SECR by tackling the ex-**London & South Western Railway** Urie 4-6-0s and in the process introducing a degree of standardisation. He was responsible for the highly successful Schools-class as well as heavy 4-6-0 and 0-6-0 locomotives for goods, but his main work was on electrification and during his tenure the Southern limited funds for steam locomotive development because of the capital demands of electrification. A major disappointment was the rejection by the civil engineer of his plans for a four cylinder 4-6-2 express locomotive and for three cylinder 2-6-2 locomotives, with the former having to wait for his successor, Oliver **Bulleid**.

Maunsell concentrated locomotive work on Ashford and Eastleigh, introducing modern line production methods, and effectively sidelined the old LBSCR works at Brighton and Lancing, although these were run down rather than closed.

He retired in 1937 and died in 1944.

Mawddwy Railway – see Cambrian Railway

Mersey Railway

Originating as the Mersey Pneumatic Railway, authorised as early as 1866, it became simply the Mersey Railway two years later. Nevertheless, it did not open its first section of 2¼ miles underground between James Street, close to the Liverpool docks, and Green Lane, Birkenhead until 1886, and in 1888 a further section opened to a surface station at Birkenhead Park, shared with the **Wirral Railway**. Later extensions were between Green Lane and Rock Ferry, with a junction with the Birkenhead Joint Railway, opened in 1891, and then between James Street and Liverpool Central (Low Level) in 1892, making a total mileage of just 4½ miles.

Originally planned as a pneumatic railway, but conventional steam locomotives were used once it opened with powerful condensing apparatus, but the result was extremely unpleasant with tunnels, stations and carriages filled with smoke and soot, so that the Birkenhead ferries advertised themselves as the 'health route', with the result that passenger traffic was so bad that the company was in receivership between 1897 and 1900. Salvation came in the form of third-rail 650 V dc electrification in 1903, which immediately turned the company's fortunes so that by 1930, it was carrying 17 million passengers annually. This was the first railway in the British Isles to convert from steam to electric traction.

Notable features were the steep gradients and US-style clerestory carriages with stable half-doors. It was not included in the grouping in 1923, but in 1938 was integrated into the newly-electrified Wirral lines of the **London, Midland & Scottish Railway**. Today it survives as the heart of the Merseyrail TOC.

Metro-land

Loosely, a word used for the area serviced by the **Metropolitan Railway**, but strictly-speaking it applies to the land obtained by the company and developed for residential purposes. During the nineteenth century, railways were not entitled to hold land for non-railway purposes and any land left over after construction had to be offered back to the original landowners within a set period, often seven years, or otherwise sold. The MR overcame this by obtaining Parliamentary powers to buy land for residential development, and in 1915 produced the *Metro-land* slogan to promote some ten estates built close to its stations by a subsidiary.

The impact of this on stimulating suburban traffic was that the company earned twice as much per third-class seat during the 1920s as the three largest main line companies, while the Metropolitan Railway Country Estates subsidiary produced an 8 per cent dividend during these otherwise lean years.

Metropolitan District Railway

Opened in 1868 as the second underground passenger railway in the world, the line was more usually known as the 'District'. The MDR was promoted separately from the **Metropolitan Railway** for financial reasons, but the two were linked as the aim was to fulfill a recommendation by a House of Lords Committee that there should be a circular railway serving central **London**. When the Inner Circle was completed in 1884, the two companies had moved apart rather than merged and the operation of the jointly-owned Circle was the result of continuous disputes.

The District was difficult to build, even though it was able to use much of the Thames Embankment, then under construction. When the section between South Kensington and Westminster Bridge opened in 1868, it was worked by the Metropolitan until it withdrew in 1971. The line was completed between West Brompton and Mansion House by 1874, after which it began to expand south of the Thames, often using lines built by companies that were nominally independent to help in raising capital. By 1889, it operated to Ealing Broadway, Hounslow, Richmond and Wimbledon in the south-west, including operation over **London & South Western Railway** metals, to Whitechapel in the east, and over the **East London Railway** to New Cross. Using the **London, Tilbury & Southend Railway**, it reached Barking in 1908, and in 1932, went further east to Upminster on what had become the **London, Midland & Scottish Railway**.

Despite its expansion, the line was seldom profitable. In an attempt to stimulate exhibition traffic, the big hall at Earl's Court was built on its property.

The extent of the disagreements between the Metropolitan and the Metropolitan District delayed **electrification** from the mid-1890s and in the end the method of electrification had to go to arbitration, but South Harrow was electrified in 1903 and all trains were electrically worked by 1905. The MDR passed to the **London Passenger Transport Board** in 1933, and later, the **Piccadilly Line** took over services to South Harrow and Hounslow. In 1933, its trains operated over 58$\frac{3}{4}$ route miles, of which 25 were on its own tracks.

Metropolitan Railway

Opened on 10 January 1863, between **Paddington** and Farringdon Street, the Metropolitan was the world's first passenger underground railway and was constructed using the cut-and-cover system running for the most part beneath streets. At the outset, it was sponsored by the **Great Western Railway** and laid a 7-ft broad gauge to enable the GWR's passengers to reach the City of **London**. Nevertheless, the relationship between the two railways was unhappy and was finally severed in 1867, when the line changed to standard gauge. A programme of expansion followed, reaching Hammersmith in 1864, Harrow-on-the-Hill between 1868 and 1880, and, using the **East London Railway**, New Cross in 1884, by which time the intention was one of creating a railway circle around central London with the **Metropolitan District Railway** that would link the major termini north of the Thames. Known as the 'City Widened Lines', the original MR was also intended to provide access to the City of London for the **Midland Railway, Great Northern Railway** and **London Chatham & Dover Railway**.

Further expansion saw the railway expand into the countryside, reaching Aylesbury from Harrow in 1892, with connections to the **Great Central Railway**, which gained its original access to London over the MR in 1899, and the two companies ran the line north of Harrow jointly after 1906. Uxbridge was reached in 1904, Watford in 1925 and Stanmore in 1932, while it acquired the **Great Northern & City** tube line, in 1913, but the two lines were never linked. More than any other railway in London, the MR was popularly associated with the expansion of the suburbs, and even had a country estates subsidiary while its catchment area became known as '**Metroland**'. Uniquely amongst the London underground railways, the MR provided three classes for its passengers, and even operated two Pullman cars, while second-class was abandoned in 1905 and first disappeared under the wartime restrictions on suburban railways in 1941. Goods and parcels traffic was also handled. Electrification of the underground section was introduced in 1905, initially with trains switching to steam at Harrow, but electrification was later extended to Rickmansworth.

Growing competition from motor buses after 1910 meant that the outer suburban services became increasingly important, and indeed the **Bakerloo Line** eventually was developed to relieve the inner sections of the MR. The company used its country routes to argue unsuccessfully against incorporation into the new London Passenger Transport Board in 1933. Under **London Transport** and later Transport for London, the MR increasingly lost some of its distinctiveness, with the Hammersmith & City Line separated, although continuing to use the widened lines along with the Circle Line. Alone amongst London's underground railways, its current stock has 2 + 3 seating, but this is likely to be sacrificed with the next generation in favour of more standing room.

Mid-Suffolk Light Railway

Authorised by a light railway order in 1901, the Mid-Suffolk opened to goods between 1904 and 1906, and to passengers in 1908. Running between Haughley, Laxfield and Cratfield, some sections were closed in 1912 and in 1915. It was acquired by the **London & North Eastern Railway** in 1924, but completely closed in 1952, some four years after **nationalisation**.

Middleton Railway

Having the distinction of resulting from the first Act of Parliament for a railway, passed in 1758, although instead of authorising construction, it simply ratified agreements with landowners. Built as a horse-drawn tramway to a gauge of 4ft 1in, it carried coal from Charles Branding's collieries at Middleton to **Leeds**. In 1812, two primitive rack and pinion steam locomotives were introduced, but these were worn out by 1835, when a sharp fall in the cost of fodder saw a return to horses until 1862, when new owners introduced conventional steam locomotives, and in 1881 converted the line to standard gauge. The coal mines that had been behind the need for the railway were all closed by 1890, but the line was used by local factories to feed into the **Midland Railway**. By 1958, most of the line was closed, but it was rescued in 1960 by the Middleton Railway Trust, the first standard-gauge preservation society to commence operations, and through working to Middleton was achieved by 1969.

Midland & Great Northern Joint Railway
The longest of the joint railways at 183 route miles, the line was an attempt by the **Midland** and **Great Northern Railways** to penetrate East Anglia, bringing Midland and Yorkshire coal to Norfolk and fish and agricultural products to the industrial centres of the Midlands and the north. Initially, the line used four short contractors' lines, promoted by Waring Brothers, to get from Peterborough to Bourne, Spalding and King's Lynn, which were opened between 1858 and 1866 and worked by the MR and GNR. Later, other lines were opened beyond King's Lynn with the Lynn & Fakenham, opened in 1882 and a line between Yarmouth and North Walsham, that had opened throughout in 1888, which combined to form the Eastern & Midlands Company, running across Norfolk and later a branch to Norwich was added, followed by one to Cromer in 1887.

Nevertheless, the EMR passed into receivership in 1890, when the MR and GNR purchased it and added the earlier sections to it to form the Midland & Great Northern Joint Railway in 1893. The following year, a branch was opened westwards from Bourne to meet the MR at Saxby, adding through services to Nottingham, Leicester and **Birmingham**. The new owners also doubled some of the line, but even so, 77 per cent remained single track, but operations were much improved after new tablet-exchange equipment was introduced in 1906. While the two owners had operating rights, the line also pursued an independent existence with its own locomotive works at Melton Constable. With the wide range of destinations served by this time, cattle and fish traffic alone required five trains daily during the summer, while the line also brought holi-daymakers to Cromer and Yarmouth. The GNR even ran through trains between **London** and Cromer, but this was a lengthy route at 174 miles, 35 more than on the **Great Eastern**.

Rivalry with the GER was left behind in 1896, when the three companies agreed to develop the Norfolk & Suffolk Joint Railway, but only two sections were completed, between Cromer and North Walsham in 1898, and Yarmouth and Lowestoft in 1903. Nevertheless, this meant that the MGHJR and its owners could reach Lowestoft. On grouping, the line remained joint, passing to both the **London, Midland & Scottish** and **London & North Eastern Railways**, but in 1936 administration and control was taken over completely by the LNER, in whose home territory the line ran. Post-war, the line passed to the eastern Region of **British Railways** on **nationalisation** in 1948, and then began a steady decline in the face of road competition and the decline of the fishing industry, eventually being closed in 1959.

Midland & South Western Junction Railway
Last to be absorbed into the **Great Western**, gaining almost an extra nine months of independence, the Midland & South Western Junction provided an important link between the Midlands and the growing port of **Southampton**, but had a difficult early life.

Due largely to the efforts of the **London & South Western Railway**, Southampton's importance as a port grew throughout the nineteenth century, so that it became a significant centre and worthy of consideration for a through line from the Midlands rather than having all traffic directed through **London**. As early as 1845, the initial plan was for a line from Cheltenham to Southampton, but in fact the line eventually had to be built in two stages, first as the

Swindon, Marlborough & Andover Railway, authorised in 1873 and completed in 1881, and then as the Swindon & Cheltenham Extension Railway which opened in 1891, and reached Cheltenham over the Great Western Railway, by which time the two lines had merged to form the Midland & South Western Junction Railway. The 62 route miles proved costly to build and the original Swindon & Marlborough received financial assistance from its contractors, although not strictly speaking a contractor's line, but once opened it passed into receivership where it stayed until 1897.

The MSWJR was rescued by Sam **Fay** who was seconded to the company in 1892 from the LSWR as receiver and general manager. Fortunately, Fay felt that the line held considerable potential, and upgraded the system including a new line to avoid the GWR at Savernake. Fay remained until after the company returned to solvency in 1897 and did not return to the LSWR for another two years, by which time one contemporary railway commentator credited him with having 'made an empty sack stand upright'. The MSWJR had branches connecting it to the GWR at Swindon and to the military base at Tidworth, the station on the line with the highest receipts. The value of the line lay in the potential for through carriages to run to and from Southampton, with Sheffield and **Birmingham** served in this way from 1893, followed later by Bradford, **Leeds**, **Liverpool** and **Manchester**, while for a period carriages ran from Whitehaven to Southampton carrying emigrants.

Midland Counties Railway

Originally intended to be a line for the owners of coal mines running from Pinxton to Leicester and mooted as early as 1832, it eventually was opened as the Midland Counties Railway in 1840, providing a link

from **Derby** and Leicester to Rugby, where it connected with the **London & Birmingham Railway**, with a branch from Nottingham. Engineered by C B **Vignoles**, the line ran through level countryside and had just two significant bridges, over the River Trent and the Warwickshire Avon. Its opening coincided with that of the **North Midland Railway** from Derby to **Leeds**, and the MCR became a vital link in the route between **London** and Yorkshire. Unfortunately, opening also coincided with that of the **Birmingham & Derby Junction Railway**, which also connected with the LBR, and although eleven miles longer than the MCR, ruinous competition was the result. The situation was not resolved until both companies merged with the NMR to form the **Midland Railway** in 1844.

Midland Great Western Railway

Authorised in 1845 as a line from Dublin to Mullingar and Longford, which opened in 1847, the Midland Great Western was then extended to Athlone, Westport and Galway and through Connemara to Clifden, Sligo and Cavan. The line eventually extended to 538 route miles by 1914. On **grouping** of the railways in 1925 in Southern Ireland after independence, it became the second largest constituent part of the **Great Southern Railways**.

Midland Railway

Authorised in 1844, the Midland Railway resulted from the amalgamation of the **Birmingham & Derby Junction**, **Midland Counties** and **North Midland Railways**, and had George **Hudson**, the 'Railway King', as its first chairman. This was the first significant merger of railway companies sanctioned by Parliament. Initially, the Midland was a regional railway without its own access to London, and acted as a link between the **London & Birmingham** at Rugby and the **York & North Midland**, another Hudson railway, at Normanton. Initially, the MR had a monopoly of traffic from London to the North East, but a more direct line, the **Great Northern**, was authorised in 1846 and opened throughout in 1852.

Nevertheless, the MR had by this time then started its own programme of expansion, reaching Lincoln in 1846, and that year leasing the Leeds & Bradford Railway, which was authorised to extend to Skipton, where it would connect with the North Western Railway (not to be confused with the LNWR) line to Lancaster and Morcambe. The MR itself reached Peterborough in 1848, and then acquired the **Birmingham & Gloucester** and the **Bristol & Gloucester**. Nevertheless, expansion was soon checked by the stock market crisis of 1847-48, and then by Hudson's downfall in 1849.

Hudson's successor was John **Ellis**, who provided the steady hand the company needed. The MR then started a period of profitable operation, and even paid a dividend in the difficult period of 1849-51, with an average of 4 per cent paid up to 1859, and then more than 6 per cent during the 1860s.

The relationship with the NWR had not worked as well as the MR had anticipated and the decision was taken to build its own line between Settle and Carlisle, which was authorised in 1866, with poor timing as this followed a collapse in the stock market. The MR tried to abandon the project, but the **North British** and the **Lancashire & Yorkshire Railways**, which had supported the measure, managed to persuade the MR to press ahead, although the line took ten years to complete because of extensive engineering works including the Ribblehead Viaduct. Meanwhile, the MR reached Manchester in 1867 running through the Peak District and with running powers over the Manchester Sheffield and Lincolnshire

Railway, forerunner of the **Great Central**. Next, the MR headed towards **London**, initially with a line from Leicester to Bedford and Hitchin, where it connected with the GNR and acquired rights to run to **King's Cross**, but finding this far from satisfactory, built a line from Bedford to London, where it opened its terminus at **St Pancras** in 1868. It was intended at one time that the head office should move from **Derby** to London once St Pancras was completed, but this did not happen and instead the building at the London terminus became a hotel. Derby did enjoy another innovation later, when in 1910, a central control office was created in an attempt to improve the poor punctuality of the MR's trains.

The **Settle & Carlisle Line** and the St Pancras extension were part of a £6 million investment programme, equating to at least £350 million today, although given the high cost of property in the London area, probably the real figure would now be very much higher. This organic growth was not the sole way forward, as the MR sought to expand. In 1875, it joined the **London & South Western Railway** in leasing the **Somerset & Dorset**, enabling it to reach Bournemouth on the South Coast. The following year, running powers were acquired that enabled the MR to reach the coalfields of South Wales.

In 1872, the MR announced that it would carry third-class passengers on all of its trains, a revolutionary move at the time when many railways regarded third-class as a nuisance. In 1875, it announced that it was scrapping second-class, which meant that third-class passengers enjoyed the comfort of former second-class rolling stock, and at the same time, the MR cut first-class fares. While this was intended to put its competitors at a disadvantage, many other companies retained second-class, in some cases as late as 1912. The MR's move had another advantage, for while it could reach **Edinburgh** and **Glasgow** by way of the Settle & Carlisle, it was a longer route, and by providing a more comfortable service, it meant that it could compete once through running started in 1875. A further step in ensuring the comfort of passengers followed a visit to the USA by the competitive general manager, James **Allport**, in 1874, which had him persuade the board to introduce Pullman cars, for which a supplementary fare could be charged: once restaurant and Pullman cars did start running on the MR, the company gained a good reputation for its food.

While the MR certainly took passenger traffic very seriously, it was also a major freight railway, and this part of its operations actually increased with the extension to London. It was amongst the first to attempt to purchase the private owners' wagons that used its rails, and while not completely successful, this was certainly a measure approved of by most railway managers.

Despite the excellence of its facilities at Derby, the MR had no hesitation in buying locomotive or rolling stock from other sources when quality, innovation or price made this attractive. Nevertheless, the company had just two locomotive superintendents between 1844 and 1903, Matthew **Kirtley** and S W Johnson. It inherited its engineer, W H **Barlow**, from the MCR in 1844, but he remained until 1857, and then continued as a consultant, building St Pancras. He was succeeded by J S **Crossley**, who was responsible for the Settle & Carlisle line. The magnificent engineering of the Settle & Carlisle and the grand St Pancras nevertheless were in contrast to the MR's policies on locomotives, which were relatively straightforward and smaller than those appearing on other railways during the late nineteenth and early twentieth centuries, so that double heading was a feature of MR expresses. There was some

logic behind this, as the MR's routes were more sharply curved than those of the other main line companies, and it was its policy to run lighter, but more frequent, trains.

As the century ended, the MR was still expanding. Its partners in Scotland were the **Glasgow & South Western Railway** and the **North British Railway**, with the latter helped by the MR contributing 30 per cent of the cost of building the **Forth Bridge**, opened in 1890. On the other side of Scotland, it acquired a 25 per cent stake in the **Portpatrick & Wigtownshire Joint Railway**, which ran from Castle Douglas to Stranraer and Kirkudbright, which took traffic that had come of the **West Coast** line at Dumfries on to connect with the packet service to Larne in Northern Ireland, a route later known as the 'Port Road'. It strengthened its hold on the Ulster market in 1903 when it bought the **Belfast & Northern Counties Railway**, the most prosperous railway in the north of Ireland. In 1904, it opened a new port at Heysham in Lancashire for packet services to Belfast. It helped to create the **Midland & Great Northern Joint Railway** in 1893 so that it could reach East Anglia. Less logical as it was isolated from the rest of its network, was the purchase of the **London Tilbury & Southend Railway** in 1912, which the MR promised to electrify, but never did. The company did, nevertheless, develop its existing network, separating slow freight trains from fast expresses, so that between London and Leeds, it had a higher proportion of quadrupled route mileage than its competitor, the **Great Northern**.

In 1923, the MR became a constituent part of the **London, Midland & Scottish Railway**, which adopted many of its ideas and practices, such as central control, but not the legacy of small locomotives.

Milne, Sir James, 1883-1958
Like **Inglis** before him, Milne was an engi-

neer. He trained and graduated in Manchester before joining the locomotive department of the **Great Western Railway** in 1904 at the age of twenty-one years. In contrast to Inglis, however, rather than continuing to rise through the engineering ranks, Milne eventually moved to the company's head office and became involved in collecting statistics and gained operational and traffic experience. He moved to the new **Ministry of Transport** when it was formed in 1919, becoming director of statistics, but returned to the GWR in 1922, on the eve of **grouping**, as assistant general manager.

On **Pole's** departure in 1929, Milne took over as general manager. He inherited a company suffering from the after effects of the miners' strike that had lost many of the export markets for coal, with output in South Wales in decline, while wider economic depression was also taking its toll, along with growing road competition for both goods and passengers. Milne was forced to find ways of reducing costs, but he consistently took a longer term view, and after railway companies were allowed to invest in road transport in 1929, he took the GWR into a greater involvement in bus operation and road haulage, while later he invested in air services both through **Railway Air Services** and Great Western Air Services, including collaboration with the **Southern Railway**. He also considered main line electrification for the GWR, but on closer examination this proved to be too costly for its less densely trafficked network, and further analysis was interrupted by the outbreak of the Second World War. He was knighted in 1932.

During the Second World War, Milne was deputy chairman of the Railway Executive Committee, but since the Minister of Transport was the chairman, he was *ipso facto* chairman. As plans for the railways post-war began to be discussed, including the strong possibility of **nationalisation**, which was Labour Party policy, he made clear his strong opposition to state ownership. Even so, no doubt because of his war service on the REC, he was offered the chairmanship of the Railway Executive of the **British Transport Commission**, but declined it, leaving the post to be offered to his counterpart at the Southern Railway.

Ministry of/Department of Transport

After four years of war and state control, Britain's railways were in a poor condition, and as a result it was decided that the state should be more active and in 1919 a separate department was established, the Ministry of Transport, under the first minister Sir Eric **Geddes**. It was Geddes who was responsible for the passage of the Railways Act 1921 through Parliament, providing the legal framework for **grouping**. Later, the responsibilities of the new department extended to include road transport, and the Road Transport Act 1930 was the first in a series of measures that brought some control to road transport, although these measures were also intended to help protect the railways as much as regulate road haulage and road passenger operations.

The **Board of Trade** retained responsibility for shipping until after the outbreak of the Second World War, when a Ministry of War Transport was formed in 1941. When the ministry reverted to its former title post-war, it retained shipping until that returned to the BoT in 1965. It became the Ministry of Transport and Civil Aviation in 1953, but aviation passed to the BoT in 1965 before returning to the MoT in 1983. Meanwhile, in 1971, the MoT had merged with the Ministry of Housing & Local Government and the Ministry of Works to form the Department of the Environment, before a Department of Transport was created in 1976, to which shipping returned.

Missenden, Sir Eustace, 1886-1973
Son of a Kent stationmaster, he joined the **South Eastern & Chatham Railway** in 1899 as a junior clerk, but made rapid progress to become a district traffic superintendent and became a divisional operating superintendent for the Southern in 1923. In the years before the Second World War, Missenden was assistant superintendent of operations in 1930, docks and marine manager at **Southampton** in 1933, and traffic manager in 1936. He became acting general manager in 1939 when Gilbert **Szlumper** was seconded to the War Office, and became general manager in 1942 with Szlumper's transfer to the Ministry of Supply.

In the preparations for **nationalisation,** Missenden became chairman of the Railway Executive, as second choice to Sir James **Milne** of the **Great Western** who had rejected the post. Missenden was a Southern man through and through, and, not surprisingly, he found the Railway Executive uncongenial and in addition he found the relationship with the **British Transport Commission,** the 'catch-all' body for all the nationalised transport industries, difficult, so he retired in 1951.

Missenden's life centred on the railway. A shy man, a competent and conscientious railwayman, a sound if not always inspiring leader, and an opponent of nationalisation, with a healthy disregard for politicians and civil servants.

Monorail
Frequently held up by enthusiasts for change as the way forward in the development of the railways, monorails have consistently continued to disappoint, despite the concept dating from at least 1821, when the London Dock Company's engineer, one H R Palmer, patented the concept. The early monorails as built by Palmer were used to carry goods, used horses and the loads were balanced as with panniers on either side of a single load-bearing rail. A man-powered monorail, with the 'driver' cycling, carried passengers and was known as the *William the Fourth Royal Car,* and ran on a circular track around the Royal Panarmonion Gardens in London: the single carriage was suspended from a single track along which two-wheeled trucks ran in tandem.

One system that did in fact become operational on a public railway was the Lartigue monorail, named after Charles Lartigue who patented the system in 1883, consisting of a single rail mounted on trestles about 3ft above ground level, augmented by a light guide and stabilising rail on either side about a foot below the main rail. This left the locomotives and rolling stock straddling the line. It was used on Ireland's **Listowel & Ballybunnion Railway** opened in 1888. An earlier version of the same system was patented by John Barraclough Fell in 1868.

Later, in 1903, Louis Brennan obtained a patent for the Gyroscopic Monorail, which was demonstrated in 1909, a year after a demonstration by E W Chalmers Kearney, whose system used a car running on a single rail but with an overhead stabilising rail. Others, using suspended cars, included the 'George Bennie Railplane', which was successfully demonstrated near Glasgow in 1929, and was powered by tractor and pusher aeroplane propellers mounted front and rear. The MAGLEV system of railcars using electro-magnetic levitation to keep them in position above a single track was also a variant on the monorail theme, but a practical system linking Birmingham International railway station with the airport, opened in 1984, was closed in 1995 due to the cost of spare parts.

Museums
There are few museums in the British Isles dedicated solely to the preservation and presentation of items of railway history and

artefacts, with the most notable example being the National Railway Museum at York. Many others are museums of transport, which include railway items, and typically include the Glasgow Museum of Transport and the London Transport Museum, or museums of science and industry, of which the most noteworthy is the Science Museum in London. Railway items also can be found in many local and municipal museums.

Those interested in railway history are fortunate in that the importance of the early locomotives and rolling stock was apparent even as early as the 1850s, and individuals and railway companies were keen to preserve this history, although there was little guarantee that the items were secure for the longer term, or that conservation techniques were understood. While railway museums were founded in Norway and Germany during the late nineteenth century, it was not until 1927 that the **London & North Eastern Railway** opened Britain's first railway museum at **York**, and eventually this was the forerunner of the present National Railway Museum.

The role of the museums is complemented by the railway preservation movement which first became significant during the 1950s. The preservation movement can take the credit for providing an experience of a steam railway for generations born after the end of steam. On the debit side, many of them are providing a steam railway experience, an up-market fairground ride, rather than an insight or introduction to railway history, and unlikely combinations of locomotives and rolling stock can be experienced. The conditions of their light railway orders and the length of line preclude high speed running. It is also the case that since this is a voluntary movement, handled and funded by individuals, the collections reflect individual interests and finances. There is an imbalance in the loco-

motives and rolling stock preserved, sometimes as a result of the movements having developed as steam was ending its days, so that interesting older locomotives were scrapped before preservationists could get to work. The absence of truly historic rolling stock also means that vacuum-brake vehicles are not as common as they should be, and locomotives have been converted to provide air braking. Finally, the passion for steam and the costs involved have meant that electric and diesel rolling stock is rare in preserved form.

It has to be recognised that in Britain's risk adverse society, much earlier railway rolling stock would be banned for health and safety reasons.

That said, some of the best preserved lines are the Welsh narrow gauge lines, whose character has lived on.

Related to railways, but apart from them, are the preserved trams at Crich in Derbyshire.

N

Naming of trains

In considering titled trains, specials such as 'Excursion' or descriptive terms such as 'Limited' or 'Mail', are generally rejected, although this does cause problems with titles such as 'Night Ferry', both descriptive and yet also official. Purists also reject informal titles, but it can surely be argued that these gain some credibility through constant use. In fact, early **Bradshaw's** did include a number of titled trains that were descriptive, and also justified their status with accelerated timings, and by 1877, there were already several of these, mainly mail trains, but the term 'Flying Scotsman' or 'Flying Scotchman' originated as a railwayman's nickname for the fastest **King's Cross** to **Edinburgh** express at around this time: it was only after **grouping** that the **London &**

North Eastern Railway made it official, and confusingly also gave the name to a locomotive.

In the north-west of England, the term 'club train' was applied to any with **club carriages**, and was informal, if also informative, but later became a general term for commuter trains into **Manchester** from **Blackpool** and North Wales.

In Scotland, many of the companies applied names as a description of the service offered, with the 'Further North Express' operating between Inverness and Dornoch.

In the south of England the first titled train arrived almost by accident. It wasn't a railwayman's idea at all, but that of a hotelier! Nor was it introduced by one of the smart, well-heeled and progressive companies such as the **Great Western** was to become, and as the **London, Brighton & South Coast** and **Midland Railway** already were, well before the turn of the twentieth century. It was the humble and poverty-stricken South Eastern Railway that introduced the first named railway train in the British Isles when, on 22 December 1876, it launched the *Granville Special Express*. The promoter of this train was the new owner of the Granville Hotel at Ramsgate, although at the time it proclaimed its address as being in the rather more up-market sounding St Lawrence-on-Sea. Its impact was such that the rival London, Chatham & Dover Railway also introduced its own competitor, the *Granville Express*, but this was the nature of the ruinous 'me too' competition between these two companies until they finally settled on a joint working arrangement as the **South Eastern & Chatham Railway**. The SECR dropped all titles abruptly in 1905, but suddenly, in 1921, the title *Granville Express* re-appeared. Many of the **Southern Railway's** named trains were Pullmans, not only because of the relative prosperity of the area throughout the twentieth century, but because the journey times were often well-suited to Pullman service, with at-seat meals and no time for more than a single sitting, which otherwise would have favoured a conventional dining car. The exception was the *Atlantic Coast Express* launched in 1926, and which could include portions for up to six branch lines in North Devon and North Cornwall.

The Great Western Railway was associated with famous expresses, most probably the *Cornish Riviera*, first used in 1904 and later becoming the *Cornish Riviera Express*, redolent of holidays in Cornwall. These were only a small part of the GWR, or even of its passenger services, but as on other railways, it was the great expresses that raised the image and were so often part of the public profile for a railway. The GWR's speciality was the 'limited' express, which ensured a seat for every passenger by requiring prior reservation, but the company did not neglect the Pullman concept entirely. **Plymouth** still had transatlantic liner traffic during the early days of the grouped railways and before **Southampton** became the dominant passenger liner port. The GWR ran boat trains and, in May 1929, as an experiment, Pullman carriages were added to the boat trains running between Plymouth and **Paddington**. This was followed in July by the *Torquay Pullman*, an all-Pullman express. This was to be the predecessor of another named express that did not have the Pullman supplementary fare; something never fully understood or appreciated by many travellers on the Great Western or elsewhere.

In 1930, the Pullman cars were removed from the boat trains and the *Torquay Pullman* was withdrawn, with all of this rolling stock transferred (since it actually belonged to the Pullman Car Company) to the Southern Railway, where it continued to operate on boat trains, but this time between **Waterloo** and **Southampton**, and on the all-Pullman *Bournemouth Belle*.

Contrary to folklore, the 'Cheltenham Flyer' was never an official title, no matter how well deserved the appellation. Certainly the name does not appear in the timetable and the train was officially known as the *Cheltenham Spa Express*. Nevertheless, the confusion over the title is understandable, as the GWR indeed did refer to the train as the 'Cheltenham Flyer' in its own internal magazine, and also sponsored a book about the train.

In 1923, the GWR decided that rather than simply speed up this service as part of its overall programme of accelerating its longer distance trains, it would aim instead to provide the fastest British express. The fastest timings for the day were those on the **London & North Eastern Railway** over the 44 miles between Darlington and **York**, against which the GWR could offer the almost level 77.3 miles between Swindon and Paddington. A morning down and an afternoon up service was selected and renamed the *Cheltenham Spa Express* to set the record for a regular scheduled service, initially taking just 75 minutes for the Swindon-Paddington section. The service was never uniformly fast, and indeed the title of express was really earned by the dash between Swindon and Paddington, although by cutting the number of stops between Swindon and Cheltenham the service did maintain a reasonable speed even at the 'country' end.

In 1927, the **London, Midland & Scottish Railway** launched the *Royal Scot*, but rather spoilt the prestige by naming the second through express of the day between **Euston** and **Glasgow** as the *Mid-day Scot*. Some names seemed set to be transient, such as the **London & North Eastern Railway's** *Silver Jubilee*, which marked the jubilee of King George V in 1935 and ran between **King's Cross** and **Newcastle**. In 1937, when King George VI had his coronation, the LNER launched the *Coronation*, while the LMS introduced the *Coronation Scot*. Perhaps there was much to be said for time-less contrived names, such as the SR's *Golden Arrow* and its French counterpart, the *Fleche d'Or*.

Named trains had locomotive and carriage headboards, while the *Golden Arrow* and *Bournemouth Belle* both had their own sets of Pullman carriages, making just one return journey a day. By contrast, when the first electric Pullman train, the *Brighton Belle* was introduced, the electric multiple units shuttled between **Victoria** and Brighton every three hours throughout the day, serving breakfast to commuters and late suppers to homebound theatre-goers.

After **nationalisation**, it took some time for named trains to gain acceptance, although a number were reintroduced by the **'Big Four'** before nationalisation. The nationalised **British Railways** reintroduced a number, but also later invented some of its own, including the *Golden Hind*, between Paddington and Plymouth; the *Red Dragon*, between Paddington and **Cardiff**; and the **Liverpool** and Manchester Pullmans, both with intensively used sets of special rolling stock, each making two return journeys a day. There were also a number of trains aimed at the business traveller, such as the *Bradford Executive* and *Hull Executive*.

Fast goods trains were also named, especially by the Great Western between the wars, while many more had working titles that were descriptive.

Nationalisation

Because the railways were often seen as having a monopoly, at least locally despite the multitude of companies, some compared the iron road with the public highway, especially when at first many railways were meant to be open to anyone who wanted to run a train, and so the railways also brought into being the concept of nationalisation, of state ownership, even though the first example of this was in another form of communications altogether, the telegraph system. The railways marked the change from the state providing a service, such as the Royal Mail, to the take over of a functioning business, or businesses.

Greater state control of the railways had been proposed almost from the dawn of the railway age by those who were concerned about the impact of the new form of transport. As early as 1836, one James Morrison wanted Parliament to revise the railway's tolls, this being the time when railways were seen as being rather like turnpike trusts with open access to anyone who wanted to put a carriage or wagon on the iron road. No less a person than the Duke of Wellington, in opposition in 1834, had urged Lord Melbourne to protect the country against the mismanagement and monopoly of the railways. This, of course, shows an early divergence of opinion between those who saw the railways as a monopoly supplier and those who felt that the monopoly was nothing more than the superiority of the railways compared with all other forms of inland transport. Certainly, throughout the early years, Parliament never intended any one railway to have a monopoly.

Outright proposals for nationalisation appeared as early as 1843, when a certain William **Galt** wrote a series of four books in 1843 and 1844 on *Railway Reform* and it was this that led **Gladstone** to include in his Railway Regulation Act 1844, a measure giving the government the power to acquire from 1865 onwards any company sanctioned following the 1844 Act. Galt was a solicitor and it is generally taken that in pressing for reform of the railways, he was more concerned with what would be best for the country as a whole, seeing the railways as similar to the highways and the Post Office, than advocating state ownership as part of a political platform. He returned to his theme in 1864 when his book was

revised and republished, providing a thorough survey of the state of the nation's railways at the time, and then went on to appear before the Royal Commission on the Railways the following year. The members of the Devon Commission certainly considered nationalisation, but decided that nothing further should be done.

The economist Walter Bagehot was another advocate of nationalisation, writing in *The Economist*: 'It is easy to show that the transfer of the railways to the state would be very beneficial, if only it can be effected.' He was unsure over just how it could be done. Advocates of nationalisation fell into several camps, and it was not until much later that this became part of a political platform, and one that contemplated state ownership far in excess of the railways. Many of the earlier advocates saw the railways as constituting a public service, rather like the Royal Mail, and in 1868, the first nationalisation appeared in the form of the government buying out the operators of the telegraph. This included the many telegraph lines operated by the railway companies, and the measure was not without benefit to many of them, with, for example, the London Chatham & Dover Railway, albeit still in receivership, using the £100,000 (around £5 million today) paid by the Post Office for its telegraph system towards the building of a much-needed new station in the City of **London** at **Holborn Viaduct**. It is not surprising, therefore, that Sir Rowland Hill, the Postmaster General, was amongst those keen on nationalising the railways, but more surprising to find that he was joined by, for example, a shipowner who was also a director of the **London & North Western Railway**. The **Board of Trade** inspector, Henry Tyler, was also pro-nationalisation, although this did not stop him from later becoming a director of the Grand Trunk Railway of Canada and a Conservative MP.

Arguments against nationalisation largely centred on the powers of patronage that it would put in the hands of politicians, as it was alleged had been the case in Belgium. The problem was, of course, that state ownership of the telegraph system was an almost instant success. It created a single unified telegraph system where before it had been fragmented. This strengthened the argument of those advocating similar treatment for the railways. On the other hand, a railway is not a telegraph system. Interoperability is far easier to ensure between railways even within different ownership, and there are even opportunities for competition that can benefit the consumer and even hasten technical progress. It is also true that the railways were not guaranteed that their predominant position in inland transport would remain forever, although this could not be foreseen at a time when even the future shape of the railways was unclear. Once again, though, we come back to another argument, which is that the railway network would have been far sparser were it not for the boom of speculation. The lines in the far north of Scotland were built with public money or relief from rates, and it would seem fair to speculate that had the railways been nationalised earlier, many uneconomic lines might have been built for social and strategic purposes, while the development of lines in the heavily industrialised and densely populated areas might have been relatively neglected. One can surmise that there would have been too few lines, with many cross-country routes not built and the trunk network having fewer sections with multiple track (i.e. more than two lines).

Nationalisation finally became a political issue in 1894, when the Amalgamated Society of Railway Servants, predecessor of the **National Union of Railwaymen**, declared in favour of state ownership. In 1899, Sir George Findlay, a director of the

London & North Western Railway, looked at the problem and, while opposed to nationalisation, worked out a system which could allow it to work. The new Labour Party made nationalisation one of its core policies early in the twentieth century.

Many advocates of nationalisation saw the railways becoming a department of state, rather like the Post Office, and one wonders just how many, especially in the trade unions, would have been so keen had they realised that it would eventually be state ownership at arm's length in what would be effectively a state corporation.

A further Royal Commission was appointed in 1913 by the then Liberal Government to consider the question of nationalisation of the railways, but its deliberations were overtaken by the outbreak of the First World War. Wartime saw the railways under state control, and in 1919 the question of nationalisation was raised again, but instead, it was decided to amalgamate the railway companies into four strong geographically-based groups, as we saw earlier. After a further spell of government control during the Second World War (see Railways in Wartime), the post-war Labour administration felt that it had a mandate for nationalisation, although, as a rear-guard action, some railway directors tried to plan a system that would transfer the infrastructure to the state, but allow the companies to remain as managers, not so different from the current situation, but this was rejected.

National Union of Railwaymen

Originally founded in 1872 as the Amalgamated Society of Railway Servants, it was renamed the National Union of Railwaymen in 1913 after amalgamating with the General Railway Workers' Union, founded in 1890, and United Pointsmen's and Signalmen's Society, dating from 1880. It no longer exists since it merged with the

National Union of Seamen in 1990 and the combined union became the National Union of Rail, Maritime and Transport Workers, RMT.

The ASRS was founded in 1872, at a time of a shortage of labour, while the previous year the Trade Union Act had eased the law relating to unions, which could no longer be accused of being illegal for acting in restraint of trade. Some of the union's early supporters would have seemed unlikely in later years, including M T Bass, the leading brewer and Member of Parliament, who objected to the excessive overtime demanded of its employees by the **Midland Railway**. Bass even subsidised the union's newspaper, *Railway Service Gazette*. Initially, the ASRS was non-militant and even published the *Railwaymen's Catechism* in 1875, which described strikes as 'evil to masters and men'. The mass of the early members were drivers, guards and signalmen, the better paid and highly skilled, as opposed to porters and other manual workers.

The welfare of the members was seen initially as reducing the number of hours worked in order to avoid the high accident rate: in 1875, 767 railwaymen were killed, or 0.3 per cent of the workforce. It even mounted exhibitions to demonstrate new safety devices, especially for such high accident areas as shunting, but little interest was shown by the companies.

Until the last decade of the nineteenth century, the ASRS was primarily a friendly society, but over those years, it became a trade union, albeit one also offering benefits to its members. The new role boosted membership from 9,000 in 1885 to 26,000 in 1990. It started with the Darlington Programme of 1887 calling for a ten hour day, reducing to eight hours in busy areas. Overtime rates of 1¼ times hourly earnings and a guaranteed weekly wage were other demands formulated around this time.

Encouraged by the outcome of a strike in the London docks, these demands were pressed upon the companies, but only on the **North Eastern Railway** did the directors agree to meet representatives of the ASRS and use arbitration. By this time, the ASRS was also advocating nationalisation of the railways.

Despite the earlier legislation, in 1901 the **Taff Vale Railway** was awarded £23,000 damages for loss of business during a strike in 1900. Nevertheless, this was rectified by the Trade Disputes Act 1906, while union financing of MPs was permitted by the Trade Union Act 1913. Meanwhile, the larger companies had already agreed to the concept of conciliation boards, long advocated by Sir Sam **Fay** of the **Great Central**, to discuss differences over pay and conditions. Despite this progress, all of the railway unions other than the Railway Clerks' Association, predecessor of the **Transport Salaried Staffs' Association**, joined the first national railway strike in August 1911. The merger with the other two unions changed the nature of the new NUR, with the General Railway Workers having catered for the less skilled and least well paid of railway workers. Membership soared to 267,611.

During the two world wars, the NUR found itself dealing with just one body, the Railway Executive, and with a severe shortage of labour, not only were woman enlisted, from 4,546 in 1913 to 55,000 in 1919, but a series of bonuses was paid. Post-grouping, the deteriorating economic situation and the growth in competition from road transport, as well as the great depression and the General Strike of 1926, combined to undermine the finances of the 'Big Four'. Wage cuts of as much as 2 shillings in the pound first appeared in 1930, and were not fully reinstated until 1937. Nevertheless, these were years of no inflation, and many prices actually fell. The movement of railway companies into bus operation after 1929 also enabled the NUR to start recruiting amongst the forty-one companies acquired by the railway companies.

However, as the Second World War threatened, the unions were about to call another national strike, and this was only averted by pleas from the government, which stressed in a meeting that it 'would need you to get the children away'. Once again wartime saw the number of women on the railways increase, rising to 114,000, while the Railway Executive again increased pay, which over the years 1939-1945 rose by 60 per cent, even though the cost of living only rose by 29 per cent, partially because of the controls imposed through rationing.

Post **nationalisation**, the NUR's membership peaked at 462,205, and extended beyond railways and buses to the nationalised hotels, canals and docks. Membership soon started to fall, dropping below 400,000 by 1952, and eventually to 70,000 by 1994.

The NUR continued its dual role of representing railwaymen in their quest for better working conditions and acting as a lobby for the railways, including proposing more electrification. Not all of its proposals were negative: a proposal to abolish guards on passenger trains on the newly-electrified line between Bedford and **St Pancras** was met by a counter-proposal that guards should become travelling ticket inspectors, and a six month trial saw revenue increased despite a static number of passengers.

Neath & Brecon Railway

One of the least hopeful projects, the Neath & Brecon Railway acquired the powers of two predecessor companies, both unsuccessful, and opened its 72 route miles between 1867 and 1873. The line ran through sparsely-populated country, with no towns of any significance and even the coal traffic was relatively meagre. The N&BR passed into receivership in 1873, despite which by 1877, costs exceeded revenue by no less than 238 per cent. The line was only saved by the **Midland Railway's** ambitions, in this case to grow traffic from **Birmingham and Hereford** to Swansea by taking running powers over the N&BR, while at the southern end of the line, coal traffic was sufficient to be profitable.

Neverstop Railway

A form of railway devised by Adkins and Lewis, with the trains propelled by a shaft laid between the tracks with which a mechanism on each car was engaged. While the shaft revolved at a constant speed, the spiral band linking the car to the shaft had a varied pitch so that when passing through stations the speed of the cars dropped to around 1 mph, while between stations it rose to 20mph. There was no need for signalling as the cars could not run into one another and it was possible to create a system that had a car available in every station for boarding.

The system was demonstrated at Southend in 1923 in the grounds of the Kursaal, after which a line was provided for the British Empire Exhibition at Wembley in 1924-25. There do not appear to have been any further examples. The limitations on speed and the mechanism indicate that it was feasible only on short routes, such as between airport terminals, for example, and it was probably more expensive than a travelator or moving pathway.

Newcastle

Horse-worked wagonways or tramways existed on both sides of the River Tyne from early in the eighteenth century, while the **Newcastle & Carlisle Railway** reached Gateshead in 1837, leaving passengers to be ferried across the river. The Tyne was bridged by the NCR in 1839, which also extended its line into the centre of Gateshead. In 1844 the **Great North of England** and the Newcastle & Darlington Junction Railways provided a through line to **York** and **London** from Gateshead, but could not bridge the Tyne because of the depth of the gorge. It was not until George **Hudson** agreed in 1844 to provide a double-deck bridge carrying trains on the upper level and wagons below that a bridge could be built by Robert **Stephenson**, completed in 1849 at the then astronomical cost of £500,000, and the following year Newcastle Central was opened.

For a while the NER had a monopoly of railway services in and around Tyneside, but this was broken in 1864 when the **Blyth & Tyne Railway** entered the city with its terminus at Picton House, but the port of Blyth did not fulfil its promise and in 1874, the BTR was purchased by the NER. It was not until the opening of the King Edward VII Bridge, west of Stephenson's high level bridge, in 1906, that trains running through to and from Scotland were spared the time-consuming reversal at Central.

Grouping had little impact on railway services in the area, but post-**nationalisation**, a number of branch lines were closed, but some were rescued by providing the route for the Tyne & Wear Metro, which opened in stages from 1980 and was the first in the revival of tramways and light railways in the British Isles. The **East Coast Main Line** was **electrified** in 1991.

Newcastle & Carlisle Railway

An east-west link across the north of England had been mooted for some time, but the end result was just the short Carlisle Canal, opened in 1823. In 1829, a horse-drawn railway was authorised, and Francis **Giles** was appointed engineer. The first section opened ion 1835 and the line was completed throughout in 1839, after problems with landowners who objected to it using steam locomotives, which were forbidden by the terms of its Act, and Giles being dispensed with due to his heavy commitments elsewhere and control being passed to John Blackmore, his assistant.

In 1848, George **Hudson** leased the company as an extension to his **York Newcastle & Berwick Railway**, but the YNBR rejected the NCR, which became independent again in 1850. The **North Eastern Railway** tried to lease the NCR, but was unsuccessful until an Act of 1862 authorised a merger. A branch was opened to Alston in 1852, but a link with the **North British Railway** followed in 1862 near Hexham.

Nock, Oswald Stevens, 1904-1994

Known as O S Nock throughout his career, he spent his entire railway career with the Westinghouse Brake & Signal Company, eventually becoming chief mechanical engineer, and travelled extensively throughout the UK, eventually claiming to have travelled on almost all of the world's railways. Nevertheless, it was his writing on railway subjects for which Nock became famous, eventually writing more than 140 books, and almost 1,000 magazine articles, most of which were in a series on locomotive performance in *Railway Magazine*, where he followed Cecil J **Allen**.

Norfolk Railway

Created in 1845 when the Yarmouth & Norwich Railway, which dated from 1844, merged with the Norwich & Brandon, which had just opened. The latter linked at Brandon with the **Eastern Counties Railway**, which ran from Cambridge to **London**. The NR built branches to Lowestoft and Fakenham between 1847 and 1849, giving it 95 route miles in total. In 1848, the ECR leased the line without first attaining Parliamentary approval, but had to rebuild much of the line during 1856-57. Both companies became part of the **Great Eastern** in 1862.

Although the second line to use electric telegraph for train control, the NR had a poor safety record, and it seems that this became even worse after the ECR took over.

North & South Western Junction Railway
Opened between 1853 and 1857, the North & South Western Junction Railway linked Willesden on the **London & North Western Railway** to Old Kew Junction on the **London & South Western Railway**, and had a branch from South Acton to Hammersmith and Chiswick. It was worked by the LNWR and LSWR, while the passenger service was provided by the **North London Railway**. Between 1871 and 1922, it was leased jointly by the L&NWR, NLR and the **Midland Railway**, while under grouping it passed to the **London, Midland & Scottish**. Mainly used by freight trains between the south and the Midlands and the North West avoiding central **London**.

North British Railway
Authorised in 1844 after the **York & North Midland Railway** was persuaded by George Hudson to provide £50,000 to complete an east coast line between **Edinburgh** and **London**, after Scottish investors had failed to provide sufficient capital. The line opened over the 57 miles to Berwick-on-Tweed in 1846, but had been poorly constructed and within three months, floods swept away many weak bridges and undermined embankments. Despite this, the NBR built branches to Duns, North Berwick and Hawick, with the last providing a link via Carlisle, the 'Waverley' route, with the west coast line when it opened in 1862. In return for allowing the **North Eastern Railway** to run over its line between Berwick and Edinburgh, the NBR was allowed running

powers between **Newcastle** and Hexham.

After an extremely shaky start, with poor punctuality and scant dividends, Richard **Hodgson** became chairman in 1855 and began to rebuild the company's operations. It acquired the **Edinburgh, Perth & Dundee Railway** in 1862, and in 1864, **Edinburgh & Glasgow Railway** in the face of fierce competition from its stronger rival, the **Caledonian**. Hodgson's reign ended in 1866 when its was discovered that he was falsifying the accounts in order to pay an improved dividend, and nearly led to a merger with the Caledonian but for a shareholders' revolt. It was not until the completion of the **Settle & Carlisle** line by the **Midland Railway** in 1876, allowing through trains from **St Pancras** to reach Edinburgh over the Waverley route, that the company's circumstances improved. Dugald **Drummond**, the NBR's locomotive superintendent, designed a new 4-4-0 express locomotive to handle the Anglo-Scottish expresses, before being poached by the Caledonian in 1882.

Competition with the Caledonian continued and proved ruinous. Both companies wanted the lucrative Fife coal market and both wanted to be the best route to **Aberdeen**, while the NBR wanted its share of the growing **Glasgow** commuter traffic. Both companies built large and prestigious hotels, with the NBR's flagship being that at Waverley Station, now known as the New Balmoral. Still more ambitious was the effort made to create a port and a resort at Silloth in Cumberland, which also included building much of the town as well as a hotel and golf course. The port attracted ferry services to Ireland and the Isle of Man, but the resort failed. Rather more success was enjoyed in developing the resort of North Berwick. The company later bought the port of Methil in Fife to handle shipments of coal from the local coalfields. The NBR even attempted to compete with the CR on the Clyde, initially putting two ferries into service in 1866, but soon had to withdraw them, and a second attempt, based on Dunoon, saw heavy losses. A later attempt in conjunction with the **Glasgow & South Western** saw steamer services from Greenock, while steamers were also operated on Loch Lomond after the NBR purchased a local company.

The heavily indented coastline of Eastern Scotland meant that the North British had substantial ferry operations of its own across both the **Forth** and the **Tay** until bridges could be built across these two wide estuaries. The first attempt at building the Tay Bridge resulted in disaster, with the bridge collapsing in a storm while a train was crossing on 28 December 1879, with the loss of all seventy-two people aboard. A new bridge was built and this was followed by the imposing Forth Bridge, completed in 1890. These two bridges meant that the NBR was the fastest and most direct route to Dundee and Aberdeen. Nevertheless, the company failed to get the NER to allow it to handle expresses from London on the stretch of line between Berwick-on-Tweed and Edinburgh.

Traffic boomed, however, with heavy congestion at Waverley that required the station to be rebuilt and the tracks to Haymarket, with the intervening tunnels, quadrupled, with the result that when the rebuilt station opened with its suburban platforms in 1898, it was claimed to be second only to **Waterloo** in size. Freight traffic also grew, and shipments of coal through the port of Methil rose from 400,000 tons in 1888 to 2.8 million tons twenty years later.

While most of the railway network had been completed by 1880, the NBR had two of the last major railway projects in the country prior to the **Channel Tunnel** Rail Link. The first of these was the West Highland Line, which ran from Craigendoran, west of Glasgow, to Fort William, and opened in 1894, and then the extension to Mallaig, completed in 1901, but which had taken Robert **McAlpine** four years for just 40 miles and almost uniquely in Great Britain, had needed a subsidy of £260,000 (about £17.5 million today) of taxpayers' money. These were followed by a line from Dunfermline to Kincardine and a small number of light railways, essentially infilling gaps in the system.

With the major naval base of Rosyth, opened in 1916, although its railway station opened the previous year, on the coast of Fife, plus the anchorages in the Cromarty Firth and at Scapa Flow in Orkney, the NBR was heavily involved in the First World War, including handling the famous 'Jellicoe Specials' which ran from London to Thurso, and put a heavy strain on a largely single track route north of the Forth. Rosyth alone received 1.25 million tons of coal from Wales in 1918. As with the other railways, the shortage of skilled men and the demands placed on the system combined to ensure that there were serious arrears of maintenance as the war ended. Nevertheless, the NBR was one of the more successful in obtaining compensation from the government, receiving just under £10 million.

The NBR was the largest Scottish railway company contributing 1,300 track miles, 1,100 locomotives, 3,500 carriages and 57,000 wagons to the new **London & North Eastern Railway** on 1 January 1923.

North Eastern Railway

Formed in 1854 when four railway companies merged their operations, the **York, Newcastle & Berwick**, the **York & North Midland**, the **Leeds Northern** and the tiny Malton & Driffield Junction, although the three larger companies did not merge their shareholdings until 1870. The NER came into being with 700 route miles, but was not a complete rationalisation of railway operations in the north-east as four other companies remained independent for the best part of ten years.

One of the independent companies, the **Stockton & Darlington**, which had supported the construction of the South Durham & Lancashire Union line, allied with the **London & North Western Railway**, but after the SDR and SDLUR merged, they were taken over by the NER in 1863. Similar action was taken by the West Hartlepool Railway, which served a port that was a strong competitor to **Hull** and Middlesbrough, and sought an alliance with the LNWR, planning to compete with the NER, and it was not until 1865 that it agreed to be taken over, and that year the **Newcastle & Carlisle** was also absorbed. This left just the **Blyth & Tyne** as an independent company within the NER area, and this was not absorbed until 1874. The acquisition of these companies was often difficult, and once in NER ownership, integration proved to be slow and difficult.

The NER was a vital link in the line from **London** to **Edinburgh**, linking the **Great Northern** in the south with the **North British Railway** at Berwick-on-Tweed, which formed what is now the **East Coast Main Line**. Between 1868 and 1871, it built cut-offs amounting to 26 miles, with the two main ones between Durham and Gateshead, and between **Doncaster** and **York**. Nevertheless, the NER was slow to introduce the block system of signalling and interlocking of points and signals, and these as well as management failings contributed to the four accidents suffered in late 1870. William O'Brien, the general manager was sacked and Henry **Tennant** succeeded him, making the necessary reforms both to the structure of the company and to its operating practices, despite which the newly integrated company managed to pay a dividend of more than 8 per cent during the 1870s. It also mounted 'The Jubilee of the Railway System' at Darlington on the SDR's fiftieth anniversary in 1875. On the other hand, possibly to appease the powerful iron masters, it was the last of the trunk railways to abandon iron rails in favour of steel. It also refused to send a delegate to the **Railway Clearing House** to discuss standardising railway telegraph codes as it could not consider any revision of its own codes.

The NER's monopoly in the north-east soon came under threat. Hull Corporation was angered by the NER entering into a traffic pooling agreement for freight receipts for all of the ports between the Tyne and the Humber. The Corporation backed plans for a new dock to ease congestion on the Humber, and a new independent railway to bring coal from South and West Yorkshire. Originating as the Hull Barnsley & West Riding Junction Railway & Dock Company, but later becoming the **Hull & Barnsley Railway**, the new 66-mile line was authorised in 1880. Railway and new docks were both completed in 1885. A rate war ensued, which forced the Hull & Barnsley into receivership during 1887-89, but an agreement was reached, and while the NER was never able to acquire the HBR, the two companies shared construction of the large new deep water dock, the King George V, which opened in 1914.

The 1870s were not a period of easy growth for the railways, and the financial performance of the NER is all the more creditable for this. Faced with a recession in mineral traffic, the company began to encourage third-class travel.

The NER gained momentum and prominence when Tennant was superseded by G S **Gibb** in 1891. Gibb believed in building a management team with diverse experience rather than continuing the NER's own introspective policies, and recruited R L **Wedgwood**, Frank **Pick** and E C **Geddes**, all of whom rose to prominence in the industry. Gibb changed the NER's working statistics, using ton-mileage rather than train-mileage to assess performance. At first other companies were dubious about the changes when introduced in 1899, but in due course these became the industry standard. Forward thinking was also evident when the NER became the first railway to negotiate with trade unions on hours and wages. Gibb himself moved on in 1906, becoming managing director of London's Underground Group of Companies.

Meanwhile, a succession of chief mechanical engineers, starting with Wilson, and then Thomas **Worsdell** and Vincent **Raven**, took the company into **electrification**. It started with the Quayside freight line at **Newcastle** in 1902, and then the suburban system north of the city in 1904, and by 1915 had also electrified the longer distance line from Shildon to Middlesbrough. The company even planned for electrification of the ECML between York and Newcastle, but in the end, this was shelved through **grouping** and **nationalisation** and did not take place until 1991.

The HBR was finally absorbed by the NER in 1922, and the NER became a constituent company of the **London & North Eastern Railway** in 1923.

North Lindsey Light Railway

Opened in 1906 between Scunthorpe and Winterton and Thealby, and extended to Winteringham in 1907, and Whitton in 1910. It was worked from the start by the **Great Central Railway**, before passing to the **London & North Eastern Railway** in 1923.

North London Railway

Authorised in 1846 as the East & West India Docks & Birmingham Junction Railway, running 13¼ miles from Camden Town on the **London & North Western Railway** to Blackwall, and opened in stages between 1850 and 1852. It was renamed

the North London Railway in 1853. Its promoters naturally enough saw freight traffic as its main business, but passenger trains operated quarter-hourly from its opening. Initially, **Fenchurch Street** on the **London & Blackwall Railway** was the terminus, but the approach was indirect and time consuming, but a two mile stretch of line was opened from Dalston to **Broad Street** in 1865, and passenger traffic grew quickly. Much of the business was generated by trains running over 54¾ miles of track belonging to other companies. By 1907, the NLR's revenue was split 50:50 between freight and suburban passenger traffic.

William **Adams** built the NLR's locomotives from 1863 at its own works at Bow. The locomotive stock was highly standardised, with 4-4-0T for passenger services and 0-6-0T for freight.

The major shareholder was the LNWR, and managed to keep **Great Northern** trains out of Broad Street, although after 1875 NLR trains were able to work to GNR stations, including High Barnett, Potters Bar and Enfield, over a curve at Canonbury. NLR trains ran over the **London & South Western** to Richmond. The NLR also provided the services on the **North & South Western Junction Railway** line between Willesden and Kew after it opened in 1853, which was jointly leased by the NLR, LNWR and the **Midland** in 1871, as well as the Hampstead Junction Railway, which ran for 6½ miles from Camden Town to Willesden and opened in 1860, which was another LNWR venture. In short, the NLR was the strategic link that was far more important than its route mileage suggested and linked the railways running to the west, north and east of London – only the **London, Brighton & South Coast** and the two south-eastern companies were not directly linked to it. An idea of its importance was that it had no less than 123 locomotives by 1908, and 620 carriages. At Kentish Town Junction, Camden Town, the NLY installed the first completely interlocked points and signals, made at its own works at Bow. In 1874, the line between Broad Street and Camden Town was quadrupled. An interesting feature was that the NLR only provided first and second class accommodation until 1875.

Generally a highly efficient and well run railway, as it needed to be given the traffic coming off other lines, it nevertheless suffered a spate of accidents with trains running into one another on the connecting curve with the GNR at Cannonbury Tunnel in 1881, and the cause was found to be GNR signalmen not understanding NLR bell codes.

By 1880, the railway had settled into a steady business which lasted until the turn of the century, and except for two years when dividends were 6³/₄ per cent, it paid 7¹/₂ per cent. Nevertheless, it was also one of the first to suffer the impact of electric tramways, and this forced it to consider electrification. The LNWR took over operations from 1909, although the LNR remained as a separate company, and electrification was approved in 1911 as part of the LNWR's scheme for its London suburban services, with electrification completed between Broad Street and Richmond in 1916, and then between Broad Street and Watford in 1922, using the third rail system.

The NLR was one of the few railway companies to suffer enemy air attack during the First World War, and occasionally had to close its passenger services.

On **grouping**, it became part of the **London, Midland & Scottish Railway**.

North Midland Railway

Authorised in 1836 to extend the **Birmingham and Derby Junction** and the **Midland Counties**, both which were exten-

sions of the still uncompleted **London & Birmingham**, from **Derby** to **Leeds**, a distance of 73 miles, and to be a vital link in a line from **London** to the North East. George **Stephenson** was the inspiration supported by the banker, G C **Glyn**, as well as other investors in London, the north-west and Yorkshire. Working with his son Robert, **Stephenson** chose an easy route rather the most direct, which would have taken the line through Sheffield and Barnsley, with a maximum gradient of 1 in 250, but even so there were three major tunnels, including one of a mile at Clay Cross.

When opened in 1840, the line had cost twice the original estimate: revenues soon proved disappointing, with an average dividend of just 3.2 per cent for the first three years. After Glyn resigned in 1842, the shareholders demanded a committee to investigate expenditure and management, and this was dominated by George **Hudson**, chairman of the **York & North Midland Railway**. The outcome was that drastic economies were introduced, with a substantial reduction in employee numbers and a reduction in the remuneration of those who remained. After a serious accident in 1843, the new policies came to the notice of the **Board of Trade**.

The situation was little better at the BDJR and the MCR, both of which also suffered financial difficulties, so Robert Stephenson and George Hudson agreed that all three should amalgamate to form a new company, the **Midland Railway**.

North Staffordshire Railway

Formed in 1845, by local industrialists to keep the Potteries free from incursions by the big companies that were emerging, the NSR used the Staffordshire Knot as its emblem and became known affectionately as 'The Knotty'. It developed a network of more than 200 route miles, and secured running rights over more than 300 route miles belonging to other companies. Although formed to transport coal, ironstone and quarried materials, it also became the largest railway canal owner, starting with an amalgamation with the Trent & Mersey Canal in 1846, but unlike other railway companies, it continued to develop the canals it bought.

The main lines linked **Crewe** with **Derby** and Colwich with Macclesfield, meeting at Stoke. The Macclesfield line was used by the **London & North Western Railway** as a cut-off to avoid Crewe and save five miles between **Euston** and **Manchester**. A loop line completed in 1875 linked all six Potteries towns, while branches connected the NSR with the **Great Western** at market Drayton and another served the Biddulph Valley. With the **Great Central**, the NSR was joint owner of the 11-mile long Macclesfield Bollington & Marple Railway. It also worked the 2ft 6in gauge **Leek & Manifold Light Railway**, opened in 1904.

Before the First World War, freight and passenger traffic combined provided an average 5 per cent dividend, while demands to reduce Sunday services were resisted and instead industrial workers were encouraged to make excursions into the countryside.

On grouping, the NSR became a constituent company of the **London, Midland & Scottish Railway**. Rationalisation and some decline followed, but during the Second World War, a branch was opened to a Royal Ordnance factory at Swynnerton, near Stone, which carried 3 million passengers a year from 1941 on trains that never appeared in the public timetables. Colwich to Stone and Macclesfield were electrified during the 1960s.

North Sunderland Railway

Opened in 1898 between Chathill on the **North Eastern Railway** to North Sunderland and Seahouses, it was managed and worked by the **London & North Eastern Railway** from 1939 before passing to **British Railways** in 1948, and closed in 1951.

North Union Railway

A merger of the Wigan & Preston railway with the Wigan Branch railway in 1834, the NUR opened in 1838, running to Preston from Parkside on the **Liverpool & Manchester**, giving a through route from **London** and an important link in the **West Coast Main Line**. It was joined at Euston Junction in 1843 by the Bolton & Preston Railway, which broke what would have been a monopoly for the NUR, and a fares war broke out for traffic between **Preston** and **Manchester**, which even extended to using road transport, before the two companies merged in 1844.

In 1846, the NUR was leased jointly by the **Grand Junction** and **Manchester & Leeds Railways**, and then the NUR passed to the **London & North Western Railway**, while the MLR became the **Lancashire & Yorkshire Railway**. An unusual feature of the former NUR's lines is a stone cutting near Chorley which is buttressed by 16 flying arches.

Northern & Eastern Railway

Originally authorised in 1836 to link **London** and **Cambridge**, it was allowed in 1839 to use the **Eastern Counties Railway** between Stratford and Shoreditch, using the same 5ft gauge as the ECR. That same year, Robert **Stephenson** replaced James **Walker** as engineer. The line had reached Bishop's Stortford, claiming to be running the fastest trains in Great Britain, with a branch to Hertford, by 1843, but there was no further progress until it was leased by the ECR and the line was extended through Cambridge to Brandon, where it met the **Norfolk Railway** running from Norwich, in 1845.

The previous year, both the NER and ECR converted to standard gauge.

The **Great Eastern Railway** acquired the NER in 1902.

Northern Counties Committee – (see **Belfast**) & **Northern Counties Railway**

Northern Ireland Railways
Formed in 1967 on the winding up of the **Ulster Transport Authority**, which had managed railways in Northern Ireland since 1949. It used the brand 'NI Railways' and operated almost 200 miles of Irish standard gauge 5ft 3in track. The main lines are from Belfast to Londonderry, with a branch to Portrush, and Belfast to the border on the line to Dublin, while there are also lines from Belfast to Bangor, seaside resort and commuter town, and to Larne, from which ferries operate to Scottish ports.

Northern Line
Renaming in 1937 of the Edgware Highgate & Morden line, which had originated from the **Hampstead Line** and the **City & South London Railway**. The Northern Line benefited from a programme of works that eventually included new rolling stock in 1938, as well as extension of its network over **London & North Eastern** branches to High Barnet and East Finchley. Plans to extend the line beyond Edgware to Bushey Heath were dropped post-Second World War. When formed, the Northern included a Northern City section that was separate from the rest of its network, but transferred to **British Railways** in 1975.

Until 1988, the tunnel from East Finchley to Morden via Bank (the City branch of the Northern) was, at 17¼ miles, the longest continuous railway tunnel in the world. Overall, the Northern consists of 40 route miles.

Notation of wheels – see **Wheel notation**

Nottingham & Grantham Railway
Opened in 1850 with a terminus at London Road, Nottingham, it was taken over by the **Great Northern Railway**, but also used by the **London & North Western** Railway running from Market Harborough.

Nottingham Suburban Railway
A railway linking Trent Lane Junction with St Ann's Well, Sherwood and Daybrook, opened in 1889 and closed in 1951.

O

Oakley, Sir Henry, 1823-1914
Joining the **Great Northern Railway** in 1849 as chief clerk in the secretary's office, he took over as secretary in 1858, and became general manager in 1870. During his period with the company, it was constantly under threat from the **Midland Railway** and the Manchester, Sheffield & Lincoln Railway, predecessor of the **Great Central Railway**, as well as from the **West Coast** companies. Growing London suburban traffic at **King's Cross** also placed a considerable demand on the company's resources.

Oakley played an important part in representing the railway case at Parliamentary hearings and was secretary to the Railway Companies Association during the 1880s, for which he was granted a knighthood in 1891. He was elected to the GNR board in 1897 and retired as GM the following year, although he then became chairman of the **Central London Railway**.

Oxford, Worcester & Wolverhampton Railway – see **West Midland Railway**

P

Padarn Railway
A private mineral line built in 1848 and

using two gauges, 4ft and 1ft 10¾ inches in Snowdonia.

Paddington

Alone amongst the 'Big Four', the Great Western had just one London terminus, Paddington. This was the result of there being only one company amongst those grouped to make the 'new' Great Western with a London connection, yet, for travellers to the City, Paddington was probably the least convenient location at which to arrive in the capital. Not for nothing did the GWR value its stake in the Hammersmith & City Line, or at one stage operate by a circuitous route through the west of London to Victoria.

Built to accommodate the broad gauge, Paddington acquired a natural spaciousness, and gave the impression of being built by an affluent railway, with the graceful roof provided by Brunel almost cathedral-like, even to the extent of having what almost amounted to transepts.

Confident that all problems would be resolved, preparatory work on the approach to Paddington was carried out even before it received Parliamentary sanction in 1837. The line reached London from Kensal Green along the alignment of the Grand Union Canal towards Bishops Walk, subsequently re-named Bishops Road and then Bishops Bridge Road, using land leased from the Bishop of London. An immediate shortage of capital meant that a temporary station had to be built, mainly of wooden construction with the passenger facilities and offices in the arches of the bridge under Bishops Road, and with just an arrival and a departure platform separated by a broad vehicle roadway. The temporary station opened on 4 June 1838, on the day that the line itself opened for business over the 22.5 miles between Paddington and Maidenhead. The line extended to Reading on 30 March 1840, and the ambition of linking London and Bristol was achieved on 30 June 1841.

Temporary it may have been, but the early Paddington Station was clearly regarded as being fit for royalty. Queen Victoria made her first railway journey on 13 June 1842, travelling from Slough, the nearest station to Windsor, behind the locomotive *Phlegethon*. Gooch drove the locomotive at an average speed of 44mph, which alarmed Her Majesty somewhat, so that Prince Albert was moved to request that future journeys be conducted at lower speeds.

The original station was perfectly adequate for the twelve trains or so on an average day, but the opening of the line to Bristol immediately put it under pressure. Enlargement was the answer, and by 1845, there were three arrival platforms and two for departures to the south of the arrival platforms, as well as a further two tracks, while at the country end of the station lay a carriage shed, and beyond that an engine shed and workshops. As an interim measure, the Great Western directors initially authorised a departure shed, hoping that, despite the line nearing completion in South Wales and to Birmingham, the original temporary station would be adequate as an arrivals shed for a while longer. In 1853, the board bowed to the inevitable, and agreed that the permanent terminus could be completed in its entirety.

Brunel's Paddington

Brunel had the wisdom to engage one of the most eminent architects of the day, Matthew Digby Wyatt, as his assistant, officially to provide ornamentation. In his design for Paddington, Brunel was influenced by his time as a member of the building committee for Paxton's famous Crystal Palace, and also by the new main station in Munich, which led him to design a metal roof, the first for a large station. The buildings at the town end of the station had to be impressive as the platforms lay in a cutting, and the station offices were alongside the main departure platform. The splendid face of Paddington to the world was that of the Great Western Hotel, later renamed the Great Western Royal Hotel, which opened on 9 June 1854. Designed by Philip Hardwick, as built, the hotel had 103 bedrooms and 15 sitting rooms, and the impact of the frontage was literally raised by two towers at each end, both two stories higher than the main building. A sculpture of Britannia surrounded by displays of the 'six parts of the world, and of their arts and commerce', stood above the pediment.

The new station was located more than 200 yards south of the temporary terminus, much of it on the old goods sidings, and was 700 feet long and 238 feet wide. Offices, some 580 feet long, were built on the southwestern side of the station along what was then known as Spring Street, but is today Eastbourne Terrace, while a cab road was built on the north-eastern side. As with the original temporary station, arrival platforms were on the northern side and departure platforms on the southern, and with royal patronage firmly in mind, the latter could be reached through a private entrance in the office building and a special royal waiting room, expensively furnished with French furniture. Above the royal entrance from the street, there was a crown, but the two doorways to the platform had one surmounted by the royal coat of arms, the other by that of the Great Western.

The greatest visual impact came from the roof, towering up to 55 feet above the platforms and with glass and corrugated iron supported by wrought iron arches. There were three spans, 70 feet, 102.5 feet and 68 feet, separated by two 50 feet transepts. The transepts were ornamental, but had the practical function of accommodating large traversers to move carriages between the tracks, but these machines were never used.

Broad gauge tracks were complemented by wide platforms, with the main departure platform next to the offices being 27 feet wide. North of the subsidiary departure platform lay another track, then five more used for storing carriages, then two more on either side of an arrival platform, 21 feet wide, with a tenth track serving a further arrival platform which, including the cab road, was 47 feet wide. The site of the temporary terminus was not abandoned, but instead became the new goods depot. To modern eyes, the unusual feature of the platforms was that the subsidiary platforms were all island platforms as there was no main concourse and the tracks extended beyond the platform ends to nineteen turnplates (some tracks had two) for horses and carriages to be loaded and unloaded. Rather than build a subway or even a footbridge, access to the subsidiary platforms was by small bridges that rested on a truck and could be lowered and raised using hydraulic power. One of these survived in use between platforms 1 and 2 until 1920, and was only finally scrapped during the Second World War.

The departure side was brought into use on 16 January 1854, followed by the arrival side on 29 May. New engine sheds came into use at Westbourne Park during 1855, allowing those by the temporary station to be closed and the entire site taken over by the new goods depot. Westbourne Park had another function, for in common with many railways of the time, tickets were not collected as trains rumbled into the terminus, impractical given the lack of corridors on early rolling stock, but at a station close to the end of the line, and a call at the ticket platform at Westbourne Park was a necessity.

Signalling at first had consisted of the disc and crossbar type using revolving posts, and semaphore signalling did not appear until 1865, with block operation introduced the following year as far out as Ealing.

The dream of a fast and spacious broad gauge railway was a nightmare for many users, and the GWR failed to make the most of its advantages either in the width of rolling stock or in achieving speed significantly higher than those elsewhere. As early as 1861, the GWR agreed to amalgamate with the **West Midland Railway**, a standard gauge line, and to enable its trains to reach Paddington, standard gauge track had to be laid between Paddington and the connecting junction thirty-seven miles out of London at Reading West. By September 1870, Paddington's suburban services were mainly standard gauge, but it was not until early on 21 May 1892 that the services to **Plymouth** and Cornwall were finally converted.

Paddington may have compared well with many of the other railway stations being built at this time, both in space and amenity, but it was far away from the West End and even further from the City of London. Appreciative of this problem, the GWR decided to invest in the new North Metropolitan Railway to the extent of £175,000. The intention was that the railway should be built as a mixed gauge line, with standard and GWR broad gauge, and a connection to the GWR just west of Paddington. Re-named the **Metropolitan Railway** in 1854, it reached Farringdon Street in 1863, although passengers from Paddington had to use a separate station, Bishops Road, to reach the underground. The Metropolitan could not introduce rolling stock of its own until late 1864, and in the meantime managed to survive using locomotives from the **Great Northern Railway** and carriages from the **London & North Western Railway**, for which the standard gauge tracks proved a blessing. The Metropolitan's other priority, in addition to

funding its own rolling stock and completing the line, was to buy out the GWR's stake in its business. This was not the only underground connection, as from June 1864, using Bishops Road Station, the **Hammersmith & City Railway** commenced operations to Hammersmith leaving the GWR main line at Westbourne Park, but it was intended to act mainly as a feeder into the Metropolitan, and enjoyed the support of both companies, which by 1867 had recovered from their earlier differences and managed the Hammersmith & City through a joint committee. Initially the Hammersmith & City was worked by GWR broad gauge trains, but from 1 April 1865, the Metropolitan used its own standard gauge rolling stock over the entire route between Farringdon Street and Hammersmith, while GWR broad gauge trains eventually ran over Metropolitan tracks as far east as Moorgate until March 1869, and then, once standard gauge rolling stock was delivered, as far east as **Liverpool Street**. In the other direction, GWR trains also ran through to Kensington. Trains from as far away as Windsor, by this time a branch off the line at Slough, ran through to the Metropolitan. The growing Metropolitan Railway was extended to Gloucester Road, and in October 1868, a new station was opened in Praed Street directly opposite the Great Western Hotel. Even so, there was no footbridge providing direct access to the services from Bishops Road, later re-named Paddington (Suburban) until 1878, and no subway between Paddington and Praed Street until 1887.

This growing network of urban services continued to use the GWR main line between Bishops Road and Green Lane Junction, near Westbourne Park, until 30 October 1871, when separate suburban lines were opened with stations at Royal Oak and Westbourne Park, but the increasingly busy main lines were crossed by the local trains until a dive-under was commissioned between Royal Oak and Westbourne Park on 12 May 1878.

It was on the lines to the underground that the worst **accident** occurred at Paddington on 5 May 1864, when a Great Northern 0-6-0 locomotive leaving Bishops Road at 09.05 for Farringdon Street suffered a boiler explosion. A number of people were injured, two of them seriously, and the station was badly damaged, with one piece of debris falling 250 yards away, penetrating the roof of the mainline station.

The Hammersmith & City Line was electrified on 5 November 1906, and once the Metropolitan Line was also electrified, GWR trains were hauled to the City of London by Metropolitan electric engines.

Paddington's isolation was eased further by the building of the deep level tube line, an extension of the **Baker Street and Waterloo**, or 'Bakerloo', proposed as early as 1899, but not actually agreed until 1911. To the dismay of the Metropolitan, which saw the new arrival as a competitor, the GWR drew the Bakerloo northwards from Baker Street with the inducement of a subsidy, and services started on 1 December 1913, with the line extended to Willesden Junction in 1915 and to Watford in 1917. The new deep level tube platforms were more than forty feet beneath a new booking hall underneath the cab road close to the arrival platforms.

The Growing Station

The original arrangement of two tracks to and from Paddington was soon inadequate as traffic continue to grow, and by 1871, four tracks were in place between Paddington and Westbourne Park, but these did not reach Slough until 1879, and Maidenhead until 1884. The new arrangement was for the fast lines, known as the 'main lines', to be on the south side and the

suburban lines, known as the 'relief lines', on the north. In 1878, a new arrival platform, No 9, was commissioned, and a new cab road approached the station using a bridge over the approaches to the goods depot. A new section of roof sheltered the new platform and roadway, albeit less grand than the original. Two new departure platforms were introduced in 1885, and some time later were re-numbered as 4 and 5. This expansion was achieved by the simple expedient of reducing the number of tracks available for carriages in the main station or train shed, and new West London Carriage Sidings to the south of the main line were commissioned during the late 1880s. In 1893, further changes enabled platform 7 to be moved southwards, with another new arrival platform. Apart from the expansion of 1878, all of these changes were accommodated under the original Brunel roof.

In 1880 Paddington became one of the first railway termini to use electric light, although unreliable. Nevertheless, in 1886 a more reliable supply was introduced using three generators installed at Westbourne Park and which lit the terminus itself as well as the offices, goods sheds and yards, and the stations at Royal Oak and Westbourne Park. The generators had to be moved in 1906 to allow Platform 1 at Paddington to be extended, and new facilities were installed at Park Royal with a fully-fledged power station.

Milk traffic became so important that it used the main terminus. The 1878 platform had a milk arrival dock completed in 1881 at its outer end, and accommodation was also arranged for this traffic on the departure side. By 1900, more than 3,000 milk churns were being handled each day at Paddington, joined by trains handling meat, fish, newspapers and horses, while there were also special flower trains during the early spring, bringing produce from as far away as the Isles of Scilly via **Penzance**.

In response to the growing number of through workings between railway companies in the north and Midlands and those in the south, early in the twentieth century, the GWR encouraged the **London, Brighton & South Coast Railway**, whose **Victoria** terminus it had used, to introduce a daily return service between **Brighton** and Paddington. The journey to and from Brighton reached Paddington using the Latimer Road spur and the **West London Railway**, with the through service taking 100 minutes, but the operation only lasted from July 1906 to June 1907, as it failed to attract sufficient custom.

The GWR had started services to and from Victoria as early as 1 April 1863, with what was essentially a suburban service from Southall where connections could be made with its main line services. Wartime restrictions saw the end of the Southall service in 1915, and in any case, such a service was really superfluous with the opening of what is now known as the **Circle Line** between Victoria and Paddington in 1868.

Edwardian Heyday and Beyond

The new century saw trains becoming longer and heavier, with corridor coaches with connections between the carriages, which especially on main line duties increasingly were mounted on bogies. Once again, Paddington was in danger of being outgrown. Before the problem could be resolved, a substantial amount of preparation had to be put in hand. In March 1906, a new locomotive depot was opened at Old Oak Common, allowing the earlier structure at Westbourne Park to be closed. New carriage sheds were also opened at Old Oak Common. There were other minor works as well, all of which contributed to the whole, so that in 1908, the main departure platform had an extension, numbered 1A, used primarily for excursion trains and, later, for

down milk traffic, although milk traffic was finally moved to the goods depot in 1923, probably reflecting the increasing use of tanker wagons. Later 1A became a platform for rolling stock waiting to be moved onto the main platform, cutting the interval between departures, and then it became a double-sided parcels platform. At around this time, island platforms 2 and 3 were extended to around a thousand feet, while platforms 1 to 5 had a luggage subway built with lifts to the platforms.

All of this really consisted of tampering with the edges. In 1906, a more comprehensive scheme was approved by the Great Western's directors. The arrival side of the station was to be extended with the addition of three new platforms under a 700 feet long and 109 feet wide steel and glass roof, intended to be in sympathy with the original, with platform 9 extended to 950 feet, while the Bishops Road platforms were also to be extended. The old overbridges with their brick arches were to be replaced by a new steel structure with long spans that would allow the tracks to be re-arranged, and would allow greater freedom for such adjustments in the future. The most radical of these changes was the construction of a new goods depot to be built at South Lambeth, as the GWR termed Battersea to avoid confusion with the LB&SCR station, which would ease the pressure on Paddington goods, and no doubt make interchange with other railways in the south easier.

These works took until the years of the First World War to complete. In the meantime the approach tracks were rearranged. As with many of the older termini, empty stock workings at Paddington for many years occupied the running lines and significantly reduced line capacity for revenue-earning trains. There had been some relief with new engine and carriage roads to serve the new engine and carriage sheds at Old

Oak, but these only ran part way on the north side of the line. Sharing of the main and suburban lines by goods trains made the problems worse. In 1911, work began on lines to segregate all empty carriage and light engine workings over the entire three miles between Paddington and Old Oak Common, hampered by the need to rebuild Westbourne Park station, but war intervened and work ground to a halt in 1916, was suspended for ten years, and the entire project was then not finally completed until 1927.

The new layout meant that there was a down empty carriage line all the way from Paddington to Old Oak Common north of the suburban or relief lines, shared by goods workings, while the old engine and carriage line was converted into a goods running line. From the junction with the subway or dive under, a second up empty carriage road was provided into Paddington. The result of these changes was that the last three quarters of a mile into Paddington was arranged, from the north, as follows:

Up City
Down City
Down carriage
Up relief (suburban)
Up main
Up carriage
Down main
Up carriage

Ten years later, the up main and up relief lines were re-signalled to enable them to be used to ease congestion on the down carriage line, and then later the down carriage line and one of the up carriage lines also became running lines.

Paddington was being transformed. The layout of the approach tracks was remodelled to provide improved connections to the **Hammersmith & City** lines and the Ranelagh engine yard on the south side of the lines at Royal Oak station, where locomotives from the provinces were turned.

The old goods yard and its approaches were replaced by three new platforms with a roadway. While the new roof was not completed until 1916, the new platforms were brought into use in stages between November 1913 and December 1915, and introduced new features to the GWR, including hydraulic buffers. Passenger amenities continued to improve, with space provided from 1910 beneath platform 1 for lavatories, bathrooms and a hairdressing salon. The new station had platforms 1 to 4 for departures on the main line, 5 to 7 for outer-suburban trains, while platforms 8-11 were for main line arrivals. Until 1923, platform 12 handled milk arrivals, and other perishable traffic such as fish, as well as mail and parcels, while the opposite face of the platform opened out onto a sunken roadway so that these goods could be manhandled easily across the platform onto the backs of road vehicles.

The First World War had far less impact on Paddington than on the termini of the southern companies, but even so the number of troop movements meant that a twenty-four hour free buffet was introduced, staffed by lady volunteer workers. There were also a number of ambulance trains, a total of 351 over the four years or so of war. Spared air raid damage, nevertheless some of the glass panels in the roof were broken by shrapnel from anti-aircraft fire. Post-war, a war memorial to members of the GWR who had fallen in combat was installed between the doors of the royal suite on the main departure platform.

Other post-war work to complete the 1906 programme of improvements saw Brunel's old cast iron columns supporting the roof between platforms 2 and 3 and between 7 and 8 replaced by steel columns on which Wyatts original decorations were reproduced. Other columns had been replaced during the construction of the new roof for the extension. Paddington also became the terminus for the **Post Office** tube railway when it opened in December 1927, with a station beneath the Royal Mail's district office in London Street. Mail chutes were installed at the head of platforms 8 to 10, while platform 11 had a bank of no less than eight chutes, and at the bottom of these were conveyors to take the mail to the tube. In the opposite direction, mail arriving on the tube was brought up from the tube by a conveyor that emerged on the departure side of the station behind the hotel.

Redeveloped Yet Again

Interrupted by the First World War, the 1906 programme of improvements had been barely completed when further work was put in hand, made possible by a combination of the removal of the passenger duty on railway travel and the Development (Loans Guarantees and Grants) Act, 1929. Neither measure had the railway passenger in mind as both were intended to reduce unemployment. The latter measure meant that the GWR's plans for a £1 million rebuild of Paddington had to be approved by the Treasury. Work began in May 1930, and was completed in 1934.

A significant feature was the extension of platforms, in this case 2 to 11 to beyond Bishops Road bridge, giving lengths of between 980 feet and 1,200 feet, with veranda-type roofing rather than a new overall roof, while the construction of a new parcels depot in Bishops Road allowed a passenger concourse to be constructed between the head of the platforms and the back of the hotel. Platform extension is often seen as an easy way of improving railway capacity, but the need to reposition signalling and points, or lineside structures, and rebuild bridges, can mean that extensions are expensive and time consuming, or bring shortcomings, and at Paddington some tight curves were inevitable. There were also new office blocks and new cab and goods depot approach roads. The tracks outside the station up to a distance of three-quarters of a mile were reconstructed, with a new parcels line on the down side and the Ranelagh engine yard was improved.

Between 1929 and 1933, electric power signals (as opposed to electric light signals) were introduced on all lines between Paddington and Southall West junction while electric motors were installed at points and track circuiting was introduced. New arrivals and departures signal boxes were needed due to the platform extensions, with the new departure box at Westbourne Bridge opened on 9 July 1933, and in addition to the down main lines, also looked after the parcels depot, Ranelagh yard and two of the carriage roads. The new arrivals box that opened on 13 August 1933, replacing the Bishops Road and Royal Oak station boxes as well as the original arrivals box, was badly affected by fire on 25 November 1938, closing the suburban station and forcing emergency signalling on all other movements. A makeshift box had to be improvised until a new one could be commissioned on 2 July 1939, and in the meantime through trains did not operate to the City. Meanwhile, a fire had broken out in the Westbourne Bridge signal box on 23 December 1938, so this also had to be replaced.

Paddington has always been the least troubled by suburban traffic. In 1903, when Liverpool Street on the **Great Eastern** had no less than 136 suburban trains arrive between 05.00 and 10.00, Paddington had just eight! Reasons for this included the slow pace at which the GWR had built its suburban stations, and the overlap of the **Great Central** and the **London & South Western** suburban networks within the catchment area for Paddington, while the proximity of the Hammersmith & City and the Metropolitan reinforced this. After the First World War, this began to change, although traffic was to remain modest by the standards set elsewhere. While the 1920s and 1930s did bring a considerable increase in Paddington's suburban traffic as speculative builders began extending the western suburbs outwards in Middlesex and the southern part of Buckinghamshire, this was nothing compared to the developments affecting many of the other London termini.

Even so, this steady growth in suburban traffic meant that new arrangements became necessary and the decision was taken to enlarge Bishops Road station as Paddington Suburban for terminating trains and those bound for the Metropolitan. The old up and down platforms were replaced by two island platforms, one for up and one for down traffic, each with two faces. These works were completed in 1933. The usual practice was for electric trains to use the outside platforms, 13 and 16, while terminating GWR steam trains used the inner platforms 14 and 15.

On the surface, the inner end of the main station had become known as the 'Lawn', possibly a reflection of the time when horses and carriages were handled on this spot, and had become something of an eyesore over the years as successive forms of business were carried out. All of this was ended with the 1933 reconstruction, with for the first time a broad new concourse extending across platforms 1 to 8, whose buffers were set back to provide extra space and a uniform ending, and stretching round to platforms 9 and 10. A new, higher, steel and glass roof was provided over the concourse, although the name of the 'Lawn' persists to this day. The office blocks on either side of the station were revamped and new steel-framed structures built at either end of the Lawn, while the hotel was also extended, being completed in the summer of 1936 with a new total of 250 bedrooms. An elec-trically-operated train indicator board was installed on the Lawn in 1934, and in 1936, a loudspeaker system was introduced. A new parcels depot with two platforms was built on the site of the former platform 1A.

Wartime

Wartime enforced many changes, and through working of trains to and from the Metropolitan ended on 16 September 1939, by which time emergency cuts were being made to timetables. Paddington did not escape its share of wartime wounds, with a parachute mine demolishing part of the departure side building in 1941, while in 1944 a V-1 flying bomb damaged the roof and platforms 6 and 7. Nevertheless, traffic was not disrupted for long.

The big problem was that with a restricted train service, commuter traffic actually increased as many of the more affluent Londoners moved to the outer suburbs or even further out to escape the worst of the bombing. For holidays and for evacuees the West of England and Wales were seen as the best options, not least because most of the South Coast was taken over for military purposes with beaches cordoned off behind barbed wire, and during the period before the Normandy invasion in 1944, only residents and those with special business were allowed near the South Coast. On the morning of 29 July 1944, a summer Saturday, Paddington was closed for three hours, and no underground tickets were sold to Paddington, because the main concourse and platforms were blocked solid with people waiting to catch trains. The problems of wartime had been compounded by government restrictions on extra trains and even on extra carriages on existing trains, added to the much reduced frequencies and extended journey times. It took three telephone calls by the general manager, Sir James **Milne**, to the Ministry of War Transport, and the threat of a visit to

Downing Street, before a man from the ministry arrived and authorised the use of the locomotives and carriages that were standing idle at Old Oak Common depot. The restrictions were eased somewhat after this, but even so, at August bank holiday weekend, then taken early in August and not at the end as today, mounted police had to be called in and the queues snaked along Eastbourne terrace, which did at least have the advantage of allowing passengers to get to and from the trains.

There was disruption of a different kind on 16 October 1944. The locomotive of a down empty carriage train was derailed outside Paddington close to the parcels depot. This was soon followed by two coaches of the down 'Cornish Riviera' express being derailed at the same point, and although there were no casualties, the line was blocked and normal working could not resume until morning of the next day.

Nationalisation brought major changes to Paddington. The new **British Railways** started to rationalise, so that what had become the Western Region eventually lost its trains to Birmingham, but in return, it became the region for all destinations west of **Exeter**, and the service from **Waterloo** was cut back to a stopping service west of Salisbury, with much of the line singled. Diesels replaced steam, as the service was not regarded as intensive enough to justify **electrification**, but Paddington eventually did find itself wired up when the Heathrow Express service began running to the station in 1998. The Heathrow Express was an operation owned by BAA, operators of London Heathrow, and was joined in 2005 by Heathrow Connect, a stopping service to the airport intended for airport workers and others living along the route.

Parliamentary Trains
The serious **accident** on the **Great Western Railway** at Sonning, east of **Reading**, on Christmas Eve 1841, with eight third-class passengers killed when their open sided wagons overturned, alerted the public and politicians to the poor conditions offered for third-class passengers. The then President of the **Board of Trade**, **Gladstone**, in 1844 obtained support for an Act that ensured that all new 'passenger railways', defined as those obtaining at least a third of their turnover from passenger traffic, operate at least one train a day, including Sundays, that would stop at every station, run at a minimum average speed, including stops, of at least 12mph, and carry all passengers in enclosed vehicles with seats. It was also stipulated that the fare would be no more than 1d per mile, including up to 56-lbs of luggage. The Railway Passenger Duty, then at 5 per cent, was not levied on these fares, and a subsequent act, in 1883, the Cheap Trains Act, exempted from duty all fares of 1d per mile or less.

In fact, most of the existing railways accepted the terms of the Act, even though it was intended at new railways because of the traditional British reluctance to embrace retrospective legislation. It was also a major factor in pushing through Sunday operations in those parts of the country where there was strong resistance to working or travelling on the Sabbath.

While the legislation was a significant step in both social provision and in government intervention in transport management, it did not mean that standards improved vastly. The enclosed vehicles often had little or no artificial lighting, wooden benches for seats, and only small windows set high. The standard was in fact lower than that of third-class, which many railways provided often on the same train. It was also unpopular in some areas, including much of Scotland, as many railway managers believed that passengers who could afford to pay more were using the Parliamentary trains. The terms of the Act were not revised other than under the Cheap Trains Act, so 12mph became very slow as the years passed, and in 1874, a court ruling upheld payment of the tax on trains that did not stop at every station.

The Parliamentary Trains began to disappear during the twentieth century, although they did not disappear completely until 1935.

Pearson, Charles, 1794-1862

Solicitor to the Corporation of the City of **London** from 1839 until his death in 1862, as well as MP for Lambeth between 1847 and 1850, he supported the improvement of public amenities as well as supporting the construction of the **Metropolitan Railway**, which he saw as giving slum dwellers the opportunity to find lower cost but better accommodation on the outskirts. He was instrumental in pushing through the concept of **workmen's trains**.

Peel, Sir Robert, 1788-1850

As a Member of Parliament, Peel did not take an interest in railways until he was encouraged to support the legislation authorising the **Birmingham & Derby Junction** line in 1835. When he became Prime Minister in 1841, he attempted to limit government intervention in railway matters, bringing him into conflict with his President of the **Board of Trade, Gladstone**. He dissolved the board headed by Dalhousie to sift railway proposals before they reached Parliament after it had worked for just a year, and allowed the **Railway Mania** to go ahead without government intervention.

Penzance

While Falmouth with its important docks and ship repair facilities was the objective of the **Cornwall Railway** running from **Plymouth**, the **West Cornwall Railway** linked up with the Cornwall at Truro. The West Cornwall had come into existence by acquiring the Hayle Railway and extending its line to Penzance, with services to Truro opened in 1852, where the standard gauge line had an inconvenient break of gauge with the Cornwall Railway. In 1864, the Cornwall Railway demanded that the West Cornwall convert to mixed gauge track under legislation acquired in 1850, but the West Cornwall lacked the funds to carry out the work, and was compelled to transfer its assets to the Cornwall Railway, which was owned by the Associated Companies, the **Great Western Railway, Bristol & Exeter** and the **South Devon**, who between them had subscribed a fifth of the Cornwall's capital.

Both Cornish railways were impoverished as the county's mineral wealth was sent away by sea, and it was not until tourist traffic grew that either showed any potential. In later years, Penzance became both the interchange point for the ferry to the Isles of Scilly, and for early spring cut flowers from the islands on their way to London and other significant mainland markets.

Piccadilly Line/Great Northern, Piccadilly & Brompton Railway

When opened as the Great Northern Piccadilly & Brompton Railway in 1906, this was the longest deep level tube line in **London** running 8½ miles from Finsbury Park to Hammersmith, with no less than 7¾ miles under ground. Its origins lay in a deep level scheme planned by the **Metropolitan District**, the Brompton & Piccadilly Circus and the Great Northern & Strand Railways, which were merged in 1902. Rolling stock was bought from France and from Hungary, believed to have been the only Hungarian stock used on Britain's railways. One innovation that never saw public service was a double spiral escalator installed at Holloway Road in 1906, but the company provided London's first railway escalator, in

1906 at Earl's Court, linking the Piccadilly platforms with those of the **Metropolitan District**, while those installed later at Leicester Square remain the longest on the London underground system. The GNPM became the **London Electric Railway** in 1910 on acquiring both the **Bakerloo** and **Hampstead** tube railways. With the other tube lines, it became part of the **London Passenger Transport Board** in 1933.

The line was extended during 1932-33, running over line abandoned by the District to Hounslow and South Harrow, and over the **Metropolitan Line** to Upminster using a new stretch of tube, while surface sections took it to Southgate and Cockfosters, giving an Uxbridge to Cockfosters run of 32 miles. A short branch was provided from Holborn to Aldwych, which was closed in 1994, although it had its services suspended during the Second World War. The Hounslow branch was extended in 1977 to London Heathrow Airport, the first deep level tube link to any airport in the world, and in 1986, a loop was added to serve Terminal 4.

Pick, Frank, 1878-1941

After serving articles as a solicitor, Pick joined the **North Eastern Railway** in 1902, and became personal assistant to Sir George Gibb in 1904. When Gibb moved to the **Underground Electric Railways** in 1906, Pick followed, and from 1909 was in charge of marketing. When the UER acquired the London General Omnibus Company in 1912, he became commercial manager for the entire group, often known as the 'Combine'. During the First World War, he was seconded to the **Board of Trade**, but returned to the UER in 1919 and was appointed managing director under Lord **Ashfield** in 1928. When the UER was absorbed into the new **London Passenger Transport Board** in 1933, he became vice-chairman, and took much of the credit for

creating the world's largest integrated passenger transport system. He was also notable for his emphasis on good design, be it in marketing material, buildings or bus and trains.

During the Second World War, he became director-general of the Ministry of Information.

Plymouth

An important naval base for many years with a less famous commercial port at Millbay, Plymouth was in fact three towns, Plymouth, Devonport (the naval base and dockyard) and Stonehouse.

Plymouth was reached by the broad gauge **South Devon Railway** running from **Exeter** in 1849, which the following year ran a short branch from its terminus at Millbay to the nearby commercial port. The SDR joined up with the **Cornwall Railway** in 1859, and stations were opened at Devonport and a branch to Tavistock was completed. In 1876, mixed gauge track was laid to allow the **London & South Western Railway** to reach Plymouth from Lydford, and much of the dockyard also had mixed gauge track. The LSWR was initially dependent on the GWR for access, but the opening of the Plymouth, Devonport & South Western Junction Railway in 1890 considerably improved matters.

In 1876, the GWR absorbed the **South Devon Railway**. Meanwhile, the **Cornwall Railway** had been authorised in 1846 to build a 66-mile line from Plymouth to Falmouth, with a connection to the **West Cornwall Railway** at Truro. The line was opened as far as Truro in 1859 and to Falmouth in 1863. The most significant engineering structure was **Brunel's** Royal Albert Bridge at Saltash carrying the line from Devon into Cornwall, but there were many other structures along the route, although mostly originally built of timber to save money. The GWR took over the

Cornwall Railway in 1889, at which time most of the line west of Plymouth was single track.

Pole, Sir Felix, 1877-1956

A protégée and great admirer of Sir James **Inglis**, Sir Felix Pole spent his entire working life with the **Great Western Railway**. At the age of just fourteen years, he joined the company as a telegraph clerk in 1891, and later worked under the civil engineer before moving to the general manager's office in 1904. For many years while he was working in the general manager's office, Pole edited *The Great Western Railway Magazine*, working on this part-time, while he had already gained a reputation as a writer on railway matters.

Appointed general manager in 1921, inevitably Pole spent most of the following year preparing for the grouping. In contrast to some of the other groupings, which were mergers of equals or near-equals, and there were two or three possible candidates for the general managership of the post-grouping company, there was no doubt that Pole of the GWR would run the new railway. His new responsibilities included taking over no less than twenty-one Welsh companies as well as a network of ports and docks, many of them in South Wales. He introduced the GWR to the concept of regular interval main line services out of **Paddington** in 1924, so that passengers did not have to carry a timetable. He was also very conscious of the importance of a good public image for the company, and in addition had also done much earlier in his career to improve communications with employees by revamping the *Great Western Railway Magazine* while working in the general manager's office. He was knighted in 1924.

The railways were not the only industrial sector to undergo mergers in the 1920s (other companies emerging at this time included Imperial Chemical Industries, ICI),

and in 1928 Pole was persuaded to leave the GWR and assume the chairmanship of another large industrial grouping, Associated Electrical Industries, AEI, where he remained. This type of move, commonplace today, was most unusual at the time.

In later life, Pole was afflicted by blindness, but even so he managed to write an autobiography, most of which was devoted to his time on the railways, clearly much more exciting to him than running factories.

Police

At the outset of the railway age, policing was largely in the hands of parish constables, a system that had not worked well in the fast growing industrial cities, but the Metropolitan Police itself only dated from 1829. In the case of disorder, which clearly overwhelmed the parish constables, the local magistrates swore citizens in as additional special constables, called in the military or, even as far north as **Manchester**, the Metropolitan Police, as happened during riots involving the **Manchester & Leeds** and **North Midland Railways** in 1838 and 1840. Under an Act of 1838, the railway companies were charged 5 shillings a day for special constables. For major events which required large numbers of policemen, railway companies would hire men from the Metropolitan Police. The Regulation Act, 1840, gave railwaymen powers of arrest for trespassers or those obstructing them in their duties.

The **Liverpool & Manchester Railway** was the first to have police of its own, but the first company to have the necessary statutory powers was the **London & Birmingham** in 1833, followed by the Great Western in 1835. In 1837, the LBR's police were given authority up to half-a-mile from the company's premises. In addition to the obvious duties of a police constable, the early railway police were also expected to patrol the line to ensure that it was clear and give hand signals to drivers, operate fixed signals if these were available, salute the train as it passed, and in some cases act as ticket inspectors and even as booking clerks. On some railways, the police were responsible to the stationmaster.

Many of these early duties passed to other railwaymen, especially signalmen, as signalling developed, but even as late as 1900, the **North Eastern Railway** expected its policemen to ring a bell to indicate the arrival or departure of a train, and to act as guards or ticket collectors when necessary.

During the early twentieth century, railway police began to belong to special departments within each company, and liaison with the new civic police forces became commonplace. There was even movement of senior officers between railway police forces and civic police forces. As early as 1863, the **London & North Western Railway** formed its own detective branch, and the following year the GWR did the same. As the railways expanded into running ferries and operating docks, their police forces were also deployed to these new operations. The NER was probably the first to have police dogs, at **Hull** in 1908.

On **grouping**, the 'Big Four' combined the police forces of their constituent companies and organised them on lines similar to those of a civic police force. In 1946, the railway companies established a joint police training school with cadet entry. It was not until 1946 that the first policewomen were appointed. **Nationalisation** in 1948 saw the police forces merged to form the British Transport Police, responsible to the **British Transport Commission**, and covering docks and canals as well as railways. The BTP survived the disbandment of the BTC and privatisation.

Pollitt, Sir William, 1842-1906
Pollitt joined the **Manchester, Sheffield & Lincolnshire Railway** (see **Great Central**) in 1857 and by 1869 was chief clerk to the accountant. In 1885, he was appointed assistant general manager and became general manager in 1886. By this time, Edward **Watkin** was chairman, and it fell to Pollitt to handle Watkin's expansive plans, including the expansion of the **Great Central** to **London**. He proved himself to be a diplomat, making peace with the **Great Northern Railway**, but found himself confronting the **Metropolitan Railway**. Knighted in 1899, he became a director in 1902.

Port Talbot Railway & Docks
Pressure for port space in South Wales during the nineteenth century saw the development of new dock facilities at a number of locations, including Port Talbot, where new docks were built from 1835 to serve the copper industry at nearby Cwmavon. Coal traffic did not become significant until 1870, and in 1894 to protect and encourage this traffic, the Port Talbot Railway was authorised and opened in 1897-98, with two lines from Maesteg and Tonmawr, to the north of Cwmavon. The railway also acquired the docks. The total route mileage was just 48 miles, but the dock and railway company was profitable, and the **Great Western** took over operation of the railway in 1908, although the docks operated separately.

Portpatrick & Wigtownshire Joint Railway
Completed as the Portpatrick Railway in 1862, it was designed to link the Castle Douglas & Dumfries Railway, completed in 1859, with Portpatrick, the Scottish port for the packet service to Donaghdee, shortest of all the sea crossings to Ireland. The line ran through Creetown and Newton Stewart to both Portpatrick and Stranraer, and the two railways combined became known as the 'Port Road'. Despite its potential, the railway was cheaply built to minimise costs on

the heavy civil engineering works needed because of the heavily undulating terrain traversed, with many tall viaducts. The **Glasgow & South Western Railway** ran to both Dumfries and Stranraer, but it was the **Caledonian Railway** that bought traffic rights for trains coming off the **West Coast Main Line**. Portpatrick lacked sufficient space for expansion either of the port or the railway terminus, so in 1874, the western terminus was moved to Stranraer, where a new port and long pier was constructed, with a branch line to the harbour, while the Irish ferry terminus became Larne. A branch to Garlieston and Whithorn, known as the Wigtownshire Railway, was opened in 1877, but neither this nor the line to Portpatrick prospered, and in 1885, the Caledonian, Glasgow & South Western, **London & North Western** and **Midland Railways** jointly acquired the line. A further branch was constructed from Tarff to Kircudbright.

Local traffic along the 80-mile line was never significant as the area was, and remains, thinly populated, but it did carry expresses with boat train traffic, although for passengers from London, the Midlands and the North West, the Lancashire ferry ports were far more convenient. The line passed to the **London, Midland & Scottish** on **grouping**, and in 1965 it was closed. Boat train traffic then travelled by the long diversion via **Glasgow** and Ayr, effectively two sides of a triangle.

Portsmouth

Portsmouth was already a substantial town and Britain's major naval base before the railways arrived. Despite this, in 1842, the first railway in the area ran from Eastleigh on the **Southampton** main line via Fareham to Gosport, a short ferry trip across the harbour. The first line into Portsmouth did not arrive until 1847, with the **London, Brighton & South Coast Railway** extending its line from Brighton, and the following year the **London & South Western Railway** line arrived via Fareham. Both routes were about 95 miles from **London**, and the two companies operated a pooling agreement from 1848, the LSWR using its rival's station in the town. The opening of the Portsmouth Direct line in 1859 cut the distance from London to 74 miles by extending the LSWR branch from Guildford and Godalming, while in 1867; the LBSCR provided an 87 mile route via Arundel.

While the services to the city were now much faster, passengers for the **Isle of Wight** still had to be conveyed by road between the train and the ferry as the Admiralty refused to allow the companies to extend their line to the harbour, although it had its own internal railway system. This eventually changed in 1876, when a high-level station with an island platform was built alongside the town station, later known as Portsmouth & Southsea, to carry the line to Portsmouth Harbour station, which was built on a pier with direct access to the Isle of Wight ferries across the concourse. The ferries themselves had been operated independently, but passed into railway control to be operated jointly by the LBSCR and LSWR in 1880.

The resort of Southsea was reached by an independently promoted branch line from Fratton from 1885 and worked by the two main line railways. It was never a success, being worked by railcars in competition with a comprehensive tramway system, and the Southern was allowed to close it in 1923 after it had been out of use for most of the First World War.

Portsmouth itself was the target for two pre-war **electrification** schemes when the 'Direct' route was electrified in 1937 and the Arundel line, with that from Brighton, the following year. The main service to **Waterloo** which had enjoyed just four fast trains a day before electrification, enjoyed as many in one hour on a summer Saturday afterwards.

Post Office Railway

Authorised in 1913, the Post Office Railway was an electric tube railway required to avoid delays to the mails on the already congested streets of **London**. It followed an earlier atmospheric tube railway authorised in 1859 when the Pneumatic Despatch Company was granted powers to build atmospheric tubes under any streets in Central London. Experiments with a 600-yard stretch resulted in a single line tunnel being built between **Euston** and Holborn, where there was a reverse to the General Post Office at St Martin's-le-Grand, some 2½ miles overall. The track gauge was 3 ft 8½ ins, while the tunnel was 4ft 6in wide and 4ft 1in high. Opened in 1873, only a limited quantity of mail was carried and the line closed the following year. By contrast, the POR was built to carry mail from **Paddington** across the West End and City to Whitechapel, and had six intermediate stations. The tunnel was completed by 1917, but was used for storage by the British Museum during the First World War, and did not open for traffic until 1928. The route was in a 9ft diameter tunnel with two 2ft gauge lines using third rail electrification at 440 v dc, with the trains operating automatically without drivers, being controlled by track circuits. The original wagons were four-wheeled, but replaced by bogie wagons in 1930, although a four-wheeled power car was placed at each end. The 'trains' were replaced in 1980, but the line was closed in 2006. Similar operations exist in Chicago and Munich.

Preston

An important port and centre for the cotton trade before the arrival of the railway, Preston was boosted still further by the Lancaster Canal, and a horse-drawn tramway was built to link the northern and southern sections of the waterway. In 1836, a local railway, the Preston & Longridge, linked the town with nearby quarries, while in 1838, the **North Union Railway** connected Preston with the lines **London, Liverpool** and **Manchester**. A link with **Carlisle** and Scotland followed between 1840 and 1849, as well as lines to Fleetwood and **Blackpool**, while more direct lines were built to Manchester and Liverpool, while a branch was built to the docks on the River Ribble. Until restaurant cars appeared, Preston was a refreshment stop on the **West Coast Main Line**.

The various railway lines around Preston soon became part of either the **London & North Western Railway** or the **Lancashire & Yorkshire**, which shared the main station and also operated the Ribble branch jointly. Between 1836 and 1900, the population grew from 14,000 to 115,000. The railway station was extensively rebuilt and extended between 1873 and 1913, but a much needed avoiding line for holiday and excursion trains to **Blackpool** was never built. The most significant event during the twentieth century was West Coast **electrification** in 1972, while the WCML has been extensively rebuilt in recent years to allow **high speed** running by Pendolino tilting trains. Preston has been spared railway closures to a great extent, although the original Longridge line closed to passengers in 1930 and to goods from 1967.

Preston & Wyre Railway

Opened in 1840 between **Preston** and Fleetwood, the line was promoted by Sir Peter Hesketh Fleetwood as part of a scheme to build a town and port on his estate at the mouth of the River Wyre. Until the **Caledonian Railway** was completed in 1848, passengers for **Glasgow** would change to a steamer to travel to Ardrossan, on the west coast of Scotland, and hence by rail to Glasgow. The PWR was acquired jointly in 1849 by the **London & North Western** and **Lancashire & Yorkshire Railways**, which built branches to **Blackpool** and Lytham, planning to develop these towns as resorts. In 1871, they also acquired a line between the two towns that had been built by an independent company.

While Fleetwood had lost its Scottish traffic, the LYR developed Fleetwood for a packet service to Ireland and the **Isle of Man**, but even so, the business of Blackpool was such that this became the main line, and in 1903 a new direct line to Blackpool Central replaced the route to Blackpool North, which was closed in 1967, while passenger services between Poulton and Fleetwood were withdrawn in 1970.

Princetown Railway

The standard gauge Princetown Railway took over the abandoned Plymouth & Dartmoor Railway above Yelverton in 1883 as the latter company was having difficulty in finishing the work. The Plymouth & Dartmoor had been promoted primarily for quarry traffic and used the unusual gauge of 4ft 6in. The route of the Princetown Railway, a subsidiary of the **Great Western Railway**, was over the 10.5 miles from Yelverton to Horridge, much of it over former Plymouth & Dartmoor infrastructure, and while some traffic from the King Tor quarry was carried, in practice the main business was carrying prison officers and convicts, and supplies, to Dartmoor Prison. It also attracted some excursion traffic.

R

Race to the North

The **West Coast** route was the first to open between **London** and Scotland, running via **Preston** and Carlisle, completed in 1848 and

through trains worked jointly by the **London & North Western Railway** and the **Caledonian Railway**. It was followed in 1852 by the **East Coast** route via **York** and **Newcastle**, in which the main participants were the **Great Northern, North Eastern** and **North British Railways**. Both routes served **Edinburgh** and **Glasgow**, and while revenues were apportioned as the result of agreements made between 1851 and 1856, there was competition between them. The ECML soon became the faster, with the day express between **King's Cross** and Edinburgh an hour quicker than that from **Euston**, but the LNWR at the time objected to fast running.

The cosy arrangement between the companies came under attack in 1876, when the **Midland Railway** completed its line to Scotland via **Settle and Carlisle**. Its line was longer and slower than the two existing lines, but it had admitted third-class passengers to all of its trains and improved their lot by abolishing second-class whilst scrapping its small stock of third-class rolling stock. By contrast, the fastest East Coast express was first-class only until 1887.

In May 1888, the West Coast companies suddenly announced that from 2 June their fastest express would run from Euston to Edinburgh in nine hours, the same time as that from King's Cross. The East Coast companies responded by cutting the through journey time to eight hours, which the West Coast matched from 1 August. On 13 August, the East Coast schedule was cut to $7^3/4$ hours, but on that day the train reached Edinburgh in 7hr 27min. Then, as suddenly as it started, the racing stopped and the two rival groups agreed minimum journey times for their trains.

Meanwhile, the NBR had been pressing ahead with its bridges over the **Forth** and **Tay**. Once completed, these cut the through journey time to Dundee and **Aberdeen**, making the East Coast line the faster to these cities. This was the spark that set off yet another 'race', between the overnight trains between London and Aberdeen. The timetable was ignored in the interest of getting the trains to their destination in the shortest possible time, but after the East Coast companies decided to stop the 'race', on the night of 23/24August 1895, the West Coast train ran the 540 miles from Euston to Aberdeen at an average speed of 63.3mph.

The races then ended between London and Scotland. On the plus side, it showed just how performance could be enhanced, if not the passengers' sleep, but on the debit side the trains used were lightly loaded and often double-headed, while all other traffic had to give way to allow the racers priority.

Racing Rivals

The railway companies, even before **grouping**, could be said to be localised monopolies with competition at the edges. A glance at the railway map shows that between several destinations, more than one route existed. While the most lucrative of these, apart from the lines between **London** and Scotland, would seem to have been between London and **Birmingham** or **Manchester**, it was between London and **Exeter** that the first race broke out between the **London & South Western Railway**, running from **Waterloo**, and the alliance of the **Great Western**, running from **Paddington**, and the **Bristol & Exeter**, starting in 1862. In 1868, the **Midland Railway** managed to compete with the **London & North Western** between London and Manchester, and, from 1880, with the **Great Northern** between London, **Leeds** and Bradford, for which an expensive line between Kettering and Northampton was constructed.

The LSWR and the GWR then competed between London and **Plymouth**, for the prestigious boat train traffic with passengers joining or leaving liners at Plymouth to save a day or so steaming to London. The GWR even constructed one of its many 'cut off' routes during the early 1900s to shorten the distance to Plymouth in 1906. Many objected to the races because of the waste, not simply because two companies were trying to provide the same service, but because they deliberately ran trains that were seldom full. There was a more pressing argument against racing: safety. On the night of 29/30 June 1906, the up boat train from Plymouth to Waterloo, with a fresh locomotive and crew, after changing at Templecombe, ran through Salisbury at excessive speed, derailing at the eastern end of the station at 2.24am, killing 24 of the 43 passengers.

Railbuses and railcars

Lightly-trafficked lines encouraged the railways to consider railbuses and railcars. The terms often become confused, especially since the advent of diesel railcars, while there were also **road-rail** vehicles able to run on both road and rail.

The original railbuses were buses converted to run on rails. Amongst the earliest such vehicles was the French Micheline, a petrol-engined bus which had solid rubber tyres fitted to the flanges of flanged wheels and could run on rails, in many ways similar to an articulated lorry in that the low-slung passenger cabin was separate from the cab and engine, with which trials were conducted in Great Britain during 1932. Later, three modifications of standard four-wheel 40-seat buses were supplied to the **London, Midland & Scottish Railway** in 1934 by Leyland. While these had basic buffers and drawgear, they lacked the power to pull a trailer. In 1936, the LMS bought two Micheline vehicles built in the UK by Armstrong Siddeley, and these achieved modest success before being withdrawn in 1939.

Nevertheless, conversions of ordinary buses proved more popular with many light railways, such as those run by Colonel Stephens, and on the narrow gauge **County Donegal Railways Joint Committee** in Ulster.

Post-**nationalisation**, **British Railways** experimented with a variety of lightweight diesel railbuses which it used on a number of branch lines during the late 1950s and through the 1960s, before withdrawing the last of them in 1968. A somewhat more substantial vehicle was developed from the Leyland National bus, but production vehicles differed from the original specification and were eventually branded as 'Pacers'.

The earliest railcars were steam-powered, with the first believed to have been *Express*, used on the **Eastern Counties Railway** from 1847. As the century progressed, many more railcars were introduced, usually consisting of a passenger carriage with a small steam locomotive sharing the same frame and having driving wheels in place of one of the bogies. The concept increased in popularity as a means of competing with tramways, and many of the later versions could be driven from either end. While cheaper to run than a full train, they nevertheless still required a crew of three, driver, fireman and guard. They were sometimes known by railway companies as steam rail motors. Few of them were completely successful as they either generated sufficient traffic to have to be replaced by push-pull two or three carriage trains, or were simply not powerful enough. Perhaps the longest-lasting were a fleet of Sentinel railcars introduced by the **London & North Eastern Railway** during the 1920s and which lasted into the 1940s.

The internal combustion engine offered a way forward, not least because it reduce the number of railwaymen by a third, and also because it only consumed fuel whilst working. The **North Eastern Railway** introduced two petrol-electric railcars in 1904, while vehicles with mechanical transmission were used by the **London Brighton & South Coast Railway** from 1905. The **Great Western** introduced a petrol-engined railcar in 1911. The early railcars suffered from the limitations of the early petrol engine, and by the time engines had become more reliable, it was the greater economy of the diesel engine that mattered. The leader in this field was the GWR, which between 1934 and 1942 introduced no less than thirty-eight diesel railcars, including two single-ended versions which, with a carriage inserted between them, became one of the first diesel multiple units, DMUs, and operated an express business service between **Birmingham** and **Cardiff**. The Northern Counties Committee in Northern Ireland also gained considerable experience with railcars. Diesel electric railcars were also built by English Electric during the 1930s and exported to Ceylon, now Sri Lanka.

Post-**nationalisation**, **British Railways** invested heavily in diesel railcars and multiple units for lines not justifying the cost of electrification, even though some of these services were fairly intensive.

Railway Air Services – see **Air Transport and Railways**

Railway Clearing House

As the number of railways grew and a network began to be created, it was clear that some system was needed to allow through booking of passengers or goods, and through working of trains. While some railway companies resisted other companies working over their lines, most came to appreciate the extra revenue while the increased number of through services benefited the railways and their passengers alike. There were other problems as well, including a lack of standardised signals or locomotive headcodes, while coupling systems and buffer positions also suffered from a lack of standardisation. Possibly the worst example of the lack of standardisation was that two red discs meant 'all clear' on the **Great Western**, but 'danger' on the **London & Birmingham**.

It was the LBR that foresaw the need to make through ticketing and running easier, almost certainly because they saw their railway as playing a strategic role in the creation of a network with longer distance services running through it. Led by the chairman, George Carr **Glyn**, representatives of nine railway companies attended an inaugural meeting of the Railway Clearing House held at 11 Drummond Street, near **Euston**, on 2 January 1842. Not surprisingly, most of the companies who attended were in the Midlands and North West. The **Great Western**, also burdened by its broad gauge, and the southern companies did not follow until the early 1860s, but by 1870, most railway companies had joined this voluntary association.

The RCH set itself five principal tasks:

1) Through booking of passengers.

2) Through booking of privately-owned carriages and horses.

3) Division of receipts on a mileage basis.

4) Encouragement of goods traffic on a rate per mile basis.

5) A system of settling all inter-company debts.

The financing of this system was twofold, with a £5 annual levy on each station belonging to the member companies augmented by a proportional levy on receipts. For the most part, the system depended on the honesty of the member companies, but from 1847 as an additional check, the RCH sent number-takers to take the numbers and check the contents of goods wagons travelling on what became known as 'foreign' lines, that is, outside their own system. Eventually, number-takers and clerks employed by the RCH totalled 3,000, with the clerks settling inter-company accounts working in what was know as the 'long office'.

One of the most enduring decisions taken was also in 1847, when the members agreed to use Greenwich Mean Time at all of their stations, which was the beginning of the end for the days when each town had its own time. That year also saw the goods managers' conference draw up an official classification of goods, but the RCH could only recommend suitable rates, and could never enforce a standard set of freight rates or of passenger fares. Ticket printing and date stamping was also standardised using the **Edmondson** system. In 1853, a book of distance tables was published. In 1867, a book of rules for working over 'foreign' lines was published, and semaphore signals were recommended, but appended were examples of the other systems likely to be found, but by 1880, the semaphore signal had become the standard. Standardising rolling stock was far harder, and in the case of locomotives, impossible, but it was also a struggle to standardise goods wagons, not least because of the high number of private owners' wagons. It took until 1902 for the RCH engineers to recommend a standard position for Westinghouse vacuum brake pipes.

The RCH did little to standardise railway accounts, and this was left to Parliament with the Regulation of Railways Act 1868.

When the First World War broke out and the railways came under the control of the Railway Executive Committee, much of the RCH role disappeared, and more than a third of its employees joined the armed forces. Nevertheless, the efficiency of the wartime railway was boosted by a common-user scheme for wagons, tarpaulins and ropes, but number-takers still had a job to do.

Post-war, the RCH acted as a catalyst in

helping the railway companies resolve many of the problems of merging more than a hundred companies into just four. A sign of the impact the **grouping** had on the RCH, with fewer companies involved, was that employment dropped from more than 3,000 in 1914 to 1,800 by 1939.

Nationalisation was seen as marking the end of the RCH, and the employees held farewell dinners and expected a final settling of accounts to keep them occupied during the first few months of 1948. In reality, the RCH still had a role to perform, helping the new **British Railways**, and so it was not disbanded until 31 March 1963. The **Irish Railway Clearing House** survived even longer, to 1974.

Railway Companies Association

Originating as a special committee of the **Railway Clearing House** in 1854, the need for the companies to consider issues relating to legislation and politics was such that it became the Railway Companies Association in 1869, with its own permanent staff situated conveniently at Westminster. The role of the RCA was primarily political, attempting to influence legislation and also, for a while, attempting to avoid recognition of the railway trade unions. It was successful for many years after the First World War in lobbying against **nationalisation**, and to some extent in lobbying for greater protection from road competition, but its 'Fair deal' campaign mounted in 1938, pressing for the freedom to fix freight rates, failed, and so too, ultimately, did the campaign against nationalisation.

Railway Mania

The term generally used to describe the fanatical passion for railways during the 1840s, when Parliament approved schemes for building 9,000 route miles of railway, not far short of the entire network today which is just over 10,000 route miles. To build these railways, more than £500 million was invested, equivalent to around £33 billion today. An earlier boom had been abruptly ended in 1825 when a succession of banking failures and a poor harvest prompted a recession, while a further boom started in 1835, lasting until 1837, with more than 1,500 route miles authorised by Parliament. Essentially railway booms were prompted by economic recovery, and while most of the early projects were sound, as the booms progressed, wilder and less well-considered projects flourished, with investors tempted to believe that this was an easy way to a fortune, not unlike the dot.com boom of recent years. The poor performance of many of the later projects and the exhausting of the supply of capital meant the end of the boom.

The growing dominance of the established railway companies later made it more difficult for newcomers to raise capital, and so many of the later projects were those sponsored or supported by the increasingly powerful companies. In a number of cases, railway contractors sponsored lines using profits made from earlier schemes to prolong the boom, leading to what became known as 'contractors' lines'. Nevertheless, there was a minor boom in the 1850s and again in the 1860s, stopped by the collapse of the bankers, Overend Gurney & Co.

Railways at War – see Wartime

Rainhill Trials

It was not until late 1828 that the directors of the **Liverpool & Manchester Railway** started to consider the means of locomotion for the line. At this early stage, horses were still regarded seriously as an option, while there were also stationary steam locomotives using cables or steam locomotives. Two engineers were engaged to visit existing lines and recommend a form of traction; they both came down in favour of stationary steam engines. One of them, James Walker, also suggested that a competition be held with a prize for the best locomotive entered: the directors agreed and fixed the prize at £500, about £30,000 by today's values. This was sufficient to attract three steam locomotives: John Braithwaite and John Ericsson's *Novelty*; Timothy **Hackworth's** *Sans Pareil*, and George **Stephenson's** *Rocket*. The trials were held on the LMR at Rainhill and lasted for seven days during October 1829.

Rocket and *Novelty* managed 30mph, a speed far in excess of that attained by other steam locomotives of the day, with the former being more consistent. The LMR thus became, from its opening, a railway with steam locomotives. The line's opening was marked by an accident to George Huskisson, President of the **Board of Trade**, and none of the speeds at the trials compared with the 36mph achieved by George Stephenson as he drove the mortally injured MP to Eccles for treatment.

Ramsbottom, John, 1814-1897

By 1846, Ramsbottom was locomotive superintendent of the **London & North Western Railway's** North Eastern Division, before being promoted to the same post for the entire Northern Division in 1857, and then taking charge of the entire LNWR locomotive stock in 1862. His inventions included the modern piston ring and the tamper-proof safety valve, while his 2-2-2 locomotives were the first to use the Giffard injector, and his DX 0-6-0, first seen in 1859, were the most numerous ever to be built in Britain. He also modernised **Crewe** works.

He resigned in 1871 after a dispute with the LNWR's chairman and became a consulting engineer, whose work included modernisation of the **Lancashire & Yorkshire Railway**, including building their new works at Horwich.

Raven, Sir Vincent Litchfield, 1858-1934

After serving an apprenticeship under Edward Fletcher at Gateshead, he became an assistant divisional locomotive superintendent on the **North Eastern Railway** in 1888, before being promoted to chief assistant mechanical engineer in 1903, and chief mechanical engineer from 1910 to 1922. He was the first to standardise the use of three-cylinder drive and built more than 200 locomotives of this type, including 4-4-2 express, 4-6-0 mixed traffic, 0-8-0 and 4-6-2T freight and 4-4-4T passenger. He was of that generation of engineers who did not confine themselves to steam, and proposed overhead **electrification** at 1,500V dc between **York** and **Newcastle**; a system used successfully on the freight line between Newport and Shildon, opened in 1915. He also introduced automatic train control between York and Newcastle. During the First World War, he was superintendent of the Royal Arsenal at Woolwich, for which he was knighted. He was after **Grouping** briefly technical adviser to the **London & North Eastern Railway**, but his plans for electrification suffered from the downturn in the economy and he left in 1924 to advise on railways in Australia and New Zealand, as well as on Indian railway workshops.

Reading

By 1838, the **Great Western Railway** was operating between **London** and a station close to Maidenhead in Berkshire, reaching Reading in 1840. The **London & South Western Railway** reached Reading in 1856, running over **South Eastern** metals from Wokingham, although it was to be another two years before the SER line from Farnborough was connected through Guildford to the rest of the company's network at Redhill. Reading was already an important calling point and junction on the GWR by this time. The LSWR line to **Waterloo** has never rivalled that of the GWR to **Paddington** in terms of speed, and the opening of the **Metropolitan Railway** also placed the latter in a better position at first for those travelling onwards to the City of London, but nevertheless, the towns along the line soon became some of the smarter London dormitories. In addition to being slightly longer, the LSWR line also suffered from severe bottlenecks, especially at Richmond. While the SER line must have counted as one of the most pointless in the country, and a millstone around the neck of the company and its successors, it also provided some useful cross-country connections, but it was to take the emergence of London Gatwick as an important international airport for the line to show serious potential, and that was long after the demise of the **Southern Railway.**

Rhondda & Swansea Bay Railway

One of the many coal lines built to by-pass the pressure on the docks at **Cardiff**, the Rhondda & Swansea Bay Railway ran from Treherbert to Briton Ferry with a two-mile tunnel. Opened in 1890, the line developed into a small system of 29 route miles. The line passed into the control of the **Great Western** in 1906, but was not taken over completely until 1922.

Rhymney Railway

The Rhymney Railway was preceded by an old tramway connecting the Rhymney Ironworks with Newport, known locally as the 'Old Rumney Railway'. In 1851, the Marquis of Bute encouraged the company to replace the tramway with a new railway to serve the new dock being built at **Cardiff**. The Rhymney Railway obtained the necessary consent in 1854-55, running down the right bank of the Rhymney Valley, and opened in 1858 thanks to running powers over part of the **Taff Vale Railway**. Finding itself hosting a competitor, the Taff Vale raised its charges, and in one case it took litigation by the Rhymney to force the Taff

Vale to reduce its charges by 80 per cent. Seeking a solution by leasing itself to the Bute Trustees, the Rhymney was refused Parliamentary consent, a measure that had it been allowed may well have forestalled the creation of the **Cardiff Railway.** Growing coal traffic solved the problem, with the Rhymney becoming profitable during the 1860s, and in 1864 obtained approval to build its own line into Cardiff, which opened in 1871. That same year also saw an extension opened between Rhymney and Nantybwch to connect with the **London & North Western Railway**, and another extension into the Aberdare Valley, largely with the help of running powers over the **Great Western Railway**. The heavily-graded Taff Bargoed line was built jointly with the GWR and reached Dowlais in 1876 and Merthyr Tydfil in 1886. Meanwhile, most of the original lines that had been laid as single track had been doubled.

The cost of this expansion was that the company could not afford a dividend as late as 1875, but tight managerial control saw this rise to 10.5 per cent before the end of the century, despite competition after 1889 from the **Barry** and **Brecon & Merthyr Railways**. The Rhymney eventually found itself with two major traffic generating points, Cardiff and Caerphilly, with locomotive repair works opened in the latter town in 1902, while the station was rebuilt in 1913 to cater for the growing passenger traffic. In 1909-10, the Taff Vale also tried to include the Rhymney in its take over of the Cardiff Railway, but as mentioned above, Parliament refused to authorise this move. Nevertheless, the Rhymney's manager, E A Prosser, became manager of the other two companies and worked all three as one, doubtless obtaining many of the benefits of a merger, possibly without some of the short term costs.

Road-rail vehicles

Passengers don't like changing, while freight customers know that transhipment between different modes is the time when goods are most likely to be damaged or suffer pilferage. There is also the question that many railway stations were built some distance from the towns or villages they were supposed to serve. These problems were reflected in interest in convertible vehicles that could switch readily from road to rail, or vice-versa, but these proved cumbersome and difficult in practice, as well as heavy. In 1931, a commercial vehicle manufacturer, Karrier, built a heavy road coach in co-operation with the **London, Midland & Scottish Railway**. This had the appearance of a conventional single-deck coach, albeit with passenger doors on both sides, and co-centric road and rail wheels, with the change requiring the steering wheel to be locked and the road wheels raised. It worked for just a few months.

A trans-modal goods vehicle was developed in the United States during the 1950s, and in the UK the Pressed Steel Company obtained a manufacturing licence. Known as the Roadrailer, it was intended to be used in multiple behind a converter wagon to provide a complete goods train, but despite trials on British Railways in 1963, it never entered revenue service.

The complication and weight involved has meant that such vehicles tend to be used for railway engineering and maintenance work, as in the type produced by Mercedes Benz.

Road Transport and the Railways

From the earliest times, the railways needed road transport for collection and delivery purposes, and the superiority of the railways over road transport was such that often very short lines could be viable because of the superior performance, comfort and reliability of the railways.

Eventually, railway companies were able to operate bus services to and from their stations, as well as having their own fleets of road vehicles to deliver small consignments to customers or collect from them.

The balance of appeal between railways and road transport began to change with the advent of street tramways, especially once these were electrified. This in turn was a major incentive for electrification of the railways' suburban routes in the major conurbations, initially with the sub-surface **Metropolitan District** and **Metropolitan Railways,** but soon followed by surface railways with the **London, Brighton & South Coast Railway** taking the lead, followed by the **London & South Western**. After the First World War, the greater reliability of the motor vehicle, and the existence of many who had learned to drive and maintain these during the war, meant that both passenger and freight traffic was under threat from the lower costs and greater flexibility of bus services and road haulage. This started a long battle between the railways and road transport, with the former pointing out that the road transport operator paid a small share of the cost of infrastructure, while the railways were burdened with their full costs and also were constrained in their freight charges.

Eventually, Parliament introduced licensing for road haulage in 1930, followed by that for bus operation in 1933. This amounted to a system of virtual rationing with operators having to prove the demand for their services. Bus operators were restricted by route and fares, while hauliers by the number of vehicles. In the meantime, the railways were allowed to operate bus services away from their stations, and all the large companies took the opportunity to buy bus companies from 1929 onwards, often incorporating their existing vehicles and routes. In due course, the railways acquired Carter Paterson, the major parcels carrier, and Pickfords, but did so acting jointly. Nevertheless, in 1938, the railways returned to the fray again, with the **Railway Companies Association** mounting a 'Square Deal' campaign, seeking the freedom to set their own freight rates, but this proved to be unsuccessful and gained little public understanding or sympathy.

Robertson, General Sir (later Baron) Brian, 1896-1974

When the new Conservative government overhauled the **British Transport Commission** in 1953, they chose an experienced military administrator, General Sir Brian Robertson, as the new chairman. He was expected to provide internal discipline within the organisation, largely through giving it strong leadership, while also decentralising much of its operations whilst denationalising the road haulage firms. In fact, his restructuring of the BTC proved cumbersome, based on army principles rather than those of a commercial organisation. His 'general staff' soon proved very unpopular with professional railwaymen. He supported the Modernisation Plan, largely because it was seen as a way of reversing a poor financial position, but the BTC was ill-equipped to drive the plan through and it was hampered further by the area boards of **British Railways** and by commercial and technological incompetence. Despite this, Robertson established the Railway Research Centre at Derby and the British Transport Staff College, both of which were judged successful.

He retired in 1961 and was created Baron Robertson of Oakridge.

Robinson, John George, 1856-1943

After serving an apprenticeship at Swindon, in 1884 he became assistant locomotive superintendent on the **Waterford, Limerick & Western Railway** in Ireland, and superintendent in 1888, when he start to reorganise

the company's workshops and renew many of its locomotives and rolling stock. He joined the **Great Central Railway** in 1900 as locomotive and marine engineer, and became chief mechanical engineer in 1902. He was credited with producing comfortable passenger carriages and large goods wagons, while he showed a preference for 4-4-2 locomotives, and his heavy freight locomotive became the standard British locomotive used by the army abroad during the First World War. His inventions included a superheater and equipment for oil-burning locomotives, as well as improved buffers and fenders for carriages in an attempt to avoid telescoping and riding over other carriages in an accident.

Romney, Hythe & Dymchurch Railway

Supported by the **Southern Railway**, which saw it as providing a feeder service, the Romney Hythe & Dymchurch Light Railway, the world's largest 15in narrow gauge line, brought railway travel to Romney Marsh in Kent, an area over which building a standard gauge line would have been impractical because of the weight of the locomotives and rolling stock. It was established by a Light Railway Order of 1926 authorising the construction of a double line of 15in gauge for eight miles between Hythe and New Romney, and was opened on 26 July 1927. A success from the beginning, it became a favourite with tourists and an attraction in its own right, so that in 1929 a seven mile extension opened between New Romney and Dungeness lighthouse, with a long turning loop.

Enthusiasts for narrow gauge railways are accustomed to the layman regarding these as 'toy' railways, but the RHDR looked like a toy railway, and still does, and it was established to carry passengers, not goods. The locomotives have always been scaled down copies of main line and US locomotives rather than something distinctive as in Wales, and, for that matter, on the Lynton & Barnstaple. This problem probably arose from the fact that it was the brainchild of Captain J P Howey, a motor racing driver who also enjoyed driving steam locomotives.

During the Second World War, it was closed to the public on 30 June 1940 and commandeered by the military and used to move troops along this vital section of coast where, it was feared, an invasion might start. It suffered considerable wartime damage, but still managed to re-open on 2 March 1946 between Hythe and New Romney, while the Dungeness extension opened the following year.

Despite this, the post-war history was by no means as happy as the early years, with the line eventually facing closure until rescued by the preservation movement.

S

St Pancras

St Pancras was built for the **Midland Railway's** extension to **London** after the original arrangement that saw trains running from Hitchin to **King's Cross** starting in early 1858, had proved expensive. The heavy excursion traffic for the Great Exhibition of 1862 also showed the limitations on capacity at King's Cross, and the growth in the **Great Northern Railway's** traffic in the years to follow would only have seen the problems repeated. It was clear that to be a railway with London amongst its destination, the MR needed its own terminus and its own approach route.

The MR already had its own goods yard in London at Agar Town, between the **North London Railway** and the Regent's Canal. It was decided to extend this line to the Euston Road, at the boundary set by the Royal Commission on London's Termini,

which effectively barred further incursions by railways into the centre of London. A 4½ acre site was found for the terminus, and the eastern part of Lord Somers' estate was acquired for a modest price. Even so, when work started in 1866, the extension required the demolition of thousands of slum dwellings in Agar Town and Somers Town, with some 10,000 people evicted without compensation. The line also infringed the cemetery of St Pancras Church, with successive layers of corpses having to be removed and re-interred, but it took complaints in the press for this to be done with any sense of reverence. The disruption to the cemetery was largely due to a double track link being constructed to the **Metropolitan Railway** on the east side of the extension, with a tunnel inside which there was a gradient of 1 in 75. Despite these problems, the line to the terminus itself had to pass over the Regent's Canal which meant both a falling gradient towards the terminus and a platform level some 20 feet above street level. Ironically, the widening of the Metropolitan (City Widened Lines) did not go further west than King's Cross and so was of more use for GNR trains than those of the Midland until further widening in 1926, and then the spur from the Midland main line was closed in 1935.

Initially, when William **Barlow** designed the station, he proposed filling the space under the tracks and platforms with soil excavated from the tunnels, but James **Allport**, the MR's general manager, saw the potential for storage space, specially for beer from Burton-on-Trent. This led Barlow to design a single span trainshed, which not only allowed greater freedom in planning the storage space beneath the station, but also meant that the layout of the tracks and platforms could be altered as needed in the years to come. A large Gothic hotel was constructed in front of the station, giving it the most impressive frontage of any London terminus. Initially, the interior of the roof was painted brown, but Allport later had this changed to blues and greys to give the impression of the sky. While trains from Bedford to Moorgate started using the tunnel under the terminus from 13 July 1868, the terminus itself was not opened to traffic until 1 October 1868, without any ceremony.

The Midland Grand Hotel was still at foundation level when the station opened, but this was intended to be the most luxurious of its kind, and a monument to its architect, Sir Gilbert Scott. The hotel also included offices for the MR in its upper storeys. Meanwhile, in the terminus itself, even the handsome booking hall was not completed until the following year.

When opened, the station had eleven roads and five platform faces. One of these, later Platform 1, was a short local platform facing the west wall, while the other face of this platform was the long main line departure platform, after which there were six carriage roads, occupying the space later used by platforms 2 to 5, and followed by the two arrival platforms, later 5 and 6, with a 25-ft wide cab road running between them. Against the east wall was the excursion platform, later platform 7. In 1892, a wooden platform was inserted in the carriage roads, later becoming platforms 3 and 4, leaving two sidings between platforms 4 and 5. A hoist provided access to the beer vaults. In this form, Platforms 1 and 2 were used for arrivals and departures, including local trains; 3 and 4 were used for departures; and 5 to 7 were used by arrivals.

The approaches consisted of four tracks, although further out these became an up line and two down lines. After Cambridge Street Junction, the line became simple double track until St Paul's Road Junction, where the lines from the Metropolitan surfaced. The main locomotive depot was at

Kentish Town, 1½ miles from the terminus. Despite not being as busy as **Waterloo**, **Victoria** or **Liverpool Street**, the approaches were congested, almost from the beginning, and difficult to operate, especially when working empty stock to and from the station. Improvements in 1907-08 helped, but the problem was never resolved during the age of steam, although in later years diesel multiple unit working with trains turned around in the station helped considerably.

The station was meant to serve the MR's long distance ambitions. The company saw its main market as the East Midlands, but while that was the basis of its traffic, its services to Scotland that started in the 1870s were also important. Despite having a local platform, there was almost no suburban traffic for many years with the MR's suburban trains, never plentiful, working through to Moorgate. Even in 1903, there were just fourteen suburban arrivals between 5am and 10am. It was not until 1910 that the Midland Railway began to encourage suburban traffic at St Pancras. The MR needed running powers into the London Docks over the **Great Eastern**, and in return the GER was able to claim that St Pancras was its West End terminus, which required some stretch of the imagination, and ran trains from Norfolk and Suffolk into the station. The GER trains were eventually suspended in 1917 as a First World War economy measure, and with the exception of a daily train to Hunstanton during the summers of 1922 and 1923, never reinstated. Nevertheless, it was St Pancras that was used by the Royal Family when travelling to and from Sandringham.

From 1894, the **London, Tilbury & Southend Railway** ran boat trains for passengers catching ships at Tilbury to Scandinavia and Australia. These services survived **nationalisation** and did not revert to **Liverpool Street** until 1963.

War and Grouping

During the First World War, St Pancras had the unwanted distinction of being the worst affected of all the London termini. On 17 February 1918, a German Gotha bomber dropped five bombs across the station, and one of these exploded in the cab court outside the booking office, killing twenty people and wounding many others. Train services were not disrupted.

Under **grouping**, St Pancras passed to the **London, Midland & Scottish Railway**, which meant that the MR was in the same group as its old rival, the **London & North Western Railway**. The emphasis was on **Euston**, and the LMS has been accused of neglecting its other mainline London terminus. Nevertheless, the company suffered greatly from the miners' strike of 1926 and the years of the Great Depression, and struggled to modernise almost anywhere.

The Second World War saw St Pancras suffer bombs and land mines, but the station's structure, despite being built over cellars and vaults, proved resilient. During the night of 15/16 October 1940, at the height of the blitz, a land mine wrecked much of the train shed roof, closing the station for five days. As the blitz drew to a close, on the night of 10/11 May 1941, the station had to be closed for eight days after a bomb passed through the station floor at the inner end of platform 3, and while no serious structural damage occurred, there was considerable damage to trains.

After **nationalisation**, **British Railways** spent much money modernising St Pancras and its approaches, especially with new signalling. Steam ended earlier at St Pancras than at many other stations, largely because the traffic was insufficient for **electrification** and introducing diesel multiple units was simpler, so that the last steam departure was on 11 January 1960. The victim of these years was the hotel, with plans to merge St Pancras with King's Cross across the road, and demolish Scott's Midland Grand Hotel, neglected and run down. The plans to combine the two termini and replace the hotel with an office block resulted in much public uproar. An alternative was to use the hotel as an exhibition centre or transport museum, close St Pancras and divert its trains to King's Cross, Euston or Farringdon. This also met resistance.

Privatisation of the railways may well have saved St Pancras, with Midland Mainline offering a much improved service with **High Speed Trains**, and during the closure of the **West Coast Main Line** for rebuilding, it was the availability of St Pancras to offer through services to **Manchester** that eased congestion. Nevertheless, after plans to build a combined station as an international terminus for Eurostar trains were abandoned as too costly, in November 2007 St Pancras emerged after a complete rebuilding as the London terminus for Eurostar. The Midland Mainline trains having earlier been evicted to a satellite station to the north of the main terminus.

Scottish Central Railway

Authorised in 1845, the Scottish Central Railway ran from Larbert and Stirling to Perth, providing the first through line between central and northern Scotland. Joseph **Locke** was the engineer with Thomas **Brassey** as contractor. The line required several bridges and tunnels, and even so had a steep gradient out of Bridge of Allan. The line opened throughout in 1848 and was an immediate success, especially for passengers from **Glasgow** to Perth, but also attracted **Edinburgh** passengers away from the shorter route of the Edinburgh & Northern as they did not have to take the ferry to Burntisland. It became a firm favourite with tourists and was soon paying a dividend of between 5.5 and 7 per cent. Later, through trains ran to **Aberdeen**, while there were branches to Perth Harbour, Denny and Plean. By 1865, when it amalgamated with the **Caledonian Railway**, the SCR had 78 locomotives, 288 passenger carriages and more than 1,300 goods wagons and vans. Before its amalgamation with the CR, the SCR acquired the Crieff Junction Railway, which left its line at what later became Gleneagles Station.

Settle & Carlisle Railway

Sponsored by the **Midland Railway** and authorised in 1866, the 72-mile line from Settle to Carlisle was essential for the Midland's ambitions to operate a **London** to Scotland service. It was joined by the **Glasgow & South Western, Lancashire & Yorkshire** and **North British** railways. The **London & North Western Railway** had opposed the Midland's ambitions, and conceded running powers to prevent the SCR being built, but the MR was persuaded to build the line by the LYR and NBR.

The engineer was the MR's John Crossley. The line has become renowned for its spectacular scenery, which also meant that construction was challenging, needing no less than thirteen tunnels and twenty-one viaducts, of which the longest is the Ribblehead Viaduct. Despite these engineering works, the line is steeply graded, starting with a 15 mile stretch from Settle, much of which is at 1 in 100, running at around 1,000-ft above sea level for much of its length, and then descending to just above sea level at Carlisle. It was meant to be completed in four years, but took more than six, and the cost escalated from the estimated £2.2 million to £3.8 million. A branch was built between Garsdale and Hawes.

Once opened in 1876, the route was still longer and slower than either the **East Coast** or **West Coast** routes, but the MR competed on superior standards of comfort, cancelling second-class fares and scrapping third-class carriages with an immediate improvement in the lot of the third-class traveller. Through trains from **St Pancras** to **Edinburgh, Glasgow, Liverpool** and **Manchester** used the route, and this through traffic was essential as there was little traffic to be found along the line itself.

The line proved difficult and costly to work, while it was often blocked by snow during the winter months. After **nationalisation, British Railways** started to reduce use of the line, and closed all stations apart from Selby and Appleby, while the vital through traffic disappeared steadily with the rationalisation of the trunk routes, so that the last through trains ran in 1982. Nevertheless, the line remained important as a diversionary route and strong local opposition to plans for closure resulted in the government insisting that the line remain open in 1989. Eight stations were re-opened and Ribblehead Viaduct, in need of costly repairs, received funding from a variety of sources. BR next tried to 'privatise' the line, but this was rejected. Local authorities have taken responsibility for many of the costly structures, working through the Settle & Carlisle Railway Trust. The line remains open and has become an important tourist attraction in its own right.

Severn Tunnel

While the River Severn had been crossed by ferry from the earliest times, and the railways were quick to install branches to the ferry crossings, it was not until 1863 that the first proposal for a railway tunnel under the river was put to Parliament: it was rejected. The **Great Western Railway's** growing traffic between England and South Wales had to take the lengthy route via **Gloucester** in the meantime, but in 1872, the company obtained authority to build a tunnel.

Work started in 1873 under Sir John Hawkshaw as consulting engineer. The project was for a seven mile length of track from Pilning on the English side to a junction at Rogiet, which was later named Severn Tunnel Junction. The tunnel itself accounted for no less than 4½ miles, of which half was under water. Designed to have gradients of 1 in 100 at each end, caution caused the section under the deepest part of the river, the Shoots, to be increased from 30ft below the river bed to 45 feet, so that the gradient on the Severn Tunnel Junction side had to be steepened to 1 in 90. To the surprise of those involved, the Shoots was not the most difficult part, instead a large spring, not surprisingly known as the Great Spring, broke into the tunnel in October 1879, flooding the workings. It took large steam pumps a year to clear the water.

Hawkshaw took a closer interest in the work as engineer-in-chief, while Thomas Walker was appointed main contractor. It was not until September 1881 that the pilot headings met. Work continued until October 1883 when the Great Spring once again broke through. Recovery was hampered by a pump breaking down, and then on 17 October, the Severn Bore, a large tidal wave, flooded the works, leaving 83 men cut off in the tunnel until they could be rescued by boat the following day. The Great Spring was later diverted and its waters are pumped out to this day.

When finally opened in 1886, the tunnel was the longest in the world.

Shipping services – see Ferries and Shipping Services

Shrewsbury & Hereford Railway
Authorised in 1846 and planned by Henry **Robertson**, work did not start until 1850, when Thomas **Brassey** was appointed contractor and also agreed to lease the line for eight years once opened. The 51-mile line opened in stages during 1852-53. At Shrewsbury, a joint station was built with the Shrewsbury & Chester and Shrewsbury & Birmingham Railways, while at Hereford it connected with the Newport Abergavenny & Hereford Railway (a predecessor of the **West Midland Railway**). The line supported and later worked an eight mile line to Tenbury, opened in 1861.

Both the **London & North Western** and **Great Western Railways** saw the line as a link between the Midlands and the expanding coalfields of South Wales, and when Brassey's lease expired in 1862, they took over, paying the shareholders a guaranteed 6 per cent dividend. The line survives and is an important link for trains between **Cardiff** and **Manchester**.

Shropshire & Montgomeryshire Light Railway
This was based on the former Potteries Shrewsbury & North Wales Railway, opened in 1866, closed that same year, and then re-opened in 1868 only to close again in 1880. Part of it was taken over by the **Cambrian Railway**, with the remainder acquired by the Shropshire Railways in 1888, before passing to the Shropshire & Montgomeryshire Light Railway in 1909, which refurbished the line and reopened it in stages during 1911 and 1912. Passenger services were withdrawn in 1933, and during the Second World War it was requisitioned by the army in 1941. Some passenger services were reinstated during the war and for some time afterwards, while on **nationalisation**, the line was worked jointly by the army and **British Railways**, although the latter had ownership. Most of the railway closed in 1960, with passenger services withdrawn some time before that.

Shropshire Union Railways & Canal
Following the merger of the Ellesmere & Chester and Birmingham & Liverpool Junction Canals in 1842, consideration was

given to converting part of the system into a railway. In 1846, the Shropshire Union Railways & Canal Company was authorised, largely based on the Ellesmere & Chester, while Shrewsbury, Shropshire and Montgomeryshire canals were added between 1847 and 1850, making an inland waterway system of 190 miles. In 1849, the company built a 19-mile railway from Stafford to Wellington. An integrated canal and railway system was the intention by this time.

The **London & North Western Railway** had leased the company from 1847, although the canal directors retained responsibility for the infrastructure and often resisted the railway interest, and the company was not absorbed by the LNWR until 1922, before being absorbed into the **London, Midland & Scottish Railway** in 1923.

Silver Arrow

An attempt to by-pass the high costs of strictly-regulated air travel, the Silver Arrow was a combined road, rail and air route between **London** and Paris, first introduced in 1956. Passengers travelled by road between London and Lydd Ferryfield Airport, were flown across the English Channel to Le Touquet Paris Plage, and then by road to Paris. The service was revamped in 1959 with rail taking passengers from **Victoria** to Margate, then a bus to Manston Airport, and on to Le Touquet, with a bus connection to Etaples for the train to Paris, with the through journey taking six hours in each direction. In 1962, the service was revised with a train from Victoria to London Gatwick Airport, then a flight by British United Airways to Le Touquet, and the following year a branch line was laid by SNCF, French Railways, into Le Touquet, with an express railcar to Paris, reducing the through journey time by about a third.

The service ended in 1981, with the introduction of hovercraft on the English Channel and improved railway timings in Northern France making it uncompetitive. It would not have survived the arrival of today's low-cost airlines and deregulation of air transport in Europe.

Sleigo, Leitrim & Northern Counties Railway

The last privately-owned railway in Ireland, the Sleigo, Leitrim & Northern Counties opened its first section in 1879 and when fully opened in 1882 provided a cross-country link between the **Midland Great Western** at Ballysodare and the **Great Northern Railway** of Ireland at Enniskillen. The Irish standard gauge line was just 43 miles long. The line survived nationalisation by either government, but closed in 1957.

Snaefell Mountain Railway – see **Manx Electric Railway**

Snowdon Mountain Railway

The only rack and pinion railway in the British Isles, it was built as a tourist railway on private land with work starting at the end of 1864 and completed in early 1896. It has remained independent. Today, it is usually worked by diesel locomotives, but steam locomotives are also used at peak periods.

Solway Junction Railway

Opened between 1869 and 1873 with running powers over the **North British Railway** line from Silloth, the Solway Junction linked Kirtlebridge, Annan, Bowness and Brayton. It was transferred to the **Caledonian Railway** in 1873. Its main structure was the Solway Viaduct, over which traffic closed in 1921, although it continued to be used by locals wishing to trek from 'dry' Scotland on Sundays to 'wet' England. The remaining parts of the SJR were absorbed into the **London, Midland & Scottish Railway** in 1923.

Somerset & Dorset Joint Railway

Created by the amalgamation of the Somerset Central, which had opened during 1854-59, running from the **Bristol & Exeter Railway** at Highbridge to Glastonbury, Wells and Burnham-on-Sea, and the Dorset Central, which opened during 1860-62, running from the **London & South-Western Railway** at Wimborne through Templecombe to meet the SCR. The new company almost immediately went into receivership for four years, and in 1874 nearly managed to do so again after opening an extension from Evercreech to Bath, which then became its main line. Salvation came when the **Midland Railway** and LSWR leased the line in 1875, realising the potential of a link between the Midlands and the South Coast.

The new ownership was marred by a head-on collision in 1875 at Radstock in which thirteen people were killed.

The SDJR consisted of 102 route miles, including the Bridgwater Railway, opened in 1890, with a 64-mile main line, parts of which were doubled, but 26 miles were single track and these, with the hilly section through the Mendips near Bath, made working difficult. The line retained its own works at Highbridge and used Midland locomotives, while carriages were painted blue. The line passed to the **Southern Railway** and **London, Midland & Scottish Railway** on grouping. The new owners made economies, with the SR taking responsibility for carriages, track and signalling, and the LMS for locomotives, but the line never made a profit. It was closed in stages by **British Railway** between 1951 and 1966. Despite carrying expresses such as the **Bournemouth-Manchester** 'Pines Express', the line did not have a good reputation, earning the nickname 'Slow and Dirty'.

South Devon Railway

Authorised in 1844 to extend the route of the **Bristol & Exeter Railway** to **Plymouth**, the broad gauge South Devon was 53 miles in length and involved tunnelling and steep gradients as it passed the edge of Dartmoor after the level first twenty miles between Exeter and Newton Abbot, opened in 1846. **Brunel** was the engineer and initially he planned to use stationary engines and pneumatic propulsion, but this was found to be impractical. A branch to Torquay opened in 1848, and the line through to Plymouth was completed the following year.

Initially, the line was worked by the **Great Western**, but between 1851 and 1866, the line was worked by contractors, including Daniel **Gooch**. Further branches were opened during this period, including an extension of the Torquay branch to Paignton, Brixham and Kingswear between 1859 and 1868 by an independent company supported by the SDR, as well as a branch to Tavistock in 1859, extended to Launceston in 1865; and branches to Moretonhampstead in 1866 and Ashburton in 1872. When completed these gave a total route mileage of 126 miles. The Tavistock and Launceston line resulted in a dispute with the **London & South Western**, which wished to use it as a route to Plymouth, and had to be converted to mixed gauge so that the LSWR could finally reach Plymouth in 1876. Meanwhile, the SDR had agreed to be absorbed by the GWR, and parliamentary authorisation was granted in 1878.

South Eastern & Chatham Railways Managing Committee

The ruinous competition between the **London, Chatham & Dover Railway** and the **South Eastern Railway** was brought to an end on 1 January 1899 by the creation of the South Eastern & Chatham Railways Managing Committee.

The South Eastern Railway came into

existence as the result of legislation passed in 1836 to build a line from **London** to Folkestone and **Dover**, but the London & Brighton Act, 1837, required both the SER and the **London, Brighton & South Coast Railway** to enter London on the same route from Redhill, forcing the SER to abandon plans for a route via Oxted. The result was that the SER reached the capital by paying tolls to the London & Croydon and Greenwich railways. The initial route from Redhill was to Tonbridge, reached in 1842, Ashford and Folkestone, reached in 1843, with the line extended along the coast to Dover the following year, with Tunbridge Wells served from 1845, the same year that the SER started cross-Channel operations using a wholly-owned subsidiary, using small paddle steamers that took 2½ hours. For the most part, the SER concentrated its efforts south of the Weald, prompting the creation of the London Chatham & Dover Railway by the disappointed people of North Kent. Even so, the SER reached Ramsgate and Margate in 1846, Deal, 1847, Gravesend, 1849, Hastings in 1851 and Maidstone via Strood in 1856, as well as extending itself west to **Reading** via Redhill and Guildford in 1858, an incredibly indirect route through a sparsely populated area that also contributed to the SER's financial weakness. One of the best positioned London termini was opened at **Charing Cross** in 1864, the only terminus actually in the West End, followed by **Cannon Street**, ideal for the City, in 1866, but it was not until 1868 that a direct route to Tonbridge was opened, by-passing Redhill and cutting 13 miles off the London to Folkestone and Dover route.

A vision for the future of the SER came with the appointment of Sir Edward **Watkin** as chairman in 1866 and he remained until 1894. Watkin wanted a route from **Manchester** to Paris using three railways including the SER and a **Channel Tunnel**.

Stirling's appointment as CME in 1878 marked the start of a series of locomotives with much improved performance, but passenger rolling stock continued to be poor for the most part, although helped by the introduction of 'American' cars for the Hastings service, and by similar British-built carriages for the Folkestone route in 1897.

The SER's concentration on the Weald route and its failure to extend the North Kent Line beyond the Medway left the field open for a rival, with the creation of the **East Kent Railway** in 1853, mainly supported by business interests in Faversham. The line opened between Strood and Faversham in 1858. The line was extended not at first in the direction of London but instead to Canterbury and Dover, which the EKR reached in 1862 and introduced its own Continental sailings with a service to Calais. The EKR's expansion had been noted with concern by the SER, and the intensive competition that ensued enabled the contractors to persuade the directors to extend the line towards London, changing the EKR's name to the London Chatham and Dover Railway in 1859. The extension reached Bromley in 1860, Victoria in 1862 and Farringdon in 1866. This rapid expansion and the reliance on contractors who had been the driving force in the development of the LCDR, placed the company under great financial strain, especially after a bank failure in 1866, which forced the company into bankruptcy that lasted until 1871. After James Staats Forbes became chairman in 1874, the competition with the SER became bitter, and extended to opening new lines to capture a share of the other company's traffic, often regardless of the likely financial benefits.

A working union between the two companies was proposed as early as 1890, by which time the LCDR's financial position was, if anything, stronger than that of the SER. This became clear later as the SER objected to the LCDR demanding 37 per cent of the overall receipts in 1890, but had to accept the LCDR having 41 per cent in 1899. In 1898, before the combining of the two companies, the LCDR had receipts of £142 per mile per week, against £87 on the SER. On the other hand, the SER had far better rolling stock, and especially locomotives. Had the SER taken a more comprehensive approach to the provision of railway services throughout Kent, the outcome could have been different, and it could even have enjoyed a monopoly within its area.

To prepare for the union, a Joint Committee was set up in August, 1898, under the chairmanship of Cosmo **Bonsor**. While the plan was that from 1 January, 1899, the two companies would operate as one, there seems to have been little stomach for strong measures. Obsolescent LCDR carriages and locomotives were scrapped, but considerable savings could have been made by eliminating competing routes, especially those to Margate and Ramsgate. Many lines had been built too quickly and too cheaply, and suffered from narrow tunnels and bridges with weight restrictions. One positive step was the linking of the two main lines by constructing four long spurs where they crossed at Bickley. Meanwhile the new CME, **Wainwright**, produced a series of 4-4-0 locomotives and new carriages, with Pullmans introduced in 1910. In 1919, Dover Marine station was opened, easing the transfer from train to ship, but before this, while still uncompleted, during the First World War Dover Marine handled hospital trains bringing home the wounded and departing for destinations throughout England.

While the improvements enhanced the quality of the continental trains, suburban operations continued to be dismal, and plans for electrification were not implemented until after the **grouping**.

South Eastern Railway – see **South Eastern & Chatham Railway**

South Staffordshire Railway

Formed in 1846 on the amalgamation of the South Staffordshire Junction and the Trent Valley Midlands & Grand Junction, the line ran from Dudley through Wednesbury and Walsall to Wichnor on the Birmingham-Derby line of the **Midland Railway**. Running powers took the company to Burton-on-Trent. The SSR opened between 1847 and 1850, and its engineer, J R Mclean, leased the line from 1850, the first individual to receive parliamentary sanction in this way. The line was notable for operating two of the first practical tank engines.

The **London & North Western Railway**, alarmed at the SSR's links with the MR, bought Mclean's lease in 1861, and in 1867, the company was acquired outright, giving the LNWR valuable access to the industrial area of the Black Country.

The South Wales Mineral Railway

The South Wales Mineral Railway operated a short line just thirteen miles in length, running from Briton Ferry to Glyncorrwg Colliery by way of Cymmer. Although nominally independent until 1923, it was taken over by the **Great Western** in 1908, and was operated using GWR locomotives.

South Wales Railway

Authorised in 1845, the SWR was supported by the **Great Western** to extend its services from Gloucester to Fishguard for the Irish packet services. Engineered by **Brunel** and opened as far as Carmarthen in 1852, the line was diverted to Milford Haven, port for a regular steamer service to Waterford. The broad gauge line required substantial viaducts at Chepstow, Newport and Landore, with a lifting bridge at Carmarthen. Locomotives and rolling stock were provided by the GWR, although the

263 route mile line had its own personnel. Operations were inhibited by the need to tranship coal and iron from the standard gauge lines in the South Wales valleys, and this may have been one reason for the line's poor financial performance, for which many shareholders also blamed the GWR. The two companies amalgamated in 1863.

The SWR was infamous for the stately progress of its passenger trains, while freight customers mounted a petition signed by 269 firms in 1866, asking the GWR to convert the line to standard gauge. This was eventually achieved in 1872, shortly before the **Severn Tunnel** was authorised and once opened the distance between Newport and London was reduced by 25 miles.

Meanwhile, a number of attempts were made to extend the line to Fishguard, and the GWR achieved this in 1899, building a new deep-water port for ferry services operated in association with Irish companies, which opened for packet services in 1906 and from 1909, also handled transatlantic traffic calling on its way to and from **Liverpool**.

Southampton

Linking Southampton to **London** was the reason why the **London & South Western Railway** came into existence. Although the town had a history as a commercial port, by the early nineteenth century this business had declined and the town was a quiet resort. The introduction of steamship services to the Channel Islands and France during the 1820s was the start in restoring the town's maritime trade, while new piers and docks were opened during the 1830s. The London & Southampton Railway was authorised in 1834 with **Manchester** businessmen taking up 40 per cent of its shares, and opened as the London & South Western in 1840 and extended to Dorchester via Poole in 1847.

As at **Bournemouth**, under the LSWR and then the **Southern Railway**, there were two main stations. The original Southampton terminus just outside the docks, and, with the Poole extension, Southampton West, or Central as it was later renamed. The former station has long been closed. The railway lines were also taken into the docks, but suffered from weight restrictions, so that when the Merchant Navy-class was introduced, these powerful Pacific locomotives could not be used on boat trains.

The railway contributed as significantly to Southampton's prosperity as the town contributed to that of the railway, as shipping services diverted to the port, cutting the long and often dangerous passage around the North Foreland to London by a railway journey of three hours. Initially much criticised for poor service and for its wider ambitions, the LSWR service improved once services operated through the town to Bournemouth.

The LSWR bought the docks, with its own railway system, in 1892. The port was the first, probably anywhere, to experience wartime traffic pressures as it handled troops going to the Boer War during 1899-1902, and then was a major port in both World Wars, being heavily blitzed during the Second World War.

Under the Southern, the new West Docks were built and the port much improved, while the railway service benefited from new rolling stock and more powerful locomotives. The port also became the departure point for the Imperial Airways services to the Empire from 1937 onwards, with special Pullman carriages attached to a Bournemouth express and detached at Southampton. Post-**nationalisation**, the Southern's new Ocean Terminal was completed, bringing fresh business to the old docks, but plans for **electrification** were long delayed, not being implemented until 1967.

Southern Railway

As the smallest of the 'Big Four' grouped companies, the Southern Railway consisted of three constituent companies, the **London, Brighton & South Coast Railway**; the **London & South Western Railway** and the **South Eastern & Chatham Railway Companies Managing Committee**, itself representing two companies, the **London & South Eastern Railway** and the **London, Chatham & Dover Railway**, that still retained their own assets and shareholders. The subsidiaries were the Bridgwater Railway; Brighton & Dyke Railway; Freshwater, Yarmouth & Newport (**Isle of Wight**) Railway; Hayling Railway; **Isle of Wight Central Railway**; Isle of Wight Railway; Lee-on-Solent Railway; **London & Greenwich Railway**; Mid Kent Railway; North Cornwall Railway; Plymouth & Dartmoor Railway; Plymouth, Devonport & South Western Junction Railway; Sidmouth Railway and the Victoria Station & Pimlico Railway. Its first general manger was Sir Herbert Ashcombe **Walker** the last general manager of the London & South Western Railway.

The Southern was the most dependent on passenger traffic of the Big Four railways. One problem was that this also meant that it had more **London** termini than any other railway company, including **Victoria, Waterloo, Charing Cross, Cannon Street, Blackfriars, Holborn Viaduct** and **London Bridge**. It inherited electrification from the LSWR and the LBSCR, but the latter used an overhead DC system and its suburban services were converted to the third-rail system favoured by the LSWR. The SECR had also planned an overhead system, but one that would have been incompatible with that of the LBSCR. Further **electrification** meant that all the inner and outer suburban lines were electrified by 1929, after which the company embarked on a programme of mainline electrification beginning with the London to **Brighton** line in 1931. Unusually, it was the only main line company to also operate its own underground tube railway, the **Waterloo & City**.

Even steam operations were marked by modernisation, but it was not until the Second World War that the CME, Oliver **Bulleid** finally gave the SR Pacific locomotives, which incorporated many advanced features and being amongst the best in terms of crew comfort, although the Leader-class that was to follow was very deficient in this respect, at least from the fireman's point of view. The Leader-class was an attempt to see if the same flexibility offered by electric trains could be found in a steam locomotive design, capable of being driven at speed in either direction and eliminating the need for turntables, which in many cases, including Waterloo, often involved running light some distance over the congested approaches.

By the outbreak of the Second World War, the SR had the world's largest suburban electric network as well as having electrified the main lines from London to the South Coast between **Portsmouth** and Eastbourne. On the two electrification projects to Portsmouth, the Portsmouth Direct of 1937 and the Mid-Sussex (via Arundel and Chichester) of 1938, it introduced corridor connections through the driving cabs, so that passengers and ticket inspectors could walk through the entire train, something not previously possible when electric multiple units were coupled together. It introduced train ferries on the English Channel, and the famous 'Night Ferry' sleeping car train used these to ensure that passengers could travel overnight without changing between London and Paris. It was a great provider of Pullman trains and even had Pullman cars inserted in many of its other trains to the Sussex coast, which also had the world's first electric all-Pullman train, the 'Brighton Belle'. At the other extreme, it looked at wider bodies for suburban carriages and also experimented with a double deck electric train, although this did not enter service until after nationalisation. With the **Great Western**, it was amongst the railway companies most involved in the development of domestic air services through first **Railway Air Services** and then Great Western & Southern Air Services, and at one time offered to buy the European services of Imperial Airways. The first airport railway stations were provided by the SR at Gatwick and at Shoreham.

More than any other railway, the SR was involved in shipping services and ports, where the new West Docks and the Ocean Terminal at **Southampton** were both the result of heavy investment and long term planning. It operated cross-Channel ferry services from Dover, Folkestone, Newhaven and Southampton, and also services to the Channel Islands from Southampton, as well as services to the Isle of Wight from Portsmouth and Lymington.

The SR built new suburban lines, notably the Chessington branch, but also closed many of its shorter branch lines as well as the narrow gauge **Lynton & Barnstaple Railway** in North Devon. Some believe that it may have been encouraged to close so many lines because of its heavy investment in bus companies, some identified by the 'Southern' prefix, as in Southern Vectis and Southern National, but nevertheless it did not close lines on the highly seasonal **Isle of Wight** network.

The company treated suburban services as seriously as its main line services, but on the Isle of Wight, with the exception of an experiment with a larger locomotive, the system was worked by carriages and locomotives from the Victorian era. Its network of services in North Devon and North Cornwall benefited from the 'Atlantic Coast Express', but in general were given a lower priority compared to those to Hampshire,

Sussex and Kent. **Grouping** was almost overlooked, despite standardisation of rolling stock and locomotives, and a new green livery, with the three operating divisions, Western, Central and Eastern, approximating to the territories of the LSWR, SBSCR and SECR respectively.

Southwold Railway

Opened in 1879, the Southwold Railway was built to a 3-ft gauge and its 8³/₄ mile line linked Halesworth on the **Great Eastern** to Southwold, conveying fish from Southwold and also handling large numbers of visitors during the summer months. The line was at best only marginally profitable, and shareholders must have regretted rejecting an offer to buy the SR by the GER in 1893. Growing road competition after the First World War resulted in closure in 1929.

Stamp, Sir Josiah Charles/Baron Stamp of Shortlands, 1880-1941

After an early career with the Inland Revenue, in 1919 he became secretary and a director of Mond Nickel Company, which later became part of Imperial Chemical Industries, ICI. He became first president of the executive and later chairman of the **London, Midland & Scottish Railway** in 1926. The LMS organised itself on US lines with a committee of vice-presidents, but suffered from over-centralisation, tight financial controls, and in-fighting between the old **London & North Western** and **Midland Railway** factions, which also showed itself in disputes over locomotive design and procurement. Stamp recruited William **Stanier** from the **Great Western**, who produced a series of classic locomotive designs, as chief mechanical engineer, and established a research department and a School of Transport.

Stamp was prominent in promoting the 'Square Deal' campaign of 1938-1939, which pressed for the railways to be able to set their own freight rates, and in 1941 was negotiating with the government over terms for the state control of the railways during the Second World War when he was killed, with his wife and eldest son, during the blitz.

Stanier, Sir William Arthur, 1876-1965

Serving an apprenticeship on the **Great Western Railway** under William **Dean** from 1892, in 1920 he became locomotive works manager in 1920, and in 1922 was appointed principal assistant to the chief mechanical engineer. In 1926, he succeeded Henry **Fowler** as CME on the **London, Midland & Scottish Railway**. The LMS suffered from the legacy of small locomotives inherited from the **Midland Railway**. Between 1932 and 1947, he produced more than 2,000 locomotives which incorporated much of GWR practice, such as tapered boilers, as well as LMS features, and while these included his famous and successful 4-6-0 Class Five or 'Black Five' mixed-traffic locomotives, Stanier also built many 4-6-2 Pacific locomotives, starting with the Princess Royal-class in 1933, and 2-8-0 goods engines, with the latter also being built by other companies as a standard wartime design. His express Pacifics culminated in the streamlined Coronation-class of 1937.

Stanier was of that generation of CMEs who also thought beyond the steam locomotive, and built some ninety diesel-electric shunting locomotives, which, along with the 'Black Fives', were adopted by **British Railways** after **nationalisation**. He also produced a prototype diesel-hydraulic articulated three-car multiple unit in 1938. During the Second World War, he became scientific adviser to the Ministry of Production in 1942, and later a director of Power Jets, the company set up to exploit Sir Frank Whittle's jet engines. He was knighted in 1943.

Stephenson, George, 1781-1848

Trained as a colliery enginewright, he invented a safety lamp that rivaled that of Davy. Nevertheless, his fame rests with his appointment as engineer for the **Stockton & Darlington Railway** in 1825. He soon realised that iron wheels could adhere to iron rails, and he developed the tubular boiler and steam blast pipe, which he combined in his famous locomotive, *Rocket*, and was responsible for both rolling stock and construction of the **Liverpool & Manchester Railway**. His other railways included the **Birmingham & Derby Junction** and **York & North Midland** in 1839; **Manchester & Leeds** and the **North Midland** in 1840; as well as many other less important railways. Nevertheless, he had to hand over the **Grand Junction Railway** to Joseph **Locke**, a sign that technology was moving on beyond his experience and ability to innovate and he was eclipsed by his son **Robert** (see below) and Locke.

Contrary to popular opinion, he amassed much of his fortune from share-dealing and his interests in collieries rather than from railways, but he remains as the 'Father of the Railways'.

Stephenson, Robert, 1803-1853

Son of George **Stephenson**, he assisted his father while he was still a colliery enginewright, and owed much to his father ensuring that he had a good training in engineering. In 1823, when his father built the world's first locomotive works, Robert Stephenson & Son, at Newcastle, Robert was put in charge. His first locomotive, *Active*, was re-named *Locomotion No 1*, and was followed by *Rocket*, *Planet* and many other famous engines. This was despite leaving the works in 1824 to work as a mining engineer in Bolivia.

After assisting with the surveying of the **Stockton & Darlington** and **Liverpool & Manchester Railways**, he became engineer in his own right for the **Canterbury & Whitstable** and **Leicester & Swannington**, but his main achievement was the **London & Birmingham**, which appointed him as engineer in 1838. In 1850, he became engineer for the **Chester & Holyhead Railway** and for the Royal Border Bridge at Berwick-on-Tweed. Less successful, his Dee Bridge at Chester collapsed, but he redeemed himself with the Britannia Bridge, linking Wales to Anglesey across the Menai Strait and the **Newcastle** High Level Bridge, as well as a number abroad. He was not above easing his father out of some major contracts. He became involved with politics as MP for Whitby between 1857 and his death in 1859.

Stirling, Patrick, 1820-1895

After serving his apprenticeship in a foundry, Stirling worked with marine engineers before moving to locomotive builders. In 1853, he was appointed locomotive superintendent of the **Glasgow & South Western Railway**, where he built a new locomotive works at Kilmarnock, and in 1857, he introduced his 2-class 2-2-2. Later, he adopted the domeless boiler. In 1866, he moved to become assistant locomotive superintendent of the **Great Northern Railway**, where he was soon promoted to chief locomotive superintendent. He produced some 2-4-0 locomotives for the GNR, before reverting to 2-2-2s in 1868, followed by 0-6-0s, 0-4-2s and 0-4-4Ts, and then, between 1870 and 1893, his 4-2-2 'Stirling Singles' which headed some of the world's fastest expresses. He produced the first dedicated **East Coast** passenger stock in 1896, but by the end of his career was falling behind thinking in mechanical engineering, objecting to bogie passenger carriages and coupled locomotives.

Stockton & Darlington Railway

When authorised in 1821, and opened in 1825, the SDR was the first railway with parliamentary approval for the carriage of passengers and goods hauled by steam locomotives. The line actually worked from collieries in south-west Durham, through Darlington and then on to Stockton, with a route mileage of around 29 miles, but in 1828, the line was extended to Middlesbrough where coal could be trans-shipped. At the time of opening, steam traction could not be taken for granted, but its engineer, George **Stephenson** and its first locomotive superintendent, Timothy **Hackworth**, used the line to develop more reliable steam locomotives which gave them an early lead. This was first and foremost a local line meeting a local need, mainly for the movement of coal, and should not be compared with the trunk routes that followed, or even with significant inter-urban lines such as the **Liverpool and Manchester**.

The SDR was financed largely by members of the Society of Friends, the Quakers, and especially by the Pease family, rather than through the stock market flotations of later years. Nevertheless, it in turn established subsidiary companies, of which the most significant was the South Durham & Lancashire Union Railway, which opened in 1861 and crossed the Pennines to Furness, bringing iron ore eastwards. The SDR and SDLUR combined kept the **London & North Western Railway** out of the North East, while Teesside was enabled to become a major iron producer.

Highly profitable with average dividends before 1860 of $9\frac{1}{2}$ per cent, and providing important routes and connections, in 1863 the line was bought by the **North Eastern Railway**.

Stratford & Moreton Railway

Authorised in 1821, the 17-mile long Stratford & Moreton Railway was built to carry coal from the River Avon to Moreton.

The railway was the idea of William James, who expected it to use steam locomotives, but when built in 1823, the engineer, J U Rastrick, planned to use horse traction. Opened in 1826, the line failed to pay its way and was neglected. There was just one branch, to Shipston-on-Stour, opened in 1836. In 1852, it was leased by the new **Oxford, Worcester & Wolverhampton Railway**, a predecessor of the **West Midland Railway**. Passenger services between Stratford & Moreton were withdrawn in 1859. In 1863, together with the OWWR, the line passed to the **Great Western**, and the SMR was wound up five years later. The GWR opened a new line between Shipston-on-Stour and Moreton in 1889 using much of the old track bed, but this was closed to passengers in 1929 and to goods traffic in 1960.

Stratford-upon-Avon & Midland Junction Railway

Created by the amalgamation of four small railways, the SMJR was connected to no less than four of the major railways, the **Midland, Great Central, London & North Western** and the **Great Western**. Its main route ran off the MR at Ravenstone Wood Junction, on the Bedford-Northampton line, to Broom Junction on the Barnt Green – Ashchurch line. Branches were built from Towcester to the LNWR at Blisworth and Cockley Brake Junction. Despite its strong connections, the line ran through sparsely-populated countryside and did not prosper, only showing its worth for freight during the two world wars. When it entered receivership, no other company was interested in buying it, but it struggled on after a reorganisation in 1908. It was absorbed into the **London, Midland & Scottish** on **grouping**, and the new owners experimented with a road-rail coach, known as a 'Ro-Railer', but most of the line was closed by 1965.

Stroudley, William, 1833-1889

After working for a millwright, he moved to the **Great Western Railway**, working in the Swindon workshops, and then to the **Great Northern Railway**. In 1861, he moved to the **Edinburgh & Glasgow Railway** as works manager at Cowlairs, before becoming locomotive superintendent on the **Highland Railway** in 1865, and finally moving to the **London, Brighton & South Coast Railway** in 1870, where he remained until his death.

He reduced costs by standardisation, and at the LBSCR this meant producing just five locomotive types, of which the most famous were his 'Terrier' tank engines for suburban trains and branch line duties, but at the upper end of the scale were his 'Gladstones', 0-4-2 express locomotives. His locomotives were economical and durable, but expensive to build.

Surrey Iron Railway

Authorised in 1801 and the world's first public railway, running 8¼ miles from Wandsworth to Croydon, it largely followed the line of the River Wandle and served the many industrial premises that had sprung up along the river. The 4ft 2in gauge line used cast iron tram-plates rather than rails, with users providing the horses and rolling stock in return for paying tolls. The line more than doubled in length in 1805 when it extended to Merstham as the Croydon, Merstham & Godstone Iron Railway, authorised in 1803 and intended eventually to reach **Portsmouth**, but this never happened.

Development of the line was overtaken by the steam railway, and the London & Brighton Railway, predecessor of the **London, Brighton & South Coast,** acquired the line while the terminus was acquired by the **London & Croydon Railway** in 1845 for its extension to Epsom. The CMGIR was wound up by Act of Parliament in

1839 and the SIR just seven years later.

Swansea & Mumbles Railway

Authorised as the Oystermouth Railway in 1804, with a five mile route along Swansea Bay, which opened in 1806 using horses to pull freight wagons. The following year, passengers were allowed to be carried on wagons run by contractors who paid a toll to the SMR. The operation was unprofitable and derelict by 1855. Nevertheless, it was repaired and reinstated so it was back in service by 1860, and in 1874, the Swansea Improvements and Tramways Company bought the right to operate services, before introducing steam locomotives in 1877, although some horse-drawn vehicles survived until 1896.

The line was extended 1¼ miles to Mumbles in 1900, and became well-known for its carriages, large double deck trams, which were hauled by small steam locomotives. **Electrification** in 1929 saw completely new trams, with traffic increasing from 700,000 passengers in 1925 to 5 million in 1945. Nevertheless, after the Second World War, traffic went into decline and the line closed in 1960.

Swansea Harbour Trust

Strictly-speaking, not one of the railways covered by the Act, nevertheless, its fleet of shunting locomotives passed into **Great Western** ownership in 1923. The Trust itself was brought into existence by Act of Parliament in 1854 to develop the port of Swansea, and initially used contractors to operate the port. After several contractors had been experienced, or perhaps suffered since the relationships seem to have been unsatisfactory, the Trust decided to operate the port itself, and acquired a stud of steam locomotives.

Szlumper, Albert W, 1858-1934

Szlumper joined the civil engineering department of the LSWR and in later years did much of the preparatory work for the reconstruction of **Waterloo**, including both the terminus itself and the widening of the congested approaches. He became chief engineer in 1914 following the death of his predecessor in a riding accident, and became chief engineer of the **Southern Railway** in 1923. He was responsible for the remodelling of **Cannon Street** and for the reconstruction of the lines in the Ramsgate and Margate areas, as well as the reconstruction of Waterloo, creating the first railway terminus designed for the electric train.

Father of Gilbert **Szlumper**, Albert Szlumper was described in one account as 'bluff, chunky and capable'; he retired in 1927 to become a consulting engineer.

Szlumper, Gilbert, 1884-1969

Unusually for someone at the **London & South Western Railway**, Szlumper reached senior level having started inside the company. Furthermore, he was the son of Alfred **Szlumper**, the LSWR's chief engineer and the brains behind the work of reconstruction at **Waterloo**.

Gilbert Szlumper's early career was in engineering, working in his father's department from the time he joined the LSWR in 1902, but in 1913, he became assistant to the new general manager, Herbert **Walker** and during the First World War he followed Walker onto the Railway Executive Committee as its secretary. Returning to the LSWR after the war, he became its docks and marine manager and started the planning for the massive extension of Southampton Docks. He rejoined Walker as assistant general manager of the **Southern Railway** in 1925, and eventually replaced Walker when he retired in 1937.

As general manager, Szlumper completed most of the Southern's electrification programme with the exception of the direct line to Hastings, for which work was prevented by the outbreak of the Second World War. Once again, Szlumper was required for the wartime railways, being loaned by the Southern to become Director-General of Transportation at the War Office shortly after war broke out, and he was retired officially from the Southern in 1942 to become Director-General at the Ministry of Supply until the war ended.

Szlumper is remembered as being quietly efficient, tireless and a clear thinker. He was very much in the mould of his predecessor and no doubt, had war not intervened, would have considerably extended the Southern electrification, possibly following Hastings with the lines throughout Kent, starting with the Thanet coast, and then probably taking on **Southampton** and **Bournemouth**.

T

Taff Vale Railway

At first, coal was moved from the valleys in South Wales to the Bute Docks at **Cardiff** by the Glamorganshire Canal opened in 1798, which moved coal and iron from Merthyr Tydfil. As production rose, the canal proved inadequate and in 1836, the Taff Vale Railway received Parliamentary approval to build a line over the twenty-four miles between Merthyr and Cardiff. Although **Brunel** was appointed as the engineer, the standard gauge was adopted, doubtless to aid construction in the narrow valleys, although the line presented no significant engineering challenges. In 1839, the new Bute West Dock opened in Cardiff, and the Taff Vale opened in 1841. Two branches were soon added, and a further branch followed in 1845, between Abercynon and Aberdare, which had been the source of much of the coal from South Wales,

although this was soon overtaken by the Rhondda.

The TVR was quick to enjoy considerable prosperity, paying an average dividend of 5 per cent during the 1850s, but by the 1880s it achieved a record of 14.9 per cent between 1880 and 1888, the highest dividend paid by any UK company over such a long period. This performance was all the more notable because of growing competition, most significantly from the **Rhymney Railway** after 1858, while the Bute Trustees, originally supporters of the TVR, soon switched to the Rhymney. The TVR responded by building a new port two miles down the River Taff at Penarth, leasing the operating company from 1862. As the congestion in the Cardiff docks continued to worsen, mine owners supported the building of yet another new port at Barry, with its own railway, which was another competitor for the TVR after 1889.

Not everything the TVR built turned to gold, and the 7 mile line built in 1892 to the small port of Aberthaw never succeeded in challenging the operations at Barry. Passenger traffic began to be encouraged during the 1890s, when services were increased by 40 per cent. Incredibly, in 1916, the TVR was able to obtain a court ruling to prevent the **Cardiff Railway** from opening a competing line near Taff's Well. Earlier, in 1908, plans to merge with the Cardiff and Rhymney railways were rejected by Parliament, but the three companies were then run by the same general manager until merged into the GWR in 1923.

Talyllyn Railway

The Talyllyn Railway was authorised by an act of 1865 and was intended both as a slate line and as a passenger line from the outset. Running from Bryn Eglwys, south-east of Abergynolwyn to Towyn on the Aberystwyth and Welsh Coast Railway. It was built to a demanding specification with many cuttings, bridges and embankments, to keep the maximum grading to 1 in 75, and to a gauge of 2ft 3ins to match that of the horse tramway in the Corris Valley (see **Corris Railway**). Unlike many such lines, it was a narrow gauge railway but not a light railway.

Lacking any association with other railways, the line never passed to the **Great Western** but remained independent, and passed into what must have been one of the first preservation societies when it was taken over by the Talyllyn Railway Preservation Society in 1951.

Tay Bridge

The **North British Railway's** route through the east of Scotland was punctuated by the wide estuaries or 'firths' of the Rivers **Forth** and **Tay**, across which the company ran train **ferries**. Nevertheless, this delayed through services north of **Edinburgh** and the crossings were often stormy and uncomfortable. Anxious to beat the **Caledonian Railway** for traffic to Dundee and Aberdeen, the North British commissioned first a bridge across the Tay from the north coast of Fife to Dundee, designed and built by Thomas **Bouch**, the bridge opened to traffic on 31 May 1878, and during summer 1879, HM Queen Victoria travelled by train across the bridge to bestow a knighthood on Bouch.

On a stormy night, 28 December 1879, the bridge collapsed as a train was running northwards across it, with the loss of all 72 people aboard. At first it was thought that the storm had blown the train over, destroying the bridge, but it soon became clear that the bridge had been badly designed, poorly constructed and without adequate supervision of its building or its maintenance. It was also the case that it was higher than it should have been to satisfy the Perth Harbour Commissioners, who were concerned that large sailing ships might not be able to proceed upstream. The train had

been derailed because of poor construction and had struck the side of the bridge, bringing it down.

Bouch was disgraced and the appalling circumstances no doubt contributed to an early death. His plans for a bridge over the Forth, a form of suspension bridge, were scrapped and the work given elsewhere. William **Barlow** built a more substantial replacement that opened in 1887. The piers and other remains of the original bridge were demolished as a condition for authorisation for the new bridge, but the base of the piers can still be seen upstream of the existing bridge.

The importance of the Tay and Forth bridges was that, once completed, the through railway line meant that the **East Coast** main line became the faster and shorter option for passengers from **London** to Dundee and **Aberdeen**, Scotland's fourth and third largest cities respectively.

Teign Valley Railway

A number of plans emerged for an inland railway between **Exeter** and Newton Abbot, but it took two railway companies to provide this line, with one of them, the Teign Valley Railway, needing no less than nine acts of Parliament to bring it to life, and another three afterwards, all for 7.75 route miles. While an alliance with the **London & South Western** railway was considered, the bankrupt company was eventually brought into the **Great Western** fold and once opened between Heathfield to Ashton in October 1882, it was worked by the GWR. Heathfield was on the broad gauge Moretonhampstead line, and the Teign Valley was standard gauge, so until the former was converted, the Teign Valley had an isolated existence with a single side tank locomotive and a handful of six-wheeled carriages. It was not until 1903 that the Exeter Railway, authorised in 1883, opened giving a through route from Exeter to Heathfield. The line's full potential as a diversionary route when the Dawlish Sea Wall was closed due to bad weather was never realised as it suffered from severe gradients, and while the GWR persisted with this, the nationalised railway preferred taking the longer LSWR route via Okehampton.

Telford, Thomas, 1757-1834

Telford was an engineer of the canal age as well as a notable builder of roads, but he designed one railway, linking Berwick-on-Tweed with **Glasgow**, 125 miles away, to be worked by horses and cables powered by stationary steam engines, but it remained unbuilt. After he became president of the Institution of Civil Engineers in 1820, he was frequently consulted on the new railways, both by the promoters of railways and by the authorities, including inspecting lines before they opened, of which the most significant was the **Liverpool & Manchester**. He always recommended horse traction, although never opposed steam locomotives, and indeed late in life he began to draw comparisons over their performance, but he was not a mechanical engineer.

Thornton, Sir Henry Worth, 1871-1933

An American, he joined the Pennsylvania Railroad in 1894, and became general superintendent of its subsidiary, the Long Island Railroad in 1911. In 1914, he was persuaded to become general manager of the **Great Eastern Railway**, where he produced a new intensive suburban timetable, launched in October 1914. By this time, the First World War had started and he was appointed by the British government to take part in the running of the railways, being later appointed as inspector-general of transport, for which he was knighted in 1919.

He returned to the GER afterwards, and his new timetable in 1920 was widely acclaimed as the best that could be done with steam traction. On **Grouping**, he returned across the Atlantic to become president of the state-owned Canadian National Railways.

Timoleague & Courtmacsherry Light Railway

Opened in stages in 1890 and 1891, the Timoleague & Courtmacsherry Light Railway was built to Irish standard gauge and linked Courtmacsherry with Ballinascarthy. It became part of the **Great Southern Railways** in 1925 and was **nationalised** in 1945, losing its passenger services in 1947 and closing completely in 1961.

Tottenham & Forest Gate Railway

Jointly-owned by the **Midland Railway** and the **London, Tilbury & Southend Railway**, the Tottenham & Forest Gate Railway opened in 1894. Control passed to the Midland in 1912, and under **grouping** it became part of the **London, Midland & Scottish**.

Tralee & Dingle Light Railway

Incorporated in 1888 to build a 3ft gauge light railway using powers from the Tramways and Public Companies Act (Ireland) 1883, the Tralee & Dingle Light Railway linked the two towns in a remote area of Co Kerry. Opened in 1891, it was a loss maker, but a subsidy from the central and local authorities and by local landowners enabled a guaranteed 4 per cent dividend to be paid. The route mileage was 37½ miles, and it never operated more than eight locomotives. In 1925, it was absorbed by the **Great Southern Railways**. Passenger services were withdrawn in 1939, but workings of cattle trains continued until the line was closed completely in 1953, by which time it had been **nationalised** and part of *Coras Iompair Eireann, CIE*, since 1945.

Transport Salaried Staffs' Association

Originally founded in Sheffield in 1897 as the National Association of General Railway Clerks, it became the Railway Clerks' Association in 1898. The creation of a union was prompted by the poor working conditions and long hours of railway clerks, whose conditions were not affected by the various Factories Acts. Recruitment at first was difficult, and the union was nearly wound up in 1898. There were fears that union members would be passed over for promotion, but this was resolved by the Trade Disputes Act 1906. The RCA adopted a policy of encouraging Labour MPs to block railway bills until companies recognised the union, and was one reason why a bill to authorise a merger of the **Great Central**, **Great Eastern** and **Great Northern** Railways before the First World War was defeated. On the other hand, the union was not unduly militant in the workplace, refusing to join the August 1911 strike over union recognition. During the General Strike of 1926, less than half of its members stopped work. Membership grew to 25,791 by the end of 1913.

The current title was adopted in 1950; so that it became clear that membership was open to all railway clerical workers. This was the period when membership peaked at 91,514, helped by recruiting amongst newly nationalised concerns such as Thomas Cook. Today, its membership is less than 40,000.

Trevithick, Richard, 1771-1833

An enginewright in a Cornish tin mine, in 1800, he built a double acting high pressure engine that was soon adopted by the mines in Cornwall and South Wales. Next, between 1801 and 1803, he patented three high pressure steam road carriages, but despite demonstrations in Camborne and **London**, the vehicles were too heavy for the poor roads of the day. In 1804, he built a steam locomotive for the Penydarren ironworks near Merthyr Tydfil, which managed to haul a ten ton load over a 9½ mile tramroad, but again suffered from weight problems as the iron rails broke. The locomotive was modified to drive a hammer. A second locomotive was built but not used.

His third locomotive was named *Catch-me-who-can*, and completed in 1808, was used for rides on a circular track close to **Euston**. He then dissipated his energies on a variety of projects, including a steam dredger on the River Thames, but his innovations such as the blast pipe and return flue boiler and coupled wheels, were adopted by others. He wasted his not inconsiderable fortune on mining projects in South America and died virtually bankrupt.

U

Ulster Transport Authority

Formed in 1948 and the following year took over the nationalised Northern Ireland Road Transport Board, the main bus operator in the province (at that time Belfast Corporation was the only other bus and tram operator), the Northern Counties Committee (see **Belfast & Northern Counties Railway**) and the **Belfast & County Down Railway**. In effect it was a small scale version of the **British Transport Commission**, from whom it received the NCC. It took over the Northern Ireland operations of the **Great Northern Railway of Ireland** in 1953. It later acquired the bus services of Belfast Corporation.

In 1966, its railway operations passed to Ulster Transport Railways, which became **Northern Ireland Railways** in 1967.

Underground Electric Railways

Formed by the American C T **Yerkes** to acquire the **Metropolitan District Railway** in 1902, Underground Electric Railways converted the MDR to electric traction, providing power from its Lots Road, Chelsea, power station and acquired the **Bakerloo, Hampstead** and **Piccadilly** Lines, still under construction. Although regarded by suspicion as profiteers at first, not least because statutory undertakings (ie. railways, authorised by Parliament) were being controlled by a non-statutory company, the company bought in a strong American management team that ensured efficiency and standardisation on its lines, with its third and fourth rail dc current supply becoming the standard for London that continues to this day. It also introduced multiple unit trains, lifts and escalators, and automatic signalling. The term 'Underground' became synonymous with the London network, especially after the other companies outside the UER group agreed to adopt the term for station signs and network maps.

The group expanded into buses, using the term 'Overground' for those which connected with the underground trains, but had also in 1912 acquired the capital's largest bus operator, the London General Omnibus Company, which also operated trams and trolleybuses, but was often referred to by its competitors as the 'Combine'. Its interests were all taken over by the **London Passenger Transport Board** in 1933.

V

Vale of Rheidol Light Railway

The only narrow gauge railway to pass into the hands of **British Railways**, the Vale of Rheidol was opened in 1902, and this 1ft 11½in line was also operated by the **Cambrian Railway**. Running from a yard next to the Aberystwyth station of the Cambrian, the line ran for twelve miles to Devil's Bridge and was built to serve iron

ore mines. The Vale of Rheidol was finally purchased by the Cambrian in 1913, which is why it was not mentioned in the 1921 Act. Under **Great Western** ownership, it continued to operate and in the late 1930s received new passenger carriages. The line not only survived nationalisation to be operated by **British Railways**, but had the dubious distinction of carrying 'British Rail' blue and the 'coming and going' logo.

Van Railway

Opened in 1871, the Van Railway was just 6.5 miles in length and was worked from the outset by the **Cambrian Railway**. Opened to goods, mainly traffic from a lead mine, in 1871 and to passengers in 1873. It was closed during the Second World War, on 4 November 1940, during the period of Railway Executive Committee control.

Victoria

Although not quite in the West End, Victoria was closer to it than any other station for the southern companies until the opening of **Charing Cross**. On the other hand, Victoria was dependent on the slow and indirect services of the **District** and **Circle lines** until the opening of the **Victoria Line** many years later.

The **London, Brighton & South Coast Railway** was unhappy with its shared terminus with the **South Eastern Railway** at **London Bridge,** as much because of the friction between the two companies that broke out from time to time as for the remoteness of the location. As happened so often in the early days of the railways, progress came from the initiative of a newcomer, and when the **London & South Western Railway** refused to support the planned West End of London & Crystal Palace Railway proposed in 1853, the LBSCR saw its chance. The WELCPR was a scheme to link the LBSCR's new Crystal Palace branch to a junction with the LSWR at Wandsworth, and with a further branch, having run for a short distance over LSWR metals, to a riverside terminus on the south bank of the Thames opposite Pimlico. The new railway opened its first stage on 1 December 1856 running from Crystal Palace to a temporary terminus at the northern end of Wandsworth Common, and was worked by the LBSCR, which introduced a new service between London Bridge and Wandsworth. The WELCPR had ambitions to extend to Farnborough in Kent and take a share of the Kent Coast business, using powers obtained in 1854, while the company obtained its second connection with the LBSCR at Norwood Junction on 1 October 1857. The through line to the riverside terminus at Battersea opened for traffic on 29 March 1858, and rejected by the LSWR, simply touched that system at what is now Clapham Junction, running parallel to it without any running connection, before passing under the LSWR towards the river. It was perhaps not quite the 'con' that it seemed since passengers could reach the north bank of the Thames by using the new Chelsea Suspension Bridge.

Although the riverside terminus was meant to be permanent and the site amounted to 22 acres, the station buildings were constructed of timber. It was later to become a goods depot. The temporary buildings indicated the sudden lack of confidence on the part of the WELCPR, because the railways were now being offered a number of schemes to take them closer to the West End. These included a Westminster Terminus Railway, which aimed to reach Horseferry Road, authorised in 1854, and then in 1857, the Victoria Station and Pimlico Railway was being actively promoted, and the necessary legislation for it was passed the following year. This new arrival immediately made much of the WELCPR plans redundant, and was immediately embraced by the LBSCR. The new

plan was for a junction with the WELCPR at Stewarts Lane, just before it ceased running alongside the LSWR, with the line climbing to cross over the main line to **Waterloo** and then continuing on a bridge over the Thames to the western end of Victoria Street, using the disused basin of the Grosvenor Canal. Construction started in 1859 and the LBSCR obligingly acquired the WELCPR line to Battersea on 1 July.

Partly to portray independence, partly to help in raising capital from investors, the Victoria Station and Pimlico Railway claimed that it would be building a terminus not only for the LBSCR, but also for the SER, the East Kent Railway (the predecessor of the LCDR) and the LSWR. The WELCPR had also another branch from Norwood to Bromley, now Shortlands, opened on 3 May, 1858, and with an adjoining section built by another railway, this was worked initially by the SER, but later the lease was transferred to the LCDR, and enabled the company to operate from Canterbury to Victoria. Despite its poverty, the LCDR realised that the new arrangement still left it at the mercy of other companies, and in 1860 obtained the necessary powers to build its own new routes to both the West End and the City of **London**, with the former achieved through a new line to the WELCPR from Beckenham to Battersea.

Such were the changing fortunes and ambitions of the railway companies, that the Victoria Station and Pimlico Railway found itself building a major terminus for the LBSCR and the LCDR plus the **Great Western**, which meant that the line from Longhedge Junction, Battersea, where the GWR would approach over the **West London Extension Railway**, had to be of mixed gauge to accommodate the broad gauge GWR trains. The LBSCR provided two-thirds of the Victoria line's capital and secured its own terminus and access lines, taking 8½ acres of the 14 acre site, so that eventually, despite the magnificent façade of the Grosvenor Hotel, Victoria was really to be two stations in one!

The approach to Victoria from Clapham Junction required both a tight curve and a steep climb, with the bridge over the river built high enough to allow passage of the largest ships likely to use the Thames, and indeed, it was unrealistically high. This was the LBSC approach, but it also had to be shared with the GWR despite that company's connection with the LCDR. On crossing the bridge, the line then had a steep descent to the station as it had been decided that an approach on a viaduct to an elevated station would have been unacceptable to the wealthy landowners in the area. Other concessions to this element included extending the train shed beyond the platforms and the early sleepers, of longitudinal design, were also mounted on rubber to minimise vibration.

The new station opened for LBSCR trains on 1 October 1860, the WELCPR having closed its riverside terminus on 30 September. The station was built from the outset on a generous scale, being 800ft long and 230ft wide, with a ridge and furrow roof having 50 foot spans covering ten tracks and six platform faces. There was a cab road from Eccleston Bridge with an exit into Terminus Place. Facilities were provided for horses and carriages to be unloaded from trains. A turntable was provided by Eccleston Bridge. The mainline trains used the eastern side of the station. The Grosvenor Hotel was constructed independently despite its obvious attachment to the terminus as the presence of several railway companies convinced the promoters of its success, and was completed in 1861, but the original hotel was along the west side of the stations and could not conceal the distinctly unattractive, even primitive, start to the station, with offices in a series of

wooden huts, for while the LCDR was indeed poverty stricken, even the more affluent LBSCR had found the cost of the move into the centre of London expensive. Matters were not improved when during February 1884, the Fenian Brotherhood deposited a bomb in a bag in the left luggage office, which also wrecked the LBSCR's cloakroom and ticket office, although fortunately the police were able to prevent similar outrages at **Charing Cross** and **Paddington**.

Last of all came the LCDR and GWR station, completed on 25 August 1862, although the LCDR had made use of a temporary station since December 1860. The LCDR made use of a modest side entrance into the station, which had nine tracks on its smaller acreage, with four of these mixed gauge. The GWR started services to and from Victoria on 1 April 1863, with what was essentially a suburban service from Southall where connections could be made with its main line services. Trains running through to **Reading**, Slough, Uxbridge and Windsor were also provided at times over the years that followed, and finally, between 1910 and 1912, a daily train in each direction between **Birmingham** and Wolverhampton and Victoria. Wartime restrictions saw the end of the Southall service in 1915, and in any case, such a service was really superfluous with the opening of what is now known as the Circle Line between Victoria and **Paddington** in 1868.

Other railway companies operating into Victoria included the **Great Northern Railway**, operating from Barnet via Ludgate Hill from 1 March, 1868, and the **Midland Railway** from South Tottenham and Hendon via Ludgate Hill from 1 July 1875, both of which used the LCDR station. **London & North Western** trains operated from Broad Street via Willesden Junction and the West London Railway from 1

January 1869 into the LBSC station, and survived the longest as an occasional service between Willesden Junction and Victoria until 1917.

Meanwhile, much had been happening with the arrangements for handling the traffic for the fast growing station. The LBSCR opened a cut-off between Balham and East Croydon, one effect of which was that the distance between that station and the two London termini became more or less the same. The LCDR also by-passed the WELPR route by building its own lines, opened in two sections, between Stewarts Lane and Herne Hill on 25 August 1862, and Herne Hill and Penge Junction at Beckenham on 1 July 1863, leaving the original WELPR approach as a purely local line. Despite these changes, or even perhaps because of them, Victoria's traffic continued to grow apace, and the approaches became a serious bottleneck, so that a leading consulting engineer, Sir Charles Fox, was asked to prepare proposals, eventually recommending new lines, including extra tracks over the Thames, and junctions. The companies accepted Fox's proposals and Parliamentary approval was obtained.

The new layout entailed removing the broad gauge tracks from two of the approach lines, providing an additional line for the LBSC, while providing three new mixed gauge lines and a standard gauge line for the GWR and LCDR. A new bridge was constructed alongside the existing Grosvenor Bridge on the downstream side. Everything was completed for normal services on 20 December 1865. The new layout meant that stations could be built at each end of the bridge, with the northern station known as Grosvenor Road and opened on 1 November 1867 for the LCDR, while the southern station was called Battersea Park and Steamboat Pier for the LBSCR, and only survived until 1

November 1870 when the LBSCR opened its own platforms at Grosvenor Road. The new station at Grosvenor Road was really too close to Victoria to be of much commercial value, with the LBSCR really using it by stopping up trains for ticket inspection, and only a few local trains called in both directions. The LBSCR stopped using it on 1 April 1907 and was followed by the LCDR on 1 October 1911.

Further additional approach lines came when the LCDR opened a new high level line, with three tracks built on a mile-long viaduct running from Wandsworth Road to Battersea Pier Junction at the southern end of Grosvenor Bridge, on 1 January 1867. This line also had a connection to the LBSCR's new South London Line.

It was soon time to consider tidying up and expanding the station itself, especially as by 1890, with all of its lines completed, the LBSCR was producing a steady return on its capital, with the annual dividend running at 6 or 7 per cent. Starting in 1892, the LBSCR acquired the houses on the west side of the station and also bought the freehold of the Grosvenor Hotel when the owners refused to sell houses owned by them. The LBSCR let the hotel to a new operator and built an impressive 150-room wing across the front of the station. The initial development of the station during the 1890s produced another 90ft in width, but only at the southern end of the station between Eccleston Bridge and the hotel. Even this was judged, rightly, to be insufficient. Unable to expand further west due to Buckingham Palace Road, or east because of the LCDR station, the only solution was to extend the station towards the river, and for this the powers were obtained in 1899, so that the station could increase from ten roads and eight platform faces to thirteen roads with nine faces, several of which could be used by two trains at once. Work started in 1901. The old roof was removed and five new ridged roofs were erected to cover the north station with a similar arrangement for what was to become the south station between Eccleston Bridge and Elizabeth Bridge. The vast project was completed in stages, starting on 10 June 1906 and followed by the five western platforms and a new cab road on 10 February 1907, and before the end of the year the new wing for the Grosvenor Hotel was completed across the front of the station. Then, on 1 July 1908, the four eastern platforms were ready and the new station enjoyed a formal opening. The LBSCR station was now worthy of the Brighton line with its luxurious trains and well-heeled clientele.

Innovations included a large departure board which showed the departure times, platforms and stops for up to eighteen trains at a time, behind which was an underground 'gentlemen's court', actually meaning a public lavatory with a hairdressing salon. The small telegraph office became the first post office on a London station on 2 October 1911. The station was screened off from Buckingham Palace Road, south of the hotel, by a wall of Portland Stone and red brick with niches for busts of the great, although these were never filled! All in all, the new station was 320 ft wide and 1,500 ft long and occupied 16 acres, almost double the area of the original. It had coaling stages at the ends of four of its platforms. It was lit by gas, and remained so until 1927 even though by then many of the trains were electric.

Of even greater value was the introduction of the first electric service on 1 December 1909, over the South London Line via Denmark Hill to London Bridge. This was an immediate success, with its 6,600v ac overhead system and countered the growing competition from the electric tramways. **Electrification** was clearly the way ahead for the suburban services, with

Victoria-Streatham Hill-Crystal Palace Low Level electrified from 12 May 1911, and on 1 June 1912, Victoria-Norwood and Victoria-Streatham Hill-London Bridge.

Meanwhile, the Chatham Station, now operated by the **South Eastern & Chatham Railway**, also underwent rebuilding, although its four storeys were dwarfed by the adjoining new wing of the Grosvenor Hotel. This work was completed in 1907, but most of the rest of the interior remained unchanged, the one area for big improvements being those for international passengers.

That the station was in mixed ownership was made clear by the signs greeting intending passengers. The SECR boasted 'THE SHORTEST AND QUICKEST ROUTE TO PARIS & THE CONTINENT SEA PASSAGE ONE HOUR,' while the Brighton proclaimed 'TO PARIS AND THE CONTINENT VIA NEWHAVEN AND DIEPPE SHORTEST AND CHEAPEST ROUTE,' all of which indicated that these were the days before advertising and trading standards since the latter route meant a sea journey of almost four hours.

The First World War saw Victoria become the main station for troop movements between London and France, with special trains for leave traffic to and from Folkestone starting in November 1914 and eventually increasing to twelve daily, with another two for **Dover**. A free buffet provided by voluntary workers served refreshments for up to 4,000 men every 24 hours. The SECR station also handled mail for the Western Front, which meant a train with some thirty vans remaining in the station each day from 11.00 to 23.00 while letters and parcels were loaded. The station escaped serious damage during the air raids, although in one case an AA shell case crashed through part of the roof, and on 1 October 1917, around 100ft of the northern end of Grosvenor Bridge was set alight when an anti-aircraft shell pierced the gas main under the disued platform.

Wartime meant disruption to traffic with Dover taken over by the Army and all of the remaining boat trains redirected to Victoria, and then Folkestone to Boulogne stopped on 29 November 1915, although the Dieppe service diverted to this port away from Newhaven until withdrawn on 13 April 1916. This left **Southampton**-Le Havre as the only route handling civilian traffic.

The SECR concentrated its cross-Channel boat trains on Victoria from 8 January 1920, while there had been a gradual reinstatement of cross-Channel services throughout 1919 and 1920, helped by the completion of the new Dover Marine station in January 1919.

The SECR main arrival platforms, then designated 1 and 2, were lengthened in 1921 to 764ft and 735ft, and the following year platforms 3 and 4, too narrow and too short were replaced by a new platform designated 3 and 4, which at 550ft long and 37ft wide was more than a third longer and three times the width.

The **Southern Railway** designated the two stations as Victoria (Eastern Section) and Victoria (Central Section), but it was not until 1924 that the first passageway was opened between the two parts of the station, with a second later in the year, and a single stationmaster appointed. The platforms were re-numbered, reversing the order used by the SECR so that platform 1 was no longer against the dividing wall, but instead its number was taken by the most easterly platform to allow numbers to run across the station. For many years, the SECR platforms had been numbered 1 to 9, with no platform 7, but now they are 1 to 8. The Central Section platforms were 9 to 17. The main arrival platform for continental trains became platform 8, and in 1930 this was roofed over and the customs examination area heated for the first time.

There was an element of tokenism about many of these changes, as separate booking offices remained and there was no operational connection between the two sections until a new line and points were installed in 1938.

In 1926, the Southern announced that it had decided to standardise on the third rail 600V dc system, and started wholesale electrification of the lines out of Victoria so that only services to Hastings via Tonbridge and the Kent Coast, including the boat trains and the *Night Ferry* were still steam hauled by the outbreak of the Second World War. Before the announcement, a third rail service was launched to Herne Hill and Orpington on 12 July 1925, while the South London Line became third rail on 17 June 1928 and the Crystal Palace Low Level service followed on 3 March 1929, working beyond to West Croydon and Beckenham Junction, as well as a new service to Epsom via Mitcham Junction. In its haste to ensure a single standard system, the Southern completed the transfer to third rail on 22 September 1929, when the last overhead train left for Coulsdon North thirty minutes after midnight.

Electrification was spreading out of the suburbs. After running services to Reigate and Three Bridges from 17 July 1932, electrification through to Brighton and West Worthing began on 1 January 1933. There was also a tremendous increase in frequencies, with four trains an hour along the main line from Victoria, including an hourly non-stop. Electric services to Hastings via Eastbourne and to Seaford started on 7 July 1935, and to Littlehampton on 3 July 1938, as well as to Bognor and Portsmouth via Arundel with the Portsmouth No2 Electrification Scheme on 3 July 1938, just in time for the start of the summer peak. Almost a year later, on 2 July 1939, Gillingham and Maidstone East services became electric, the last scheme to be completed before the outbreak of war.

The 'sparks effect' produced a dramatic increase in traffic, with the numbers arriving at Victoria in the height of the peak rising from 10,200 in an hour in 1927 to 17,200 in 1937. There would also have been a significant saving in costs, with fewer operational personnel and the end of shunting mileage as locomotives moved to turntables.

Growing competition from air transport led to a number of developments intended to improve the quality of the continental services, with an all-Pullman train introduced to Dover in 1924, and in 1929 the famous *Golden Arrow* was introduced, followed on 14 October 1936 by the *Night Ferry* through sleeping car service with specially-built *Wagons Lits* rolling stock.

Imperial Airways opened a London terminal in Buckingham Palace Road in 1939, and the so-called *Flying-Boat Train* from Waterloo was augmented by a service from Victoria during that summer. This was replaced during wartime by *Air Specials* from Victoria to Poole to connect with flights by the newly-formed British Overseas Airways Corporation, BOAC, to Baltimore, on which accommodation was usually reserved for VIPs.

The Second World War brought about major restrictions with train services cut back and, of course, not only did the Continental traffic end on the outbreak of war, but trains carrying service personnel to Europe also disappeared with the fall of France. The heavy air raids during the Blitz of 1940 and 1941 saw Victoria closed at times as bombs and parachute mines closed the approaches, but the station itself was spared serious damage, despite a crashing Dornier Do17 hitting the Eastern Section on 15 September 1940. Later, a flying bomb hit the Eastern Section on 27 June 1944, destroying offices and also damaging the booking office.

The invasion of France soon brought back the daily leave trains, and a limited service for civilian traffic to Europe started after German surrender, but a more complete service did not follow until 15 April 1946, including the reinstatement of the *Golden Arrow*. The *Night Ferry* was reinstated only a little more than a fortnight before nationalisation.

Victoria Line

Authorised in 1955, the Victoria Line was the first new tube railway in central **London** since 1907, and when opened in 1968-69, provided the capital with its first fully automated passenger trains, allowing one man operation. It provided interchanges with all of the other underground lines and initially ran from Walthamstow via **King's Cross, St Pancras** and **Euston** to **Victoria,** but an extension to Brixton opened in 1971, giving a route mileage of 14 miles.

Volks Railway

A short stretch of railway running along the seafront at **Brighton** and the first electric railway in the UK to survive to the present day, it was built in 1883 using a 2ft gauge. The following year it was modified to 2ft 9in gauge. It continues to run during summer.

W

Sir Herbert Walker, 1868-1949

Sir Herbert Ashcombe Walker was the last general manager of the **London & South Western Railway,** and followed in that company's tradition of recruiting its general managers from outside, in his case from the **London & North Western Railway** which he had joined at the age of 17 years. He joined the LSWR in 1912 when he was 43 years old, at a time when it had already started on third rail **electrification** and on the massive and desperately needed reconstruction of **Waterloo**. Despite being one of the youngest general managers, during the First World War he became acting chairman of the Railway Executive Committee, the body that ran the railways on behalf of the government, and his valuable work was recognised by a knighthood in 1917.

Walker has become famous for his extensive system of third rail electrification, completing that of the suburban network and extending it to the coast so that by 1939, the third rail covered the Sussex coastline as far east as Hastings and extended into Hampshire as far as **Portsmouth** and, well inland, Aldershot and Alton. He also took the credit for the extension of the docks at **Southampton** that enabled it to become Britain's premier passenger port at a time when overseas travel meant travel by sea. Others credit him with even interval or 'clockface' scheduling, on which he insisted, but many of the early railways had operated on such a basis, especially on suburban services where high frequency lent itself to even interval operations.

It is true that Walker deserves acknowledgement for all of these, and indeed for the strong leadership that he provided throughout his time at the **Southern Railway**. Yet, to confine any appraisal of him to these matters alone is to overlook his other qualities. He had a strong grasp of financial matters coupled with what can only be described as common sense. Typical of him was the decision not to rebuild the whole of Waterloo because the 'Windsor' station was at the time a new structure and could be incorporated into the design for the reconstruction without damaging the completeness of the new terminus. Equally, one suspects that his enthusiasm for third rail electrification was based on the economy of a system that did not require the wholesale reconstruction of tunnels and overbridges, the cost of which could well have changed

the economics of the programme completely. In many cases, carriages originally built for steam haulage were rebuilt as suburban electric multiple units, again a worthwhile economy, especially as the newer rolling stock was selected that otherwise could have been wasted by premature retirement. Walker also had an eye for publicity and recruited the young journalist John **Elliott** to handle the Southern's publicity. The LSWR had no great history of named trains, but the Southern Railway soon established a range of named expresses, showing that Walker did not adhere blindly to every LSWR tradition.

That Walker also took the long view and was aware of developments in transport generally can be gathered from the Southern's keen interest in acquiring bus companies, and where the entire company could not be purchased, taking a substantial shareholding, and, of course, its interest in air transport and airports. The enthusiasm for main line electrification has led many to believe that his ultimate ambition was that of complete electrification of the Southern, but this seems unlikely given the sparse service and poor business prospects of many of the lines in Devon and Cornwall.

As a man, Walker has been described as quiet but authoritative, a consummate professional with a strong grasp of all aspects of railway operation, and a leader who always got the best from his management team. He had a strong sense of duty towards his shareholders and the travelling public. A weakness was the failure not to look for greater integration of the old companies that could have rendered economies in management. Integration was carried through efficiently in such places as the **Isle of Wight**, where the three companies rapidly became one. It also has to be accepted that communications and automation were less sophisticated than today, so that keeping distinct divisions would have been seen as a practical approach rather than allowing over-centralisation. Undoubtedly, the network could have taken more line closures than was in fact the case, with branches such as those to Bembridge and Ventnor West proving a drain on the finances of the Southern Railway at a time when market conditions were far from buoyant, while those closures that did take place could have been accelerated. There was a curious contradiction in that the man who managed a railway and shipping concerns, and several ports of which the most significant by far was Southampton, believed that airports should be provided by the state, rather like roads.

Walker retired in 1937 and became a non-executive director of the Southern until **nationalisation**. He died in 1949.

Wantage Tramway

Linking the town of Wantage with Wantage Road Station on the **Great Western, London to Bristol** line, this 2½ mile line initially used horses when it opened in 1875, but steam locomotives were introduced the following year. It was unusual in that it ran alongside the highway, and railway goods wagons could be disconnected from trains and shunted along the tramway. Until after the First World War, the company enjoyed modest prosperity, paying an annual average dividend from opening to 1914 of 4.6 per cent. It was an early victim to the motor bus, passenger services ceasing in 1925, but goods continued until 1945, and the company was wound up in 1947.

War and Railways

The railways did not seek a role for themselves in warfare, and at first both the Admiralty and the War Office were hostile to the approach of the railways at **Portsmouth** and Shoeburyness respectively. Yet, as early as 1842, legislation was passed that allowed the government emergency

powers over the railways: but at first the reason was that of internal security. It was not until invasion fears arose again in 1859 that consideration was given to the use of the railways in wartime.

Many of the early ideas were grandiose, including the proposal for a circular line built around London to allow armoured trains carrying artillery to defend the capital. None of this should have been too surprising as the American Civil War, 1861 to 1865, showed that the railways were of supreme importance to army commanders, who could have the men and the material that they wanted, wherever they wanted it and when they wanted it: troops arrived ready to fight, rather than tired from a lengthy forced march. It was easier to keep armies supplied, and the size of armies grew as it became possible to cope with their massive appetites for food and ammunition. The wounded could also be moved away more speedily and with less risk of further injury from being bounced around in a wagon.

In the UK, Parliamentary scrutiny of legislation authorising new lines began to take defence requirements into account. The War Office accepted the **London, Tilbury & Southend Railway**'s extension to Shoeburyness in 1882. The War Office joined those opposed to the **Great Western Railway**'s broad gauge, seeing it as delaying the movement of men and equipment in an emergency.

The original emergency powers simply gave the government of the day the authority to direct how the railways should be run, leaving operational control in the hands of the companies. This remained true with the legislation of 1844 and 1867, and even with the Regulation of the Forces Act 1871. Other recognition of the importance of the railways to the military included the creation of the Engineer & Railway Staff Volunteer Corps in 1865, so that experienced railwaymen would be on hand when needed. Amongst those who helped plan for the use of the railways in wartime was Sir Myles **Fenton** of the SER. In 1896, an Army Railway Council was established, which later became the War Railway Council.

Britain's railways had played a minor role in the Crimean War, although its supply needs swallowed up shipping, but this changed with the Boer War, although this was confined to the workings of one company, the **London & South Western Railway**, with the majority of troops sent to Southampton to embark for South Africa between 1899 and 1902 travelling through London's **Waterloo** Station, while the cavalry took their horses with them through Nine Elms. Over three years, no fewer than 528,000 men were moved over the LSWR to **Southampton.**

The First World War
Throughout the Boer War the LSWR remained under the control of its own management, but the big lesson was that concentrating so much traffic on London was inefficient, and in the years leading up to the outbreak of the First World War in 1914, the railway links between the coast and the military training and rear concentration areas on Salisbury Plain were improved.

War in Europe was widely expected. The Liberal government had begun to consider nationalisation of the railways, but this was put aside as war loomed. The state took far more extensive powers over the railways than had ever been anticipated, with the President of the **Board of Trade**, whose department was responsible for the railways, as well as ports and shipping, taking control of the railways and acting as nominal chairman of the Railway Executive Committee, REC, formed as early as 1912, to run the railways on behalf of the government. Membership of the REC included the general managers of the ten most important railway companies, and one of their number, Herbert Ashcombe **Walker**, general manager of the **London & South Western Railway** since 1910, was chosen as acting chairman, despite being one of the youngest general managers. It could have been the LSWR's experience of the demands of the military during the Boer War that had resulted in Walker becoming acting chairman, or it could have been the commonsense argument that since so much traffic would travel over the company's metals and it owned the port of Southampton, that it would be best placed to co-ordinate matters and liaise with both the Army and the Royal Navy. Everything suggests that Walker was a great success in this post, for which he received a knighthood in 1917.

The REC's remit initially only covered railways in Great Britain, and it was not until 1917 that the Irish railway companies also came under its control – Ireland at that time being united and all of it part of the United Kingdom. Two of the Irish railways, the **Northern Counties Committee** and the Dundalk, Newry and Greenore were owned by 'mainland' railways. The **Great Southern & Western** had a close relationship with the **Great Western Railway**, but it was a working relationship, not a financial arrangement. Control of the railways in Ireland was necessary not just for the war effort, but also because of the internal security situation.

Of course, the LSWR had no monopoly of cross-Channel traffic, which was also shared with four other railway companies, the **Great Eastern,** with its port at Harwich; the **South Eastern & Chatham,** with its ports at **Dover** and Folkestone; and the **London, Brighton & South Coast Railway,** with its port at Newhaven. The LSWR operated cross-Channel and Channel Islands services from Southampton, while the Great Western operated to the Channel Islands from Weymouth. Other shipping services were bringing men and horses across the Irish Sea, with Ireland an important source for both, while the entire railway network was pressed into service to meet the needs of industry as well as the armed forces. Wartime innovations across the English Channel included train ferries between a new port at Richborough in Kent and France to help speed deliveries of rolling stock. This was not the first train ferry, as the concept had been pioneered many years earlier.

Few had any real idea over how modern warfare would affect the railways. The shelling of east coast towns by German naval forces was not unexpected, although no one had really considered just how much naval gunnery had increased in potency over the previous century. Only a few considered attack from the air to be a serious threat, but as early as October 1914, the SECR had a lookout posted on Hungerford Bridge, carrying the line from **London Bridge** and what is now Waterloo East (then known as Waterloo Junction) into **Charing Cross**. The lookout was expecting bombers' Zeppelin airships, ready to stop trains running across the bridge.

There was little damage to the railways from bombing during the First World War, despite being recognised by both sides as legitimate and significant targets. Aircraft were in their infancy, and even a Zeppelin could only carry a limited bomb load. Most of the action affected **Liverpool Street**. On the night of 8/9 September 1915, several bombs fell on Liverpool Street, damaging the suburban and through lines, and fracturing a water main that flooded the suburban tracks. Nevertheless, partly because of the small size of the bombs, repairs were put in hand and a full service restored by 11am on 9 September. The bombs also demolished a wall and shattered glass at **Broad Street** next door, where some horses were

injured. A more significant incident followed during the air raid of 13 June 1917. Again the City was the target, and again three bombs landed on the GER's terminus at Liverpool Street: one of the bombs was a dud and failed to explode, another exploded on a platform and a third hit the dining car of the noon express to King's Lynn and Hunstanton, setting it alight. Two carriages between platforms 8 and 9 were being used for medical examinations, and these were smashed. All in all, sixteen people were killed and another thirty-six wounded, making it one of the worst bombing casualty rates in England during the First World War.

During the First World War, the **Great Northern Railway** at **Kings Cross** used Gas Works Tunnel as a shelter for main line trains whenever enemy aircraft approached, but the station was untroubled by German bombing during the war, even though a massive volume of freight traffic passed through the station on its way to the SECR, including train loads of explosives for the British forces fighting in France.

Unfortunately, accidents were a far more serious threat to the railways and those using them than enemy action. On 22 May 1915, at Quintinshill, near Carlisle, on the **Caledonian Railway**, Britain suffered its worst ever railway disaster (see **accidents**) with several trains involved and at least 227 people killed with another 245 injured. Most of those who died were soldiers on their way to France from Scotland, and as their unit records were destroyed in the fire that engulfed the wreckage, completely accurate figures have never become available. The signal box covered not just the main line but two passing loops to allow expresses to overtake the slower goods trains and local stopping trains. At the time both loops were occupied by goods trains, so that a northbound local train had to be reversed on to the southbound mainline to allow a double-headed express, to pass it on the way to **Edinburgh** and **Glasgow**, but the local train was promptly forgotten by the signalman. A crowded troop train raced downhill from Beattock, with no less than twenty-one carriages, mainly elderly six-wheelers built largely of wooden construction and with gas lighting, and struck the local train with such force that the troop train was compressed to a quarter of its original length. Worse was to follow, when the double-headed northbound express ran into the wreckage before it could stop, glowing coals from the fireboxes created an inferno as they ignited the ruptured gas pipes for the lighting of the troop train. The resulting fire was so severe that it did not die down for twenty-four hours.

Both signalmen were negligent and convicted of manslaughter, but the real culprit was the railway company's failure to pay for any form of automatic train control.

State control of the railways was intended to ensure that the system operated as one: an excessive measure as the pre-war railways had co-ordinated themselves very well indeed, partly through the workings of the **Railway Clearing House**, which did more than simply balance inter-company tickets and freight receipts, and several companies did collaborate, especially to ensure the smooth through running of the Anglo-Scottish expresses, of which the most complicated was that from **Aberdeen** to **Penzance**, a distance of well over 800 miles. Nevertheless, state control enabled resources to be directed to wherever they might be most needed rather than companies keeping their equipment to themselves while another part of the system suffered under wartime pressures. Many railwaymen had volunteered to join the armed forces while others were mobilised because of their reserve obligations, so that no less than 184,475 – 45 per cent of railwaymen of military age - had enlisted. The military had

also helped itself to locomotives and rolling stock for service as far away as Mesopotamia: more than 600 locomotives were pressed into military service overseas as the 1/2 inch or so difference between British and French track gauges mattered little.

Despite cutting or reducing many ordinary services to free men and equipment for military use, there were increased pressures on the system over and above the obvious need for troop trains. Unforeseen by the planners on the outbreak of war was that the role of coastal shipping, in peacetime so important for the movement of bulk commodities such as coal, was severely restricted by enemy activity in the North Sea and the English Channel.

Few warships were fuelled by oil at this stage in the Royal Navy's history, because of fears that sufficient oil might not be available in wartime. The Grand Fleet had moved to its forward wartime base at Scapa Flow in Orkney, not the most convenient location for supply by railway, but coal had to be carried from South Wales to Grangemouth, where it was transferred to coastal shipping, on the so-called 'Jellicoe Specials', named after the admiral commanding the Grand Fleet. All in all, no less than 13,630 coal trains were run for this purpose alone between August 1914 and March 1919, with Pontypool Road on the Great Western Railway being the main loading point. Grangemouth had to be the main transhipment point because further north the railways, with most of the route mileage single track, could not have coped, and there were insufficient port facilities in the far north of Scotland. Despite the shortcomings of the largely single-tracked line north of Perth, naval manpower was moved further north by rail, putting the **Highland Railway** under great strain between Perth and Inverness and then north to Thurso. This required 'naval specials' to be operated every night, covering the 717 miles from Euston to Thurso in 21½ hours, an average speed of just over 33 miles per hour.

Routine operations were severely affected as railway workshops were converted to help with the war effort, including the manufacture of armaments, while rolling stock was converted to provide ambulance trains. Some minor railway lines, as far apart as near Dumfries in the south-west of Scotland and at Southsea on the South Coast, were closed in wartime never to reopen, but the creation of new manufacturing plant, such as an ordnance factory near Gretna close to the border between Scotland and England, also meant that additional facilities had to be created quickly.

Economy in manpower, fuel and materials all meant that services elsewhere had to be reduced. There were fewer trains, and as the Quintinshill accident showed, many were lengthened or combined, while overall speeds were reduced, although none of these measures were as restrictive as those imposed during the Second World War. Dining car and sleeping car provision was also reduced, but again, the cuts were not as severe as those that came in the early 1940s and these facilities never quite disappeared completely. First-class travel survived the war years, even on inner suburban lines and those parts of the London Underground offering this facility, but eventually cheap day return tickets were withdrawn to discourage leisure travel.

New, rebuilt or reconditioned steam locomotives appeared in a drab grey colour scheme.

Despite it being a truly global war, the main centre of activity was in Europe, and the greatest pressure fell on the Channel Ports, with first Dover and then Folkestone closed to civilian traffic. The SECR became Britain's frontline railway, with the heaviest responsibility for the movement of men and materials to the coast. In London, **Charing Cross** also had the role of being Westminster's local station, and a special train, code-named *Imperial A* was held ready at all times for VIP journeys to the coast, being used for 283 journeys during the war years. Charing Cross was also the arrival point for many of the casualties of war: On 7 June 1917, after the start of the Battle of Messines at dawn, the first wounded arrived at Charing Cross at 2.15pm that same day.

The state was to prove to be a short-sighted and improvident proprietor, so that financially, the war years were a disaster for the railway companies, despite compensation being based on pre-war earnings, ones of prosperity for the railways. Post-war, one general manager noted that the combined profits for the railway companies in 1913 had totalled £45m, but that by 1920, these had dropped to less than £7m, owing to improved rates of pay during WWI when the railways were under direct Government control. By 1921, immediately prior to government control ceasing, the railways were running at a loss overall of around £9 million. Part of the reason was almost certainly the cost of manpower. Railway wages in 1913 had totalled £47m, but by 1920 had risen to £160m.

The Second World War

Before the outbreak of war, the **Ministry of Transport**, later to become the Ministry of War Transport, seized control of the railways on 1 September 1939, using powers granted under the Defence Regulations Act 1939. As before the minister operated through a Railway Executive Committee, which included the general managers of the four main line railways and of **London Transport**. The railways evacuated many of their administrative personnel. The Railways Executive Committee used an abandoned underground station on the

Piccadilly Line at Down Street, between Green Park and Hyde Park Corner stations, converted to provide office accommodation and dormitories.

State control made the railways contractors to the government, with all revenue passing to the government which then allocated shares from a pool, initially set at a guaranteed £40 million (around £2,152 million today). The **Southern** share of the pool was fixed at 16 per cent, the same as for the **Great Western** while the **London Passenger Transport Board** received 11 per cent, the **London, Midland & Scottish** 34 per cent and the **London & North Eastern** 23 per cent. These percentages were based on the average net revenues for the companies and LPTB during 1935-37, which the government took as each company's standard revenue. Once the guaranteed £40 million had been paid, any balance was allocated to the five train operators on the same percentage terms up to a maximum of £3.5 million. After this, if there was a further balance, the revenue over £43.5 million would be divided equally between the government and the pool until the pool total reached £56 million. At this stage, if the revenue share allocated to any of the companies then exceeded its standard revenue, the excess would be shared out proportionately among the other companies.

Costs of maintenance and renewals had to be standardised, while the cost of restoring war damage would be met up to a total of £10 million in a full year. Privately-owned wagons were also requisitioned by the Ministry of War Transport, and the individual companies had to meet the costs and revenue attributed to the wagon owners out of their share of the revenue pool. The Railway Control Order also applied to other lines, including the **East Kent, Kent & East Sussex**, and **Shropshire & Montgomery** light railways, the King's Lynn Docks & Railway

and the **Mersey Railway**. The **Romney, Hythe & Dymchurch Railway** was requisitioned by the military, becoming a vital link in the defences of the Kent coast.

This was a 'take it or leave it' type of agreement, with the government leaking threats of nationalisation if the companies failed to agree, although these were officially denied. While the years in question had been bad ones for the British economy, the final year 1938, had been even worse and the railways had difficulty in getting the government to understand this. The government had earlier warned the railways that as many as 800 locomotives might be required for service overseas, but as the war did not follow the pattern of 1914-18, not all were required.

Some 110,000 men had to be given up for national service, with more than 100,000 actually conscripted into the armed forces, while 298 steam and 45 of the still rare diesel locomotives, mainly shunting engines, were also taken for service overseas. These figures were in addition to the use of railway workshops for war work, which naturally moved a further substantial number of personnel away from railway work.

Once again the railways had to economise in the provision of their services, saving fuel and making locomotive power and rolling stock available for the many specials required by the armed forces. For the first time the railways had to participate in a massive evacuation programme, moving children and expectant and nursing mothers away from areas judged to be at risk from enemy bombing. Evacuation was to be a problem that recurred during the war. As France fell, a further evacuation moved many evacuees away from what had now become an endangered zone, the coastal and country districts in the South East and South of England, as well as evacuating many of the residents of those areas. A further evacuation later in the war was caused as the V-weapons took their toll on London and the South East.

Evacuation was ordered on 31 August. In London alone, 5,895 buses were required to move 345,812 passengers to the stations. During the four days of the operation, from 1 to 4 September 1939, only a skeleton service could be provided for the public outside the rush hours. Elsewhere were moving children from the Medway towns, from **Southampton, Portsmouth** and Gosport. The railways also had to arrange 34 ambulance trains for the partial evacuation of hospitals.

Initially, excursion and cheap day tickets were withdrawn, but day tickets were reintroduced on 9 October, although with tighter conditions.

On the eve of war, 2 September, black out was enforced. Drivers had to pull up their trains beside oil lamps placed on the platform as markers. Steam locomotives had canvas draped between the engine cab and tender to hide the light of their fires, while the side windows on the more modern locomotives were blanked out. Colour light signals had long hoods fitted over them so that they could not be seen from the air. At first trains ran at night without lights, but later shaded lights were introduced.

On 11 September, government-inspired cuts were imposed, inflicting hardship on passengers as normal commuter traffic remained virtually at pre-war levels. Twenty minute suburban frequencies were cut to half-hourly, while off-peak and Sunday services became hourly. This led to unacceptable levels of overcrowding with many passengers left behind, and station dwell times were extended as passengers struggled to alight from trains or climb aboard. Normal services were reinstated on weekdays from 18 September, before new reductions in passenger services followed during September and October. Catering arrangements were reduced.

The impact on longer distance services included, for example, on the GWR, between London and **Bristol**, the number of daily trains falling from 20 to 14, while the average journey time for the 118 miles extended from 135 minutes to 178 minutes, but pre-war journeys included a fastest time of just 105 minutes. There were many 'temporary' speed limits, while war damage became extensive, especially in the London area and along the south and east coasts. Trains had extra stops and extra carriages. Long distance trains from some London termini would have to be divided in two to fit the platforms, with the first half pulled out of the station, and then backed on to the second half to be coupled, before the journey could start. At intermediate stations, such over-long trains had to make two stops so that passengers could board and alight.

By the time of Dunkirk, many railway ships had been requisitioned by the government, but as the situation in France began to spiral out of control, the signal was received that 'all available railway steamers of 1,000 tons gross with a range of 150 miles are required for immediate Government service.' At 17.00 on 26 May, the code-word 'Dynamo' was sent to the railways, warning them that the evacuation was due to start. The operation ran from 27 May to 4 June, and the difficulty of organising it was made worse by the sudden realisation on the part of the authorities that a second evacuation was needed of many children moved from London. In the end, more than 338,000 troops were carried. The railway companies quickly agreed amongst themselves to provide a large pool of carriages. The GWR provided sufficient for 40 trains, the LMS 44, the LNER 47 and the Southern 55, a total of 186 trains with a total of almost 2,000 carriages.

Throughout the war years there was an almost constant trimming of services to reduce fuel consumption. At the same time, the changing traffic patterns created by wartime saw new stations opened and some new lengths of track to meet the needs of war workers and the military. The Elham Valley line was one of a number taken over completely by the military. In addition, as the war progressed, other restrictions were applied. On 6 October 1941, under the directions of the Minister of War Transport, all suburban trains became third class only. While mainline trains retained first class accommodation, on 22 May 1942, many lost all catering facilities, although some service was maintained on the longer distance services.

On 5 October 1942, off-peak cheap returns were finally scrapped, leaving seasons as the only discounted tickets.

The financial basis of state control had been imposed, but the original scheme had many deficiencies. Instead of the original agreement of a £40 million guarantee and a share in net revenue in excess of that amount up to £56 million, there would be a fixed annual guarantee. Division of the £43 million and the relative shares were to be:

Great Western	£6,670,603	15.5%
Southern	£6,607,639	15.4%
London, Midland, Scottish	£14,749,698	34.3%
London & North Eastern	£10,136,355	23.6%
London Transport	£4,835,705	11.2%

Further adjustments were not made in the later stages of the war, but even so surplus profits taken by the government for 1943, 1944 and 1945, reached a total of £155 million.

Traffic rose dramatically. The number of originating passenger journeys on the GWR in 1938 was 129 million, but by 1944 this had increased to 190 million. On the LMS the figures were a smaller rate of increase, from 421 million to 456 million, itself down 2 million on 1943, but static on the LNER

at 281 million, but again down on 1943. The big exception was on the Southern, where passenger journeys fell from 361 million to 347 million, due in no small part to the loss of the holiday and excursion traffic. For all of the railway companies, the number of coaching train miles fell between 1938 and 1944, including empty stock workings.

Freight increased overall by 46 per cent between 1938 and 1943, with the biggest increase, 86 per cent, in merchandise, which doubtless included manufactured items such as munitions. While coal and coke traffic only rose by 13 per cent, the length of haul rose by no less than 30 per cent

Overall, in 1935-37, the five railway undertakings had average annual total operating receipts of £195,236,000 and expenditure of £158,500,000, which gave them net operating receipts of £36,727,000 and net revenue of £39,903,000. By 1944, the annual figures had risen to total operating receipts of £394,360,000 and expenditure of £301,200,000, giving net operating receipts of £93,193,000 and net revenue of £90,256,000, but, of course, of the last figure, they were only allowed to keep £43,469,000, with the rest going to the government. Overall, for 1941-44, the railways received a total of £173,876,000 and the government received £176,199,000, and these figures ignore the sums for 1939-40 and for 1945.

Waterford & Kilkenny Railway
Opened in 1848, the Irish standard gauge Waterford & Kilkenny became the Waterford & Central Ireland Railway in 1868, and was absorbed by the **Great Southern & Western Railway** in 1900.

Waterford, Limerick & Western Railway
Originating as the Waterford & Limerick Railway in 1846, the first section to be opened was between Limerick and

Tipperary in 1848, but it was later extended and renamed the Waterford, Limerick & Western Railway in 1895, by which time it was opened throughout from Waterford through Limerick to Sligo, and had branches to Foynes, Killaloe, Thurles and Tralee. Built to Irish standard gauge, it was absorbed by the **Great Southern & Western Railway** in 1901.

Waterloo

In some ways, the history of Waterloo is similar to that of **London Bridge**, with the station being fairly remote from the destinations of most of the travellers arriving off its trains, but having replaced an earlier and even less satisfactory terminus, in this case at Nine Elms. The station also grew piecemeal, with four separate stages of construction and was extended to provide through running, and with the creation of a station just outside at Waterloo Junction on the line from London Bridge to **Charing Cross**, so it was also used by two railway companies. Here, however, the histories of the two stations differ considerably. The through connection for trains to run beyond Waterloo was relatively short-lived. More important, Waterloo was taken in hand and the **London & South Western** terminus completely rebuilt by a vigorous and determined new general manager, Sir Herbert **Walker**, so that for more than eighty years it has represented a dignified and cohesive whole, clearly showing that it was the first terminus designed for electric trains.

The predecessor of Waterloo, Nine Elms, was chosen as the terminus for the new London & Southampton Railway, first mooted in 1831, largely because it meant that costly disturbance to business and residential property would be minimal. Its position, close to the southern end of Vauxhall Bridge, meant that passengers could make their way to the West End, while boat services were envisaged for those travelling to the City. The new terminus was opened on 21 May 1838, by which time the railway was open as far as Woking. The following year, the London & Southampton unveiled its ambitions with a new name, the London & South Western Railway, although it did not reach its original objective until 11 May 1840. The first train, carrying guests, took three hours for the journey of just under eighty miles between Nine Elms and **Southampton.**

The new railway soon found that its heaviest traffic was short distance between what would now be the outer suburbs and **London.** Many of the station names of the early LSWR differ from those of today, with the original Kingston now being Surbiton. The first branch line was opened on 27 July 1946 from Clapham Junction to Richmond, and soon provided a quarter of the company's traffic. The lack of appeal of the railway for much of the other traffic was largely due to the remote location of Nine Elms, and the LSWR admitted to the Metropolitan Termini Commission in 1846 that road coaches had survived between Chertsey and the City because of this. The original promoters of the branch to Richmond had also proposed a line from Nine Elms to a supposed 'West End' terminus near Hungerford Bridge. Having taken over the Richmond branch before its completion, the LSWR obtained powers in 1845 for a new terminus in York Road, close to the southern end of Waterloo Bridge, and a further act in 1847 increased the number of lines to the new terminus to four and also the size of the site. The reasons for the LSWR choosing Nine Elms in the first place can be the more readily understood when it is realised that the extension to Waterloo, then requiring far fewer tracks than exist today, required the demolition of 700 houses and the crossing of 21 roads, despite the 1³/₄ mile railway using a viaduct with more than 200 arches for most of its length. Obstacles that affected the alignment included Lambeth Palace, Vauxhall Gardens and a gas works. One intermediate station was built at Vauxhall, while a bridge over Westminster Road was on the skew with the then unprecedented span of 90ft. The size of the undertaking was partly because the LSWR was encouraged by earlier negotiations with the **London, Brighton & South Coast Railway** that would have seen the latter share the new terminus, but despite legislation being passed, the concept was dropped, largely because of objections from the **London & Croydon Railway** before that company was absorbed by the LBSCR. A few years later, another scheme surfaced that would have seen the LBSCR use Waterloo, but this was also dropped and eventually **Victoria** became the objective of the Brighton Company's ambitions. The South Eastern Railway also considered an extension to Waterloo from Bricklayers' Arms, but Parliament rejected the proposal. The interest in using Waterloo can be understood, with Robert **Stephenson** telling a Royal Commission in 1846 that there was 'no point on the South side of the Thames so good for a large railway station, as the south end of Waterloo Bridge'.

The first Waterloo Station opened on 11 July 1848, with Nine Elms having closed the previous day, although being available for VIP use and visiting royalty. Initially, Waterloo was designed not as a terminus but as a through station and under a two span 280ft iron and glass roof were six tracks and six 300ft platform faces, although the length of these was soon doubled, while a spur towards the river suggested that the LSWR was attempting to keep every option open. The catchment area for the new terminus was soon growing again, with an extension of the Richmond branch to Windsor on 1 December 1849, by

which time an additional up line had been installed.

The LSWR itself, not withstanding the opinion of Stephenson and the interest displayed by other companies, was not content with Waterloo, and instead wanted to get closer to the City. Even at this early stage, the LSWR claimed that there was no room for goods traffic at Waterloo, especially since access to the river was blocked by the Lion Brewery. Acts of 1846 and 1848 provided for an extension to a site just west of London Bridge and property acquisition started, but a financial crisis in 1848-9 undermined these plans. The plans for an extension and the financial crisis doubtless also delayed the construction of permanent buildings on the site.

By this time, the rapid expansion of London and the tremendous growth in population combined to put extreme pressure on cemetery space. This was solved in 1854 when the London Necropolis & National Mausoleum Company opened a private cemetery at Brookwood, conveniently on the LSWR mainline west of Woking, and a private station was built at Waterloo for the special trains with their hearse carriages.

Expansion continued at Waterloo as the LSWR network grew. Four additional platform faces were built in 1860, in what was to become known as the Windsor Station and separated by the original station, now known as the 'Main Station' by its own cab road. The opening of the **Charing Cross** extension in 1864 was accompanied by a short spur into Waterloo, and this could have enabled passenger trains to work through to London Bridge and, later, to **Cannon Street**, thus providing the long sought after City extension of the LSWR, but instead it was rarely used by passenger trains, although it was the route taken by Queen Victoria when travelling from Windsor to the Channel ports. In 1868, a service from Kensington to Cannon Street was introduced over the connection, but this was cut back to Waterloo in February 1869, no doubt influenced by the opening of an SER station, known as Waterloo Junction for many years, on the Charing Cross extension, although at first passengers interchanging between the two companies were forced to rebook, and only later were through fares offered for those attempting to reach the City. For the most part, the connection was used for the occasional goods working.

Yet another Waterloo station was added in 1878, opening on 16 December, but on this occasion, new offices were opened and a refreshment room, with a cab yard under a new 300ft frontage on Waterloo Road. In 1885, a further final extension was added, with the North station built as an extension of the Windsor Station and opened in November, with six new platform faces, so that by now Waterloo had a total of eighteen, and unusually for the day, all of them suitable for arrivals and departures, but still served by just four approach tracks, which were the cause of much delay as by this time Waterloo was handling 700 trains daily. As was the custom at the time, and as we have seen at **Victoria**, Waterloo was an open station, with tickets being checked at Vauxhall, and this no doubt added to the delays. The station itself was a mess, not least because of an eccentric platform numbering system that meant that many platforms used the same number for two faces, and this, with a paucity of departure information, meant that even if the intending passenger found the right platform, there was a 50 per cent risk of boarding the wrong train. Between 1886 and 1892, a further two approach tracks were added for trains off the South Western main line and a third for trains on the Windsor line, necessitating the rebuilding of Vauxhall station. Once again, there was massive destruction

of housing, so that the LSWR had to provide new property in 1890 for more than a thousand people. In 1900, the number of approach lines was increased to eight for part of the approach, reducing to seven as far as Queen's Road. Progress was uneven, and it was not possible to ease the lot of all passengers at once. Passengers for the City were growing in numbers, and were also people of considerable influence. The need to rebook at the South Eastern station was a nuisance, and although later through season tickets did become available, the service from Charing Cross to Cannon Street was unreliable, especially in thick fog since the railways of the day did depend entirely on enginemen being able to see signals, and Cannon Street was not by any means a convenient terminus for all City workers. An idea of the character of the typical LSWR City-bound passenger can be gained from one event in 1880, when a group of them formed the Metropolitan Express Omnibus Company to operate horse buses between Waterloo and the City, and even though this company was taken over within a year by the Railways & Metropolitan Omnibus Company, within five years it was operating eighteen twenty-six seat buses and carrying 2.5 million passengers annually. The LSWR itself calculated that of the 50,000 daily arrivals at Waterloo, a quarter of them were heading for the City, divided equally between the buses and the SER. As early as 1882, plans were considered for an overhead railway, but rejected as too costly, and no doubt hazardous given the technology of the day, and these were revived in 1891, but still considered too costly. Relief was soon found in plans for a **Waterloo and City** tube line, authorised in 1893. The new company was clearly attractive to the LSWR, which provided much of the capital and five of the eight directors, and agreed to operate the line for 55 per cent of the gross receipts after payment of a 3 per cent dividend. The line opened in 1898, providing a direct non-stop link between a station not strictly deep underground but in Waterloo's basement and a point just across the road from the Bank of England, appropriately enough known as Bank. Open air carriage sidings were constructed at the Waterloo end, and rolling stock could be moved using a hoist. This was also the LSWR's first experience with electric train operation. In 1907, the company took over the line completely.

Even earlier plans had attempted to introduce a tube line between Waterloo and the West End. A pneumatic tube was begun, but this, the Waterloo and Whitehall, was abandoned in 1868. At this stage the LSWR was probably being cautious in the middle of a depression in railway financing, but there seems little explanation for its neglect of the **Bakerloo Line**, originally known as the Baker Street & Waterloo Railway, which opened on 10 March 1906 between Lambeth North and Baker Street, with a station deep below Waterloo which was reached at first by means of lifts.

Waterloo was to experience the demands of wartime traffic before any other London terminus, simply because all of the troops sent to the Boer War between 1899 and 1902 passed through Southampton, and the majority of them also went through Waterloo, while the cavalry boarded with their horses at Nine Elms.

The LSWR was not blind to the shortcomings of its only London terminus, and as the 1890s drew to a close and the railway enjoyed considerable prosperity, powers were sought from Parliament to extend the station by purchasing an additional 6½ acres to the south of the terminus, including six streets and parts of two others, a church and church schools, and in return the LSWR erected six blocks of flats to accommodate 1,750 people, allegedly more than the number displaced by the expansion. From

contemporary accounts, little of worth was lost in the exercise since the area around Waterloo was as much a mess as the stations themselves, with such an unsavoury reputation that it was sometimes known as 'whoreterloo'.

Site clearing had already begun in 1901 when the new chief engineer, J W Jacomb-Hood was sent to the USA to study American termini. He returned to design a magnificent twenty-three platform station with a single roof, a wide passenger concourse running uninterrupted across the platform ends, and opposite them a substantial office block that also accommodated the station facilities. This was thinking on a grand scale that had no precedent in the design of the London termini at the time, and, some might suggest, or since! It required massive strengthening of the foundations, with additional foundations being dug thirty feet deep to get below the marshy ground, while the bridge over Westminster Bridge Road was widened to take eleven approach roads. The Necropolis station was demolished, with a new structure built on the south side of Westminster Bridge Road, and opened on 16 February 1902, and powers obtained to buy more land to the north of the terminus and to abandon the through line to the SER. When Herbert Walker joined the LSWR in 1912, the plans were scaled back, but only slightly, since Walker, who was a man who knew how to get the best value out of any investment, decided that the 1885 north station, still relatively new, should be untouched and retain its own roof, although the concourse would still continue unbroken across the station, and this reduced the number of platforms to twenty-one.

Much of the new roof had already been completed by the end of 1907, followed by a new cab road that ran from Westminster Bridge Road along the side of the new terminus and then turned left to run in front of what were to be the new offices. The first four platform faces were ready in stages during 1909, with another early in 1910, all with conventional numbering of each face. Parts of the new frontage block were also ready in 1909, although the new booking hall was not ready until 11 June 1911, with doors both to the cab road and to the main concourse. The LSWR obviously had other priorities, as a new 'gentlemen's court' was opened under the new building and reached by a stone stair case from the main concourse: described by *Railway Magazine* as 'perhaps the finest in England', it also included a hairdressing salon, shoe cleaning room and bathrooms, while the air could be changed by electric fans.

A far-sighted feature of the first fifteen of the new platforms were steps running down to a subway that ran under them and provided access to the tube stations, both speeding up the progress of those wanting to travel on the underground and also easing pressure on the platform barriers. Less far-sighted were the platform lengths, and given the amount of work undertaken both within the new terminus and on the approach roads, this oversight is all the more difficult to understand. Already, main line trains often consisted of twelve corridor carriages and a locomotive at each end, with that at the buffers having brought the train into the station. Already trains could easily be 750ft in length, but the platforms were as short as 635 ft, with those for the West Country and **Portsmouth** at 728ft and 735ft, with just one, reserved for boat trains to **Southampton**, at 860ft, although later extended to 946ft, with across the central cab road from this, another platform of 843ft. The end of the cab road also had two short loading docks. The legacy of the Southern and its predecessors on nationalisation would have been almost perfect but for this, especially in recent years as pressure on existing train lengths have lead to

calls for longer trains. Additional office accommodation was provided in a two storey office block completed in 1920 between platforms 15 and 16, and marking the boundary between the all-new platforms and the Windsor Station, which also had a further loading dock on its north side, beyond which the carriage and engine sidings, hoist to the Waterloo & City and locomotive turntable were little affected by the changes. Changes to the approaches allowed greater flexibility in operations and allowed parallel working at some of the platforms.

Once completed and opened on 21 March, 1922, by Queen Mary, Waterloo stood comparison with the best anywhere, and there could be no doubt that this was a single large terminus, since the concourse, 120ft wide, ran for 770ft across the platform heads with a single long block of offices and amenities behind it, which included the first London terminus branch of a bank when the National Provincial (now RBS NatWest) opened it in 1923. The economy made by Walker on the Windsor platforms was not apparent to the casual observer, but simple good housekeeping with so much else to spend money on, modernising and standardising the now grouped railway. In addition to access from the cab road, there was the Victory Arch, the war memorial to the LSWR dead in the First World War, and staircases opposite platforms 8 and 12 led down to Waterloo Road. Given the SER's penchant for building riverside termini in prominent positions, it seems a shame that the view of Waterloo, set back somewhat from the banks of the river, was marred by the viaduct carrying the former SER lines from Waterloo to the Hungerford Bridge.

During the First World War, Southampton had handled the embarkation of the British Expeditionary Force in 1914, followed by many of the reserves in 1915, and was the main port for those going to other theatres of war, especially in the Middle East. The presence of the Royal Navy at Portsmouth, as well as the flood of men going for training on Salisbury Plain or into the many garrisons in the south, meant that there was considerable strain on the entire system. As at **Victoria**, there was a free buffet staffed by volunteers for troops and this was opened in 1915 and not closed until 1920, some eight million meals later. The numbers returning from leave was such that on Sunday nights as many as thirty extra trains had to be organised.

Despite its importance, Waterloo suffered bomb damage just once, when on the night of 29/30 September 1917, a number of bombs dropped in the sidings to the north of the station – the damage was repaired within a day.

The LSWR was an energetic proponent of the electric railway, and Walker's eye for value meant that this was done on the 600-volt dc system using a third rail. This was certainly economical and straightforward. Wimbledon via East Putney was electrified on 25 October 1915, and on 30 January of the following year it was joined by the Kingston Roundabout and its Shepperton branch. On 12 March 1916, the Hounslow Loop was electrified, followed by the Hampton Court branch on 18 June. The so-called 'new' Guildford line, running via Cobham, was electrified as far as Claygate on 20 November 1916, and initially there was a steam push-pull service beyond for stations to Guildford, but the line had to return to steam working in July 1919, as demand on the other routes meant that the rolling stock could be used more effectively elsewhere. After **grouping**, the line through to Guildford via Cobham was completed, as was the line from Raynes Park to Dorking North, and electric services inaugurated on these routes on 12 July 1925. After some delay while competing methods of electrifi-cation were evaluated, services to Windsor were electrified on 6 July 1930.

In 1924, improvements were made to the booking hall, with the original wood block floor replaced by coloured glass tiles and plaster columns replaced by marble capped with bronze, while the doors to be cab road were replaced by windows. Of possibly greater importance, on 13 September 1926, the Hampstead Tube, now the **Northern Line**, opened an extension from Charing Cross to Kennington, with a station beneath Waterloo, providing a direct service from Waterloo to **Euston**, but it was not until the following year that the escalators were ready with a new booking hall beneath the Windsor platforms.

Possibly bearing in mind that many longer distance passengers would have a wait for a train, and of course there were those waiting to greet arriving passengers, a newsreel and cartoon cinema had been built at the end of the concourse next to platform 1 and opened on 27 August 1934. Announcements of arriving trains would be flashed up at the side of the screen if requested from the cashier.

In 1935, twelve years after the grouping, the name Waterloo Junction was dropped for the old SER station, which had lost its line into the terminus in 1911, and plat-forms were designated A to D to avoid confusion with those of the terminus. As at Victoria, the process of integration seems to have been piecemeal and patchy.

New signalling and layouts were brought into use on 17 May 1936 as steady growth in traffic, boosted by electrification, needed changes to the approaches to the station. Given the congested nature of the surround-ing area, this required a flyover at Wimbledon, the nearest point at which the work could be carried out, to carry the up main local over the up main line. These were joined at Vauxhall by a relief line between the up main through and the down

Windsor through, while at Waterloo **electrification** was extended to platforms 7, 8 and 9. Colour light signalling was introduced between Hampton Court Junction and Waterloo, although those at the terminus were delayed until 18 October.

Electrification had continued to spread, so that from 3 January 1937, Windsor electrics divided at Staines, with the rear portion serving Chertsey and Weybridge. Next, came Waterloo's first main line electrification, and the longest on the Southern, with introduction of the third rail for the Portsmouth Direct, the line running through Woking and Guildford to Portsmouth Harbour, brought into service on 4 July 1937. This was done in conjunction with electrification to Aldershot and Alton, with the stopping trains dividing at Woking into Portsmouth and Alton portions. Once again there was a massive increase in frequencies, with summer Saturdays seeing four fast trains an hour on the Portsmouth line, which had seen just four fast trains a day in steam days. As war approached, further electrification followed, with services to Reading from 1 January 1939, and these trains also divided, at Ascot with a portion continuing to Guildford by the roundabout route of Camberley and Aldershot. As the suburbs grew, a new line was needed branching off the Dorking North line to Tolworth, reached on 29 May 1938, and Chessington South, reached on 28 May 1939, and, of course, electrified throughout.

Loudspeakers had been introduced and used from 9 March 1932, which was probably an ideal day since the Oxford and Cambridge boat race coincided with a rugby international at Twickenham. Waterloo's business could be sporty as well as commuting, for there were also occasions when trains were needed for races at Ascot and Epsom. In 1937, the Southern experimented with music over the loudspeaker system, often using light opera, but the idea was to have marches to encourage arriving passengers to leave the station briskly in the morning and something soothing to calm them and entertain them as they waited for their evening train home. The announcer was also responsible for the musical programme – although recordings were never announced – and at first was based in a booth over the news stand opposite platforms 8 and 9, but the announcer's box was later moved to a position above the station offices between platforms 15 and 16.

As war approached, the Southern started to take precautions, with air raid shelters for around 6,500 people constructed in the arches underneath the station, doubtless with the idea that there could be trainloads of passengers to protect at busy periods, but in fact many of the users were to be local people, and those bombed out of their homes sometimes took up permanent residence.

The Second World War was one in which few places escaped the bombs, and Waterloo was a primary target. On 7 September 1940, a bomb fell just outside the station and seriously damaged the viaduct over John Street. Railwaymen and the Royal Engineers worked to restore services, but the station was closed until 19 September, and services could not be fully restored until 1 October. The disruption affected more than just passengers, and at one stage there were 5,000 bags of unsorted mail. The overnight newspaper trains switched to Clapham Yard, and after further enemy action moved to Wimbledon, and then to Surbiton after bombing destroyed the roads around Wimbledon station. Waterloo was the worst affected of the Southern termini in London, as it was out of action due to incendiary bombs from the night of 29/30 December 1940 until 5 January 1941, which itself was not a quiet night as the old LSWR offices in

York Road were destroyed that night and the underground lifts and booking hall badly damaged. A further closure came after the raid on the night of 10/11 May 1941, when around 50 high explosive and incendiary bombs and parachute mines set fires blazing and destroyed the Necropolis Station, and penetrated to the basement arches setting alight large quantities of spirits stored there: the station could not function until a partial re-opening on 15 May. The disruption to services was severe, with many passengers delayed by several hours as the crowds overwhelmed the replacement bus service from Clapham Junction, with a queue of more than a mile in length at one point and the road towards Waterloo difficult to drive over as it was cluttered with many fire hoses. One unexploded bomb was to remain undetected until work started on an office building in York Road in 1959: at 2,000-lbs, had it exploded during the intervening years, the destruction and loss of life at the height of the rush hour would have been terrible. The original LSWR terminus at Nine Elms also lost its roof on 10/11 May.

There were few changes at Waterloo after the war, and only the most essential tidying up between the end of the war and nationalisation. For many years, Waterloo was largely neglected by the new **British Railways,** and it took almost twenty years before any further electrification, with the line through to **Bournemouth** finally being electrified in 1967, and later the third rail was extended to Weymouth. The most significant change came with the completion of the **Channel Tunnel,** which until late 2007 saw the Eurostar services from Paris and Brussels using a new Waterloo International station built over the old Windsor station and the sidings on the other side of the wall. Since Channel Tunnel services have been diverted to **St Pancras,** this station with its very long platforms remains unused, as indeed do many of the junctions created to allow trains to travel from near Folkestone to Waterloo.

Waterloo & City Railway

The only tube railway not to pass into the control of the **London Passenger Transport Board** in 1933, the line opened in 1898 to give direct access to the City of London from **Waterloo** Station, isolated south of the Thames. The line was independent but worked by the **London & South Western Railway** which took it over in 1907. Initially, specially-built four car trains were used. The line ran for 1½ miles under the Thames without intermediate stations from Waterloo to the Bank, which passengers could interchange with the **Central Line.** An electric hoist at Waterloo enabled vehicles to be removed for overhaul. The line passed into the control of the **Southern Railway** in 1923. Increasingly, as traffic grew and its equipment aged, its reputation with City commuters fell, but new American-built rolling stock was introduced in 1940, and this remained until the line was transferred to **London Transport** in 1994, before railway privatisation, and four car electric trains based on standard LT tube rolling stock were introduced and the line converted from third rail to third and fourth rail.

At least twice in its history, once during the Second World War, the line has had to be closed due to flooding from burst or damaged water mains.

Watkin, Sir Edward, 1819-1901

After working in the family cotton merchants, he became involved in campaigns including one against the Corn Laws. At the age of twenty-six, he became secretary of the Trent Valley railway, before becoming assistant to Mark **Huish** general manager of the **London & North Western Railway.** In 1854, he became general manager of the Manchester, Sheffield &

Lincolnshire Railway, predecessor of the **Great Central**. He spent some time away from the GCR working in Canada, where he attempted to rescue the Grand Trunk Railway, and on his return in 1862, disagreed with the decisions taken during his absence and resigned. He returned to the GCR in 1864 as chairman. This was the first of a string of chairmanships, followed by that of the South Eastern Railway (see **South Eastern & Chatham Railway**) in 1866, and the **Metropolitan Railway** in 1872. He saw these railways as forming a continuous link leading to a **Channel Tunnel**, with through trains between **Manchester** and Paris via **London**, and this drove his ambitions to extend the MSLR to London, which was finally achieved in 1899, by which time the company had been renamed the Great Central. His approach to railway management was grandiose and expansionist, which led to much ruinous competition.

He was knighted for his services in Canada in 1868. Involved in politics, he was at different times MP for Yarmouth in 1857, Stockport from 1864 to 1868, and finally, Hythe from 1874 until 1895.

Although he lived to see the GCR reach London and was present at the celebrations for the opening of its terminus at **Marylebone**, ill health forced his retirement from all of his chairmanships in 1894.

Wedgwood, Sir Ralph Lewis, 1875-1956

After graduating from Cambridge, he became a traffic apprentice at the **North Eastern Railway**, after which he made rapid progress, becoming company secretary in 1905 and chief goods manager in 1911. He worked for the government during the First World War as director of ports, and on his return to the NER he became deputy general manager, and general manager in 1922, before becoming the first general manager of the new **London & North**

Eastern Railway in 1923, the same year that he was knighted.

Under Wedgwood, the LNER operated a policy of decentralised management, leaving a small team to look after finance and policy matters. He also found time to be a member of the Weir Committee on main line electrification in 1931, and in 1936 visited India with a team investigating the state of the country's railways. On his return, he was one of the figures behind the 'Square Deal' campaign in which the railways pleaded unsuccessfully for the freedom to set their own freight rates. When he retired in 1939, he was appointed chairman of the Railway Executive Committee, which oversaw the running of the railways in wartime, before finally retiring in 1941.

Welshpool & Llanfair Light Railway

The 2ft 6in gauge Welshpool & Llanfair Light Railway was completed in 1903. Unlike most of the Welsh narrow gauge lines, it was not built primarily for mineral or slate traffic, although it did have traffic from the Standart Quarry, but operated through an agricultural area. The line was built to link the small town of Llanfair Caereinion to the nearest large (the terms are relative) town of Welshpool, and using the Light Railways Act, 1896, a Light Railway Order was obtained in 1899. One term of the order was that the railway would have to be worked by an existing company, and so the following year it was leased to the **Cambrian Railway** for ninety-nine years in return for 40 per cent of the receipts. Only three passenger carriages and two locomotives were built.

West Clare Railway

Opened in 1887, the West Clare was a light railway using a 3ft gauge running from Ennis on the Limerick to Sligo branch of the **Great Southern & Western Railway**, initially to Miltown but later an extension was opened in 1892 to Kilrush, on the Shannon estuary, and to Kilkee, with the line dividing at Moyasta Junction. A levy on the population of Co. Clare, half of which was refunded by the British government, enabled a guaranteed 4 per cent dividend to be paid on this otherwise unprofitable line. Just eleven locomotives were operated. Subject of a song by Percy French, *Are Ye Right There, Michael, Are Ye Right?* It passed to the **Great Southern Railways** in 1925, and was nationalised in 1945. It closed in 1961.

West Coast Main Line

Often known in railway circles as the WCML, the term is of comparatively recent origin and refers to the main line from **Euston** to **Glasgow**, or what would at one time have been known as the West Coast Group of Companies. The companies involved originally were the **London & North Western** and **Caledonian Railways**.

The line was amongst the early railways and a number of companies built stretches of it between 1837 and 1850, initially running through **Birmingham**, but in 1847 the LNWR provided a cut-off route between Rugby and Stafford through the Trent Valley. Another cut-off followed north of Warrington. At Carstairs, the line divided, with a line to **Edinburgh** in competition with the **East Coast** route, while the line to Glasgow continued to **Aberdeen**, and until the opening of the **Forth** and **Tay** bridges, was the quickest route to that city. The terminus in Glasgow was the Central Station.

The line was opened throughout in 1858, and between 1860 and 1870 what was known as the Scotch Railways Agreement confined Glasgow and Aberdeen traffic to Euston and that to Edinburgh to **King's Cross**. Nevertheless, old habits died hard and afterwards there were occasions when the competing main lines tried to provide the fastest expresses (see **Races to Scotland**). This was despite the problems of the steep gradients at Shap and Beattock.

Not all of the traffic was between London and Scotland, as the line carried heavy traffic between London and the Midlands and to the North West, and the traffic to Ireland via Holyhead. Post-**nationalisation**, Aberdeen services were concentrated on the East Coast route. Between 1959 and 1974, the line was electrified, starting with services to the Midlands and ending with those to Glasgow, while that between Carstairs and Edinburgh was electrified in 1991, but another route from Carlisle closed earlier as part of the post-**Beeching** cuts.

In more recent years, the entire route has been through the most extensive rebuilding and modernisation of any route in British railway history, to the extent that many believe that a completely new line would have been less expensive. The current operator post-privatisation is Virgin Trains, which operates 'Pendalino' tilting trains between London and the main cities along the route.

West Cornwall Railway

Authorised in 1834 as the Hayle railway, the 17-mile standard gauge West Cornwall opened for goods traffic during 1837-38 to take tin and copper mined around Redruth to the port at Hayle. Two miles of gradient were worked by stationary steam locomotives, but standard locomotives were used on the remainder. Passenger services did not begin until 1843.

The West Cornwall itself was authorised in 1846 to purchase the Hayle Railway, eliminate the gradients and extend the line westwards to Truro and **Penzance**. Although W S Moorsom was appointed engineer, he was replaced by **Brunel**. The line as completed was entirely single track, and for economy, its nine viaducts were built of wood. Operations were complicated by the opening of the broad gauge **Cornwall**

Railway between **Plymouth** and Truro in 1859, and to avoid a break of gauge, the CR had been empowered to require the WCR to lay a third rail to allow mixed gauge operations, but the company could not afford to do this and so its property was transferred to the supporters of the Cornwall Railway, known as the Associated Companies. Nevertheless, the WCR existed on paper until nationalisation, not being formally grouped in 1923.

West Highland Railway – see **North British Railway**

West London and West London Extension Railways

An important strategic link in the railway network, these two lines of just seven route miles linked the trunk routes approaching London from the north and west with those from the south and south-east. Originally authorised in 1836 as the Birmingham Bristol & Thames Junction Railway to link the **London & Birmingham** with the Kensington Canal. The canal was bought in 1839 and the railway became the West London Railway. When it opened in 1844, it crossed the **Great Western** main line on the level. At first, only freight was carried, and after six months the line closed until reopened in 1862 as part of a West London Extension Railway that reached Clapham Junction where it connected with the **London & South Western, London, Brighton & South Coast** and **London, Chatham & Dover railways.**

Passenger traffic became important after this, with a station built at Kensington which served the site of the second Great Exhibition and later the Olympia exhibition centre. Long distance expresses from the Midlands and the North West to the South Coast used the line as well as suburban services. Nevertheless, the passenger services dwindled away for many years and only since privatisation has the line been electrified on the third rail system and used by passenger trains once again.

West Midland Railway

The result of an amalgamation of the Oxford, Worcester and Wolverhampton, authorised in 1845, Newport, Abergavenny & Hereford, authorised in 1846 but not completed until 1852, and Worcester & Hereford Railways, dating from 1858, in 1860.

The OWWR was originally intended to be part of the **Great Western** broad gauge network, running from Oxford into the Black Country and with **Brunel** as its engineer. There was a considerable cost overrun with both the GWR and the contractors, Peto & Betts and Treadwell, providing considerable additional capital. The 92 route miles were completed in 1854 using mixed gauge, although no broad gauge trains ever used it, and by this time supported by the **London & North Western Railway.** The OWWR did not prosper and there were changes to the board, while in 1859, the GWR agreed that all but two miles of the line could be converted to standard gauge, while the line from Oxford to **Paddington** would become mixed, allowing through trains from the OWWR to run to **London.**

By contrast, the Newport, Abergavenny & Hereford Railway and Worcester & Hereford Railway were both standard gauge. The former was built with the support of the LNWR which needed access to South Wales, and opened in 1854, while a branch was built to serve Quaker's Yard, completed in 1857, which included a grand viaduct at Crumlin. The Worcester & Hereford Railway had a difficult passage through Parliament, but the OWWR and NAHR undertook to work the line jointly with the **Midland Railway.** Although the first seven miles were completed by 1860, the tunnels at Ledbury and Malvern proved difficult and the line was not completed until 1861 after the creation of the WMR. While the LNWR had designs on the WMR, proposing a connecting line from **London** to Oxford, the WMR was acquired by the GWR in 1863.

West Somerset Railway
Built to broad gauge, the West Somerset Railway was authorised in 1857, although work did not start until 1859, and then suffered difficulty in raising the £160,000 needed, so it was not opened from Norton Fitzwarren to the small port of Watchet until 1862. A further extension, the Minehead Railway, had an even longer gestation period, authorised in 1865, dissolved in 1870, revived in 1871 and finally opened in 1874. From the start, both lines were worked by the **Great Western Railway**, and the two railways were converted to standard gauge in 1882. The GWR took over the Minehead Railway in 1897, but the West Somerset remained independent until 1922.

Traffic on the line was always light, partly as there was no connection with the West Somerset Mineral Railway at Watchet, and little onward railway movement of cargo arriving at the docks. It was not until the early years of the twentieth century that passenger traffic began to grow as Minehead developed as a resort, and in 1933 the number of passing loops was increased from four to six, and in 1934 and 1936 stretches of the line were doubled.

Weston, Clevedon & Portishead Light Railway
Not one of the grouped companies, as most light railways slipped through the net and retained their independence, doubtless to the relief of everyone, and especially the '**Big Four**'. Nevertheless, under the control of the Railway Executive Committee, the compa-

nies were not quite their own masters. The **Great Western Railway** took over the Weston, Clevedon & Portishead Light Railway in 1940 and traffic was discontinued on 18 May. The line had been built using powers obtained in 1885 as a tramway to replace a horse bus service, but the 8½ mile stretch between Weston-super-Mare and Clevedon did not open until December 1897, and the rest followed later giving a 14½ mile route with no less than seventeen stopping places. In 1899, its own Act of Parliament authorised the conversion to a light railway, and at the time of the GWR acquisition, there were five steam locomotives, of which three were immediately condemned, and a Fordson rail tractor, as well as an ex-**Southern Railway** Drewry petrol railcar. Passenger carriages included three with bogies, while the rest were four and six wheelers.

Wharncliffe, Lord/James Archibald Stuart-Wortley-Mackenzie, 1776-1845
A career politician, Wharncliffe had already been elevated to the Lords when the **Great Western Railway's** second bill was proceeding through Parliament in 1835. He chaired the committee that examined the proposals and discovered falsehoods amongst the objections to the bill, and as a result, the bill was enacted. As a mark of gratitude, the viaduct at Hanwell, completed in 1837, was named after him. His name entered railway terminology as he was instrumental in getting the Lords in ensuring that railway companies needing to extend their powers should first obtain the agreement of a minimum of 60 per cent of the shareholders in a special meeting before starting the Parliamentary processes – these meetings became known as 'Wharncliffe meetings'.

Wheel and Axle Notation
1) Diesel and Electric
The notation of wheels for electric and

diesel locomotives is different from that used for steam locomotives. This is because it is important to distinguish between motored and unmotored axles. A single motored axle is denoted as 'A', two coupled motored axles by 'B' and three by 'C'. If the axles are individually driven rather than coupled, which is the more usual form except for shunting locomotives, the same form is used for the number of powered axles but they are followed by 'o'; so a locomotive with two powered axles on each bogie and no other axles would be Bo-Bo, and with three powered axles, Co-Co, for example. The other wheels on the bogie that simply bear weight are denoted by the number, so that two unpowered axles followed by three coupled powered axles, with the same layout at the other end of the locomotive, would be 2C-C2. A train with three axles on each of two bogies, but with just the outer axles on each bogie powered, would be A1A-A1A.

2) Steam

The wheel notation for steam locomotives is also known as Whyte's Notation after the inventor, F M Whyte (1865-1941), who was general mechanical engineer of the New York Central Railroad. It was introduced in the United States around 1900, and adopted in the UK around 1903. The notation works from left to right, with the left being the front of the locomotive and right being the back, usually the driving cab. The total number of wheels, if any, at the front is given, then those which are coupled driving wheels, and then the trailing wheels. This means that a Pacific locomotive would be described as 4-6-2, that is a four-wheeled leading bogie, followed by six driving wheels (three on each side), and then a small bogie or pony truck with a wheel on each side. Large articulated locomotives such as those produced by Beyer-Garratt, would be 4-8-8-4, for example, denoting a bogie first

and last and in between two sets of four coupled driving wheels on each side.

A commonly used refinement applied to tank engines, with the suffix 'T' for a standard tank engine; 'ST' for saddle tanks; 'PT' for pannier tanks; and 'WT' for a well tank. This means that an 0-4-4T tank locomotive would be one with a standard tank, no leading bogies, four driving wheels and a trailing bogie.

It has become the custom to assign names to the main notations, so that a 4-6-2 locomotive is generally known as a 'Pacific', while other significant notations mentioned in the British Isles include 'Atlantic' for 4-4-2; 'Baltic' for 4-6-4; 'Mogul' for 2-6-0.

In mainland Europe, a different notation is used based on axles, so that a Pacific would be 2-3-1.

Whitby & Pickering Railway

Authorised in 1833 to carry passengers, lime and stone, from the Vale of Pickering to the port of Whitby, 24 miles away. The line was engineered by George **Stephenson**, but was initially worked by horses except for the Goathland incline, which was worked by cable haulage. Completed during 1835-36, the line was acquired by the **York & North Midland Railway** in 1845, and by 1847 had been strengthened for steam locomotives. In 1854, it became part of the **North Eastern Railway**, and subsequently became part of the **London & North Eastern Railway**. Closed in 1965, the 18-miles from Pickering to Grosmont became the preserved North Yorkshire Moors railway which reopened in 1973.

Whitechapel & Bow Joint Railway

An important strategic link in the capital's railway network, the line was supported by the **Metropolitan District** and **London, Tilbury & Southend Railways**. When the two-mile long railway opened in 1902, it relieved the pressure on **Fenchurch Street** and gave commuters from southern Essex easier access to the City of **London**. It is now part of the London **Underground** system.

Whitelaw, William, 1868-1948

A landowner and bank director, Whitelaw became a director of the **Highland Railway** in 1899, becoming chairman in 1902 until he became a director of the **North British Railway** in 1912. He next became chairman of the **London & North Eastern Railway** in 1923, staying until 1938, where he was a popular and successful figure. The LNER was over-capitalised and he insisted on dividend restraint, as well as restricting investment, although he took great pride in the high speed trains.

Wirral Railway

Formed in 1891 from a number of short lines, one of which was the Hoylake Railway which had opened in 1866 to link Hoylake with the docks at Birkenhead. Eventually the WR had 13½ route miles with connections to the **Great Western** and **London & North Western** joint line at West Kirby and extensions to Birkenhead Park, New Brighton and Seacombe, where passengers could transfer to a ferry service to **Liverpool**. The line was mainly used by passenger trains.

Although powers to electrify the line were obtained in 1900, **electrification** on the third rail system did not come until 1938, by which time it was part of the **London, Midland & Scottish Railway.**

Wrexham, Mold & Connah's Quay Railway

Opened in 1866, the Wrexham, Mold & Connah's Quay Railway linked the tidal port at Connah's Quay with the coal mines and iron and steel works. It was under financed and provided an indifferent service as a result until it was taken over by the **Great Central Railway** in 1905.

Y

Yerkes, Charles Tyson (1837-1905)

Although born in Philadelphia, the financier Yerkes was initially involved in tramcar operation in Chicago before becoming involved in the development of the London underground system. He sought authorization for the **Charing Cross & Hampstead** tube line in 1900, and the following year he established the **Metropolitan District Electric Traction Company**, putting these ventures into a new company, the **Underground Electric Railways Company** of **London** in 1902. He moved quickly to electrify the District and build and equip three tube lines, the Hampstead, **Bakerloo** and **Piccadilly**. His methods of financing his enterprises were new to British financiers and treated with suspicion, with most of his funds being raised in the United States. Nevertheless, he succeeded in raising £16 million (about £1,100 million by today's prices). Possibly his somewhat racy personal life and lavish personal expenditure was not to the taste of Edwardian London, and certainly his private art collection had to be auctioned after his death to pay his debts, but there seems to be no record of any fraudulent dealings.

Yerkes transformed transport in London, providing relief from the congested streets and connecting the main railway termini while standardising operating systems on the lines under his control, aided by a strong team of American railwaymen brought to London to ensure operating efficiency and overcome resistance to new ideas. His lines continued to develop after his death and his company expanded into trams, buses, known as the 'Overground', and trolleybuses, attracting much jealousy and becoming known as the 'Combine' to his competitors. Nevertheless, any monopoly positions were strictly local. The entire transport empire passed into the control of the **London Passenger Transport Board** in 1933.

York
Before the railway, York was already an important religious centre, market town and commercial centre with good water transport links via the River Ouse which connected it to the Humber and **Hull**. During the 1830s, York had first the **York & North Midland Railway** and then the **Great North of England Railway**, so that the city had lines radiating from it to **London**, **Leeds** and Hull, while local lines followed linking the city to Scarborough, Harrogate, Market Weighton and Beverley, and by 1850 there was a line northwards to **Edinburgh**. These lines were promoted by a single man, George **Hudson**, whose activities benefited York most of all, and made the city the most important railway junction between **Newcastle** and **London**. His influence was such that the railway was able to site its station actually inside the ancient and confined city, even to the extent of breaching the city walls. By 1854, the **North Eastern Railway** had a monopoly, but another seven railway companies had running powers into York. New lines to the south were built twice to reduce mileage, while the station eventually had to be rebuilt outside the city walls to ensure that enough space was available for the growing demand and to avoid the need for trains to reverse. It eventually reached 16 platforms, but was built on a sharp curve.

More than a major junction, York also had railway workshops built from 1842 onwards, but in 1905, lack of space meant that locomotive building had to be moved to Darlington, but York continued to produce carriages and wagons. **Grouping** meant that York ceased to be the NER's headquarters, but after **nationalisation**, York became a regional headquarters for the North Eastern Region of **British Railways**, and when the Eastern and North Eastern Regions were merged, they

remained at York. Nevertheless, overall, railway employment in the city was falling.

In addition to the mainline railways which placed York firmly on the **East Coast Main Line**, in 1913 a light railway, the Derwent Valley, was opened, mainly an agricultural line. This evaded grouping and **nationalisation**, but lost its passenger services in 1926 and closed in stages between 1965 and 1981.

The **London & North Eastern Railway** opened a museum in York in 1928, and this has developed over the years to become today's National Railway Museum, opened in 1975 on a much larger site.

York & North Midland Railway
Authorised in 1836 to run from the **North Midland Railway** at Castleford over the 32 miles to **Leeds**, with both companies promoted by George **Hudson** and with George **Stephenson** as engineer. Construction of the line was easy, and it opened in 1839, a year before the longer NMR, and when both were opened a new trunk route linked **York** and **London** via **Derby** and Rugby. The line was linked to the **Leeds & Selby** and the **Hull & Selby** at Milford. When the NMR opened, the Hull & Selby was leased to it and the YNMR jointly. Hudson remained as chairman from 1836 to 1849, and during that time the YNMR was extended to Pickering and Scarborough in 1845, an additional 49 miles, with Robert Stephenson as engineer. That same year, the Leeds & Selby and **Whitby & Pickering Railways** were purchased.

When Hudson was removed from office by suspicious shareholders in 1849, the YNMR had concluded an agreement with its old rival, the **Great Northern Railway**. The **East & West Yorkshire Junction Railway**, which ran from Knaresborough to York, was acquired in 1851, giving a total route mileage of 113 miles. In 1854, the YNMR amalgamated with the **York, Newcastle & Berwick** and the **Leeds Northern** to form the **North Eastern Railway**.

York, Newcastle & Berwick Railway
The outcome of the merger of the York & Newcastle and Newcastle & Berwick Railways in 1847, engineered by George **Hudson**. This gave Hudson a line from **London** to Berwick on Tweed, but his ambition to reach **Edinburgh** and beyond was foiled when the **North British Railway** rejected his offer. At the same time, he gained the support of **Newcastle** Corporation with his promise of a high level bridge that would not interfere with shipping on the Tyne and would also carry a road as well as a railway. The new railway had 149 route miles, and leased the **Newcastle & Carlisle** and **Maryport & Carlisle Railways**, as well as acquiring a number of smaller railways within its area.

After Hudson fell from grace, the NCR and MCR regained their independence.

The YNBR was amongst the first railways to use three cylinder locomotives, and also a leader in attempting to buy out as many private owner goods wagons as possible.

Between 1852 and 1854, protracted negotiations with the **Leeds Northern Railway** resulted in a merger to form the **North Eastern Railway**, approved by Parliament in 1854.

Yorkshire Dales Railway
Opened in 1902, the original Yorkshire Dales Railway connected Skipton with Grassington and was worked by the **Midland Railway** until it was absorbed into the **London, Midland & Scottish Railway** in 1923. Subsequently, the title was adopted by the Embsay Steam Railway, a preserved line opened in 1979 and which became the ESR in 1988, using the former Embsay Junction to Ilkley line.

CHRONOLOGY

1814 – Killingworth Colliery wagonway: George Stephenson's first locomotive *Blucher*, introduced.

1820 – Patent for rolled rails awarded to John Birkinshaw, Bedlington Iron Works.

1825 – Stockton & Darlington Railway opened: George Stephenson's *Rocket* used at the opening, pulling passengers and freight.

1829 – Rainhill: Liverpool & Manchester Railway, locomotive trials.

1830 – Liverpool & Manchester Railway opened. First casualty on a steam railway was the President of the Board of Trade, William Huskisson, knocked down and killed by a steam locomotive.

– Dublin & Kingstown Railway opens, Ireland's first railway.

1836 – Festiniog Railway opened: first narrow gauge public railway in the world. Steam introduced 1863.

1837 – Grand Junction Railway opened throughout.

– First section of Great Western Railway opened.

1841 – Semaphore system first used on railways.

– Clay Cross Tunnel: on North Midland Railway, block system first used with electric telegraph.

1842 – Railway Clearing House starts business.

– HM Queen Victoria makes her first railway journey, travelling between Slough and Paddington.

1843 – Crewe works opened by Grand Junction Railway.

1844 – Dublin & Kingstown Railway opens Dalkey extension using atmospheric traction, which only lasts for ten years before being abandoned.

– Midland Railway formed on amalgamation of Birmingham & Derby Junction, Midland Counties and North Midland Railways.

1845 – London: Gauge Commission starts work, and in twelve months supports 4ft 8¹⁄₂in as standard gauge, but makes exception for Great Western and its associated lines, while the Irish standard gauge is set at 5ft 3 ins.

1846 – London: London & North Western Railway formed on amalgamation of Grand Junction (which included the Liverpool & Manchester), London & Birmingham and Manchester & Birmingham Railways.

1850 – Opening of Britannia Bridge across Menai Strait completed route for the Irish mails.

– First trials of locomotives with compounded cylinders on the Eastern Counties Railway.

1853 – Trains controlled by line staff working on single lines introduced by the London & North Western Railway.

1855 – World's first special postal train introduced by the Great Western Railway between London and Bristol: no passengers carried until 1869, when first-class accommodation added.

1856 – John Saxby patents interlocking of signals and points.

1857 – Derby: First steel rail laid experimentally on a busy stretch of line by Midland Railway.

1859 – Saltash: Royal Albert Bridge completed.

1860 – London & North Western Railway installs first water troughs.

1862 – Chalk Farm: London & North Western Railway lays first standard production steel rails.

1869 – Birdswood Junction: London & North Western Railway builds first fly-over.

1872 – Third-class passengers conveyed by all trains on the Midland and Great Eastern Railways.

1873 – First-class sleeping cars introduced on services to Scotland from King's Cross. Two months later, Euston follows.

1874 – Midland Railway introduces Britain's first Pullman cars.

1875 – Bogie coaches appear.

– Midland Railway abolishes second-class fares and scraps or upholsters third-class carriages.

– First electrical passenger emergency communication introduced on London, Brighton & South Coast Railway.

1878 – First Tay Bridge opened, designed by Thomas Bouch.

1879 – Dining cars introduced by Great Northern Railway between King's Cross and Leeds.

– Tay Bridge collapses in storm while train is crossing.

1881 – London, Brighton & South Coast Railway experiments with electric lighting in Pullman car.

1884 – London: Metropolitan and Metropolitan District Railways complete Inner Circle and connection with East London Railway.

1885 – First mail train between King's Cross and Aberdeen, but no passenger accommodation.

1886 – Severn Tunnel opens, construction having taken fourteen years. At the time, the longest underwater tunnel in the world.

1887 – Present Tay Bridge opened, designed by William Barlow.

1888 – 'Race to the North' between Euston and King's Cross Anglo-Scottish expresses.

1889 – Regulation of Railways Act enforces the use of block system, interlocking of signals and points, and continuous fail-safe brakes on passenger trains.

1890 – Forth Bridge opened, designed by William Barlow.

– London: City & South London Railway opened, the first underground electric railway.

1892 – Great Western Railway introduced corridor carriages, although initially only guards can use corridor connections.

– Great Western Railway completes conversion to standard gauge.

1893 – Liverpool: first section of overhead railway completed, the first elevated electric railway.

1895 – Race to Aberdeen with West Coast train covering 541 miles in 8 hrs 32 mins against East Coast train covering 523½ miles in 8 hrs 38 mins.

– Fastest Great Western trains cut out refreshment stop at Swindon.

1897 – Manchester, Sheffield & Lincolnshire Railway renamed Great Central Railway.

1903 – Mersey Railway electrified.

1904 – Great Western *City of Truro* sets unofficial speed record of more than 100 mph.

– Great Western Railway inaugurates non-stop running between Paddington and Plymouth.

1905 – London: Inner Circle electrified.

1906 – Henley; Fairford: Great Western Railway introduces first audible cab signalling.

– Lancashire & Yorkshire Railway first in Britain to use Schmidt superheater on locomotives.

1908 – Britain's first all-Pullman train, the *Southern Belle*, introduced between Victoria and Brighton by London, Brighton & South Coast Railway.

1914 – First World War begins; Britain's railways pass into government control.

1917 – Irish railways also taken into government control.

1919 – Ministry of Transport formed.

1921 – Government control of railways in Great Britain and Ireland ends.

– Railways Act requires formation of Southern; Western; North Western, Midland and West Scottish; and North

Eastern, Eastern and East Scottish 'groups' in Great Britain.

1922 – Irish Free State formed, with Great Northern Railway of Ireland, Londonderry & Lough Swilly and County Donegal Railways running across border between Northern Ireland and the South.

1923 – Grouping sees 123 railways companies combined into four, although many joint railways continue.

1928 – London & North Eastern Railway introduces world's longest non-stop service between King's Cross and Edinburgh.

– London & North Eastern Railway introduces first all-steel carriages on the Pullman *Queen of Scots* between King's Cross, Edinburgh and Glasgow.

– Third-class sleeping cars introduced by Great Western, London & North Eastern and London Midland & Scottish Railways.

1933 – London Passenger Transport Board is formed.

– Southern Railway completes Britain's first mainline electrification between London (Victoria and London Bridge) and Brighton.

– Great Western Railway inaugurates Cardiff-Torquay-Plymouth air service, the first by a British railway.

1935 – London & North Eastern Railway introduces Britain's first streamlined train, the *Silver Jubilee*, and on trials runs at average of 100 mph for 43 miles and reaches 112^1/2 mph twice.

1937 – London Midland & Scottish Railway introduced *Coronation Scot* streamlined express between Euston and Glasgow, and on trials reaches 114 mph near Crewe.

1939 – Second World War breaks out and railways taken into government control, although serious delays in fixing compensation.

– Restricted timetables introduced.

– Catering services cut back.

1941 – Ministry of War Transport, includes Ministry of Transport and takes shipping from the Board of Trade.

– First-class abolished on London suburban services.

1945 – Second World War ends.

– Labour government vows to nationalise transport.

– Travelling post offices reinstated.

– Railways nationalised in the Irish Republic with the exception of cross-border lines, and *Coras Iompair Eireann, CIE,* Transport Company of Ireland, formed.

1946 – Ministry of War Transport abolished and Ministry of Transport reformed.

1947 – Transport Bill enacted setting up British Transport Commission and preparing for nationalisation of railways, canals, railway-owned assets such as ports and bus companies, and for later nationalisation of road haulage.

1948 – The 'Big Four' railway companies nationalised, including joint lines, and some other smaller railways. The new British Railways divides itself into six regions.

– In addition to British Railways, the British Transport Commission finds itself with the Northern Counties Committee and the Belfast & County Down Railway; as well as the Dundalk, Newry & Greenore Railway, which it has managed by the Great Northern Railway of Ireland.

– Ulster Transport Authority formed to take over Northern Ireland Road Transport Board.

– Non-stop services between King's Cross and Edinburgh reinstated.

1949 – Ulster Transport Authority acquires the Northern Counties Committee and the Belfast & County Down Railway from the British Transport Commission, as well as the Dundalk, Newry & Greenore Railway, which remains managed by the Great Northern Railway of Ireland.

1953 – Bankruptcy of Great Northern Railway of Ireland prompts final nationalisation of Irish standard gauge railways on both sides of the border.

1954 – Electric passenger services introduced between Sheffield and Manchester.

1956 – British Transport Commission plans most future electrification to be 25kv ac overhead.

1958 – *Coras Iompair Eireann, CIE,* Transport Company of Ireland, takes control of former GNR(I) services in the Republic, while the Ulster Transport Authority has all railways in the North transferred to it.

1960 – Last steam locomotive completed, Class 9 2-10-0 goods *Evening Star.*

– Inauguration of electric services between Euston and Manchester via Crewe on the London Midland Region, British Railways.

1963 - *Reshaping of British Railways,* the 'Beeching Report' published.

– London: District Line train conducts trials with automatic driving equipment.

1964 – London: Central Line conducts trials with automatic train operation using Woodford-Hainault shuttle.

1966 – Freightliner service introduced between London and Manchester.

– Electric service introduced from Euston to Manchester and Liverpool.

– Ulster Transport Railways formed to take over Ulster Transport Authority Railways.

1967 – Northern Ireland Railways, NIR, formed.

1974 – Electric services inaugurated between Euston and Glasgow.

1986 – Railways in Irish Republic pass to *Iarnrod Eireann, IE,* Republic of Ireland Railways.

1991 – Electric services inaugurated between King's Cross and Edinburgh

1994 – British Rail restructured ready for privatisation.

– First services through Channel Tunnel, running to Waterloo International.

1996 – First privatised railway begins operations.

2007 – Channel Tunnel trains transferred from Waterloo to St Pancras International.

BIBLIOGRAPHY

Given the wide scope of Britain's railway history, it is not possible to provide a complete list of books on the subject. Old copies of *Bradshaw's Railway Guide*, originally published monthly, when they can be found, are illuminating, and the reprints by David & Charles are better value than the originals, now collectors' items. A good sample of books would include some at least of the following:

Allen, Cecil J, *Salute to the Southern*, Ian Allan, Shepperton, 1974.

– *Titled Trains of Great Britain*, Ian Allan, London, 1946-67.

– with Townroe, S C, *The Bulleid Pacifics of the Southern Railway*, Ian Allan, Shepperton, 1951 & 1974.

Allen, P C and Macleod, A B, *Rails in the Isle of Wight*, Allen & Unwin, London, 1967.

Barman, Christian, *The Great Western Railway's Last Look Forward*, David & Charles, Newton Abbot, 1972.

Beaumont, Robert, *The Railway King: A biography of George Hudson railway pioneer and fraudster*, Review, London, 2002.

Bishop, D and Davies, W J K, *Railways and War since 1917*, Blandford, London, 1974.

Bonavia, M R, *A History of the LNER*, 3 vols, George Allen & Unwin, London, 1983.

Bradley, D L, *Locomotives of the Southern Railway*, 2 vols, The Railway Correspondence & Travel Society, 1977.

Christiansen, Rex, *A Regional History of the Railways of Great Britain: Volume 7 – The West Midlands*, David & Charles, Newton Abbot.

Course, Edwin, *The Railways of Southern England: The Main Lines*, Batsford, London, 1973

– *The Railways of Southern England: Secondary and Branch Lines*, Batsford, London, 1974.

– Crump, N, *By Rail to Victory: The story of the LNER in Wartime*, London & North Eastern Railway, London, 1947.

Darwin, Bernard, *War on the Line, The Story of the Southern Railway in War-Time, including D-Day on the Southern*, Southern Railway, London, 1946.

Dendy Marshall, C F, *A History of the Southern Railway*, Southern Railway Company, London, 1936.

Elliot, Sir John, *On and Off the Rails*, George Allen & Unwin, London, 1982.

Glover, J, *London's Underground*, Ian Allan, London, 1999.

Gordon, D I, *A Regional History of the Railways of Great Britain: Volume 5 – The Eastern Counties*, David & Charles, Newton Abbot.

Gould, D, *Bulleid's Steam Passenger Stock*, The Oakwood Press, Salisbury, 1980.

– *Maunsell's Steam Passenger Stock, 1923-1939*, The Oakwood Press, Salisbury, 1978.

Gourvish, Terry, *British Railways 1948-73*, Cambridge University Press, 1987.

– *British Rail 1974-1997*, Oxford University Press, Oxford, 2002.

Hamilton Ellis, C, *The Trains We Loved*, Allen & Unwin, London, 1947.

Haresnape, Brian, *Maunsell Locomotives*, Ian Allan, Shepperton, 1977.

– *Bulleid Locomotives*, Ian Allan, Shepperton, 1977.

Haswell, E G F, *Great Western Shed Designs*, Ian Allan, London, 1969.

Hoole, K, *A Regional History of the Railways of Great Britain: Volume 4 – The North East*, David & Charles, Newton Abbot.

Jackson, Alan A, *London's Termini*, David & Charles, Newton Abbot, 1969.

John, E, *Timetable for Victory: A brief and popular account of the railways and railway-owned dockyards of Great Britain and Ireland during the six years' war, 1939-1945*, The British Railways, London, 1946.

Jones, Richard Bagnold, *British Narrow Gauge Railways*, Adam & Charles Black, London, 1958.

Joy, David, *A Regional History of the Railways of Great Britain: Volume 8 – South and West Yorkshire*, David & Charles, Newton Abbot, 1975.

Kidner, R W, *The Southern Railway*, Oakwood Press, Salisbury, 1958 and 1974.

Klapper, Charles F, *Sir Herbert Walker's Southern Railway*, Ian Allan, Shepperton, 1973.

Maggs, Colin G, *The GWR Swindon to Bath Line*, Sutton, Stroud.

Moody, G T, *Southern Electric 1909-1979*, Ian Allan, Shepperton, 1979.

Nash, G G, *The LMS at War*, London, Midland & Scottish Railway, London, 1946.

Newberry, Peter, *The Vectis Connection: Pioneering Isle of Wight Air Services*, Waterfront, Settle, 2000.

Neele, George Potter, *Railway Reminiscences*, 1904.

Nock, O S, *A History of the LMS*, 3 vols, George Allen & Unwin, London, 1983.

– *Britain's Railways at War, 1939-1945*, Ian Allan, Shepperton, 1971.

– *Sixty Years of Western Express Running*, Ian Allan, London, 1973.

– *The Great Western Railway in the Twentieth Century*, Ian Allan, London, 1971.

Peacock, A J, *The Rise and Fall of the Railway King*, Sutton, Stroud, 1995.

Smullen, Ivor, *Taken for a Ride*, Herbert Jenkins, London 1968.

Robertson, Kevin, *Signalling on the Great Western Railway*, Sutton, Stroud.

– *GWR Gas Turbines*, Sutton, Stroud.

– *Odd Corners of the GWR from the days of Steam*, Sutton, Stroud.

– *More Odd Corners of the GWR*, Sutton, Stroud.

Russell, J H, *A Pictorial Record of Great Western Coaches, Part II (1903-1948)*, Oxford Publishing Company, Oxford, 1973.

– *A Pictorial Record of Great Western Absorbed Engines*, Oxford Publishing Company, Oxford, 1978.

Simmons, Jack, and Biddle, Gordon, *The Oxford Companion to British Railway History*, Oxford University Press, Oxford, 2000.

Tavender, L, *HRMS Livery Register No3, LSWR and Southern*, Historical Model Railway Society.

Thomas, David St John, *A Regional History of the Railways of Great Britain: Volume 1 – The West Country*, David & Charles, Newton Abbot, 1960.

Thomas, John, *A Regional History of the Railways of Great Britain: Volume 6 – Scotland*, David & Charles, Newton Abbot.

Tomkins, N S, & Sheldon, *Swindon & the GWR*, Sutton, Stroud.

Townroe, S C, *The Arthurs, Nelsons and Schools of the Southern*, Ian Allan, Shepperton, 1973.

Vinter, N S, *Railway Walks GWR & SR*, Sutton, Stroud.

White, H P, *Regional History of the Railways of Great Britain, Vol 2, Southern England*, David & Charles, Newton Abbot, 1966.

– *A Regional History of the Railways of Great Britain: Volume 3 – Greater London*, David & Charles, Newton Abbot.

Wilson, Roger Burdett, *Go Great Western*

– *A History of GWR Publicity*, David & Charles, Newton Abbot, 1970.

Winkworth, D W, *Southern Titled Trains*, David & Charles, Newton Abbot, 1988.

Wragg, David, *The Great Western Railway Handbook 1923-1947*, Sutton, Stroud, 2006.

– *Wartime on the Railways*, Sutton, Stroud, 2006.

– *Signal Failure – Politics and Britain's Railways*, Sutton, Stroud, 2004.

– *The Southern Railway Handbook 1923-1947*, Sutton, Stroud, 2003.